'Get Away!'

THE
CARRY ON
COMPANION

ROBERT ROSS

Exclusive Carry On memories from...

Terence Alexander, John Antrobus, Janet Brown, Dora Bryan, Simon Callow, Roy Castle, Julian Clary, Bernard Cribbins, Barry Cryer, Alan Curtis, Jim Dale, Larry Dann, Ed Devereaux, Angela Douglas, Jack Douglas, Dave Freeman, Hugh Futcher, Jack Gardner, Mike Grady, Fred Griffiths, Sheila Hancock, Carol Hawkins, Melvyn Hayes, Frankie Howerd, David Kernan, Dilys Laye, Maureen Lipman, Jimmy Logan, Victor Maddern, Bill Maynard, Norman Mitchell, Richard O'Brien, Richard O'Callaghan, Milo O'Shea, Brian Oulton, Bill Owen, Lance Percival, Bill Pertwee, Jon Pertwee, Leslie Phillips, Wendy Richard, Cardew Robinson, Anton Rodgers, Alexei Sayle, Terry Scott, Julie Stevens, Marianne Stone, Eleanor Summerfield, Stanley Unwin, Kenneth Waller, Gwendolyn Watts, June Whitfield and Barbara Windsor.

Dedicated to the memory of Sid James, Peter Butterworth, Hattie Jacques, Talbot Rothwell, Kenneth Williams, Charles Hawtrey, Frankie Howerd, Bernard Bresslaw, Kenneth Connor, Gerald Thomas, Terry Scott and Joan Sims. Without whom....

Acknowledgements

With much love and thanks to my Dad, Mum and sister, Fiona, for their belief in me and the unflagging support and encouragement through thick and a lot of thin. Thanks to Phil Collins for his kind support and interest; the many invaluable contributors of Carry On memories; Peter Rogers and Audrey Skinner - Pinewood Studios; Janet Moat and Saffron Parker - British Film Institute (Special Materials Unit); Richard Reynolds and Martina Stansbie at B.T. Batsford Ltd for being the best in the business; Carol Thorn and Tony Gale - Pictorial Press Limited; Jon Keebel - Polygram Video; Alan Coles; for use of photographs, Lumiere Pictures (*Sergeant-Screaming*), Rank Film Distributors (*Head-Emmannuele*), United International Pictures UK (*Columbus*); Robert Cope; Michael Fury; Jason Hobbs and with love to my lucky charm, Mabel... we'll see you again.

Front Cover:
Bernard Bresslaw – *Carry On ... Up the Khyber*
Hattie Jacques – *Carry On Teacher*
Kenneth Williams – *Carry On ... Up the Khyber*
Sidney James – *Carry On Loving*
Barbara Windsor – *Carry On Abroad*
Charles Hawtrey – *Carry On Up the Jungle*

First published 1996, reprinted 1996, 1997
Revised edition 1998, paperback edition 2002, reprinted 2003, 2004
© Robert Ross 1996, 1998, 2002

ISBN 0 7134 8771 2

A CIP catalogue record for this book is available from the British Library

Printed in Singapore by Kyodo Printing Ltd.

for the publishers B T Batsford Ltd
The Chrysalis Building, Bramley Road
London W10 6SP
www.batsford.com
An imprint of Chrysalis Books Group plc

Distributed in the United States and Canada by Sterling Publishing Co., 387 Park Avenue South, New York, NY 10016, USA

'Matron!' 'Oh! Hello!' 'Charming!' 'Stop messin' about!' 'Get Away!'

CONTENTS

Foreword
by Phil Collins

The very first film I ever saw in a cinema was *Carry On Regardless*. It was in the days when families still went to the cinema *together*, and the team and their films still conjure up memories of me, mum, dad, brother and sister queueing up to get in, then, sitting in a *crowded* cinema laughing at the innuendo delivered by Kenneth Williams, Sid, Hawtrey, Connor *et al.*

What appeals to me about the *Carry Ons* is the repertory company that goes from film to film with such ease. It is easy to dismiss the dirty jokes as tasteless or corny, but even the biggest cynic must at least chuckle when the lines are delivered by Williams or Hawtrey. The *Carry On* team were the great example of English cinema humour, possibly without the satirical edge of Ealing, but very British.

This book is a labour of love for its writer Robert Ross, whose knowledge of English comedy is formidable. He has compiled a collection of everything you might have wanted to know but were afraid to ask about a cinema institution. Even if you *weren't* going to ask, it's an interesting read!

Enough from me... carry on.

'Matron!' 'Oh! Hello!' CARRY ON

INTRODUCTION

COR! 'Charming!'

'Stop messin' about!' 'Get Away!'

'Cor! Blimey, What A Carry On!': words of innuendo-sodden anticipation and affection that capture the essence of a series of low-brow British comedy films which kept a generation laughing and continue to enthral a new one. But why are the *Carry Ons* so popular and who needs a companion to the series? Well, you do for one! This is the essential guide to every entry in the *Carry On* canon, containing a bundle-load of facts in a handy pocket-sized publication. The humour of the *Carry Ons* taps into everybody's basic love of life and the good times - it's a world of sexually keen men, scantily-clad but in control women and a community spirit which is proud to be British and proud to shout about it. A world of Brighton holidays, seaside postcards, kiss-me-quick hats and fish 'n' chips, where the idea of true happiness is over-excess in everything - eat, drink and be merry for tomorrow we snuff it!

This book is not an attempt to analyse the eternal appeal of the *Carry Ons* but simply aims to present the facts in all their glory and prove an invaluable source of reference for the fan and the historian, for the enlightened and the uneducated. Having searched through this volume you need never feel ill-informed again when the topic of conversation at your office party turns towards the merits of *Carry On Screaming!*.

Nor need you pace around à la Hancock and James in search of that bit part player's name in *Wagon Train* when all you have to remember is the character Patricia Hayes played in *Carry On Again Doctor*. Everything you need know is in your hands now, Matron! Each film is looked at in turn, skating through the major elements and achievements, and culminating with a few scraps of detail: the favourite bit, a 'did you know?' section, notable things to look out for and the finest performance. Each is a very personal choice and sure to cause hours of happy banter and mindless argument in the households of particularly sad followers of the *Carry On* legend. The treatment of television and stage productions is conducted in a similar manner, and every *Carry On* has a marking out of five, based on the number of Sids scored! Bearing in mind that for the die-hard fan one Sid must constitute that the film is at least pretty damn brilliant, the system is just a rough guide to ferret out the classic entries in the series from those more routine examples of the genre.

Finally, it is a great honour you have done me in buying this book, and if you're just browsing through it in the shop, do me a favour and take it to the assistant and part with your cash. Happy reading and the best of British!

'Matron!' 'Cor!' 'O,

'Charmin

'Stop messin' about!'

CARRY ON FILMS

Hello!'

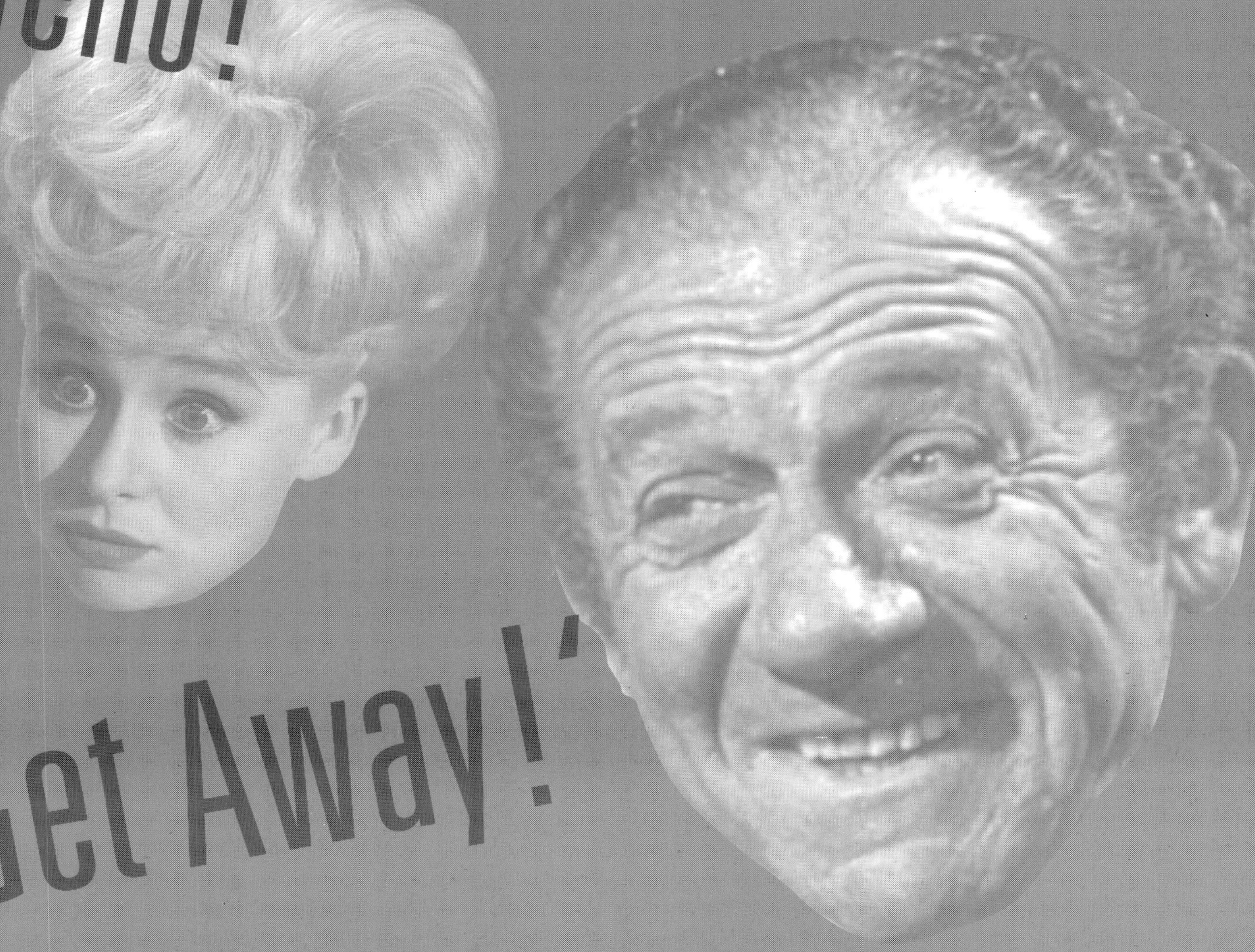

Get Away!'

IN THE BEGINNING

'Matron!' 'Oh! Hello!'

'Stop messin' about!'

or how do you start a comedy legend anyway?

'Get Away!'

In 1958 an economically-made comedy about life in an army barracks called *Carry On Sergeant* was released in cinemas across Britain. Produced by Peter Rogers and directed by Gerald Thomas, it was to begin the longest, most successful and best-loved series of films in British cinematic history. It was an immediate success story and the series it launched would divert almost out of recognition from the coy warmth of this entry. The actors, jokes and characters, however, would stay reassuringly the same.

As with most of the best things in life, the *Carry On* films were not particularly original, wallowing in a collection of tried and tested comic ideals and stereotypes. Whereas *Doctor Who* must tip its hat to H.G. Wells and Nigel Kneale, The Beatles grab inspiration from Elvis Presley and Gene Vincent, and *Monty Python* tug its comedic forelock to Marty Feldman and Spike Milligan, the *Carry Ons* got their lead from the explosive combination of William Wycherley and Max Miller. The last glorious flourish for traditional clowning and farcical innuendo, the *Carry On* team embodied the spirit of Shakespearian jesters and music-hall smut.

It was comedy in its simplest form: low brow and unassuming but speaking directly to the average person in the street. It was working class and energetic, where pomposity was deflated and drinking lads were king. Or to put it simply, Sid James. This was not drawing room comedy or light romance, but barrel-scraping one-liners and an obsession with bodily functions, sex and having a good time - or, ideally, all three! In the tradition of George Formby, Gracie Fields, The Crazy Gang and Frank Randle, the *Carry On* team trundled out the groanworthy gags time after time and got the audience on their side.

By the time the *Carry Ons* appeared, the music-hall glories of the pre-war years were a very distant memory and the surviving old clowns like Formby and Miller were struggling for uneasy television spots. When the series hit its peak, England was the centre of the universe as 'the swinging sixties' swung all around, but even in this era of change, that giggling, winking and none-too-serious manifestation of *Carry On* reached its audience.

The secret, of course, was an unrepeatable combination of class comedy actors who fused as a unit immediately. In retrospect, the main gang - Bernard Bresslaw, Peter Butterworth, Kenneth Connor, Jim Dale, Charles Hawtrey, Hattie Jacques, Sid James, Joan Sims, Kenneth Williams and Barbara Windsor - steamrolled through 20 years of farce without taking a breath, and for those few, those precious few, who spanned the entire run, their wildly flared nostrils and long drawn out cries of 'Cor!' became as much part of the British way of life as strikes and talking about the weather.

The men behind the films were also, naturally, behind the camera, and are seldom praised even by the die-hard *Carry On* fan. However, without the creative genius of Peter Rogers and Gerald Thomas, British innuendo would have been deader than a certain parrot. Although *Carry On Sergeant* was their first major hit and out-and-out comedy production, both Rogers and Thomas were already experienced film craftsmen. Peter Rogers, a Fleet Street journalist, broke into cinema in 1942 when he began writing *Thought For the Week* - five-minute religious shorts for Methodist, flour merchant and film mogul, J. Arthur Rank. Rogers enjoyed muted success with stage productions of his play *Mr Mercury* which led to such work as *The Man Who Bounced*, *Mr South Starts a War* and *Cards on the Table* making it to BBC radio. However, his major breakthrough came with a position as writer for Gainsborough Studios, during which time he met and married Betty Box and saw his name co-credited for hits like *Holiday Camp* (1947) with Jack Warner and Dennis Price and *Marry Me!* (1949) with David Tomlinson and Susan Shaw. By 1953 Peter's Children's Film Foundation production, *The Dog and the Diamond* had won The Venice Film Festival Award and in 1954 he wrote and produced *To Dorothy a Son*. Casting John Gregson fresh from his *Genevieve* success, Rogers continued his use of ensemble comic acting teams with roles for Alfie Bass and such future Carry Oners as Wilfrid Hyde-White, Joan Sims and Charles Hawtrey.

Meanwhile, across a crowded lot at Pinewood Studios, a young assistant editor by the name of Gerald Thomas was getting established in his own methodical way. Having started his career at Denham Studios in 1946, he cut his teeth on such prestigious productions as Laurence Olivier's *Hamlet* (1948) and *The October Man* (1949) with John Mills. Eventually Thomas graduated to editor on the 1949 Margaret Lockwood melodrama *Madness of the Heart* for writer/director Charles Bennett.

A competent editor, Thomas continued accepting assignment after assignment, notably cutting the Walt Disney live-action adventure *The Sword and the Rose* in 1955 and gaining useful experience as both editor and second director on *Above Us the Waves*. The director was his elder brother, Ralph Thomas, and the two would join forces on several stiff-upper-lipped British military adventures during the 1950s. However, this partnership, although fruitful, wasn't on an equal footing which simply wasn't enough for Gerald Thomas. His wish was to sit in the director's canvas chair and a meeting with a certain Peter Rogers presented the ideal route.

Both had ambitions to take full control of their movies and a producing/directing venture was the only way forward. The Children's Film Foundation offered Rogers a featurette called *Circus Friends* and, as it was a comparatively low-budget movie, Rogers gave Gerald Thomas the chance to make his director-ial debut. The film was released in 1956 to fairly high praise and dealt sympathetically with the plight of a tired old circus pony and the devoted children who love it. This typically saccharine short tale from the CFF is given a touching treatment by Thomas and a plum comic element is injected by the support performances from Meredith Edwards, John Horsley and, particularly, Sam Kydd. From a Peter Rogers script and boasting work from *Carry On* composer Bruce Montgomery and editor Peter Boita, the 63-minute production is a minor gem. Notable in the more youthful cast is the very young Carol White in her first movie. A few years later she would crop up in *Carry On Teacher* and would later bask in the light of stardom, albeit briefly, after the television landmark *Cathy Come Home*. Even at this stage, prolific character actor Hal Osmond, who had worked on several Rogers films including *Marry Me!* and *To Dorothy A Son*, allegedly told Gerald Thomas that he considered the 13-year-old temptress 'pure jail bait'. The ill-fated spiral of her life is clearly light years away from her unassuming picture of childhood affection: a star, fallen angel and natural actress caught in her early days by Thomas' lenses.

The muted success of *Circus Friends* led to the feature film debut for the Rogers/Thomas partnership for Romulus Films. *Time Lock* (1957), based on a minor Canadian television thriller by Arthur Hailey, dealt with the suspense-laden tale of a young boy trapped in an air-tight bank vault. Full of Hitchcockian chills, shadowy, atmospheric direction, moments of tension from cast members Robert Beatty and Vincent Winter and a stirring score from Stanley Black, its chief interest now lies in the small part allotted to a fresh faced actor by the name of Sean Connery. A very low-key British B picture, it can arguably be cited as Thomas' most effective director-ial performance, capturing the eerie unease and white-knuckle panic of the situation with precision.

The film was critically applauded, if less successful commercially, and the team continued the mysterious mood with the John Mills thriller *Vicious Circle*. Another adaptation from a television original, this time *The Brass Candlestick* by Francis Durbridge, the whodunit format is given the full treatment by Thomas who tells this story of a departed thespian at break-neck speed. The film was blessed with an experienced cast including Derek Farr, Roland Culver, Wilfrid Hyde-White and Lionel Jeffries, the music was again from Stanley Black and the turn-stiles did veritably spin.

Settling on the notion of churning out further British film noir productions, Rogers and Thomas established their own production company 'Insignia' (in the wake of Michael Powell and Emeric Pressburger's Archers) and immediately turned out *Chain Of Events* and *The Solitary Child*. This was all very well and good, the partnership was a success and the punters were enjoying the product. However, both quickly became tired of re-treading old murder mysteries and whodunits - humour was the name of the game. They enjoyed each other's humour socially, Thomas' brother and Rogers' wife were steering the hugely successful *Doctor* films, and the men at Insignia decided to jump on the bandwagon.

The order of the day was down-to-earth working-class comedy, ensemble playing and feel-good community spirit. Rogers and Thomas decided to embrace the contemporary scene by combining the basic ingredients of British film comedy with the essence of teenage rock 'n' roll. So it was that the young Tommy Steele, fresh from starring in the film of his very brief life story in 1957, was cast in *The Duke Wore Jeans*. It was the first and only pre-*Carry On* comedy film from Insignia and a milestone in British cultural history for presenting the initial teaming of producer Peter Rogers, director Gerald Thomas and writer Norman Hudis. Steele's co-stars included future *Carry On* players Michael Medwin and Eric Pohlmann, while the success of the film led to the Rogers/Thomas partnership becoming fully dedicated to comedy and their grooming for film stardom of another 1950s' teen idol, Jim Dale.

The Tommy Steele movie was released in early 1958, by which time a much-rejected film treatment of R.F. Delderfield's *The Bull Boys* had found its way onto the desk of Peter Rogers. It dealt with the forced enlistment of a ballet dancing team into National Service and lacked any sense of innuendo comedy or 1950s' awareness - Leslie Caron had been considered for the female lead. Though it had been rejected by almost every producer in the business, Peter Rogers saw a distinct possibility in the piece and approached several writers to liven up the antiquated dialogue.

Inspired by the new generation of comedians, Rogers turned towards the anarchic voices of the new war-weary age behind *The Goon Show*. Eric Sykes was considered, as was Spike Milligan - who had been voted 'Comedy Writer of the Year' for 1957. Both were asked to mould something out of the script but nothing came of it, bar a manic on-screen cameo from the pair in the Rogers/Thomas naval comedy *Watch Your Stern*. Fellow Goon personage and all round good egg John Antrobus wrote a treatment for a film based on *The Bull Boys* which led Rogers in the right direction - some of the material remains in the finished film and Antrobus retained an 'additional dialogue' credit. Finally, Norman Hudis looked over the script and cut out the inner soul of Delderfield's work, bringing out the working-class ideals and struggles of the squaddies. The ballet dancers are forgotten for a newly married couple desperately trying to consummate their union while hubbie is trapped in the army routine.

Now that sounded more like the sexually coy and frustrated state of 1950s' British comedy.

The film was ready for shooting and the direction was naturally left in the capable hands of Gerald Thomas. The major decision now was a title: *The Bull Boys* was out of the question, as it smacked of old fashioned values and war-time unity. This was to be a comedy of contemporary comment: National Service exposed, the bubble of pomposity burst. Eventually the team of Rogers, Thomas and Hudis embraced the snappy title of *Carry On, Sergeant*. It was a familiar army cry and summed up the aggressive authority of enforced service. Unfortunately it was also a title that had been used before - or at least, the all important *Carry On* bit had. Indeed, the title *Carry On!* had been used for a film as early as 1927, when Moore Marriott and Wally Patch teamed up for some fun and games for director/producer Dinah Shurey, while 1937 saw Kenneth More and Carry Oner Eric Barker star in D.R. Frazer's filmed Windmill revue *Carry On London* - later to become the title of the first *Carry On* stage show in 1973.

However, the major legal problem facing Rogers in 1958 was that a similarly structured comedy had been released in 1957 under the title of *Carry On Admiral* - indeed, distributor Stuart Levy had suggested the title change to Peter Rogers due to the success of *Admiral*. Starring A.E. Matthews, David Tomlinson, Alfie Bass, Reginald Beckwith, James Hayter and a certain Joan Sims, *Admiral*'s director was Val Guest who had graduated from scriptwriter for Will Hay, Arthur Askey and The Crazy Gang to directing such diverse work as Frankie Howerd's *The Runaway Bus* and Hammer's *The Quatermass Experiment*.

In order to avoid problems, Rogers approached Val Guest to direct his army comedy. As it happened, Guest refused the offer and Gerald Thomas gratefully returned to the fold. In an attempt to cash in on Rogers' success, *Carry On Admiral* was re-released in 1959, though to little effect. Eventually Peter Rogers registered the title 'Carry On' with the Film Production Association of Great Britain, thus preventing any other company using it.

So it was that Rogers, Thomas and Hudis saw their production filmed in six weeks during the March and April of 1958 at Pinewood Studios. A broad comedy of uneasy sexuality, innuendo, pathos and social comment, the film cost a meagre £74,000. It was released by Anglo Amalgamated in August 1958 under the title of...

'Matron!'
'Oh! Hello!'
'Cor!'
'Charming!'
'Stop messin' about!'
'Get Away!'

CARRY ON FILMS

CARRY ON SERGEANT

Bearing in mind *Sergeant*'s chequered pre-production history and that it is the seed for a long series, this is pretty good stuff. Remaining fresh and funny while wallowing in 1950s' nostalgia, the film stands as an invaluable social document as the blueprint of *Carry On*. Peter Rogers was no mug, and immediately realized what the British cinema audience wanted: low-brow comedy delivered by talented low-brow comedy actors in a familiar and much-debated environment. In 1958 everybody had either served, were serving or knew somebody who had served in the army. The war was just over a decade past and community spirit was still in the air. Of equal importance was the emergence of television as the major source of entertainment. In 1958 the most popular series on the small box was the ITV situation comedy *The Army Game*. Peter Rogers knew that to lure the home-based

viewers back to the big screen one needed to embrace the new threat rather than shun it. So it was that his team of farceurs were gleaned from television and, in particular, *The Army Game* itself. The television series had already enjoyed a Hammer film version, *I Only Arsked!*, and Peter Rogers simply followed the format for his first major screen comedy. The result was, of course, a huge hit, with *Sergeant* becoming the most popular film comedy in Britain for 1958 and making its money back within the first few days of release.

Rogers' main coup was his casting of William Hartnell in the title role. Before becoming everybody's favourite Time Lord, Hartnell was everybody's favourite army sergeant in everything from Carol Reed's morale booster *The Way Ahead* (1944) to the Ralph Richardson melodrama *The Holly and the Ivy*. For all his deserved fame and assurance, Hartnell was always whimsical about his success, having been invalided out of the army due to a nervous breakdown. As the actor explained, 'The strain of training was too much. I spent twelve weeks in an Army hospital and came out with a terrible stutter. The Colonel said, "Better get back to the theatre. You're no bloody good here".' It was perhaps fitting that Hartnell would build his arrogant officer into a comic icon by starring with Dennis Price and Ian Carmichael in the Boultings' *Private's Progress* in 1957, taking the lead in *The Army Game* and, during a brief sabbatical from the show, storming into the Pinewood field of dreams to kick-start the *Carry Ons*.

His combination of aggression and affection is invaluable and, allegedly, Hartnell worked the actors in his squad like the real thing - painful but productive. Fellow refugees from ITV's Nether Hopping transit camp were Norman Rossington and Charles Hawtrey, while others along for the ride included Bob Monkhouse, Gerald Campion, Terence Longdon, Kenneth Williams and Kenneth Connor. All were familiar faces and voices but, with the exception of Hawtrey, not established in films. Even Hawtrey had seldom again aspired to his early heights as the irritating schoolboy of four Will Hay movies, though his fame had received a much needed boost with casting in *The Army Game*. Connor was much respected as a radio voice grotesque in the mould of Peter Sellers and Jon Pertwee - creating a string of over-the-top figures to annoy Ted Ray - while Kenneth Williams was brilliantly performing the same feat opposite Tony Hancock.

What Peter Rogers did was to spot a collection of hugely talented actors who were not top billing stars in their own right. Cast in their ideal comic stereotype position - Williams (the snobbish intellectual), Connor (the bumbling bag of nerves),

Hawtrey (the slightly effeminate beanstalk), Campion (the mouthy fat boy), Longdon (the wolfish dandy) - the squad represented the complete spectrum of the British class system in all its glory. Monkhouse, the young scriptwriter and comedian, was tossed into the cocktail as the token 'star' romantic lead, while all the elements of working Britain were kept firmly in control by Hartnell's booming voice of authority.

While the comic vignettes were given the full flamboyant treatment by the eccentric squad members, Monkhouse wanders through the proceedings as an everyman caught up in frustrating bureaucracy. It is he who is separated from his young wife (the ultimate sex symbol for a coy Britain, Shirley Eaton) and bluffs and whines his way through the hellish National Service system. Like a watered down Kenneth Connor, Monkhouse battles against the iron door of army oppression with no real power.

It is undoubtedly Connor who leaves the deepest comedic paw print on the film. The straight romance between Monkhouse and Eaton has its comic equivalent in the coupling of Connor and Dora Bryan, and such straight romantics would be quickly side-stepped by Rogers, later re-surfacing in the brilliantly comic misunderstanding of Jim Dale. Shirley Eaton's contribution remains important in the *Carry On* canon, setting up the glamorous blonde leading lady who would run throughout the majority of the series, developing from Eaton's sexually naive, eyelash fluttering darling to the more forthright and vitally comic figures of Liz Fraser and Barbara Windsor.

The film injected shades of Ealing-like small town Britain and community spirit, while throwing in every corny gag which could get past the censor or the groaning audience. We were eventually spared such terrible one-liners as when Connor's squaddie complains he suffers from vertigo and Hartnell tells him vere to go: more's the pity it wasn't kept in. That was the whole point of the film's success - the jokes *were* very old hat but the fact remains that they were very funny and safe in the hands of an experienced and competent team of performers. While the dubious romantic ducking and diving and stolen kisses of Monkhouse and Eaton are at the plot's centre, the real joy of the script is the army environment and the battle between officialdom and the man in the street. No one really cares if Monkhouse has his way with Eaton or not but we cheer when Kenneth Williams tells the bemused and amazed figure of Hartnell where to get off. It's the individual debunking the powerful; simple but it works.

The entire film is stolen by the trio of fresh-faced recruits in the form of Williams, Hawtrey and

Ex *Army Game* cohorts Charles Hawtrey and William Hartnell relax on the set for *Carry On Sergeant*. Note Hawtrey sitting on assistant director Geoffrey Haine's chair!

Connor. All have a touch of camp about their personae, even though Williams here is the supercilious know-all of his Hancock days rather than the flamboyant mincing machine of later *Carry Ons*. The film's major comic line is the combination of these outsiders and the inner sanctum of army discipline in the shape of Hartnell, Bill Owen and Eric Barker (the latter embodying the old guard with his pride in his high rank, tapping his stripes and muttering, 'Look at this man'. Williams counteracts, 'you've nothing to complain about, look at the suit they've given me!'). It is the individual winning the game of life and the audience rejoices together with one almighty cheer and an 'up yours!'.

The finest moments come from the recruits' failure at every turn of their basic training: the priceless unease of Connor as he swings on the rope, Williams' high-brow objections to the bayonet practice, Rossington's bumbling and eventual, quick skill at dismantling the rifle. The ultimate message of the film is the love and affection that the recruits hold for the dreaded figure of Hartnell who has a wager of £50 with the sardonic figure of Sergeant Terry Scott that this, his last batch of recruits before retiring, will win the title of 'star squad'. Kenneth Williams' knowledge of sociology and his plan to celebrate the low-key efforts of Hartnell to instil army know-how into his squad, leads to a concerted effort to become real soldiers. If the final blast of soldiering expertise seems a little far-fetched, well, it is, so what - if it's logic and realism you're after, don't go to the movies.

The film's climax is a heart-warming union between all the social representives in the army barracks and a fond salute to a retiring figure of authority who, after all, only did his best. The stirring refrain of a military march, with the cast strolling through the parade ground, allows the patriotic viewer to puff out his chest and say, that's British determination for you! It's glorious stuff and culminates in the tender moment when Hartnell is presented with an inscribed lighter bearing the legend, 'For Sgt Grimshawe from the boys'. Feel that lump in your throat and cheer for a classic British comedy which started something very big!

Best performance

Kenneth Connor as Horace Strong. A masterpiece of jittering nerves and hypochondriac panic, Connor is the first of the team to appear, brilliantly decrying his fitness to a bemused Bob Monkhouse during the train journey to the Heathercrest National Service Depot. 'You going to hospital?'/'Into the army.'/'The army!'/'Yeah'./'Hah! So am I! How'd you pass the medical - influence.'/'Medical. Ehh... a farce, a criminal farce. A1 - me! A flaming 1. I tell you mate, two of everything you should have two of and you're in!'. The first moment of pure, or should I say, impure, *Carry On* innuendo. It's wonderfully undiluted and played to the hilt by Connor through his shivering ill health and mad angst. He's the source of doom and gloom throughout the film and puts a damp blanket over every adventure. Monkhouse suggests a drinking bout: Rossington licks his lips but Connor cries out, 'Dangerous, very dangerous!'. Battling the hapless Hattie Jacques (in a brief but effective bit as the army Medical Officer), Connor stumbles through the gamut of ill health and eventually becomes a herculean figure of soldiering prowess due to the love of Dora Bryan. As the epitome of the small man that makes good, Kenneth Connor steals the first film with a concentrated performance of energetic helplessness.

Favourite bit

The glorious highlight of the film is, naturally enough, concerned with the bumbling troops in Hartnell's control and is enlivened by an inspired piece of farce acting from Charles Hawtrey. The bayonet sequence boasts a myriad of helpless attempts at piercing the enemy sack figure after Hartnell's patriotic pep talk. Connor fumbles and crawls through the motions, Campion just keeps on running and Williams turns on the self loving knowledge by decrying the whole operation as outmoded ('Don't you think this is a trifle out of date in a world bristling with H-bombs, Sergeant?') However, it falls to Hawtrey's lovable half-wit to valiantly attack the figure with bloodthirsty vengeance, combining over-the-top anger and a passion for a much praised possession: 'Now then you beast, peasant, commoner, have at you, varlet. Hand back that cup final ticket!'/Hartnell (to Williams): 'In answer to your question, I'll back him against the H-bomb any day.'/'You beast, peasant, commoner.'/'Well don't just stand there, help me get him out.'/'Got you. You pirate. Take that and that... let go this is my turn.' Pure *Carry On* comedy in gloriously definitive terms.

Did you know?

Kenneth Williams, the mainstay of the subsequent team, earned the princely sum of £800 for his role in the first of the series. The wage remained the same until a turning point in 1962, when the fee was raised to £5,000 - a sum matched by Sid James' *Carry On* pay packet.

In the 1950s, Joan Sims and Dora Bryan were often mistaken for each other, indeed, Bryan's *Sergeant* role is the blueprint of the Hudis *Carry On* characters Sims would tackle. In 1971, during the Brighton location work for *At Your Convenience*, the *Carry On* crew stopped at Dora Bryan's hotel, Claridges, and Sims ran towards Bryan shouting 'Oh! Joanie!' as Bryan ran towards Sims crying 'Oh! Dora!'

Actor Terry Skelton was credited as the Fourteenth Recruit in publicity material although he failed to film his role, leaving the cast a few weeks before the shot so he could appear in a stage show.

Carry On music man, Bruce Montgomery, was also a popular detective fiction writer under the pseudonym of Edmund Crispin. His books included such complex whodunits as *The Moving Toy Shop* and *Buried For Pleasure*. In 1967 Montgomery became the mystery fiction reviewer for *The Sunday Times*, while Julian Symons summed up his style with, 'at his weakest he is flippant, at his best he is witty, but all his work shows a high-spiritedness rare and welcome in the crime story'. His single screenplay would be filmed by Gerald Thomas as the outlandish music college comedy, *Raising the Wind*.

The box-office success of the film began a nationwide craze, with the dramatic Laurence Olivier/Burt Lancaster/Kirk Douglas movie *The Devil's Disciple* (1959, director Guy Hamilton) receiving unscheduled bursts of applause and loud laughter when John Dighton's script presented the immortal phrase, 'Carry On, Sergeant!'. At the 1958 Last Night of the Proms concert, conducted by Sir Malcolm Sargent, one witty wag held aloft a banner with the slogan 'Carry On Sargent!'. William Hartnell himself would deliver the line, 'Carry On!', at the end of the 1959 Peter Sellers comedy *The Mouse That Roared*.

Look out for...

There's a quickly ad libbed piece of vocal comedy from Kenneth Williams as the new squaddies are kitted out. As a 'large' sized cap is plonked on his head, Williams mutters 'Charming!'. He was almost out of shot when he delivered the line and Gerald Thomas considered re-shooting the sequence, but the gag was brilliantly effective, Thomas thought it would work and so he wisely left it in.

Carry On memories

'*Carry On Sergeant* was nothing out of the ordinary - I was making loads of films at the time and they all seemed to be the same character... all the parts were waitresses, barmaids or ladies of easy virtue!'
Dora Bryan

'My particular memory of the *Carry On* films was the first, *Carry On Sergeant*. I remember that we weren't particularly welcome at Pinewood Studios, with a limited time in which to make the film. If I remember correctly this was due to the type of film - a "corny comedy" was considered a little "below stairs" for Pinewood. They were fun to be in'.
Bill Owen

'I met with Peter Rogers and Gerald Thomas at The Dorchester a couple of times. I wrote a version of *Carry On Sergeant* for them and some of it was incorporated into the film. I was offered to write three more *Carry On* screenplays for the princely sum (then!) of £5,000. For some reason I declined!'
John Antrobus

Stuart Levy and Nat Cohen Present
A Peter Rogers Production

CARRY ON SERGEANT

Sergeant Grimshawe **WILLIAM HARTNELL**   Charlie Sage **BOB MONKHOUSE**
Captain Potts **ERIC BARKER**   Mary Sage **SHIRLEY EATON**
Norah **DORA BRYAN**
Horace Strong **KENNETH CONNOR**   Peter Golightly **CHARLES HAWTREY**
James Bailey **KENNETH WILLIAMS**   Corp. Bill Copping **BILL OWEN**
Miles Heywood **TERENCE LONGDON**   Herbert Brown **NORMAN ROSSINGTON**
Andy Galloway **GERALD CAMPION**   Captain Clark **HATTIE JACQUES**
Gun Sergeant **CYRIL CHAMBERLAIN**   1st Specialist **GORDON TANNER**
2nd Specialist **FRANK FORSYTH**   3rd Specialist **BASIL DIGNAM**
4th Specialist **JACK GATRELL**
5th Specialist **ARNOLD DIAMOND**   6th Specialist **MARTIN BODDEY**
Medical Corporal **IAN WHITTAKER**   Injured Recruit **BERNARD KAY**
Stores Sergeant **ANTHONY SAGAR**   1st Storeman **ALEC BERGONZI**
2nd Storesman **GRAHAM STEWART**   3rd Storeman **ALEXANDER HARRIS**
4th Storeman **PAT FEENEY**   5th Storeman **EDWARD JUDD**
6th Storeman **RONALD CLARKE**   7th Storeman **DAVID WILLIAMS**
Mr Sage **MARTIN WYLDECK**   Mary's Mum **HELEN GOSS**
Sgt Paddy O'Brien **TERRY SCOTT**   Sgt Matthews **JOHN MATHEWS**
Sgt Russell **ED DEVEREAUX**   Sheila **LEIGH MADISON**
Recruits **JACK SMETHURST   BRIAN JACKSON   DON McCORKINDALE
LEON EAGLES   MALCOLM WEBSTER   PATRICK DURKIN
JAMES VILLIERS   HAYDN WARD   GRAYDON GOULD
JEREMY DEMPSTER   TERRY DICKENSON   HENRY LIVINGS
BERNARD KAY & MICHAEL HUNT**

Based on *The Bull Boys* by **R.F. Delderfield**   Screenplay by **Norman Hudis**
Additional Material by **John Antrobus**
Music composed & directed by **Bruce Montgomery**
Played by **The Band of the Coldstream Guards**

Director of Photography **Peter Hennessy**   Art Director **Alex Vetchinsky**
Editor **Peter Boita**
Production Manager **Frank Bevis**   Camera Operator **Alan Hume**
Assistant Director **Geoffrey Haine**
Sound Editor **Seymour Logie**
Sound Recordists **Robert T. MacPhee & Gordon K. McCallum**
Continuity **Joan Davis**   Make-up **Geoffrey Rodway**
Hairdressing **Stella Rivers**
Dress Designer **Joan Ellacott**   Casting Director **Betty White**
Set Dressing **Peter Murton**
Titles **Pentagon Film Titles Ltd.**   Producer **Peter Rogers**
Director **Gerald Thomas**

A 1958 Anglo Amalgamated Release 'U' Cert.
Black & White Running Time - 83 mins. 7,505ft

NURSE

The immense success of the first film came as a huge surprise to most of the people concerned - only Kenneth Connor had sensed that something special was in the air on the army set, and it wasn't the smell from the Pinewood canteen! Once it became clear that their first fully-fledged comedy film was a hit, Peter Rogers and Gerald Thomas set about planning a further project. As with the Marilyn Monroe song, when a film-maker senses the big time from one film it has to be a case of do it again, again and again, and for an astonishing 20 years, that's what happened.

The touchstone for the series came in the shape of a medical comedy based on *Ring For Catty* by Jack Beale and Patrick Cargill. As with the Delderfield manuscript, Hudis took his basic premise from this equally rejected film script and broadened the comic ideals to produce *Carry On Nurse*. Once again, the setting was familiar, the jokes were corny and the emphasis was lavatorial/anal, and the cast was fairly similar to a collection of bumbling eccentrics who had just been in the army. The combination of a cheery community of male bonding and lustful dreams, the man in the street battling against authority (this time the stern figure of Matron Hattie Jacques), regular chats with jolly rogue Leslie Phillips and nurses such as the gorgeous Shirley Eaton is almost enough to break your leg for and get in.

Norman Hudis always considered *Nurse* to be the best screenplay he wrote, and such notables as Leslie Phillips and Gerald Thomas believed the film to be the peak of the *Carry On* series. For me it is a reasonable reassessment of the characterizations and ideals of *Sergeant* but is somewhat swamped by the huge amount of time handed over to the romance - this time between Eaton and a somewhat low-key Terence Longdon. It's all very coy and 1950s' England, while the comedy is again left in the hands of a clutch of spirited eccentrics, although even Kenneth Williams is allowed a brief vignette of serious romance with the stunning Jill Ireland.

However, it falls to Connor, Hawtrey and a maniacally anxious Williams to bombard the medical profession with camp innuendo, pathetic whining, oneupmanship and childish play. The scenario is pure soap opera and clearly basks in the television success of *Emergency Ward 10* - *Carry On* newcomer Joan Sims was plucked from the 1959 film version, *Life in Emergency Ward 10* - while Shirley Eaton's friendly and overtly seductive nurse is pure melodrama. *Nurse* was also clearly trading on the success of the *Doctor* series but brilliantly steered clear of fluttering hearts over the operating table and flighty romance between the medical staff. Rogers' masterstroke was a rare concentration on the frustrations and opinions of the patients - usually relegated to brief one-liners and two-dimensional characters. In *Nurse* the patients are the mainstay of the comedy and literally take over from the medical staff in a half-hearted, nightmarish attempt at a bunion operation, enough to bring tears to the eyes of Leslie Phillips.

Although the character names have been changed to protect the innocent, the *Carry On* regulars again roll out the stereotypes as Hawtrey minces and giggles from his hospital bed (locked into his radio headphones and living outside of the male community for most of the film), Connor stumbles and bumbles as an unwilling and sexually uneasy boxer with a broken hand (memorably covering his face with his towel as he walks towards the ward: 'I'm not going in there, it's full of sick people!') and Williams plays his big-headed bookworm with sardonic relish. As with his memorable attack on Hartnell and the military state of mind, Williams throws himself energetically into a battle of wills with frosty Hattie Jacques: 'if a doctor asks me to hang by one arm from a ceiling wearing an aqua lung with my birthday tattooed on my left buttock in shorthand, I'll do it. He aims to cure me. Your rule has nothing to do with my cure, therefore it has no meaning in here.' Williams in full flow.

Most comic mileage is made from the inspired

Kenneth Williams, Cyril Chamberlain and Terence Longdon have a bash at Leslie Phillips' bunion in *Carry On Nurse*, while the bemused Kenneth Connor looks on.

contrasting of the Williams and Connor characters: intellect versus brain-bashing. Connor gurgles and chirps his way through the indignities of hospital life, seeing the bright side of everything and debunking the stone-faced absurdity of the medical employees, notably in a memorable duologue with the trolley lady (Lucy Griffiths). Connor: 'Got any fruit bars.' Griffiths: 'No, I've got a sliced nut.'/'Come to the right place to have it mended haven't you!' A sequence with Williams looking on in disgust as Connor tries to unpeel a banana with his one good hand is superb visual comedy in the Buster Keaton league: the look of pure joy on Kenneth C.'s face as he manages to rip away the skin by using his fist and teeth and go for a bite is perfectly timed. The final deflation, as the banana falls from its skin and Connor's grimaces are matched by Williams disgusted look, encapsulates the essence of *Carry On* class system comedy.

As with most of the early *Carry Ons*, there is no real story to this production: just a host of outstanding comic actors playing their camped-up characterizations with innuendo-guns ablaze, here trying to live their lives while trapped in the authoritative clutches of the National Health Service. Hudis takes as his lead role the figure of Terence Longdon's newspaper reporter and thus, a semi-autobiographical approach creeps into the plot. Hudis, at one stage dejected and unable to mould *Ring For Catty* into the *Carry On* format, was admitted to The Peace Memorial Hospital, Watford, for an appendicitis operation and his encounters there brought a touch of lowly realism to the *Carry On* ethos, while his wife, Rita, a nurse, would offer him episodes from her own experience.

The combination was a sketchy but effective backdrop for a collection of bed-pan jokes, randy male

patients, sexually-swaying nurses and frustrating public visitors. At the epicentre of all this mad carrying on is Jacques' Matron, a towering performance of dedicated control and straight-faced authority. However, even Jacques has a sense of humour, and just as Hartnell's sergeant is embraced in the warm family community of the squaddies, Jacques is highlighted as a lovable old softie via the film's final gag, a landmark in *Carry On* comedy based on an idea by Hudis' mother-in-law, Ethel Good.

Centred round the overtly awkward Colonel, a guest-starring turn from Wilfrid Hyde-White, the rushed-off-their-feet nurses (Joan Sims and Susan Stephen) set up a bizarre sight gag with a daffodil, a bare Hyde-White bottom and an unusual way of taking a temperature. The sequence has passed into our filmic culture. Jacques bursts into this pretty scene as the camera cuts to the cheekily worried faces of Sims and Stephen. Giving a priceless look of anguished surprise, Hattie blurts out the immortal line, 'Colonel, whatever's going on?!'. The scene is cut to a close-up of the helpless Colonel as he murmurs, 'Come, come Matron, surely you've seen a temperature taken like this before!', to which Jacques mutters, 'Yes Colonel, many times - but never with a daffodil'. Giving a delightfully beaming smile, Hattie holds the offending stem in her hand as the screen fades to black. It remains one of the most celebrated frames from the series, from what is, after all, a fairly average sort of comic situation.

Nevertheless it caught the tide at the right time and secured *Nurse* a major success both in England and, amazingly, America. The film became the highest grossing in Britain for 1959 and single-handedly saved the independent American distribution company, Governor Films. Its owner, David Emanuel, had seen and enjoyed *Carry On Nurse* and secured the rights to take it across America. Lacking financial security and finding it hard to convince major cinema chains to take the film on, Emanuel displayed *Nurse* at hospitals, fun fairs and university campuses. The Crest Cinema in Westwood, Los Angeles, ran the film for over a year and the visual gag that closed *Nurse* struck such a chord with American audiences that millions of plastic daffodils were especially manufactured for sale at theatres screening the film.

Initially this all-important sequence was situated just before the end and considered funny but fairly ordinary by the makers. Anglo's head, Stuart Levy, thought the scene inspired and advised Peter Rogers to make it the final explosive shot and so leave the audience laughing. This Rogers agreed to do, so the penultimate scene in the final print concerning the projected romance between leaving patient Longdon and nurse Eaton was, in fact, the original ending.

Clockwise:

Medical madness: Marriage In Bed – Anita Harris, Frankie Howerd, Joan Sims and Bernard Bresslaw in *Carry On Doctor*

That dirty old man Wilfrid Brambell gets cheeky with Elizabeth Knight – *Carry On Again Doctor*

Sid James, Jacki Piper and Hattie Jacques block up Bunn Ward in *Carry On Matron*

(Previous page) Sid! *Carry On Again Doctor*

Note the louder than usual crescendo at the scene's close, suggesting the final image of black and the end title card.

Arguably the most successful film in the entire series, *Nurse* began its most popular sub genre, the medical *Carry Ons*, and secured the long-term future for the Rogers and Thomas formula. Some jealous guy commented that 'the way Peter Rogers makes money out of illness makes me sick!' - nothing succeeds like success.

Best performance

Leslie Phillips strolls through the cheerful men's ward atmosphere in his flamboyant, wolfish, RAF-type fellow persona, chatting up the nurses and bouncing comic banter off Williams and Connor with perfect timing. His entrance is inspired: 'Hello chaps!' Nurse: 'Mr Bell?' / 'Ding Dong, you're not wrong!'. His jolly, all-round good egg character is dampened by the persistent bunion on his foot which puts a question mark over his weekend away with girlfriend June Whitfield. However, he seems more at ease with the male community of the institution and gleefully gets carried away with the flowing booze in the climactic mock operation sequence.

Favourite bit

The drunken attempted operation on Phillips' foot is an inspired piece of nightmarish surrealism, from a world populated by madly obsessed bumblers among whom Kenneth Williams is the most outstanding. Williams, taking Connor, Longdon and Cyril Chamberlain along, leaves the wonderfully camp figure of Hawtrey in a nurse's uniform to guard their venture. Kenneth W., with a handy medical do-it-yourself book and a belief in his own ability, leads the increasingly more uncertain Phillips into the operating room. It is a masterly directed sequence: the shot of the illuminated room sparkling with equipment is cut quickly to a close-up of the beaming face of Williams - all 'Stop messin' about!' grin and chuckles. The already drunken state of our heroes is worsened when Connor accidentally leaves on the dispenser of laughing gas, leading to Williams' increased enthusiasm for the job in hand and Leslie delightfully joining in with the laughs and japes while still projecting cheerful apprehension. It's classic stuff as Kenneth C. suppresses further giggles and Kenneth W., finally dropping his rather superior drunken veneer and in a splendid mockery of himself, laughs joyfully behind his surgeon's mask. Priceless.

Did you know?

Carry On Nurse saw one of the final screen appearances of the glamorous young actress Susan Shaw, as Kenneth Connor's wife. Having been a rank starlet, notably starring opposite Jack Warner and Kathleen Harrison in the Huggett films (often co-scripted by Peter Rogers) she made her final film, *The Switch*, in 1963. She died penniless in 1978 and her funeral expenses were paid for by The Rank Organisation.

Kenneth Connor's son is played by his own three-year-old son, Jeremy. Turning in a delightfully natural performance, he was fascinated by Susan Shaw's sparkling shoes and would only perform his few lines and a nifty boxing punch to his dad after a promise of a present from Gerald Thomas - some sweets hanging behind the camera. Jeremy would later join Kenneth for a run of three further *Carry Ons* some 15 years later: *Dick*, *Behind* and *England*.

When the finished print was shown at the cinema, Wilfrid Hyde-White's outraged agents tried to sue Rogers and Thomas for exposing their client's bare backside without his permission. Knowing full well that Hyde-White hadn't agreed to such an image, or indeed, filmed one, his agents believed that some stand-in bottom had been superimposed on the print! In fact, Thomas doesn't show anybody's bare bottom - Hyde-White's or not - the image appears in, perhaps, the best place for it, your imagination! Eventually his agent was chuffed with *Nurse*, its success in the States would lead to the unlikely but inspired casting of Wilfrid opposite Marilyn Monroe in *Let's Make Love*. Peter Rogers himself turned down many an offer to take the *Carry Ons* to America and film in Hollywood with Hollywood stars - it would have been interesting to see Marlon Brando and Monty Clift tackling roles in *Carry On Constable*!

Like Joan Sims, *Nurse* guest star Wilfrid Hyde-White appeared in the 1959 film *Life in Emergency Ward 10*.

The profitable daffodil that made the film such a success was also a symbolic throw-back to an incident in Peter Rogers' life. In his late twenties, he was seriously ill with meningitis. As patients around him died, a sole daffodil by his bedside grew stronger and flourished even in that atmosphere of disease. The sight of this beautiful flower inspired Peter to look to the future and conquer his illness.

Following the popularity of *Nurse*, Peter Rogers announced the titles of the next four films in the series and the official *Carry On* team to be Kenneth Williams, Kenneth Connor, Charles Hawtrey, Hattie Jacques, Bill Owen, Leslie Phillips, Terence Longdon and Joan Sims. Each was offered an exclusive film contract and a percentage of the money each film made. None of the actors accepted the proposal but the majority of the names did appear in the subsequent films for the usual no-strings-attached fee. Only *What A Carry On!* failed to materialize and even Peter Rogers has forgotten what the subject was going to be. The title had earlier been used for a Jimmy Jewel/Ben Warris army comedy film.

Amidst *Carry On* fever, Rogers and Thomas were swamped with letters suggesting further entries in the series. The topics ranged from a *Carry On Stamp Collecting* to a *Carry On Cesspool Cleaning*. Neither got further than Peter Rogers' file 13!

A sight gag involving Bill Owen's broken leg and the spilt ball bearings from his leaded weight was cut by the censors. The pay-off line of 'Pick up Mr Hickson's balls' was thought unsavoury!

As the director of the most popular film in Britain for 1959, Gerald Thomas negotiated a percentage from the profits of each subsequent *Carry On*. By *Cruising* in 1962, Rogers and Thomas were on equal percentages from the series' profits. The two became known in the industry as Rogers and Thomastein!

While the film was a huge success in America, there was just one gag that didn't translate - the 'L-plate' plastered on young and inexperienced Joan Sims.

Look out for...
A memorable in-joke from horse-racing-mad Wilfrid Hyde-White. In one of several scenes where the Colonel places bets with a friendly medical orderly (Harry Locke), Hyde-White changed the horse's name from the scripted, 'Bloody Mary', to 'Rambler'. This was a real horse who Wilfrid had backed earlier in the day and Locke's blank expression as he stares at his notebook is real shock. Ever the professional, Harry Locke didn't ruin the take. 'Rambler' won at Nottingham at odds of 100-8.

The cartoon sketches during the film's opening titles were the first illustration of the debt the *Carry Ons* owed to the seaside postcard and would crop up in another nine films. Initially depicting several comic moments from the films, under the control of brilliant cartoonist 'Larry' for films like *Up The Khyber* and *Girls* these cartoons became risqué and funny in their own right.

Carry On memories
'The cosiest job I ever had was in *Carry On Nurse*. I used to roll out of bed in my own home in the morning, into a car to take me to Pinewood, onto the film set and to another bed, and finally out of that bed and into my own bed again. I thought I had done a hard day's work. Peggy Thorpe-Bates, my wife, who had been cooking and cleaning and also rehearsing a long and exhausting part on the stage, wasn't quite so sure!'
Brian Oulton

'After *Carry On Sergeant* Peter Rogers wanted me for a part in *Carry On Nurse*. He told me he wanted me to play a character with one "boss-eye". Now I could cross both eyes but crossing just one was hard to manage. I practised for days and finally achieved it. Triumphantly I told Peter Rogers and only then it transpired it was a joke - he really wanted me to play a character who was impotent! I can still do the eye bit!'
Ed Devereaux

Stuart Levy and Nat Cohen Present
A Peter Rogers Production

CARRY ON NURSE

Nurse Dorothy Denton **SHIRLEY EATON**   Bernie Bishop **KENNETH CONNOR**
Humphrey Hinton **CHARLES HAWTREY**   Oliver Reckitt **KENNETH WILLIAMS**
Matron **HATTIE JACQUES**   Jack Bell **LESLIE PHILLIPS**
Ted York **TERENCE LONGDON**   The Colonel **WILFRID HYDE-WHITE**
Nurse Stella Dawson **JOAN SIMS**   Mick **HARRY LOCKE**
Jane Bishop **SUSAN SHAW**   Sister **JOAN HICKSON**
Percy Hickson **BILL OWEN**   Madge Hickson **IRENE HANDL**
Frances James **SUSAN BEAUMONT**   Henry Bray **BRIAN OULTON**
Nurse Georgie Axwell **SUSAN STEPHEN**   Bert Able **CYRIL CHAMBERLAIN**
'Ginger' **MICHAEL MEDWIN**   'Norm' **NORMAN ROSSINGTON**
Jill Thompson **JILL IRELAND**   Alec Lawrence **ED DEVEREAUX**
Helen Lloyd **ANN FIRBANK**   John Gray **FRANK FORSYTH**
Tom Mayhew **JOHN MATHEWS**   George Field **GRAHAM STEWART**
Jackson **PATRICK DURKIN**   Andrew Newman **DAVID WILLIAMS**
Meg **JUNE WHITFIELD**   Alice Able **MARIANNE STONE**
Rhoda Bray **HILDA FENEMORE**   Perkins **MARTIN BODDEY**
Rose Harper **MARITA STANTON**   Nurse Nightingale **ROSALIND KNIGHT**
Miss Winn **LEIGH MADISON**   New Nurse **STEPHANIE SCHILLER**
Fat Maid **CHRISTINE OZANNE**   Porter **CHARLES STANLEY**
1st Ambulance Driver **ANTHONY SAGAR**
2nd Ambulance Driver **FRED GRIFFITHS**
Attractive Nurse **SHANE CORDELL**   Stephens **JOHN VAN EYSSEN**
Anaesthetist **JOHN HORSLEY**   Trolley Lady **LUCY GRIFFITHS**
Jeremy Bishop **JEREMY CONNOR**

Based on an idea by **Patrick Cargill and Jack Beale**
Original screenplay by **Norman Hudis**
Music composed and directed by **Bruce Montgomery**

Director of Photography **Reginald Wyer B.S.C.**
Art Director **Alex Vetchinsky**   Editor **John Shirley**
Production Manager **Frank Bevis**
Camera Operator **Alan Hume**   Assistant Director **Stanley Hosgood**
Sound Editor **Roger Cherrill**
Sound Recordists **Robert T. MacPhee & Bill Daniels**
Make-up **George Blackler**   Hair Dressing **Pearl Orton**
Dress Designer **Joan Ellacott**   Casting Director **Betty White**
Set Dressing **Arthur Taksen**   Continuity **Penny Daniels**
Nurse's Uniforms **Courtaulds**   Producer **Peter Rogers**
Director **Gerald Thomas**

A 1958 Anglo Amalgamated film released in 1959 'U' Cert.
Black & White   Running time - 86 mins. 7,771ft

TEACHER

'You roared at *Carry On Sergeant*, howled at *Carry On Nurse*, you'll be convulsed by *Carry On Teacher*'- well... quite! So screamed the advertising hoarding for the third offering from the Rogers and Thomas school of comedy and even though the seductive Shirley Eaton-like schoolmistress on the poster didn't feature in the film, the school of fools was a worthy continuation of the line.

Following the pattern of earlier films, *Teacher* was a coy, cosy look at the world of mortar-boards and chalk dust and tackles the less troublesome elements of youth culture by steering the comic style via 1930s' friendliness. Charles Hawtrey has ample opportunity to emulate his comic master, Will Hay, and sweep through the school room with flowing cloak and sweeping cane. While Glenn Ford was dealing with sluggish teen angst and Bill Haley-obsessed rocking rebels in *The Black Board Jungle*, the experienced farceurs at Pinewood struggled to survive itching powder and a defaced piano: more Billy Bunter and Greyfriars than James Dean and the juvenile court. Falling into line with the hugely popular *St Trinian's* series and even incorporating a clutch of Ronald Searlesque school brats for the poster and opening credits (written in effective chalk print and billing the school children as 'The Saboteurs'), this film concentrated on the mild nightmare situation between the overtly adult school kids (all cocky guys and mini-skirted girls with a watered-down line in acid put-downs) and the childish bumbling of the teaching staff (brought to life by all the current Carry Oners). The pivot for the action, and thus as with Hartnell and Jacques, the centre of authority for the others to battle around, is Ted Ray - timidly trying to hold his school together while deliberating over whether to leave his community spirit post for a super-duper new school.

Teacher is largely overlooked by followers of the series as it can lay claim to little importance for the structure of the series as the *Carry On* style was already in full flow. However, as a rose-tinted social document of the British way of life in the 1950s, it is hugely enjoyable and hilariously played. The kids are effective and Gerald Thomas handles the innocent plotting and school yard discussion sequences very well. Having displayed excellent ability in coaxing strong child performances in his earlier films like *Circus Friends* and *Time Lock*, he creates a collection of likable youngsters who contrast the comic masters with tongue-in-cheek obedience and superior understanding. The likes of Carol White and Richard O'Sullivan would, of course, go on to greater things.

Naturally enough though, it is the main team members who inject touches of manic humour and delightful prat-falling to the scenario, but with the exception of moments of babyish bickering between Hawtrey and Williams, these characters are not the clumsy eccentrics of the initial films. The comedy does come from camp outbursts and accidents but this is due to the actions of outsiders (the children) rather than the masters' own incompetence. Even the ultimate dithering science master, Kenneth Connor, is a brilliant and clever teacher who battles with love sickness (when faced with Rosalind Knight) and tongue-tieing spoonerisms (all jittering mistakes, long drawn-out 'Cor's and muttered 'Ho, ho's) to create a likable figure of bumbling nervousness. However, his intellect is never questioned and although his home-made rocket contributes to another farcical episode, the fact remains that his ingenious experiment does *work*.

Despite the old fashioned values of this warm good-time English community, Hudis includes touches of feminist thought and radical debate in the staffroom antics. Both Hattie Jacques and Joan Sims crusade through the blinkered men's world of education with comments about beating the men at their own game and sorting out the school's problem for the feminist course. Jacques' wildly uncontrolled maths mistress is the chief harridan of cane-mad authority although, as with her Matron, little

Good morning boys! Charles Hawtrey in Will Hay mode - Carry On Teacher.

tap dance!'/'He could toy with his dirk.'/'Or he could chuck it at you!'.

The disastrous staging of the Bard forms the, by now standard, explosive *Carry On* ending and Connor deflates the wide-eyed pomposity of the two organizers by dropping in subtle and, more importantly, unsubtle references to Shakespearian glories (calling Williams 'Sir Laurence'/moaning 'If music be the food of love - belt up!'). Ted Ray's amazed and totally dumbfounded headmaster meanwhile, sinks deeper and deeper into his front row seat and literally eats his handkerchief in embarrassment. Marvellous stuff!

The tear-jerking finale has the children's bad behaviour explained away as a plan to distress the visiting school inspector and thus destroy Ted Ray's dreams of leaving Maudlin Street School. In an echo of the fond farewell for Hartnell's sergeant, this unites the battling elements that have created the bulk of the film's chaotic comedy. *Teacher* is a delightfully naive vision of the education system and was another top money earner for the *Carry On* stable. The team had developed a style of outrageous retelling of the same story through similar characters in various locations and occupations. The series was in the ascendence and everybody was happy.

Best performance

Kenneth Williams walks about the film in his flamboyant, energetic personification of the dedicated and understanding teacher. While his colleagues are clad in the flowing robes of Will Hay education, Williams tries to get closer to his pupils by dressing in casual, contemporary clothing. His controversial theories on the dangers of caning is at loggerheads with the 'whack and be damned' ideals of the rest of the staff, but Hudis gives him the most powerful line of argument: 'Extraordinary theory, you bend a child double in order to give it an upright character!'. Having the perfect character name for an English teacher - Milton - Kenneth throws himself gleefully into the staffroom madness of itching powder, sabotaged telephones and an enforced conga of relief with Connor, Sims and the gang. It's vintage Williams without the eye-popping innuendo of later productions.

Favourite bit

Kenneth Williams is also at the centre of the film's finest moment while his overtly enthused dialogue about the glories of Shakespeare bore and bewilder his pupils. Their witty comments and deliberately naive questions bring Williams down dubious avenues of debate as Leslie Phillips looks on, fascinated. Diana Beevers: 'Act I Scene V, Sir.' Williams:

traces of endearing glee are apparent in her performance, notably when one of her pupils (Paul Cole) fools confident child psychiatrist Leslie Phillips. Joan Sims takes over the mantle of glamour girl from Shirley Eaton before being tossed into a long-running collection of *Carry On* ogresses, although her girlish games mistress is firm with the wolfish advances of Phillips and energetically stubborn - memorably incorporating Joyce Grenfell-like touches when she castigates her pupil, Monica.

The film's chief asset is an inspired tooth-and-nail battle of oneupmanship between Hawtrey's music master and the flamboyant English master played by Kenneth Williams. Complete with over-the-top arty temperaments and allowing the full camp elements of their *Carry On* personae to engulf all reasonable thought, the two create a number of priceless vignettes within the sanctuary of the staffroom. Williams is in full disgruntled mood and Hawtrey's mad twittering creates moments of inspired comedy. Their tense relationship is strained even further through disagreements over the school play, *Romeo and Juliet*: Charles: 'The star-cross'd lover scene is vital to my integrated musical interpretation.' Kenneth: 'And what may I ask does the actor do all this time,

'Ah yes, your sweet little scene with the Nurse, yes?' Beevers: 'Go ask her name - If he be married, my grave is like to be my wedding bed.'/'Well, what's your question?'/'What's a wedding bed?'/'What do you mean - what's a wedding bed'./'Well, what's it like? What's special about a wedding bed?'/'Really dear, I don't see what that's got to do with *Romeo and Juliet!*' Paul Cole: 'Cor! Hell of a lot if you ask me.'/'Nobody did ask you Atkins - be quiet!' In a wonderful, tongue-in-cheek homage to the pressures of Shakespearian teaching, Kenneth pulls off an ever mounting picture of panic with great style.

Did you know?

Rosalind Knight, memorable in the film as the snooty school inspector who melts Kenneth Connor's heart, is the daughter of much respected thespian Esmond Knight whose credits included a leading role in the Peter Rogers co-scripted classic *Holiday Camp*.

The comic genius of Ted Ray was replaced by Sid James in the *Carry On* movies due to a legal problem over the former's film contract. Ray, a prized radio and variety comedian, was officially under license to ABC Films who had seldom used his talents. Rogers, admiring his quick-fire work in Ray's *A Laugh* with Connor and Hawtrey, cast him as the flustered father at the centre of a family scandal in the Rogers/Thomas/Hudis film *Please Turn Over* (based on the West End hit, *Book of the Month* by Basil Thomas). Pleased with his comic acting talents, Rogers cast him as the lead in *Teacher* and planned to launch him as a mainstay of the series. However, seeing a lapsed contract player making good in another producer's movies enraged ABC and they instructed Stuart Levy that a law suit would be the result. The fact that Anglo had no cinema circuit and relied on the display of their movies on ABC screens meant that the Rogers camp had to back down or face non-distribution. Levy, anxious to avoid the nose-diving of his movies, instructed Rogers to drop Ted Ray from his films. This reluctantly was agreed upon and the central role in the next film was destined to go to another fine comic talent who was enjoying some friendly banter with Tony Hancock on television.

Although Ray's role in *Constable* was unceremoniously curtailed, his son, Robin Ray, appears briefly in the film as a junior store executive faced with a 'dragged-up' Kenneth Williams and Charles Hawtrey.

Kenneth Williams, Joan Sims, Kenneth Connor, Charles Hawtrey and Hattie Jacques in your average staffroom discussion - *Carry On Teacher.*

Ted Ray's starring credit in the film, highlighted by his name occupying an opening title card to himself while the other stars are grouped as a team, was only apparent in the series on two other occasions - the last billing, special appearance from Bob Monkhouse in the first film and the imported Hollywood name of Phil Silvers for *Follow That Camel*.

Upon the completion of filming *Teacher* the cast and crew enjoyed a lavish party in Harrow which later moved on to the nearby home of Kenneth Connor. It started a trend of family unity between the *Carry On* personnel which enhanced the feel-good factor of the series.

Look out for...

There's a fine supporting turn from George Howell as a bespectacled, supercilious school boy battling with the hapless Charles Hawtrey in a homage to Hawtrey's old frustrating persona towards Will Hay's dithering school teacher in *Good Morning Boys!* and *The Ghost of St Michael's*.

Cyril Chamberlain, a regular face throughout the first seven *Carry Ons*, turns in his most effective support as the kindly school caretaker, passionately discussing the appalling performance of the local football team and delightfully pocketing some mildly risque pin-ups that the kids have pinned to the notice board. Clearly the inspiration for George A. Cooper's performance in *Grange Hill*!

The young Larry Dann pops up as a nervous schoolboy who pleads with Kenneth Williams to take notice of his raised hand. Williams determinedly tells him to put his hand down but the shuffling anxious figure of Dann indicates that he must be excused fairly quickly. These few lines led to Dann's profitable association with three later *Carry Ons*, notably in tackling the romantic lead cum bumbling youth figure in *Emmannuelle*. Ten years later he would be a passing member of *The Bill* cast.

Carry On memories

'I was fortunate to have been in four: *Carry On Teacher*, *Carry On Behind*, *Carry On England* and *Carry On Emmannuelle*, my memories are of just having a good time and laughing a lot. The films were always shot on a "tight" budget and usually took four weeks to make, so there wasn't much time for too much detail. I think that's part of their English postcard humour fun. I was very sad at the death of Kenneth Williams, he was always wickedly charming, a great tease and also an authority on history.'

Larry Dann

A Peter Rogers Production

CARRY ON TEACHER

William Wakefield **TED RAY**   Gregory Adams **KENNETH CONNOR**
Michael Bean **CHARLES HAWTREY**   Alistair Grigg **LESLIE PHILLIPS**
Edwin Milton **KENNETH WILLIAMS**   Grace Short **HATTIE JACQUES**
Sarah Allcock **JOAN SIMS**
Felicity Wheeler **ROSALIND KNIGHT**
Alf **CYRIL CHAMBERLAIN**
Robin Stevens **RICHARD O'SULLIVAN**
Billy Haig **GEORGE HOWELL**
Harry Bird **ROY HINES**
Penny Lee **DIANA BEEVERS**   Pat Gordon **JACQUELINE LEWIS**
Sheila Dale **CAROL WHITE**
Atkins **PAUL COLE**   Irene **JANE WHITE**   Boy **LARRY DANN**

Screenplay by **Norman Hudis**
Music composed & directed by **Bruce Montgomery**

Poster tag-line - 'You roared at Carry On Sergeant,
howled at Carry On Nurse, you'll
be convulsed by Carry On Teacher'

Art Director **Lionel Couch**
Director of Photography **Reginald Wyer B.S.C.**
Editor **John Shirley** Production Manager **Frank Bevis**
Camera Operator **Alan Hume**   Assistant Director **Bert Batt**
Sound Editor **Leslie Wiggins**
Sound Recordists **Robert T. MacPhee & Gordon K. McCallum**
Continuity **Tilly Day**   Make-up **George Blackler**
Hairdressing **Olga Angelinetta**   Casting Director **Betty White**
Wardrobe **Laurell Staffell**   Set Dressing **Terence Morgan**
Producer **Peter Rogers**   Director **Gerald Thomas**

A 1959 Anglo Amalgamated Release 'U' Cert.
Black & White Running time - 86 mins. 7,771ft

CARRY ON CONSTABLE

Gaining an extra Sid for... well, having an extra Sid in the cast, this is a major milestone in the *Carry On* legacy, introducing the guiding light of the series in the shape of Mr James himself. Sid's down-to-earth, laid back approach to comedy acting was ideal for the *Carry On* style and he complemented the established farceurs to perfection. Familiar with Williams' pompous figures of authority and Jacques' larger-than-life touches of gentle anguish from *Hancock's Half Hour*, Sid storms through Hudis' comic homage to *Dixon of Dock Green* with all-out innuendo firmly in mind. He hits the floor running while the likes of Williams, Hawtrey and Connor are happily set in their familiar characterizations: this is a series entry that is confident with itself, relaxed in the knowledge that it's a winner. It is the first true blue *Carry On* classic.

The film's basic premise is vintage Hudis, dealing with the urgent need for replacement police staff to plug the gap caused by absentees down with flu. Sid is the main man who stands as the pillar of authority around whom the bumbling incompetents bumble. In a nutshell, it's *Sergeant* in helmets!

However, the stern figure of James is never really the aggressive enemy that Hartnell is initially. Instead Sid turns on the amazed authority because of his love of the job and his need to cover the sheer bullheaded incompetence of his superior (Eric Barker). The two share at least one priceless moment of pure *Carry On* fun when Barker gabbles on about his prized exotic fish and gleefully asks Sgt James: 'Would you like to have a look at my cherbunkin?' James: 'If it will give you any satisfaction!'. Together with his only real ally, the coyly loving and similarly minded Hattie Jacques, James keeps a firm hold on the policing of the area while all the praise goes to Barker and all the problems are directed at him.

Into this unstable but controlled situation stumble three recruits from nightmare city in the shape of Kenneth Williams, Kenneth Connor and Leslie Phillips. They are brilliantly introduced: as Sid talks with Cyril Chamberlain and confidently explains that the new boys will be great - 'I hope!' - Thomas cuts to the imposing image of the three eccentrics in uniform heading towards the station and stopping off to help friendly robber (boxing legend Freddie Mills) get away with a huge haul.

Into this bubbling cocktail of madness and mayhem stumbles experienced but camply unsuitable policeman, Charles Hawtrey, who memorably turns on the full effeminate mincing for an effective contrast with the gruff, no nonsense figure of Sid. Strolling throughout the film with flowers, scooter antics and banter with his budgie, Bobby, Hawtrey even manages to inject the first intertextual reference in the series. In a direct evocation of *Sergeant* he gurgles cheerfully on parade, 'I haven't done this since the army!'. Although the main protagonists had hardly steered off the tried and tested characterizations from the first film, Hawtrey's delightful delivery and knowing look is the first sign that *Constable* is a direct descendant of the first film and happy to look over its shoulders to past glories. In the future, amidst the cinematic in-jokes and innuendo, most films would contain a reference to the deep and distant past of *Carry On* comedy.

Although James stands firmly at the centre of this film, it is the playful and dubious misadventures of Williams, Connor, Hawtrey and Phillips that signal most of the fun. Williams is back to his high-and-mighty, superior self, mocking old fashioned policing methods and dedicating his life to spotting the criminal by mere observation (notably arresting CID undercover man, Victor Maddern), while Connor twitches in the background, living his life through astrology, jittering around in his zodiac pyjamas and frequently rubbing his rabbit's foot. Phillips, in his last *Carry On* for 32 years, turns on the wicked charm with effortless ease.

In *Constable*, for the first time, the romantic interludes that had to some extent got in the way of the innuendo in the earlier films were relegated to a

Kenneth Connor, Kenneth Williams and Leslie Phillips are the new recruits in *Carry On Constable*.

sub-plot concerning Leslie's tongue-in-cheek attention to a scantily-clad Shirley Eaton. Thus with the glamour of Eaton suitably decorative on the sidelines, Hudis can turn to the more comically fruitful fun of the bashful advances of Kenneth Connor towards dedicated policewoman Joan Sims (Kenneth's *Teacher* relationship with Rosalind Knight resurrected without the pathos) - the moment when Connor pours out his heart to Sims as she walks up a flight of stairs and he carries on along the path is touchingly real but totally hilarious. True love wins out in the end as always!

The inexperienced policemen wander through a host of outlandish vignettes, including Hawtrey's camp rescue attempt on a cat stuck in a tree, Connor's forced entry into a house after hearing a supposed murder which turns out to be a radio show and Williams' joyous act of helping a deaf old lady (Esma Cannon) across the road after she had just spent minutes crossing in the other direction. The three join forces with Leslie Phillips to pull off the classic shower sequence in the police cells. This begins with Charlie's annoyingly cheerful personality waking up his fellow officers. As the four wander into the shower, Williams urges Hawtrey to stick the water on: 'Come on, turn it on!'. In so doing, cold water shoots out and a bedraggled Hawtrey explains: 'Oh, I'm frightfully sorry. I remember now. It only comes on hot at certain times. Williams: 'You maniac!' Connor: 'We'll all catch f...f...flu' (refer to *Teacher*'s staff room madness with Kenneth's stutter on f...f...fifth formers!). Phillips: 'Let's get out of here!'. Cue four bare bottoms!

The redemption of the four bumblers comes with a tense operation in a deserted house in search of a dreaded criminal gang. Montgomery's musical score is full of sinister passages and stunned silences as the intrepid coppers stagger around the building and eventually save the day, see Sid promoted to Inspector, find permanent positions at the station and bring Hattie's love for Sgt James out in the open. It was all fun and games in the early days of *Carry On* comedy and this film remains the most enjoyable, effective and entertaining Hudis entry. When you have Sid tackling the innuendo with gusto and Williams and Hawtrey mincing around in women's clothes where can you go wrong?

Best performance

It just has to be Sid's Sergeant Frank Wilkins, an instantly likable, heart-warming, streetwise, in-control debut contribution. While the more experienced *Carry On* farceurs run through every manic police misadventure in the book, Sid simply strolls around the madness with a bemused shake of the head. Whether it be his initial brilliantly underplayed and innuendo-encrusted line concerning Mrs Bottomly and the suspicious behaviour round the rear of her property, or the split second of stunned anger as Leslie Phillips tosses a bucket of water into his face, Sid stands tall amidst the camp one-liners and frustrated couplings.

Favourite bit

The legendary introductory sequence with the raw recruits battling Sid is one of the finest moments of *Carry On* comedy - certainly from this early era. Authority versus bumblers in definitive terms. Williams: 'I'm Benson, Sergeant. This is Constable Potter and this is Constable Constable.' Sid: 'Who?' Connor: 'Charlie Constable!'/'Oh I get it, that's your name!'/'Yeah! and I'm fed up with it - everybody keeps taking the mickey.'/'Nobody will do that here Constable Constable.'/'Oh, I'm very pleased to hear it Sergeant Sergeant!' It cracks me up every time!

Did you know?

When working on the script, Norman Hudis found inspiration hard to come by and so organized a few days alongside the force at Slough Police Station. After a few days of hard work and serious crime he came away believing that no *Carry On* humour could be fashioned from the profession. Peter Rogers advised him to leave the theme for a while but after several viewings of BBC television's adventures of Jack Warner down at Dock Green, Hudis wrote the ultimate police comedy in a few weeks!

A prophetic writer reviewing *Constable* for *Monthly Film Bulletin* wrote: 'The *Carry On* series looks like becoming an anthology of all the slap-and-tickle music hall jokes that have ever been cracked.' Get away!

Carry On make-up artist George Blackler bitterly complained about one assignment on the film - powdering the bare bottoms of the four new coppers to stop the studio lights flaring during the shower sequence. With tongue planted firmly in cheek (although I'm not sure whose!), Blackler complained that he had made up Margaret Lockwood, Jean Kent and every beauty in British film but had quite clearly reached the bottom now!

Following the restriction of Ted Ray's casting, Peter Rogers looked for a way to attract wider audiences and searched for a Scottish comedian to act as the comedy's pivot. The choice was Chic Murray. The idea is certainly relishable but Rogers abandoned the thought and approached Sid instead - an inspired move.

Look out for...

Gerald Thomas takes full advantage of the comic impact of Charles Hawtrey and builds up his entrance into a major event. Carrying his budgie cage in one hand and a huge bunch of flowers in the other, Charlie minces into view with a cheerful and flamboyantly camp greeting. Later films like *Cowboy* and *Up the Jungle* would see Hawtrey's first appearances become major comic statements.

There's a classic of longing sexuality as Kenneth Connor spins out his belief in the supernatural and the fact that Eric Barker was a Roman gladiator in a past life. As Connor closes his eyes to imagine the scene, Sid James shakes his head in disbelief until Connor mentions the scantily-clad vestal virgins. Immediately Sid closes his eyes to get the vision in a superb piece of visual comedy - look out Cleopatra, Sid is on his way!

Terence Longdon, initially shortlisted as a major *Carry On* team member, crops up in *Constable* as a cocky, cheerfully sympathetic confidence trickster who convinces PC Williams that he has a mountain of money owing to him. It's an effective cameo gag appearance from the romantic lead of the first two films who found his position comedically expanded and filled by the wolfish figure of Leslie Phillips.

Carry On semi-regular Lucy Griffiths injects an American television in-joke when she signs off from her telephone conversation to the police with a knowing '10-4' - the national catchphrase continually used by Broderick Crawford in *Highway Patrol*.

Charles Hawtrey incorporates a stunning ad lib when he gets out of bed, chats to his budgie and bangs his concealed chamber pot. After the planned gag of a china clink is captured, the object refuses to stop rolling on the floor and Hawtrey barks, 'Be quiet'. In these early days such moments of improvisation were allowed to stay in, later on, the script would be a restricting bible.

Carry On memories

'One will always have happy memories of the three *Carry Ons* that I made in the early days - they were fun, *and very badly paid* - the people I worked with were a joy - but it was a long time ago! One has thankfully moved on.'
Leslie Phillips

'I only ever had one or two days' work on those very funny films. Going into a long running team show is a frightening experience and so it was that each time I was lucky enough to be invited to play in a *Carry On* I always arrived at the studio with a certain amount of trepidation. I first met Sid James very early one morning when we were on location for my very first *Carry On, Carry On Constable*. We were comparatively young then and

Lock up your daughters! The arrival of Sid James with Hattie Jacques in *Carry On Constable*.

Hello, hello, what's all this then - Kenneth Williams misjudges Victor Maddern in *Carry On Constable*.

able to talk as buddies. I was greatly in awe of all that talent. Let me quote you an example of what I mean: I had been at RADA with a young man who played the 'Lonely Man' in the advert for the cigarette, 'Strand'. Terence Brook was a very good looking young man with a charming personality; when he was cast as The Lonely Man I was very happy for him. But then the cigarette did not sell well because the public never wanted to feel lonely. The ads went on and on, and nobody was buying the product and the ads became a bit of a joke. One morning on the set I was chatting with Kenny Connor whom I had known for many years. I talked about Terence Brook and suddenly, right there on the spot, Kenny made up the following limerick:

There was a hernia patient named Rand,
Who had all the hairs shaved off round his gland.
He looked with despair,
And said, 'There's still one hair there!',
But you're never alone with a Strand!'.

On the set it seemed to me that Kenneth Williams' mouth was never closed - except when he was swallowing lunch. Sometimes I had to walk away for fear of the laughter pain becoming too much to bear. All this ad lib comedy gave me the most extraordinary complex to add to my own home-grown inferior one. Each and every one of the team was a member of the most elite band of thespians in the world. They all had huge talents.
Victor Maddern

A Peter Rogers Production

CARRY ON CONSTABLE

Sergeant Frank Wilkins **SIDNEY JAMES**
Inspector Mills **ERIC BARKER**
Constable Charlie Constable **KENNETH CONNOR**
PC Timothy Gorse **CHARLES HAWTREY**
PC Stanley Benson **KENNETH WILLIAMS**   PC Tom Potter **LESLIE PHILLIPS**
WPC Gloria Passworthy **JOAN SIMS**   Sgt Laura Moon **HATTIE JACQUES**
Thurston **CYRIL CHAMBERLAIN**   Sally Barry **SHIRLEY EATON**
Mrs May **JOAN HICKSON**
Distraught Woman **IRENE HANDL**   Herbert Hall **TERENCE LONGDON**
Crook **FREDDIE MILLS**   WPC Harrison **JILL ADAMS**
Store Manager **BRIAN OULTON**   Criminal Type **VICTOR MADDERN**
Suspect **JOAN YOUNG**   Deaf Old Lady **ESMA CANNON**
Agitated Woman **HILDA FENEMORE**
Vague Woman **NOEL DYSON**   Assistant Manager **ROBIN RAY**
Matt **MICHAEL BALFOUR**
Honoria **DIANE AUBREY**   Eric **IAN CURRY**
1st Shop Assistant **MARY LAW**
Miss Horton **LUCY GRIFFITHS**   Thief **PETER BENNETT**
Cliff **JACK TAYLOR**
Shorty **ERIC BOON**   Girl with dog **JANETTA LAKE**
Young Woman **DORINA STEVENS**
Citizens **TOM GILL**   **FRANK FORSYTH**
JOHN ANTROBUS & ERIC CORRIE

Based on an idea by **Brock Williams**
Screenplay by **Norman Hudis**
Music composed & directed by **Bruce Montgomery**

Poster tag-line - 'That hilarious Carry On shower in another riot of laughter!'

Art Director **Carmen Dillon**   Director of Photography **Ted Scaife B.S.C.**
Editor **John Shirley**
Production Manager **Frank Bevis**   Camera Operator **Alan Hume**
Assistant Director **Peter Manley**
Sound Editor **Leslie Wiggins**
Sound Recordists **Robert T. MacPhee & Bill Daniels**
Continuity **Joan Davis**   Make-up **George Blackler**
Hairdressing **Stella Rivers**
Dress Designer **Yvonne Caffin**   Set Dressing **Vernon Dixon**
Casting Director **Betty White**
Producer **Peter Rogers**   Director **Gerald Thomas**

A 1959 Anglo Amalgamated film released in 1960 'U' Cert.
Black & White
Running time - 86 mins. 7,781ft

CARRY ON REGARDLESS

This is a mad, mixed-up, rag bag of *Carry On* delights with a totally meaningless title for a totally plotless collection of brief comic situations and familiar character players. If hardly the 'funniest Carry On ever!' as the poster would lead us to believe, *Regardless* is a timelessly funny encapsulation of the best elements of vintage *Carry On* - a complete cast of flamboyant team members, lowly British characters joining forces to make good, a few moments of gentle sniggering at beloved and belittled institutions and a feast of good time fun through boxing matches, chatting up women, getting drunk and demolishing a house. What a way to spend a Saturday night!

As the title suggests, this film is devoid of any real thematic focus, and wanders aimlessly but memorably through a myriad of various occupations and bizarre scenarios in which anything can happen and the best thing to do is to sit back, enjoy the experience and simply carry on regardless! It was Hudis' least favourite of his films, as he believed that the comedy lost its edge through the film's rambling narrative and disjointed approach. However, I disagree with this comment: clearly the film has less structure than the earlier *Carry Ons*, but the central plot - that of Sid James and his 'Helping Hands' agency - is a worthy peg on which to hang the various sketches.

An attempt to address some of those thousands of letters Peter Rogers had received suggesting further *Carry On* subjects, *Regardless* is a real curate's egg of surprises and dubious gags delivered with style by the team in definitive stereotype mode. Kenneth Connor bumbles around nervously as women make advances (a particularly lush Fenella Fielding), Kenneth Williams stomps through the working-class masses with his nose in the air, Joan Sims has the frumpy female gags thrown at her as her sexy figure of the past two films begins to transform into the battling harridan of the Rothwell era and Charles Hawtrey minces about in the background with a constant smile and a wickedly sparkling glint in his eye. Bill Owen and Terence Longdon, by now merely token familiar faces from an earlier era, have little of note to do and do it with little note. All the funniest and most carefully written vignettes go to either Hawtrey, Williams or Connor, as the others struggle through some minor low antics and make the best of a less-than-excellent deal. The seventh and most glamorous 'Helping Hand' is series newcomer Liz Fraser, who resurrects the girl-next-door sex symbol Shirley Eaton role with an injection of acting confidence and good natured comedy. In fact this role was a very hasty re-write of a major 'Helping Hand' position for Hattie Jacques who had to pull out shortly before filming began due to illness. Jacques, a popular part of the series at this point, did want to make an appearance, however brief, and fittingly crops up as the Sister in a hospital sequence with Sid James and Joan Hickson - Hickson ironically playing Matron in a role reversal with Jacques from their work in *Nurse*.

The element of stability in the film is in the office sequences where boss Sid James and flustered assistant Esma Cannon dish out the various odd-ball assignments and try and tie the whole into a seamless comedy of community and innuendo. If you're willing just to enjoy a handful of totally committed and peerless comedy actors go through their paces, then *Regardless* is a real treat.

Sid's brilliantly laid back, underplayed and slightly off-centre lead role is the catalyst for some priceless moments. He himself only tackles one assignment, when Kynaston Reeves makes his rather confusing request for Sid to take his place in a hospital waiting room. This inadvertently develops into a situation where James is happily examining the nurses in their underwear - tough work but somebody has to do it! Hudis' most memorable comedy moments are given to the camp clowns but there's no denying that Sid is the guy in charge. After all, he selects his new employees, even though he does take on every-

Give us a job! Bill Owen, Kenneth Connor, Kenneth Williams and Terence Longdon lack satisfaction in *Carry On Regardless*.

masses with his unique gobbledegook talk. Sid James turns on his down-to-earth, no-time-for-this-idiot style and brilliantly debunks Unwin's surreal trains of thought. As Unwin walks out and Williams walks in, the eager Kenneth asks, 'Was that a job? What did he want?' Sid, straight-faced, sighs, 'A new set of teeth by the sound of it!'. Class!

Of course, towards the close, Kenneth is present while Stanley speaks and it turns out that Unwinese is a language Williams speaks like a native. 'He gobbledegooks', he explains to James. 'I don't care what he eats!' groans Sid. All is fine and dandy as the problems are resolved and the job of cleaning (read, demolishing) one of Unwin's properties creates a whiz bang, dust covered, gloriously messy climax which ends the only way it can - Kenneth W. translating Unwin's last words as 'carry on regardless'. Well who wants originality anyway!

Best performance

Kenneth Connor grabs a host of Hudis' funniest vignettes and injects them with fruitful nerves, manic bumbling and jittering giggles to create a string of hilarious moments. The wild attempts at giving up smoking create a memorable atmosphere of obsessed angst directed against an understanding Joan Sims, with Kenneth's befuddled and totally out-of-control few minutes creating a fine piece of comic madness. *The Thirty Nine Steps* scenario, while tipping its hat to Hitchcock, allows Kenneth to enact the heroic ideals of Robert Donat through his little man persona - a double-edged moment in the train washroom with Kenneth breaking off his super cool pep talk to his natural bag-of-nerves self is particularly fine. Great scenes like a sexy encounter with a panting Fenella Fielding and a host of jabbering Chinese stand alongside one of the milestone Connor moments - the Ruby Room scene when his suppressed giggles and uncontrollable reaction to the antics of the ancient buffers get him thrown out. Connor's reaction to a member's attempt to reach for a book is expertly timed and note the reference back to *Sergeant* with his addressing of the attendant as Sarge!

Favourite bit

Despite Connor's claim to a clutch of prime Hudis situations, the finest of these is given to Kenneth Williams: the now legendary chimp-walking sequence. Rather uneagerly taken from owner Ambrosine Phillpotts, the chimp accompanies Kenneth as he wanders around London looking for a jolly outing on a bus (although driver Tony Sagar is less than impressed: 'Great hairy thing!'/'I am not!') while typically down-to-earth cabbie Fred Griffiths

body that turns up for the job interview where he attracts sexual offers from Liz Fraser ('Delia King... Miss!') and flamboyantly conceited boasts from Kenneth W. with his wealth of knowledge and amazing command of a host of languages.

In the largest cast of well-known actors ever assembled for a *Carry On*, every new venture or unusual job introduces a few brief lines from such popular character stars as Sydney Tafler, Molly Weir and Jerry Desmonde. Hugely welcome performers wander through the proceedings as the seven 'Helping Hands' eagerly try and complete their assignments. Liz Fraser's whistleworthy figure is used to stunning effect in a seductive sequence with Jimmy Thompson while her every line is misinterpreted as a sexual advance in a mixed-up meeting with Ian Curry (here giving a restrained performance after his rather stilted contribution in *Constable*). He is expecting a visit from his marriage agency lady friend, a scenario later resurrected with Richard O'Callaghan and Jacki Piper in *Loving*. Joan Sims enjoys herself in the classic winetasting sequence with Nicholas Parsons, David Lodge and spiked glasses of Pinewood mock plonk, while Williams grins and giggles with snide-like uncertainty in his translation of Julia Arnall's dubious foreign utterances. Charles Hawtrey gets entangled in a spirited boxing match with resident muscle man Tom Clegg and there is a wonderful brief bit from Norman Rossington as the referee - the simple phrase 'Ahh!' has never been so funny!

However, the enjoyable goings-on of the various clients and Sid's bumbling employees could not go on for ever - an element to bring the events and the principal actors together is needed. That linking force comes from Stanley Unwin's guest starring turn as Sid's landlord who confuses the assembled

tells it as it is ('I'll take you but not your brother!'). Finally Ken and the chimp arrive at a rather uncivilized tea party at London Zoo, and as the other chimps go ape, Williams and his companion sip their tea with calm decorum. Kenneth enjoyed filming this most-loved piece of *Carry On* capering: note the affectionate moment when he saves the chimp from getting his toes clipped by Griffiths' cab!

Did you know?

The fairly minor role for Terence Longdon is a radically cut back version of a major part originally earmarked for Leslie Phillips. Unhappy with a typecast future as a *Carry On* cad, Leslie decided to quit before *Regardless* started shooting and Hudis reshaped the part for Longdon to play. A Bristol newspaper still managed to pan Leslie Phillips' performance in the film even though the poor lad wasn't in it!

While filming *Regardless* Charles Hawtrey had a mild disagreement with Peter Rogers over what would prove a long-running subject - his billing. Charles complained about his low position and the lack of funny lines Hudis had given him in the new script, after all, he explained, 'I am a comedian!'. Rogers was not impressed. As it was, Hawtrey had less to do than usual in *Regardless*, but milked his boxing scene well, wonderfully camping through the stripper/exotic birds misunderstanding with Sydney Tafler - blue tits will never be the same again!

In fact one of Charles Hawtrey's funniest scenes was cut by the British Board of Film Censors and in the process, an entire performance, that of Eleanor Summerfield, was completely lost to the cutting room floor; a pity when you sample a brief extract from the original script. Summerfield: 'You'll be able to do your part from the wardrobe!' Hawtrey: 'You flatter me Madam!' Obviously too hot for the audiences of 1961. An exchange from the Connor/Fielding seduction scene which originally read 'Oh please Mr Twist don't make it hard for me.'/'Oh... actually you're making it a little bit hard for me Madam!' was quickly changed to the totally unfunny '...making it a little bit difficult for me!'. Fans of the film series and, indeed, of the joke, had to wait until *Emmannuelle* and a scene with Suzanne Danielle and Larry Dann to hear the original version.

Many of the frumpy jokes originally intended for Hattie Jacques were tacked on to Joan Sims' role, allowing the stunning Liz Fraser to stand as a sexy contrast. Initially, Sims would have been the muted object of the male gaze, but Fraser's casting enabled the use of more forthright sexual comment.

Look out for...

A cutting comment on the lack of equality between the sexes when Liz Fraser and Joan Sims barge into the 'Men's' section of the job centre - much to Kenneth Connor's chagrin. Liz mutters, 'It's a man's world!'.

During the photographer sequence with a pompous, self-loving Kenneth Williams, Ian Wilson and Michael Ward, Bruce Montgomery injects a musical joke to complement Williams' shocked amazement at the product in the form of a snatch from 'The Flight of the Bumble Bee'.

While Kenneth Connor is caught up in Hitchcockian intrigue in *The Thirty Nine Steps* parody, a further Hitchcock reference is conjured up by Betty Marsden's continually flickering eye: 'You're not Chinese, so what!'. This links to the all-important sign of the killer in *Young and Innocent*. The huge frame of Eric Pohlmann controlling the whole sequence is, of course, a nod to Hitchcock himself.

Also during *The Thirty Nine Steps* sequence, look out for Cyril Raymond as a bemused army officer resurrecting train-based memories from his best-loved role as Celia Johnson's husband in *Brief Encounter*.

Carry On memories

'The sheer fun of it all has packed so many memories that it's not easy to select one. However, I do recall strongly the expression on the face of Sid James (the cast reckoned it resembled a squashed grapefruit) when, in *Carry On Regardless*, the

Give us a clue! Kenneth Connor does his stunning fly impression to a totally bemused Charles Julian in *Carry On Regardless*.

mercurial and excruciatingly funny Kenneth Williams translated my dialogue with Sid when I played the part of Sid's landlord and was interviewing him in order to get some renovating work done on my property. At the end of the interview, which contained several interruptions when Kenneth explained the meaning of a particularly difficult word, Sid's goodbye to me which was less than friendly was followed by Kenneth wishing me a "Goodly byelode". Kenneth, like so many other comic pros, understood the "conscious stream" of sense concealed in my dialogue and it was always inspiring to work with him'.

Stanley Unwin

'I was only in one of the films - *Carry On Regardless*. The only thing I can tell you about it is that Julia Arnall had to hit me over the head with a vase which was obviously made of wax and quite harmless. Even so she managed to hit me with the edge and cut my head. She always was a bit silly! The only other thing was I had a long chat with the boxer Freddie Mills who was a lovely fellow but later was found shot dead in his car outside his night club.'

Terence Alexander

'The particular story line in which I was involved was cut from *Carry On Regardless*. The few days I spent working in the studio was great fun - they were such a nice team of actors - any spare moments were spent being regaled with hilarious stories from Kenneth Williams and watching Sid James and the other men playing poker behind the set!'

Eleanor Summerfield

'My old mates have passed on but they will be in my memories until I slip the anchor. Sid James, Charlie Hawtrey and Kenneth Williams *et al* are some of my fellow artistes who have a special place in my mind. Sid with his horses, Charlie with his troubles and Kenny with his comedy. They were a happy crowd, no bitchiness, no temperaments - we all mucked in together and did a job of work which was to make the public laugh. We must have done a good job because the public still love them!'

Fred Griffiths

A Peter Rogers Production

CARRY ON REGARDLESS

Bert Handy **SIDNEY JAMES** Sam Twist **KENNETH CONNOR**
Gabriel Dimple **CHARLES HAWTREY**
Francis Courtenay **KENNETH WILLIAMS** Lily Duveen **JOAN SIMS**
Delia King **LIZ FRASER**
Montgomery Infield-Hopping **TERENCE LONGDON**
Mike Weston **BILL OWEN**
Miss Cooling **ESMA CANNON** Penny Panting **FENELLA FIELDING**
Sister **HATTIE JACQUES**
Landlord **STANLEY UNWIN** Mr Panting **ED DEVEREAUX**
Policeman **CYRIL CHAMBERLAIN** Yoki's Owner **AMBROSINE PHILLPOTTS**
Matron **JOAN HICKSON** Bird Owner **MOLLY WEIR**
Strip club manager **SYDNEY TAFLER** Sinister Man **ERIC POHLMANN**
Nurse **JUNE JAGO** Referee **NORMAN ROSSINGTON**
Trevor Trelawney **TERENCE ALEXANDER**
Martin Paul **JERRY DESMONDE** Mr Delling **JIMMY THOMPSON**
Bus conductor **TONY SAGAR**
Wine organizer **HOWARD MARION CRAWFORD**
Taxi Driver **FRED GRIFFITHS**
Wine waiter **BERNARD HUNTER** Connoisseur **DAVID LODGE**
Wolf **NICHOLAS PARSONS**
Wine bystander **MICHAEL NIGHTINGALE**
Raffish customer **PATRICK CARGILL**
Testy old man **KYNASTON REEVES** Houseman **FRASER KERR**
Fanatic patient **DOUGLAS IVES**
Pretty probationer **MAUREEN MOORE**
1st Sinister passenger **VICTOR MADDERN**
2nd Sinister passenger **DENIS SHAW** 'Mata Hari' **BETTY MARSDEN**
Lefty **FREDDIE MILLS**
Massive Micky McGee **TOM CLEGG** Dynamite Dan **JOE ROBINSON**
Auntie **LUCY GRIFFITHS**
Shop Assistant **IAN WHITTAKER** Trudy Trelawney **JULIA ARNALL**
MC/Policeman **JACK TAYLOR**
Club receptionist **GEORGE STREET** Army Officer **CYRIL RAYMOND**
Old lady **NANCY ROBERTS** Photographer **MICHAEL WARD**
Advertising Man **IAN WILSON** Chinese lady **MADAME YANG**
Formidable lady **JUDITH FURSE** Distraught manager **DAVID STOLL**
Helen Delling **CAROL SHELLEY** Old man in Ruby Room **CHARLES JULIAN**
Leonard Beamish **IAN CURRY**

Screenplay by **Norman Hudis**
Music composed & conducted by **Bruce Montgomery**
Poster tag-line - 'Funniest Carry On ever!'

Art Director **Lionel Couch** Director of Photography **Alan Hume**
Editor **John Shirley** Associate Producer **Basil Keys**
Assistant Director **Jack Causey** Camera Operator **Dudley Lovell**
Sound Editor **Arthur Ridout**
Sound Recordists **Robert T. MacPhee & Gordon McCallum**
Unit Manager **Claude Watson** Hairdressing **Biddy Chrystal**
Continuity **Gladys Goldsmith**
Make-up **George Blackler** Costume Designer **Joan Ellacott**
Casting Director **Betty White**
Producer **Peter Rogers** Director **Gerald Thomas**

A 1961 Anglo Amalgamated Release 'U' Cert.
Black & White Running time - 90 mins. 8,100ft

CARRY ON CRUISING

All aboard for a fun-filled cruise on the SS *Happy Wanderer*, with Sid James and his hapless new recruits sailing around the Pinewood back lot with cheerful grins and bumbling antics. Or how to mark the end of an era with a special occasion, for *Cruising* does mark the end of an era in the *Carry On* series, boasting the sixth and last script written by Norman Hudis. The film also marks the first venture into colour for the *Carry Ons*, allowing the viewer to enjoy the rippling shades of blue from the studio water tanks as they complement the still fairly mild shades of blue humour from the gang.

As with all Hudis' work, *Cruising* sets up the experienced figure of authority (in this case James again) and allows a collection of fresh-faced, eager but incompetent assistants to make his life hellish. Again, as with *Teacher*, the established figure has something to prove - Sid wants to gain control of a brand new oceanliner - and the bemused, confused and, ultimately, endearing meddlings of those around him sees these plans changed. The scenario is simply a very enjoyable retread of past glories and the initial sequence when Captain Sid welcomes his new crew is practically a slightly re-written remake of the introduction sequence from *Constable*.

Kenneth Williams is there again as a big-headed, supercilious, warmly flamboyant officer, as is Kenneth Connor as the nervy, big-hearted, love sick medical man. However, of the firmly established *Carry On* team, that's all we get. The film is a vital watershed for the regulars. For the first time since the series began, Charles Hawtrey was absent from the cast, a further dispute over billing causing his decision to turn down a role. Hawtrey, stating quite rightly that he had been with the films since the beginning, firmly believed that he should have top billing and a star on his dressing room door. As Gerald Thomas later commented, this was impossible, 'with the best will in the world we could never have cast him above Sid James', while restlessness in

the camp was not tolerated by Peter Rogers. The *Carry On* name was always the star, and although the team was essential, no one single performer was considered indispensable. So it was that Hawtrey saw his role occupied by one-off Carry Oner Lance Percival, who also crops up in the Rogers/Thomas films *Raising the Wind*, *Twice Round the Daffodils* and *The Big Job*. Percival does a good job in the Hawtrey shoes, mincing about with his toothy grin, lanky clumsiness and outlandish cooking ideals, while allowing the bulk of the laughs to fall on the shoulders of James, Williams and Connor.

In a major breakthrough in the structure of the series, the need to spread the good lines over fewer number of actors built up a solid contrasting relationship between Sid James and Kenneth Williams. While Kenneth Connor is spooning about with besotted love for Dilys Laye, walking round the deck with pseudo-energetic style and forcing buckets of sea sickness pills down Percival's throat, James and Williams have the opportunity to establish their classic love-hate, working class-educated class, macho-

A priceless shot of Captain Sid James explaining a movie camera to 'Miss Loughborough' on the set of *Carry On Cruising*.

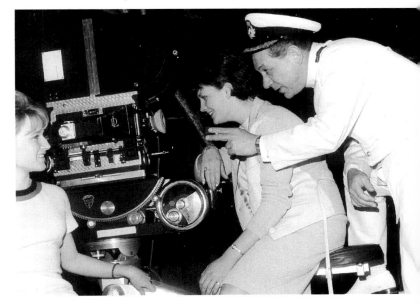

The power game - Gerald Thomas, Stuart Levy and Peter Rogers on the set of *Carry On Cruising*.

mincing contrast that would develop further during the Rothwell golden era. In the earlier movies, Connor was the chief comic name at the top of the team billing. Now he was lowered to make room for the explosive team of James and Williams - so it would be for the majority of films to come.

Ironically Kenneth Williams almost joined Charles Hawtrey on the walk-out on *Cruising*. Unhappy with his unchanging and lowly wages for the series, he told Rogers that he would only make the film if he had a pay rise. Peter assured him this would be considered (it later came into effect with *Jack*) but promised Kenneth that the filming would get out of the studio and on to a real ship for an exotic Mediterranean cruise. Williams agreed to star. Eventually the cruise around the Med became simply a cruise around Britain, which, to Williams, was better than nothing. Finally, of course, the money wouldn't stretch to even that and the entire interior and deck of the ship (complete with bar and swimming pool) was designed by Carmen Dillon and built at Pinewood Studios. The initial shots of a liner were filmed at Southampton by kind permission of P&O Ferries - none of the cast were present.

Like the past *Carry Ons*, *Cruising* sees the smooth running of a national institution disrupted and destroyed by a mad collection of comic situations, misadventures and memorable characters - tirelessly cheerful Cyril Chamberlain, Jimmy Thompson's sympathetic bar man, Ronnie Stevens' pathetic drunken traveller, Brian Rawlinson's comic shyness, Liz Fraser, seductively resisting male temptation and Esma Cannon as the frenzied aged passenger who leaves the younger guests standing. But it is moments like the inspired serenading from Connor ('Oh Bella Flo, Oh Bella Flo, I need you so, Please

let's have a...I love you so!'), the manic bull-fight sequence with Williams and Connor ('he was the biggest bull shipper in the business!'), joyful banter with Williams and James ('I always find the first few days make me feel quite drowsy'/'Shut your porthole!') and Sid's solid but sympathetic authority, that hold the film together. When Sid complains of things happening behind his back and Kenneth Connor helpfully offers to massage his clavicles, you know this is class *Carry On* and the company are true pros. Raise the anchor!

Best performance

Sid James - for a sterling job in cementing the whole plot together and remaining the one fixed point in a chaotically changing world. Brilliantly mixing streetwise cheerfulness with biting satire and angry put downs, Sid grins, grimaces and crawls through Hudis' scenario basking in his power and proud military past: 'During the war I did Arctic runs which would have made HMS *Ulysses* look like a trip to Brighton!'. Sid also displays an untypical fear of female advances in his battles to avoid the affection of a lovelorn Dilys Laye; his belief in the power of thought and the flamboyant psychoanalysis of his dreams by Kenneth Williams adds a touching edge of uncontrolled attraction and intellectual overtones: 'I'm not a Jung man!'.

Favourite bit

The peak of *Cruising* comes, naturally, in a priceless piece of by-play between Sid James and Kenneth Williams. In a desperate attempt to impress the Captain, Kenneth teams up with that mad little pixie Esma Cannon for a wild game of table tennis. Esma quickly shows her firm grasp on the game and gives Williams a clear run for his money. Angered by his impending defeat, Kenneth puts in more effort and whacks the ball into Sid's open mouth. Cannon's delight: 'Oh clever! Do it again!' is greeted by stunned disbelief as Sid spits out the offending object.

Did you know?

Still basking in the glory of his script for *Nurse*, Hudis began visiting America from 1964 where his work was much praised. Finally in 1966 he moved there permanently to work on American television including several episodes of *The Man From U.N.C.L.E.* and, most notably, the classic adventure *The Five Women Affair* released in British cinemas as *The Karate Killers*, with Herbert Lom, Terry-Thomas and *Nurse's* Jill Ireland.

Cruising was based on an idea by *Carry On* actor and radio clown Eric Barker. He actually suggested a film

Admiral Peter Butterworth gets an eyeful in *Carry On Girls*

The Ship of Fools – *Carry On Cruising* with Kenneth Connor, Kenneth Williams, Ed Devereaux, Vincent Ball and Sid James

A Touch of the Historicals – Charles Hawtrey and Kenneth Williams in *Carry On Jack*

based around a touring coach holiday but Rogers gave him suitable credit for the basic idea of a *Carry On* holiday. The coach scenario would feature, albeit briefly, in both *At Your Convenience* and *Abroad*.

On the release of the film P&O ran a £500 'Carry On Cruising' holiday of a lifetime on the *Canberra*.

Look out for...

A nod to the linear pattern of working class British film comedy when Kenneth Connor's figure of bumbling incompetence falls on to the vast stomach of Willoughby Goddard and pays homage to the late George Formby with a stuttered 'Turned out nice again!'.

A memorable cameo comes from popular comic actor, frequent stooge for Tony Hancock and resident *Army Game* star, Mario Fabrizi as a humourless cook under the bizarre and inspired control of Lance Percival.

Carry On memories

'1. The larking about and jokes between Kenneth Williams and Kenneth Connor when we were not filming were far more outrageous than when we *were* filming.

2. I was playing the chef and one important scene was when the cake I'd made blew up in my face. It was done by a pressure pump underneath with the cake mixture sitting in the pot on top of this air pipe. When they pressed the button the mixture

shot up in my face. However, every time I leaned over to "smell the aroma" just before it exploded, I *blinked* as it actually shot up, i.e. I knew it was coming! Therefore it took 9 takes to get a scene which lasted 10 seconds!'
Lance Percival

A Peter Rogers Production

CARRY ON CRUISING

Captain Wellington Crowther **SIDNEY JAMES**
Leonard Marjoribanks **KENNETH WILLIAMS**
Dr Arthur Binn **KENNETH CONNOR**   Glad Trimble **LIZ FRASER**
Flo Castle **DILYS LAYE**
Bridget Madderley **ESMA CANNON**   Wilfred Haines **LANCE PERCIVAL**
Sam Turner **JIMMY THOMPSON**   Drunk **RONNIE STEVENS**
Jenkins **VINCENT BALL**
Tom Tree **CYRIL CHAMBERLAIN**   Very Fat Man **WILLOUGHBY GODDARD**
Young Officer **ED DEVEREAUX**   Steward **BRIAN RAWLINSON**
Young Man **ANTON RODGERS**
Cook **TONY SAGAR**   Passerby **TERENCE HOLLAND**   Cook **MARIO FABRIZI**
Bridegroom **EVAN DAVID**   Bride **MARIAN COLLINS**
Shapely Miss **JILL MAI MEREDITH**   Kindly Seaman **ALAN CASLEY**

From a Story by **Eric Barker**   Screenplay by **Norman Hudis**
Music composed & conducted by **Bruce Montgomery & Douglas Gamley**
Poster tag-line - 'That Carry On crew in a luxury laughter-cruise!'

Director of Photography **Alan Hume B.S.C.**   Art Director **Carmen Dillon**
Editor **John Shirley** Production Manager **Bill Hill**
Camera Operator **Dudley Lovell**   Assistant Director **Jack Causey**
Sound Editors **Arthur Ridout & Archie Ludski**
Sound Recordists **Robert T. MacPhee & Bill Daniels**
Continuity **Penny Daniels**   Make-up **George Blackler & Geoff Rodway**
Hairdressing **Biddy Chrystal**   Costume Designer **Joan Ellacott**
Casting Director **Betty White**
Beachwear for Miss Fraser & Miss Laye by **Silhouette**
The Producers wish to acknowledge with grateful thanks the
kind assistance of P & O - ORIENT LINES in the making of this film
Producer **Peter Rogers**   Director **Gerald Thomas**

A 1962 Anglo Amalgamated Release 'U' Cert.
Colour Running time - 89 mins. 8,009ft

Delighted chef Lance Percival looks on as Kenneth Williams and Kenneth Connor tell him what to do with his cake in *Carry On Cruising*.

CARRY ON
CABBY

Powerful women establishing a local business and cocking a snook at arrogant male domination may sound like a plot for a Ben Elton play, but it is, in fact, the outline for this landmark *Carry On*. As the first of the totally invaluable feast of scripts submitted by writer Talbot Rothwell, *Cabby* is the seed for the future of the series.

Its longwinded pre-production history is well documented, beginning life as a script that Rothwell had worked on at the request of Peter Rogers, *Call Me A Cab*, with the original idea from Morecambe and Wise screenwriters Sid Green and Dick Hill. With the absence of Norman Hudis from the *Carry On* typewriter, Rogers asked Rothwell if he could restructure the screenplay as a *Carry On*, initially with the working title of *Carry On Taxi*.

Thus a legend was born. Although following directly the Hudis premise of an established authority figure (Sid James) and a collection of clumsy bumblers (Charlie Hawtrey prominent among them), this script rings the changes and dismisses coy 1950s' sentimentality in favour of gritty 1960s' 'kitchen sink' realism. The moving portrayal of the marriage on the rocks between Sid and Hattie Jacques is at the heart of the film and even the well-organized revenge on Sid's love of taxi driving has a sense of pathos and guilty emotion. The times were certainly a'changing from the community mugging of earlier films, and the experienced team members eagerly turned on the serious acting skills to get the full benefit of Rothwell's beautifully crafted script. Cleverly interwoven into the fabric of social realism, Sid's spiral into alcoholism and the pressures of fading affection, are handfuls of typically low-brow *Carry On* humour and delightful farcical sequences with Kenneth Connor in drag, Charles Hawtrey spilling his cups of tea all over the place and a debuting Jim Dale (all wildly spinning arms and youthful panic) as an anxious father-to-be with his expectant wife.

It's all gloriously spirited stuff, superbly played by its semi-seriously minded cast (only Hawtrey turns in a fully comic performance), and stands as arguably the most polished and, importantly, beloved of the early *Carry Ons*. The film marks a welcome return for Hawtrey and Jacques and a reversion to black and white (due to both the original plan to make the cheaply-filmed quickie *Call Me A Cab* and an attempt to address comedically the working-class dramas of Osborne). *Cabby* is a bittersweet comic-drama which injects a more forthright attitude to sex into the scenario and presents the much appreciated stereotypes of the previous films in a new, more three-dimensional fashion. Rothwell was the man with the steering wheel firmly in his hands.

No one could have bettered the performance of Sid James as the ultimate rogue talking, man-about-town, war weary, quick thinking, unromantic battler of the black cabs. In a multi-layered character, Sid's usual chuckling persona is contrasted by a softer trait, naming his first cab PEG 1 after his wife, and sincere friendships with his workers. Whether it be seductively chatting to Hattie over his taxi radio, doggedly trying to whip his new recruits into shape, performing a brilliantly timed chain-smoking sequence with Charles Hawtrey and Jim Dale or spiritedly reliving old army campaigns by rounding up the crooks during the climax, Sid shines throughout.

Kenneth Connor acts as Sid's comrade-in-arms, fighting the restrictions of female ties from Jacques and Fraser and continually trying to brighten Sid's spirits with outlandish ideas and helpful opinions. In a change of pace for Connor, his performance is more bitingly cynical with social comment rather than the friendly bumbling of earlier films. In perhaps his most polished character study, flashes of sarcastic wit when faced with the incompetence of Charles Hawtrey or heart-warming attempts at cheering up Sid James stand side-by-side with a complex and floundering relationship with Liz Fraser. Rothwell highlights the moments of typical

Carry On comedy within a believable scenario to bring the flamboyant style of the Hudis movies into the swinging sixties.

Gerald Thomas' sparkling homage to the Hollywood Western, as Sid's hoard of cabs come to the aid of the hapless heroines (Jacques and Fraser - thus defusing any feminist tendencies in the script!), is a typically fun-filled and touching community-geared close to an early *Carry On*. Thomas orchestrates the sequence with subtle skill, and it remains one of his most polished and exciting cinematic contributions. Hawtrey's final line, linking back to Rothwell's original title, brings on a Sid guffaw and the audience are left chuffed and cheering.

Best performance

Hattie Jacques turns in her most impressive *Carry On* performance, with touching expressions of love towards her preoccupied husband, energetic attempts at getting her own back, a memorable attempt to fool Sid with a Fenella Fielding-like telephone conversation and a final collapse into wedded and blessed bliss. For the first time, Hattie's size is not used as the source of gags or comic by-play as with Tony Hancock and the earlier *Carry Ons*. The only overweight joke comes from Hattie herself, bemoaning her physique due to Sid's insistence to crawl about under his cab tinkering - 'he knows I can't get under one!'. Hattie's awareness of her sexual and romantic needs, her tongue-in-cheek attempts at glamorizing her image and knowing ability to use the sexy image of youthful females to attract taxi business, make her contribution likable and rounded. Justifiably Hattie's favourite *Carry On* assignment, her role in *Cabby* illustrates the sincere actress behind the monstrous authority.

Favourite bit

The peak of *Cabby* comes with the male viewpoint of the feminist movement. Dismayed by the seductive techniques of Hattie's Glamcab drivers, Sid calls a meeting of the men in the taxi company canteen. Fifth columnist Liz Fraser even advertises the rival company in Sid's midst and the poster is quickly ripped down for closer inspection. Sid: 'Here, listen to this. "Glamcabs" the modern efficient way to travel. No draughty old taxis. Ring 32323 for prompt and pleasant service. No waiting. No tipping... no tipping!' Kenneth Connor: 'Cor!... look at this bit though. Our drivers are there to please, just ask for what you want!' Charles Hawtrey: 'Really! Cor! What was that number again!'. Even a brief interruption from Liz Fraser cannot deter this male examination of the competition and Hawtrey's delightfully sexually charged delivery is outstanding.

You what mate! Sid James takes *Carry On* debutant Jim Dale for a ride in *Carry On Cabby*.

Did you know?

Talbot Rothwell served with the RAF during the Second World War and, following his capture, spent time at the Stalag Luft 3 camp. He became involved with the camp concert shows and a myriad of attempts to escape; among his colleagues were Rupert Davies and future *Carry On* master, Peter Butterworth. The latter helped to organize 'The Wooden Horse' ploy and made his performing debut opposite Rothwell with the comic song 'The Letter Edged With Black'.

Before becoming the finest *Carry On* writer, Tolly Rothwell had worked on scripts for such comedians as Arthur Askey, Ted Ray, Terry-Thomas and The Crazy Gang. His West End successes included *Once Upon A Crime* and *Queen Elizabeth Slept Here*. Rothwell saw the *Carry On* films as a continuation of the music-hall legacy of his hero, Max Miller, who died on 7 May 1963 - the last day of filming for *Cabby*.

At the time of filming, Sid James was starring in the BBC television comedy drama *Taxi* with Bill Owen, Ray Brooks and Alan Curtis - *Carry On Cabby* saw a similar performance and tied in with the popular Lord Ted Willis-devised TV show perfectly.

Charles Hawtrey couldn't drive before the filming of *Cabby*. For his priceless role as a hapless cabbie, Hawtrey was given a crash course by Pinewood staff - with manic results. Lock up your bumper!

Kenneth Williams turned down a leading role in *Cabby* due to the inferior quality of the script! The subsequent part was stripped of its best lines (which were given to Hawtrey) and was eventually played by reliable character actor Norman Chappell. He proved a particularly memorable foil for the down-to-earth wit of Kenneth Connor.

Is it green for oily skin... Hattie Jacques prepares for a nightmarish anniversary in Carry On Cabby.

The film sees Eric Rogers gain his first credit for musical score although he had helped a flagging Bruce Montgomery on the previous three films. Montgomery was unable to get the contemporary feel that Peter Rogers wanted, so Eric Rogers worked on his basic score and added flashes of ingenious style. Eventually Montgomery decided to throw in the towel and the full-time job went to Eric Rogers who enjoyed a close association with Peter Rogers - he often included musical touches from the producer. Eric Rogers would work on a further 22 films in the series and his ability to write the perfect Carry On score in two weeks was unbeatable.

Did you know that Eric Rogers wrote every note of Lionel Bart's groundbreaking musical Oliver!. Bart, unable to read or write music, sang the songs to his friend Rogers who transcribed them on to manuscript paper! For the original 1960 production, Sid James was considered for the role of Fagin, while in 1995's revival a certain Jim Dale would take on the role in the West End.

Look out for...

Michael Ward camping and mincing around opposite a bemused Kenneth Connor. As Ward wanders away, cabbie Connor sees something in his vehicle and picks it up. Shouting after Ward he cries, 'Excuse me sir, but does this pearl ear-ring belong to you?'; with perfect timing, Michael answers, 'What, with tweeds!'. Pure magic.

Cyril Chamberlain plays his last Carry On role as Sid's radio operator - the fact he is called 'Sarge' by his workmates highlights the military past of his character and links to his Gun Sergeant in the first film.

Carry On memories

'We shot Carry On Cabby and were called in for dubbing at the end of the filming. I had to get back to Dublin immediately to start rehearsing a stage show with Jimmy O'Dea. However, I was going to be held up because my dubbing was scheduled after Sid James who had booked to go away to Spain with his wife for a holiday. Now Jimmy O'Dea was an old mate of Sid's from variety, and somehow, he had got to hear that I was in a show with him. So you could have bowled me over when Sid came up to me and said, "Look, I believe you're doing a show with my old friend Jimmy O'Dea in Dublin. Why don't I postpone my holiday plans in Spain for a couple of days and you do your dubbing first - that way you can get back to Dublin and start rehearsing with Jimmy".
This was such a kind thing to do - but that's the sort of atmosphere that I found with the Carry On people. They were so kind, thoughtful, generous and professional'.
Milo O'Shea

A Peter Rogers Production

CARRY ON CABBY

Charlie Hawkins **SIDNEY JAMES**   Peggy Hawkins **HATTIE JACQUES**
Terry 'Pintpot' Tankard **CHARLES HAWTREY**
Ted Watson **KENNETH CONNOR**
Flo Sims **ESMA CANNON**   Sally **LIZ FRASER**   Smiley **BILL OWEN**
Len **MILO O'SHEA**   Expectant Father **JIM DALE**   Battleaxe **JUDITH FURSE**
Molly **RENEE HOUSTON**
Aristocratic Lady **AMBROSINE PHILLPOTTS**   Anthea **AMANDA BARRIE**
Dumb Driver **CAROL SHELLEY**   Sarge **CYRIL CHAMBERLAIN**
Allbright **NORMAN CHAPPELL**   Dancy **PETER GILMORE**
Man in tweeds **MICHAEL WARD**   District Nurse **NOEL DYSON**
Bespectacled Business Man **NORMAN MITCHELL**
Business Man **MICHAEL NIGHTINGALE**
Clerk **IAN WILSON**   Bridegroom **PETER BYRNE**   Punchy **DARRYL KAVANN**
Tubby **DON McCORKINDALE**   Geoff **CHARLES STANLEY**
Bride **MARIAN COLLINS**
Car Salesman **PETER JESSON**   Chauffeur **FRANK FORSYTH**
Glamcab Drivers **VALERIE VAN OST** & **MARIAN HORTON**

Screenplay by **Talbot Rothwell**
Based on an original idea by **S.C. Green & R.M. Hills**
Music composed & conducted by **Eric Rogers**
Poster tag-line - 'They're Here Again'

Associate Producer **Frank Bevis**   Art Director **Jack Stephens**
Editor **Archie Ludski**
Director of Photography **Alan Hume B.S.C.**   Camera Operator **Godfrey Godar**
Unit Manager **Donald Toms**   Assistant Director **Peter Bolton**
Sound Editor **Arthur Ridout**
Sound Recordists **Bill Daniels & Gordon K. McCallum**
Hairdressing **Biddy Chrystal**
Make-up artists **Geoffrey Rodway & Jim Hydes**   Continuity **Penny Daniels**
Costume Designer **Joan Ellacott**
The Producers wish to acknowledge the kind assistance
of The London General Cab Co. Ltd. and The Ford Motor Company Limited
in the making of this film
Producer **Peter Rogers**   Director **Gerald Thomas**

A 1963 Anglo Amalgamated film released through the
Warner-Pathe Distribution Ltd.
'U' Cert. Black & White Running time - 91 mins. 8,230ft

CARRY ON JACK

It's a life on the ocean waves again, and the film screenplay that officially brought Talbot Rothwell into the *Carry On* fold. Peter Rogers had read the first three pages of the script, initially titled *Poop-Decker RN*, and decided to film it. Once the taxi movie had proved popular, Rogers approached Rothwell with the idea of making his naval comedy part of the *Carry On* series. Rothwell readily agreed and the film was set to be made as *Carry On Up The Armada*, but problems with the censors led to a title change, *Carry On Sailor*. Eventually, in order to avoid any confusion with the contemporary style of *Cruising*, this was changed again to the more historically-geared *Jack*.

As the first historical parody from the *Carry On* series and the official debut of Tolly Rothwell, this film should be among the classics. However, while there is no denying its place as a milestone, *Jack* is simply too restrained and lacking in painfully awful puns to be a typical Rothwell comedy. Without doubt the film remains one of the most polished and impressively mounted films in the series but it misses several intrinsic stars and takes huge chunks of screen time for dramatically straight explanation.

Taking its influence from the Captain Hornblower stories of C.S. Forester via the cinematic antics of Errol Flynn, Charles Laughton, Burt Lancaster and Douglas Fairbanks, the film's basic premise is a fresh-faced new naval officer taking a post on the HMS *Venus*. Due to a dubious meeting with the glamorous temptress-cum-heroine (Juliet Mills) and a disbelieving second-in-command (Donald Houston), our hapless hero finds himself stuck with the lowly ranks on a perilous galleon.

The roster of true blue Carry Oners was low for *Jack*, with only a scene-stealing Kenneth Williams as the gloriously sea-sick charlatan and an ever cheerful Charles Hawtrey to keep the flag of innuendo flying. For the audiences in 1963 this must have been a bit of a shock after the cosy community and bumbling antics of the earlier movies. History was surely something for the schoolroom and high-brow intel-

lects, not for film fans after a few cheap laughs and familiar situations. As it happens, the film scored heavily at the box office and kick-started a very profitable trend for comical looks at historical traditions - wisely tackling subjects which were fresh in the mind due to current film/television productions.

While it remains for Williams and Hawtrey to battle and bungle their way through a rather unfamiliar scenario of bloody deaths, blown-up ships and murderous pirates, the central role of Poop-Decker goes to newcomer and brief team member, Bernard Cribbins. In an effective combination of Kenneth Connor nerves and naivety and Terence Longdon romantics, Cribbins carves a brilliantly funny creation which injects several, albeit few and far between, priceless lines of comic dialogue - notably when he tries to identify someone on the bridge (Mills in heavy disguise): 'Let me see, ah... ah, it is Nelson? No, he's got too many arms!' In a stunning debut performance, Cribbins goes throughout the film with a bemused, hard-done-by cheerfulness, and his comic ineptitude is highlighted by the heroic adventurers and buccaneers around him. Like a bumbling, Chaplinesque clown tossed into a subtly comic version of *Mutiny On The Bounty*, it is Bernie's clumsy, tongue-tied performance that links the realistic images of death, destruction, dodgy operations and derring-dos to *Carry On* tomfoolery. While the casting of Williams and Hawtrey is the crucial connection with earlier movies, it is really the nervous hero of Bernard Cribbins that taps completely into the old ethos.

Memorably, it is the mincing, sickly, bag of nerves of Kenneth Williams (beautifully parodying Laughton's Captain Bligh as the more than terrified Captain Fearless) who turns in a superb character study of mixed-up command and Freudian childhood memories: 'Oh goody, goody, Daddy going to make me a rocking horse!'. Only Williams can make such corny nautical gags as the throwing the book joke and the 'cat' misunderstanding work so

Jigging in the rigging - Bernard Cribbins swings into action in *Carry On Jack*.

Woodbridge and a superbly ragged Jim Dale creating an aura of murky British back streets and a fruitful life on the ocean waves. Perhaps all it really needed was a totally out-of-context but hugely welcome pirating Sid James to make it a true Rothwell classic.

Best performance

Despite the sterling work of Bernard Cribbins, the most effective and rounded contribution to *Jack* comes from a delightfully eccentric Charles Hawtrey. In one of his most interesting screen performances, Hawtrey moves away from the camp vocals of earlier films to play a sort of bumbling, Jewish confidant and friend who does his best to please Cribbins while making his life a lot less easy. Touching and emotional rather than out for major belly laughs, Hawtrey's pathetic, painfully unaware character is happily ignorant of his low social standing and proud of his work: notably, when the less than friendly Officer Houston comes a' press-ganging. 'You a sailor?' Charles: 'Who me! No, I'm a cesspit cleaner!' / 'I wondered why there wasn't anybody else about! Wouldn't you like to go to sea friend?' / 'Like to go to see what!?'. It's a knowing, awful pun, which Hawtrey delivers with perfect timing, culminating in an infectious giggle of simple amusement. Pure class.

Favourite bit

Although most of the action takes place on the open sea (or at least, on the Pinewood Studios set), the funniest sequence comes at the very beginning in the seedy dock area, when young and inexperienced Cribbins comes across ladies of easy virtue, drinking at 'Dirty Dicks' and, best of all, a couple of money-grabbing sedan chair carriers, played by Jim Dale and Ian Wilson. 'I'll get in if I was you, they'll be shut!'. The *Monthly Film Bulletin* commented that the sequence 'is probably as good as anything the series has yet produced'.

Did you know?

Liz Fraser was originally cast to play the female lead in *Jack* but other work commitments and a plan to move away from comedy roles led to Peter Rogers casting Sir John Mills' daughter in her only *Carry On*. Juliet was a natural choice, having excelled in starring roles in Rogers/Thomas hits, *Twice Round The Daffodil* and *Nurse On Wheels*.

The film was retitled *Carry On Venus* for several international screenings.

The casting of guest star Cecil Parker linked back to his naval authority performance in Ken Annakin's

brilliantly. It's all great stuff and stands as Kenneth's first real *acting* screen work, happily moving away from his Hancockian men of superiority to a fine interpretation of a man of character.

Elements of down-to-earth death and suffering would, of course, invade all subsequent historical *Carry Ons*, where the innuendo-drenched dialogue would be contrasted with serious moments of high drama and low adventure. Realistic danger sequences were crucial for these historical, filmic action parodies to work, whereas in the contemporary entries no such serious messages emerged. Indeed, the only deaths to occur in twentieth century-based films were in the utterly fantastic situation of *Spying* where death was treated with cartoon-like Wile E. Coyote homage.

This first foray into the world of history is complemented by an astounding cast of seasoned film *actors* rather than comic stars, with Donald Houston, Cecil Parker, Percy Herbert, Peter Gilmore, George

Disney adventure *The Swiss Family Robinson* (1961). Janet Munro's cross-dressing persona found a spiritual relation in Juliet Mills' *Jack* creation.

Look out for...

The stirring Eric Rogers title theme score combines elements of *Life on the Ocean Waves* and *God Save The King* to enhance the authentic sea-faring prints and paintings, selected by Gerald Thomas to set the scene for his historically-geared *Carry On* debut.

A brilliantly evil supporting turn from Peter Gilmore as the sexually charged, typically arrogant pirate.

Patrick Cargill, whose *Carry On* association dates back to his play *Ring For Catty*, the springboard for *Nurse*, excels as the flamboyantly floppish Spanish Governor. He had earlier cheekily chatted up Liz Fraser in *Regardless*.

Carry On memories

'The first *Carry On* I did, *Carry On Jack*, was my favourite. We worked on the lot, on the ship - we had days on location - the weather was beautiful and the laughs went on from morning til eve. Great Fun!'
Bernard Cribbins

'As it happens, I have quite an amusing tale to tell about one of the *Carry On* films. I appeared, albeit briefly, as Captain Hardy in the opening of *Carry On Jack*, and I formed part of the title credit sequence where Nelson, played by Jimmy Thompson, asks Hardy to kiss him. The director decided to use the very famous picture of the dying Nelson, and cross-fade from the painting to a live interpretation of it. This meant that we had approximately 30 or 40 extras grouped in various positions around Nelson. Nelson asks Hardy to kiss him and Hardy says, "I beg your pardon, Sir!", and Nelson keeps repeating "Kiss me Hardy!" Hardy does everything he can to get out of this, eventually saying that he doesn't think it will be very good for him. Notwithstanding this, Nelson asks him yet again, and so reluctantly Hardy kisses him, at which point Nelson dies. Then Hardy says, "I told you so!" and the film proper begins. Needless to say, this shot took an awfully long time to set up, as it had to be so accurate in terms of the real painting. By the time we got to the first take, Gerry Thomas was getting extremely annoyed at the amount of time it was taking and was very tetchy. Each time we tried to do the scene one of the extras would start to shake with laughter, thereby ruining the shot. I think it eventually took us all

day to do this one scene. I look back on it as one of the most enjoyable days I have spent filming'.
Anton Rodgers

'I loved working on *Carry On Jack* because it was a lovely little cameo - I loved that part. It wasn't very long on screen but they incorporated one of my jokes in it which was when I was bowing to Bernard Cribbins and he was bowing back and I was bowing and he was bowing and I finally said - "I'll get in if I was you, they'll be shut!". It was just a throw away line but they let me keep it in the film which was very unusual, because as you know, no-one was allowed to improvise in the *Carry Ons*. It was great working opposite little Ian Wilson - well, opposite, he was opposite much further down because he was a wee little fellow and he probably still is, getting smaller every day! But it was lovely to actually have a sedan chair with no bottom and you only charged half fare because the passenger was partly driving. It was a wonderful gag, it was fun to do that sort of lovely *Carry On* humour. My main memory is of racing along the quayside with Ian Wilson inside and Bernard Cribbins and myself carrying the damn thing!'
Jim Dale

A Peter Rogers Production

CARRY ON JACK

Captain Fearless **KENNETH WILLIAMS**
Midshipman Albert Poop-Decker **BERNARD CRIBBINS**
Sally **JULIET MILLS**   Walter Sweetley **CHARLES HAWTREY**
Mr Angel the Bosun **PERCY HERBERT**
1st Officer Jonathan Howett **DONALD HOUSTON**   Carrier **JIM DALE**
1st Sealord **CECIL PARKER**
Spanish Governor **PATRICK CARGILL**   Hook **ED DEVEREAUX**
Patch **PETER GILMORE**
Ned **GEORGE WOODBRIDGE**   Ancient Carrier **IAN WILSON**
Nelson **JIMMY THOMPSON**
Hardy **ANTON RODGERS**   Town Crier **MICHAEL NIGHTINGALE**
2nd Sealord **FRANK FORSYTH**
3rd Sealord **JOHN BROOKING**   Coach Driver **BARRIE GOSNEY**
Spanish Captain **JAN MUZURUS**
Spanish Secretary **VIVIANNE VENTURA**
Girls at 'Dirty Dicks' **MARIANNE STONE**   **SALLY DOUGLAS**
DORINA STEVENS   **JENNIFER HILL**   **ROSEMARY MANLEY**
DOMINIQUE DON   **MARIAN COLLINS**   **JEAN HAMILTON**

Screenplay by **Talbot Rothwell**
Music composed & conducted by **Eric Rogers**

Art Director **Jack Shampan**   Director of Photography **Alan Hume B.S.C.**
Editor **Archie Ludski**
Associate Producer **Frank Bevis**   Assistant Director **Anthony Waye**
Camera Operator **Godfrey Godar**
Sound Editor **Christopher Lancaster**   Sound Recordist **Bill Daniels**
Unit Manager **Donald Toms**
Make-up Artists **Geoffrey Rodway & Jim Hydes**   Continuity **Penny Daniels**
Hairdressing **Olga Angelinetta**   Costume Designer **Joan Ellacott**
Technical Advisor **Ian Cox**
Producer **Peter Rogers**   Director **Gerald Thomas**

A 1963 Anglo Amalgamated film released through the
Warner-Pathe Distribution Ltd.
'A' Cert. Colour Running time - 91 min. 8,190ft

CARRY ON SPYING

This is the stuff to give 'em: Talbot Rothwell fully comfortable in his writing for the series, film noir, a flamboyantly and beautifully crafted parody of a swinging sixties icon and a small but compact cast of regular team members. The last black-and-white entry in the film series, it was also the only time Rothwell collaborated on a film script - with his old *Ray's A Laugh* and *The Army Game* cohort Sid Colin. It is the work of a man relaxed and happy with himself and his position, with a string of non-stop one-liners, farcical situations and nostril-flaring innuendo.

The seed for inspiration, of course, comes from the hugely popular James Bond series, which had started in 1962 with the Sean Connery action-packed yarn, *Dr No*. In the world of *Carry On*, the evil mastermind becomes the bizarre cross-gender figure of a growling Judith Furse - memorably introduced as just a sinister hand in a direct resurrection of Terence Young's Bond direction. The train sequence stems from the Robert Shaw/Connery clash in *From Russia With Love* while the foreign powers using chemical warfare under the guise of secret organizations and Jim Dale's handsome, adventurous crusader are direct homages to the Bond legend.

However, the filming in black and white and a myriad of in-jokes dictate that for the real film buff, this is an inspired salute to Hollywood film noir, train-based chillers (*Rome Express*, *Terror By Night*), Hitchcock (*The Thirty Nine Steps*, *The Lady Vanishes*) and war-torn British thrillers. The Bogart duo of dread, Sydney Greenstreet and Peter Lorre, are clearly represented by Eric Pohlmann and John Bluthal, the trenchcoated figures of Williams and Hawtrey also give a nod to Bogart, James Cagney is misquoted and misrepresented in Williams' 'dirty rat' threat and a sizable chunk set in Vienna is a perfectly directed and lit tribute to *The Third Man*. Thomas, who had worked as associate editor on the 1949 classic, recreates the atmosphere of Carol Reed's masterpiece with memorably subtle references: the

Cafe Mozart meeting; the cuckoo clock in shot for a few seconds; Jim Dale's greeting of Williams from the Vienna train; a superb meeting between a disguised Jim Dale (his ancient bearded vendor comes direct from *The Third Man*) and Bernard Cribbins as the latter emerges from a man-hole cover (an echo of the original's climax sequence) and a black cat (from Lime's first appearance) that strolls through the rain-soaked back streets of Vienna. It's simply breathtaking stuff.

Into this montage of classic movie images, Rothwell tosses a tongue-in-cheek salute to the *Carry On* style of Norman Hudis by resurrecting the premise of authority surrounded by incompetents. In an inspired twist on the theme, Rothwell makes the figure of authority (Kenneth Williams) even more stupid than his assistants who include Cribbins, Hawtrey and newcomer Barbara Windsor. Although they are in continual contact with befuddled superiors - Eric Barker, again, and Richard Wattis - it is the team of four who career through the scenario, dodging the bullets and drugged drinks with a beautiful lack of elegance. Suspicion is aroused when a 'reserved for British agents' place card appears on their table. 'Oh I say, do you think they may be on to us!?' Hawtrey asks Williams. 'Don't be silly, how can they be on to us! We don't even look British!'. It is a celebration of the absurd dogged attitude of the British: gullible, likable, bumbling and inexperienced but always certain to pull through in the end.

The duologues between Kenneth and Barbara Windsor have spiralled to near legendary status amongst fans ('Number?'/'38-22-35'./'No, your number, not your vital thingammyjigs!'/'Oh Mr Simkins that was wonderful - I'm sure I'll never get my draws off as slickly as that!'), and from her first appearance it is clear that Barbara was the perfect actress for the *Carry On* style - all cheeky grin, hourglass figure and, importantly, able to compete for the laughs opposite such established scene-stealers

Taking over from where Carol Reed left off - Jim Dale, 'Our Man in Vienna', in heavy disguise for *Carry On Spying's* *The Third Man* homage.

as Williams and Hawtrey. In a further nod to equality, Windsor is the smartest agent of the bunch.

Bernard Cribbins, in his last *Carry On* appearance for almost 30 years, returns to his lovable bumbler of *Jack* and successfully chats up Windsor while also indulging in inspired bits of horseplay with the lads - notably when he attempts to escape from jail with a spoon! Some of his coy observations with the overly keen and energetic Kenneth Williams are priceless. When the gang arrive at an exotic 'Hakim's Funhouse' after friendly guidance from Norman Mitchell, Ken gushes, 'They've got a place like that in Blackpool', to which Cribbins mutters, 'I wouldn't bet on it if I were you!' - a perfect evocation of British sea-side postcard fun in a foreign climate. However, even at this early stage, it was clear that Jim Dale was enforcing his position as the ultimate *Carry On* hero. Straightfaced and determined, he battles through the farce and innuendo to give a subtle performance of bemused bravery. Jim's pivotal role is essential as a justification for the bumbling Englishness of Williams and his pals.

Spying is what the great *Carry Ons* are all about: jam-packed with spirited performances from everyone involved; a subtle musical score; directorial touches that enhance the less-than-subtle jokes, moments of real tension and a script of grease-lightning wit and fun that leaves the audience gasping! Vintage.

Best performance

No-one comes close to the firing-on-all-cylinders performance of Kenneth Williams as he barges his way through the Bondian plot with wide-eyed amazement. Taking the 'snide' vocal characterization from *Hancock's Half Hour* and putting visual meat on the bones, Williams epitomizes the bumbling British hero, getting through danger with grinning confidence and flamboyant luck. Rife with painful puns (the 'hair today!' line with Cribbins) and constantly lecturing on the rigours of life as a secret agent, Kenneth's role is the ideal vehicle for a really over-the-top, arms flying, hair akimbo *tour de force*, which he seizes with both hands. Whether it be in his pratfalling scenes with Eric Barker or his gleefully authoritative display of the agent's secret weapons, Kenneth is a scriptwriter's dream come true. Every word of dialogue is instantly hilarious through his exaggerated performance, as he never lets a gag slip, such as when he emerges bemused from a filing cabinet: 'I'm a man who knows where he's going... by the way, where are we going!' A master of disguise with delusions of grandeur, his slightly tanned and fez-topped Arabian is a stroke of genius. In the classic Cafe Mozart sequence, he reads a note 'You're being watched!' and, blessed with a sudden sinister

What big secrets you've got! - Bernard Cribbins and Barbara Windsor play the espionage game in *Carry On Spying*.

halt in Rogers' score, his eyes crease in dogged determination to get the villains caught. It is a superb performance that has the Williams touch all over it - 'Stop Messing About!'

Favourite bit

It has to be *The Third Man* parody in Vienna, and features a delightfully dragged up Jim Dale and the coy embarrassment of Charles Hawtrey. Culminating in the tyre of Hawtrey's bicycle bursting while he thinks he's being shot at, the misunderstood duo-logue between the two - with Hawtrey believing Dale is a real woman - is simply tear-jerkingly hilarious. Charlie, shy and nervous, gulps when the seductive blonde asks him to look at her etchings. Hawtrey's shocked and confused, 'Beg your pardon?!' is pure *Carry On* genius.

Did you know?

In a camp twist on the James Bond theme, Peter Rogers wanted to call Charles Hawtrey's character Charlie Bond - 001 and a half. However, incensed and humourless Bond producer Harry Saltzman threatened legal action and Rogers changed it to Charlie Bind - O.O.O. (delivered as 'Oo-oo, Ooh!').

Fittingly, for one of its European releases the film's title was changed to *Agent Oooh!*

Charles Hawtrey was the first member of the *Carry On* team to play a character with his own first name. In the footsteps of comic heroes like George Formby, Laurel & Hardy and Tony Hancock who were always, basically, themselves to an audience, Charles added an extra dimension of familiarity to his role. Later on, Sid James would invariably play 'Sid' and other Carry Oners would follow suit - notably most of the cast of *Camping*. Just remember, Charlie was first!

Spying saw the usually hostile critics finding moments to enjoy. *The Times* commented that the film was 'very British, very much a Bank Holiday film and, yes, when all is said and done, very funny!'.

Bernard Cribbins would recreate his man-hole cover entrance in the 1967 Bond parody, *Casino Royale*.

Look out for...

As the gorgeous Dilys Laye smoothly puts over the song 'The Magic of Love' from Eric Rogers, Kenneth Williams melts and the real players in the spy game (Dale, Laye, Victor Maddern), exchange knowing looks in a quickly cut episode of suspicious glances.

There's a gloriously surreal touch of Goonish comedy with Bernard Cribbins and Jim Dale. Meeting during *The Third Man* parody, Cribbins approaches

Dale's filter tip bootlace seller, with the line 'I cannot smoke those, they make me deaf!' It's pure Spike Milligan, an element which may have formed more of the series if he had written *Sergeant* back in 1958. Bernard Cribbins' codename, 'Bluebottle', is another link to Sellers Goonery.

The first coy sequence suggesting that a sexual relationship is going on between the film characters crops up with Barbara Windsor and Bernard Cribbins during the Algiers section of the film. As intimate dialogue is spoken off camera, the shot pans down to show the two, in the company of Kenneth and Charles, trying to get the right wavelength on their radio set. Later examples would include a card game between Hawtrey and Renee Houston in *At Your Convenience*, another card game with Peter Butterworth and Joan Sims in *Behind*, television viewing with Hawtrey and Jacques in *Matron* and a darkened projection room in *That's Carry On* with Williams and Windsor.

Victor Maddern is a brilliant endearing villain, beginning the film as a sinister milkman (note his fingers in ears, cartoon-like reaction to the explosion) and ending with a feast of 'ooh' and 'ahhs' as Hawtrey thinks the Chinese are involved and Williams continues to pin down the enemy. Following on from Hitchcockian criminals you love to love/hate (Edmund Gwenn in *Foreign Correspondent*, Norman Lloyd in *Saboteur*) Victor enjoys a visually breathtaking death.

Carry On memories

'Bernard Cribbins was a big help on my first one, *Carry On Spying*, because he knew them all and I had just done *Crooks In Cloisters* with him. I mean, he was my mate, my china. I'd known Bernie for years and he just told me what to look out for. It's funny though, because he wasn't employed for years after by Gerry Thomas because Bernie offended him on set. In the scene when we're running at the end and they're shooting at us, the blanks went a bit hay-wire and they went off near Bernie. He screeched and shouted and the *Carry On* people didn't like it. He'd lost his temper and Gerry found somebody else. I think I was just being tried out for the team, but Kenny Williams later told me that I wasn't used again for some years because I had upset Gerry Thomas. He brought out this motoring magazine during a break on *Carry On Spying* and started talking about cars. I said, "Ooh! How boring to be talking about that!" and Kenny said that was the reason. I'm not too sure!'

Barbara Windsor

A Peter Rogers Production

CARRY ON SPYING

Desmond Simkins **KENNETH WILLIAMS**
Daphne Honeybutt **BARBARA WINDSOR**
Charlie Bind **CHARLES HAWTREY**
Harold Crump **BERNARD CRIBBINS** Carstairs **JIM DALE**
The Chief **ERIC BARKER** Cobley **RICHARD WATTIS** Lila **DILYS LAYE**
The Fatman **ERIC POHLMANN** Milchmann **VICTOR MADDERN**
Dr. Crow **JUDITH FURSE**
The Headwaiter **JOHN BLUTHAL** Madame **RENEE HOUSTON**
Doorman **TOM CLEGG**
Code Clerk **GERTAN KLAUBER** Native Policeman **NORMAN MITCHELL**
Professor Stark **FRANK FORSYTH** Algerian Gent **DEREK SYDNEY**
Cigarette Girl **JILL MAI MEREDITH** Cloakroom Girl **ANGELA ELLISON**
Bed of Nails Native **HUGH FUTCHER** Elderly Woman **NORAH GORDON**
Thugs **JACK TAYLOR & BILL CUMMINGS**
Guards **ANTHONY BAIRD & PATRICK DURKIN**
Funhouse Girls **VIRGINIA TYLER** **JUDI JOHNSON & GLORIA BEST**
Amazon Guards **AUDREY WILSON** **VICKY SMITH**
JANE LUMB **MARIAN COLLINS**
SALLY DOUGLAS **CHRISTINE RODGERS** & **MAYA KOUMANI**

Screenplay by **Talbot Rothwell & Sid Colin**
Music composed & conducted by **Eric Rogers**
Songs - "Too Late" by **Alex Alstone & Geoffrey Parsons**
"The Magic of Love" by **Eric Rogers**

Poster tag-line - 'They're at it again - O.O.Oh!'

Associate Producer **Frank Bevis** Art Director **A. Vetchinsky**
Director of Photography **Alan Hume B.S.C.** Editor **Archie Ludski**
Camera Operator **Godfrey Godar** Assistant Director **Peter Bolton**
Unit Manager **Donald Toms** Continuity **Penny Daniels**
Hairdressing **Biddy Chrystal** Sound Editor **Christopher Lancaster**
Sound Recordists **C.C. Stevens & Bill Daniels**
Costume Designer **Yvonne Caffin**
Make-up **W. T. Partleton** Producer **Peter Rogers**
Director **Gerald Thomas**

A 1964 Anglo Amalgamated film released through the
Warner-Pathe Distribution Ltd.
'A' Cert. Black & White Running time - 87 mins. 7,840ft

CARRY ON CLEO

😊 😊 😊 😊 😊

This is a film bristling with comic assurance, in the same laugh-a-second mood as *Spying* but with the bonus of a much welcome return from Sid James. Boasting one of Rothwell's most sparkling and inventive deconstructions of popular dramatic culture, *Cleo* is a rip-roaring production which knows it's good and enjoys itself throughout. The series had come of age with this, the tenth entry in the series, which gained frosty but grudging respect from the critics while the public embraced the ethos of *Carry On* as an essential part of the British identity. The earlier sense of development and construction had given way to a colourful confidence and feel-good innuendo with a practised and recognizable team. Kenneth Connor and Joan Sims rejoined the fun and games while Jim Dale graduated to official romantic lead and the Williams/James contrast reached definitive terms.

The film was, of course, a timely deflation of the mega-production *Cleopatra* with Elizabeth Taylor and Richard Burton. The out-of-this-world sets built at Pinewood for the 20th Century-Fox blockbuster were left standing when the film moved back to Hollywood, and for Peter Rogers, it was the perfect chance to make an immediate comic reply. Thus, the sets (exteriors from Fox, interiors from Victor Maddern) were of an amazingly high quality and the costumes were fresh from the backs of Burton and Harrison. Legal problems, when the James/Williams/Amanda Barrie parody of the Howard Terpning painting which inspired the artwork for the official Burton/Harrison/Taylor poster, caused a few tense moments for Rogers, before the poster was changed to a merry-go-round image with James, Williams, Connor and Hawtrey holding the poles! This was given limited distribution and the major advertising was redesigned as a Sid James-like sphinx. The court hearing occurred at 10.30 am on 15 January 1965. The *Carry On* ethos was brilliantly defended by an ideal eccentric, Lord Hailsham, who pointed out to the prosecuting counsel, Sir Andrew

Clark QC, that as the Sid adventure was a *comedy* consciously spoofing the established drama, everybody had made the connection and the poster offended nobody. Case dismissed by Justice Plowman, sitting bemused on the bench.

Secondly, Rogers came under fire from Marks & Spencer for using the company's official colours, green and gold, for *Cleo*'s slave market, Marcius & Spencius. The jokey treatment of the company name wasn't a problem, but the use of their logo colours was. The all-powerful Sieff family caused problems and demanded that a public apology be printed in *The Daily Express*. Their in-house lawyer calmed them down and got the concern curtailed. The situation was amicably resolved and Marks & Spencer enjoyed free and regular publicity for the next 30 years!

At the heart of *Cleo* is the stunning and delightfully dotty performance of Amanda Barrie as the seductive Queen of the Nile, cleverly constructed as a naive and childish figure (an idea used 20 years later in the Ben Elton/Richard Curtis/Miranda Richardson interpretation of Elizabeth I for *Blackadder II*). Amanda's simple minded commands and fluttering eye-lids are a masterly piece of work and her relationship with Sid James (especially the poisoned asp sequence/close liaison with Tom Clegg's mute slave in attendance) is priceless.

James comes fully to the fore in this, his first venture into *Carry On* history, which sees the first outing for his wide-boy, sexy rogue figure from the Hancock days. In contrast to his merely cocky cockney characters of old who, as in *Cruising*, actually shied away from female company, Sid is now the Sid we all know and love: the ever laughing, never tongue-tied, ultimate low-brow hero. When he joins forces with Amanda Barrie's mindless Cleo, the gags flow thick and fast, with Sid's streetwise hold on the situation highlighting the childish naivety of Barrie during the 'loan' word play. It is this full inclusion of the naturalistic Sid which makes the James/Williams relationship click into place.

Kenneth, in arguably his finest role as the manic Caesar, has the perfect sounding board for his camp, flamboyant outbursts. While the out-of-control, frenzied figures of say, Bob Hope or Daffy Duck need the confident calm of Bing Crosby or Bugs Bunny to reach full comic potential, then the out-of-control, frenzied figure of Kenneth Williams needs that confident calm of Sid James. In *Cleo* their relationship reaches the peak of comic timing: the in-depth description of Cleo's beauty is a Rothwell gem. 'They call her the Siren of the Nile!'/'Ooh! I hope she don't go off, I mean they do tend to in these hot countries don't they?'/'Oh, you don't have to worry about that, she's got a deep frieze running all around the walls of the Palace'. Dialogue doesn't come any better than this!

While these characters run the Roman Empire, back home in stone-age Britain, bumbling Kenneth Connor and hot-blooded hero Jim Dale are enjoying the quiet life. Once the wires cross and the two elements combine, the Connor/Dale contrast comes brilliantly into effect. While Jim is the typical dashing hero (a sort of battling Tony Curtis let loose in a trouser-dropping farce, answering Sid's comic question of 'What do you hunt?' with the deadly serious bark: 'Romans!'), then Connor is the *Carry On* version of these action-packed Hollywood heroes. It's the cue for various misunderstandings, a hatful of corny puns and the most polished comic epic ever filmed.

The main coup in *Cleo* is the down-to-earth playing of the entire cast: this isn't the realist dramatics of *Jack* but practically a contemporary *Carry On* filmed in funny costumes. All the stereotypes of old are kept in aspic and let loose in an unfamiliar environment. Thus Sid's Roman villain is the usual lovable laughing Sid with his cockney cry of 'Blimus!'; Williams is all childish camping about and nostril-flaring; Connor is really Horace Strong in a fur outfit, bumbling through the misunderstood heroics; and Hawtrey contrasts his wide-eyed effeminacy with an energetic gusto when the leggy blondes crop up, giggling as he proclaims Williams' death and ending up surrounded in a broken Roman vase with the immortal last words, 'Just call me Urn!'.

In fact, most of the cast act like Shakespearian travelling players, interpreting the historical in the style of the English stage via their own eccentric British traits. Though Joan Sims turns in a totally convincing representation of historical realism as she wails and bemoans her fate, she is basically the nagging wife/mother-in-law comic figure of McGill postcards and Les Dawson sketches. However, it is Connor's bumbling Englishman abroad that gets the funniest lines, when these Anglicized Romans don't

understand his cultural references ('Ices - they're lovely!'). The knowing opening credit, 'based on an original idea by William Shakespeare', tipped an affectionate nod to the master and at least there's no serious mention of Sam Taylor anywhere!

Cleo is quite clearly a landmark in the history of *Carry On*, with a perfect cast of expert players, a well rounded, do-anything-for-a-giggle screenplay and sets that the usual budget could never have afforded. All the elements come together superbly for one of British cinema's most respected and effective comedy movies. Salute!

Best performance

While everybody in the cast, particularly the four principals, is outstanding, *Cleo* quite simply sees *the* comic performance of Kenneth Williams' career. His Julius Caesar oozes innuendo and breathtaking

'Oh! Hello!' A pot of Charles Hawtrey in 'dirty old sage' over-drive for *Carry On Cleo*.

and Kenneth Connor. The moment when Williams notices something odd about Connor's bizarre female is outstanding. 'Ah, good evening', (note the 'snide' catchphrase), 'I wanted to ask' (realization of strange looking virgin) ' ...are you really a vestal virgin?'/'Oh no... no I'm a eunuch!'/'Oh I see... you're a what!' Of course, the film's most prized line comes as bodyguard David Davenport pulls out his sword, much to Kenneth Williams' dismay: 'Err... what are you doing with your thing!' Davenport: 'I am sorry sir but for the good of Rome you must die!'/'But you're my personal bodyguard and champion gladiator. I don't want to die. I may not be a very good live Emperor but I'll be a worse one dead. Treachery! [wait for it!] Infamy! Infamy! They've all got it in for me!' - what a brilliant deconstruction of Shakespearian technique. Priceless stuff.

Did you know?

Talbot Rothwell often asked his friends Frank Muir and Denis Norden if he could incorporate some of his favourite gags from their popular Jimmy Edwards radio show *Take It From Here*. Due to the ephemeral quality of radio, Muir and Norden were more than happy to see the jokes given a more permanent place in the movies. One of these lifted comic exchanges was the earth-shattering 'infamy' line immortalized by Kenneth Williams in *Cleo*. The joke has come to epitomize *Carry On* comedy.

Talbot Rothwell throws in every corny gag in the book, although the corniest 'What's a Grecian Urn!' line is surprisingly left out. But lovers of the best of the worst need only refer to Rothwell's Frankie Howerd triumph *Up Pompeii* - the line's in the first episode!

The straight-laced narration for *Cleo* is delivered by E.V.H. Emmett, much respected voice of Gaumont-British news during the 1930s and 1940s. His distinguished tones bring a tongue-in-cheek touch of contemporary authenticity to the ancient Roman ethos.

On 30 October 1964 Kenneth Williams had to do some extra dubbing work on *Cleo* concerning this comment to Joan Sims about the complete lack of women during his travels: 'They don't have them abroad you know, they're a very backward people there!'. The censor rejected the line due to its homosexual implication, and the offending word 'backward' was changed to 'bashful'.

Despite the problems with 20th Century-Fox concerning *Cleo*'s original poster, the design was used in

conceit, mincing throughout the proceedings with a self-loving, totally flamboyant air of pompous authority. Again, as in *Spying*, his ruler is both incompetent and unliked, but Williams, ever the optimist, jaunts along without a care in the world. However, at the first sign of real danger he is a self-protecting mass of panic, relying on double-crossing friends like Sid and Kenneth Connor's bag of nerves for protection. His contrast with James is legendary, but heights of camp comedy are reached in his partnership with Connor: the meeting with Cleo's vision is a classic example of Williams' mock sexual energy. Typified as a hen-pecked husband in the highest position of power, Williams is really a childish emperor with an ever loosening grip on his empire. 'I even failed my XI plus', he moans in a subtle touch amongst the barrel-scraping gags. From his immortal introductory line, 'Ooh, I do feel queer!', through his babyish sulking at not getting his own way, a brilliantly manic mock death scene ('Lend me your ears!' Hawtrey: 'Don't you, you'll never get them back!') and on to his final and wonderfully hammed real death, this is treasurable Kenneth Williams. 'Friends, Romans... Countrymen... I know!' - gets them every time!

Favourite bit

This has to involve Kenneth again, in one of the most prized sequences in the series as the Emperor gatecrashes into the holy temple of the vestal virgins to find the totally unconvincing 'virgins' of Jim Dale

the late 1970s when the film (along with *Nurse*) was the first *Carry On* available to buy on home video. The cost was £39.50.

Although *Cleo* remains one of the most lavish films in the series, the budget was still only a very reasonable £194,323. Rogers and Thomas were on £7,500 each, James and Williams received their usual £5,000 a piece, while Charles Hawtrey got a pay packet of £4,000. Likewise, Talbot Rothwell was paid £4,000, Jim Dale's major supporting role earned him £1,000 and title siren, Amanda Barrie, got £550. Even regular Joan Sims was employed on a basic rate of £125 per day.

Kenneth Connor's contract included a clause detailing that the making of *Cleo* would not disturb his West End work in *A Funny Thing Happened On The Way To The Forum*. Connor continued in his starring role opposite Frankie Howerd, eventually took over directing the show on tour (with Charles Hawtrey in his old role) and still managed to earn his £4,500 for *Cleo* in between.

The original screenplay included the coda, 'Carry On Cleo. A Funny Sort of Screenplay by Talbot Rothwell'.

Despite its now-classic status, *Cleo* was on the receiving end of some damning criticism on its first release. *The Times* commented that 'the formula does not really lend itself to this particular form, and in addition there are distinct signs of tiredness in the scripting', while D. Fletcher of Lincoln told one film magazine that the film was 'a lot of silly vulgar tripe; a complete waste of time, money and talent. The cast was terrible - especially Sid James'. Ooer! - how wrong can two people be?!

Look out for...

A fine address by Kenneth Williams to the Roman senate: as he gets more and more involved he lapses into Churchillian interpretation. Throwing in Macmillan dialogue and flamboyant delivery, Kenneth gets supporting player Brian Oulton giggling. Desperately trying not to spoil the take, Brian just about holds in the guffaws and the scene is a encapsulation of the Pinewood set fun and games.

Note Kenneth Williams' muffed line, 'What slay... what say you!' as Sid James interrupts his initial death scene.

There's a reference to Beatlemania, as the fan worshipped hero of Kenneth Connor is stripped of his possessions by adoring souvenir hunters to the sounds of twangy guitars! Far out man!

Jon Pertwee, in his first and funniest *Carry On* cameo, shuffles and moans away opposite Kenneth Connor, Kenneth Williams and Charles Hawtrey as an ancient soothsayer. Successfully following the lead roles in playing his historical part with a contemporary British edge, Pertwee croaks with perfect timing, 'Well gather round and 'ave a butchers!'.

Pertwee's vision acts like a Shakespearian play within a play, but Rothwell, keeping it in the tradition of contemporary comedy, fashions the piece in the style of a television interlude, with Williams' anxious 'We're missing all the best bits!'. Within the vision sequence, Williams becomes the confident Emperor he longs to be, while Connor keeps his bumbling persona reassuringly intact, clipping his finger as he hands over the sword.

There's a fine support from big and burly Francis de Wolff as Agrippa, to whom Connor replies in mock heroics, 'And I know one or two holds myself, so you better watch it!'.

Delight in Michael Ward's major *Carry On* contribution, wandering through Cleo's palace with superior bemusement. It is a stunning comic performance which works brilliantly off the chuckling rogue of

Kenneth Williams returns to his dramatic roots but only for publicity purposes - *Carry On Cleo*.

Another day at the office: Sid James and Kenneth Williams lock innuendo horns for *Carry On Cleo*.

James and the manic camping of Williams. His slightly disgusted look as Sid and Victor Maddern stroll by is particularly treasurable.

The film contains an inspired piece of by-play between Kenneth Connor and Jim Dale as they await their fate in the slave cells of Marcius & Spencius. Fearful discussions about going to the lions ('Well, I hope they're a nice family!') culminates with a brilliant evocation of a lion from Jim as he explains, 'it's quick anyway, the old head in the mouth, quick snap of the jaw and it's all over', and Kenneth moans 'but how am I going to get his head in my mouth!' It's so corny it's hilarious.

Take note of Charles Hawtrey, sitting in all his finery in the Senate as Williams makes a speech with Connor's mock muscleman in support. Hawtrey has no dialogue and is easily missed but his comic expression is one for the scrapbook.

Watch for Joan Sims' mouthed command to 'Piss off!' when she notices the bumbling bodyguard Kenneth Connor camped on top of her bed.

Also note the splendid duologue between returning conquering hero Kenneth Williams and cheerful street heckler, Norman Mitchell. 'I have taken Spain, England, Gaul what will you have me take next?'/'A running jump!' Priceless.

Carry On memories

'I enjoy my daughters' company. They have always been with me at work whenever possible. In fact, two weeks after Ellie-Jane was born... I was acting in the film *Carry On Cleo* and would rush off the set every three hours to feed her in the dressing room where she was waiting impatiently with my mother. On the frequent embarrassing occasions that film is repeated on television, should Ellie-Jane dare to criticize my definitive rendering of Senna Pod, wife of Hengist Pod, inventor of the square wheel in early Britain, I remind her that it was her greed that prevented me etching in the finer details of my role!'
Sheila Hancock

'I only did one *Carry On*, *Carry On Cleo*, and in fact it was my only film. I went for a fitting at Pinewood, and on arrival was told they were looking for a long-legged blonde ingenue. As I was 27, and overweight following the birth of my son, and brown haired to boot, I realized that I was not right for the part of Gloria. We had a hilarious time together at that interview, and I even gave them some giraffe and mouse impersonations (I was doing *Playschool*, a programme for 3-5 year olds, at the time!) By the time I had got home, my agent phoned to say they had given me the part! Julie Harris, the costume designer, was horrified by my short sturdy functional legs! She promptly put me into high-heeled shoes, which as you can imagine were perfectly in keeping with the Roman costumes! She made no bones about the rotten job the casting people had done... choosing such legs. I felt like a horse having its fetlocks examined! The cast were incredibly nice, and in spite of the constant laughter and jokes, very professional when it was time to work. Sid James took pity on me at the end of each day, and let me shower in his dressing room. The one I was given was really a chorus type room, with only a wash basin, and as I was covered in brown make-up wherever skin showed, I was grateful for his kindness. The most memorable moments were with Kenneth Williams. He was two men. One was shy, studious, well read and cultured; the other was a naughty boy, into "rude" jokes, being the centre of attention and very funny. I kept meeting the "naughty boy"! For most of the film he wore a short Roman skirt, and whenever he passed me in a corridor and we were alone he would lift the skirt, under which he wore nothing. Although I was a married woman, with a baby and 27 years old, I never failed to jump and squeal, which is why he enjoyed doing it so much! I vowed that "next time" I would just ignore it and behave as though he hadn't done it; I never managed to. I got my own back though, when he announced one day that his mother, of whom he was extremely fond, was coming to visit the set. I pretended outrage that she did not realize what her son was really like and threatened to tell her of his behaviour. For days he followed me

Carry On Cleo – Amanda Barrie as the alluring Siren of the Nile.

A series highlight as wannabe hero Kenneth Connor protects Emperor Kenneth Williams and boy wonder Jim Dale

Above: Ooh! What a couple of braves – Bernard Bresslaw and Charles Hawtrey in *Carry On Cowboy*

Right: The Kid is back in town! Sid James is every inch the Western dude in *Carry On Cowboy*

around begging me not to say anything, which I really enjoyed. When Mrs Williams appeared I went up to her and said, "Oh. I would love to tell you something about your son". Kenneth went white, and I continued, "He is so lovely to work with". He was so relieved and I got flashed at severely during the next day! I recall it with great affection. We worked together on many occasions after and he was always charming. One other recollection... Although I had just had a baby and my boobs were at their largest ever, it was not enough for the scene where they comment that I come from Bristol...get it...Bristol City...! They padded out my fur bikini (Diana Dors was not the only one to wear one) with so much cotton wool that I was in danger of popping out mid scene if I merely breathed, let alone acted! So much for *art*!'
Julie Stevens

'I went off to wardrobe to have my armour fitted. The suit I was given had Richard Burton's name inside. He had worn it in *Cleopatra*. I felt so privileged. The only trouble was that it was made of leather. The scene in the bathroom where Cleo is bathing in milk was very embarrassing. Not because of the nakedness, but from a sound point of view. We rehearsed several times, then took Take One - and Two - and Three - and so on, until Gerry Thomas walked over to the sound man, ear-cupped in his hand, saying quietly - "What!?" It turned out that there was a squeaking noise somewhere. Gerry asked for us all to be quiet on the set so that they could trace this noise. We all held our breath and the sound man said that it had cleared. We repeated the procedure - another few takes, and the drama was repeated. Finally it was decided to rehearse again without film; people were delegated to walk round the set while we worked, trying to identify the squeak. Yes, it was Richard Burton's armour. I was the culprit. Every time I breathed in and out there was a creak from the leather. Gerry said, "Hold your breath right through the scene." We got it in the next take. I had been working previously in a play in London called *Caligula*. At the end of the production which only ran two or three weeks, I asked the producer what happened to expensive sets like the one we were using, which had been built especially for the play at a huge cost of £40,000. "Oh, we've sold that - I think", he said. "How much?" I asked. "About - no, exactly £150, that's all we could get. Plus the get-out, of course" (the get-out is the money it costs the crew to take the set to pieces and load it onto a lorry). "Yes, £150 - couldn't get a penny more. £40,000... and look what they get!"

I offered £155 and the deal was struck. I no sooner got the lot home and stored in an old coach-house than I heard that a film called *Carry On Cleo* was being made soon. I phoned Pinewood Art Department and they came to my home to have a look. I loaned it out to them for £800 so, you see, the set was very familiar to me!'
Victor Maddern

'Kenneth Williams was disgraceful in that particular film. There was one scene when he backed me into a doorway while Kenneth Connor was fighting in the bath with a nubian slave. Kenneth Williams had backed me into a corner and was standing in front of me and it was outrageous what he was doing with his rear end! It really was embarrassing. I was trying to push him away from me... It's all on film if you look carefully that's what he's doing, but then they speeded the film up and it looks quite funny... that's if you know what to look for!'
Jim Dale

A Peter Rogers Production

CARRY ON CLEO

Mark Antony **SIDNEY JAMES** Julius Caesar **KENNETH WILLIAMS**
Seneca **CHARLES HAWTREY** Hengist Pod **KENNETH CONNOR**
Calpurnia **JOAN SIMS** Horsa **JIM DALE**
Cleopatra **AMANDA BARRIE** Sergeant Major **VICTOR MADDERN**
Gloria **JULIE STEVENS**
Senna Pod **SHEILA HANCOCK** Soothsayer **JON PERTWEE**
Brutus **BRIAN OULTON**
Archimedes **MICHAEL WARD** Agrippa **FRANCIS de WOLFF**
Sosages **TOM CLEGG** Virginia **TANYA BINNING**
Bilius **DAVID DAVENPORT** Galley Master **PETER GILMORE**
Messenger **IAN WILSON** Heckler **NORMAN MITCHELL**
Hessian Driver **BRIAN RAWLINSON** Markus **GERTAN KLAUBER**
Spencius **WARREN MITCHELL** Companion **PETER JESSON**
Caveman **MICHAEL NIGHTINGALE** Gloria's Bridesmaid **JUDI JOHNSON**
Seneca's Servant **THELMA TAYLOR** Antony's dusky Maiden **SALLY DOUGLAS**
Pretty Bidder **WANDA VENTHAM** Willa Claudia **PEGGY ANN CLIFFORD**
Guard at Caesar's Palace **MARK HARDY** Narrator **E.V.H. EMMETT**
Hand Maidens **CHRISTINE RODGERS GLORIA BEST & VIRGINIA TYLER**
Vestal Virgins **GLORIA JOHNSON JOANNA FORD**
DONNA WHITE JANE LUMB & VICKI SMITH

Screenplay by **Talbot Rothwell**
From an original idea by **William Shakespeare**
Music composed & conducted by **Eric Rogers**
Poster tag-line - 'The Funniest film since 54 B.C.'

Associate Producer **Frank Bevis** Art Director **Bert Davey**
Director of Photography **Alan Hume B.S.C.**
Editor **Archie Ludski** Camera Operator **Godfrey Godar**
Assistant Director **Peter Bolton**
Unit Manager **Donald Toms** Continuity **Olga Brook**
Make-up **Geoff Rodway**
Sound Editor **Christopher Lancaster**
Sound Recordists **Bill Daniels & Gordon K. McCallum**
Hairdressing **Ann Fordyce** Costume Designer **Julie Harris**
Whilst the characters and events in this story are based
on actual characters and events,
certain liberties have been taken with Cleopatra
Producer **Peter Rogers** Director **Gerald Thomas**

A 1964 Anglo Amalgamated film released through Warner-Pathe Distribution Ltd.
'A' Cert. Colour Running time - 92 mins. 8,247ft

CARRY ON COWBOY

After the warm Englishness of *Cleo*, this film transferred the regular team way out west and way out of their usual characterizations. With a script of Western ideals and violently staged sequences, this is innuendo in the real world. Whereas everybody knew the chuckling old Sid was really behind that cowardly villain Mark Antony, in *Cowboy*, James is a convincing, blood-chilling bandit who fully deserves his baddie black hat. Although his performance is jam-packed with low-brow gags and male fantasies, Sid actually goes round killing people here with a cold grin on his face.

From that first sequence, as the Roy Rogers-like voice imparts the *Carry On* song for the wide open spaces and the camera follows Sid on horseback, the audience knows this movie means business. The gags and comic situations are there merely to counterbalance an evil plan of American domination, greed and murder, and attempts at dispatching favourites like Jim Dale and Kenneth Williams. In contrast to *Cleo*'s cheerful mugging, *Cowboy* allows the gang to flex their acting muscles and, naturally, as a result it remains most of the team's favourite entry. Joan Sims relished the chance to turn on seductive Mae West-like charms (introduced by a sexy Eric Rogers score) and works brilliantly off Sid - 'My, but you've got a big one!' - oozing glamour in her tight, black low-cut gown. Kenneth Williams enthused in his diary that the film was 'the best one of the lot. At last the *Carry Ons* have found the juveniles... all the character actors are marvellous, including me!'. Sid considered that his stunning central performance 'was like going back to the type of parts I used to play before I started this light comedy stuff'; an achievement brilliantly supported by a hand-picked group of characterizations.

Not least among these are two fine minor turns from a couple of valued newcomers: Bernard Bresslaw (booming and yelling his Red Indian anger at every opportunity) and Peter Butterworth (quietly fidgeting in the background and stealing every scene

he appears in). The delightful Angela Douglas, in a return to the straight leading ladies of Shirley Eaton and Juliet Mills, throws another log on the feminist fire with her rebel rousing, gun-wielding heroine.

The Pinewood version of John Wayne's America is populated by well-loved farceurs playing dramatic comedy rather than comic drama. Gone are the knowing winks to the audience and tongue-in-cheek references to English tradition; the gang are playing for real. The regular foreigner abroad character is brilliantly brought to life by Jim Dale, finally gaining a major romantic lead role and playing it to perfection. It is Jim's naive attitude to women, westerners and the American way of life that links the comic scenarios to the old *Carry On* style. As the token English character, Jim's mistaken hero tackles all the Western cliches and cinematic echoes (notably when the time of Sid's arrival is given as high noon, Williams muttering, 'I know - I told him it was a most unoriginal time for that sort of thing!').

While not denying the film's superb style, perhaps the very believability of all the Americanized characters blurs the edge of the Englishness of the scripted comedy. The script sparkles with entertaining scenarios and memorable one-liners, the cast is ripe with *Carry On* favourites, the direction is inspired, but somehow that feel-good comic embrace is muted. Though we can applaud the film for showing Sid as the great *actor* we all knew he was, *Cowboy* unquestionably misses the fun and frolics of the chuckling, fun-loving Sid of old. While still enjoying his womanizing, drinking, gambling and, indeed, rooting shooting persona, Sid's *Cowboy* contribution is breathtakingly naturalistic. The only *American* character to inject elements of his cliched persona is Indian chief Charles Hawtrey. Although the actor regretted missing the chance of acting with dignity - Gerald Thomas preferring to have Hawtrey continue to turn on the camp mincing - the fact remains that as Charles stays his constant self, his performance shines against the semi-serious Western

characterizations of Sid, Kenneth and the rest. His 'Oh! Hello!' entrance from his teepee is inspired: the entire film establishes the idea of the Carry Oners as Americans and Thomas cunningly builds up the tension for the first appearance of a fearsome Indian. The fact that we get the small cough, twinkling grin and sparkling eyes of Charlie Hawtrey is a peak of contrasting comic effect.

Celebrated as one of the most professionally produced and effective films in the series, *Cowboy*'s magic is there in heaps (if only little ones): it's a western field of dreams where Sid's dark villain literally gets away with murder, Jim Dale gets the gal of his cowboy fantasies, Charles Hawtrey happily drinks away the Indian blues and the character skills

of Bresslaw and Butterworth get a memorable baptism of fire. Wagons roll!

Best performance

While Sid James chews up the scenery with western realism and Charles Hawtrey delights the *Carry On aficionado* with his camp deconstruction of the American legend, the finest performance comes from Jim Dale - finally grabbing his high billing romantic hero and milking the opportunity for all it's worth. His delightful Englishness and clumsiness leads to a brilliant combination of Kenneth Connor and Gary Cooper, giving the series that vital ingredient of dashing heroics. His manic and muddled Drainage, Sanitation & Garbage Disposal Engineer

Sid James in superb villainous mood for his blacker than black character study in *Carry On Cowboy*.

Forget Gary Cooper - here's Jim Dale to save the day in Stodge City... *Carry On Cowboy*.

Favourite bit

Cowboy's finest moments come with the contrasting performances of Charles Hawtrey and Sid James. In their first scene together Sid bumbles through pidgin Indian speech before the ever cultured Charlie reveals his distinguished tones. The sexual energy when Charlie offers the panting Sid his gorgeous squaw (Sally Douglas) is hilarious ('How!'/'Never mind how... Where?!'). When the two get down to business, as the bemused Percy Herbert looks on, Talbot Rothwell lets rip with the British slant on western iconography. Charles: 'Well, what do you want?' Sid: 'Certain fellow got rid of!'/'Where is this fellow?'/'On the stage.'/'Oh, I don't blame you, I can't stand actors myself, peculiar lot!'/'The stage coach coming in from Denver today. All you got to do is raid it and get 'um!'/'Oh, I don't like the sound of that - I'm told they carry guns on these stages, it might get rough!' *Carry On* pride meets Lee Van Cleef! Charles is all affectionate hand shakes, good manners, whiskey-gurgling and wide-eyed fun - a simply outstanding comic support who leads the mighty Sid a wonderfully merry dance.

Did you know?

The basis storyline for the film, that of a confused British gentleman caught up in the wild west, was inspired by the Jayne Mansfield/Kenneth More film *The Sheriff of Fractured Jaw* (1957). And who should appear briefly as a drunken stage coach passenger but your very own, Sid James!

The teaming of Charles Hawtrey and Bernard Bresslaw creates a link with their hugely successful ITV situation comedy *The Army Game* which set the ball rolling with its influence on *Sergeant*. The two shared the limelight with Hattie Jacques and Joan Sims in Norman Hudis' *Our House* before forging an essential comic relationship in the *Carry On* gang.

Cowboy was the only film in the series to fall behind its tight shooting schedule. Heavy rain during the initial stages of location filming caused the loss of the first day. It was a period that Gerald Thomas was never able to make up and resulted in the finished film coming in one day late. Mind you, one day over 31 movies ain't bad folks!

Cowboy was not Jim Dale's first brush with tongue-in-cheek Western ideals. On the tide of his success as a pop singer in the late 1950s Jim was hired by Cadbury's to advertise their Nux Chocolate Bar. Playing a cowboy singing a song about 'Injuns' Jim's fresh-faced glee sadly didn't give the bar a huge sales boost, but I'm sure they were delicious!

(1st Class) injects elements of bumbling British pratfalling and perfectly-timed tongue-in-cheek innuendo. Painfully unaware of the dangers to come ('Stodge City... Oh, right in the country, should be nice and peaceful') and fearfully ill at ease with the dangerously geared heroine of Angela Douglas, this is the ultimate innocent abroad. The role spans a priceless duologue with Sid James concerning his cattle rustling ('Bullocks!'/'I know what I'm talking about!'); having to hide his embarrassment at getting locked in his own jail; and a beautifully timed sequence when Jim is surrounded by the trio of glamorous Western belles in his bedroom. With a touch of comic genius, Jim nervously turns the photo of his mother to the wall. Technically, of course, the greatest achievement of the part is the fabulous display of gun skills after Angela's quickly dispatched lessons. Jim's skill is amazing but, as the late Sammy Davis Jnr would say, 'hell, if I wasn't good at it I wouldn't do it!'. The film's climax gives Jim a rousing finale as he pops up from various man-hole covers, quickly decreasing Sid's band of western baddies: it's Gerald Thomas direction and Jim Dale acting at their peak.

For its release in Germany, *Cowboy* was re-titled *The Rumpo Kid*.

The vocal characterization of Kenneth Williams' Judge Burke was inspired by legendary Hollywood comedy producer Hal Roach (a genius for bringing together Stan Laurel and Oliver Hardy in 1927). Roach had offered Kenneth the chance to travel to Hollywood and star in his latest slapstick production and although the supercilious actor declined the offer, he stole the distinctive gravelled vocals of the film maestro. Incidentally, the delivery of the accent - out of one side of the mouth - led to the irritation of Kenneth's painful mouth infection.

Cowboy features the only Western town in film history with a left-hand turn at the end of the main street. This was simply to mask the fact that no sprawling wilderness happened to be available on the Pinewood back-lot.

Carry On fan Ben Elton included a subliminal image of the end title from *Cowboy* in an episode of *The Young Ones* - 'Nasty'.

The composer of Angela Douglas' saloon song, 'This is the time for love', was Alan Rogers, the brother of main *Carry On* music man, Eric. Look closely during this sequence and you will spot the portly figure of Eric Rogers as the saloon pianist.

Edina Ronay gives a slinky support performance as Dolores, and was described by Peter Rogers as 'the new Brigitte Bardot'. Before *Cowboy* she had just filmed Rogers' *The Big Job* with Sid James and Jim Dale. She is now a successful fashion designer.

Following the popularity of the Hawtrey singing sequence in *Cleo* where he joyfully warbles 'There's no place like Rome!', Peter Rogers wanted his Indian brave to sing a snatch of 'Rose Marie' in *Cowboy*. Sadly the American publishing house which owned the rights wouldn't give permission.

Look out for...

There's a memorable piece of visual comedy between Sid James and Charles Hawtrey. When the drunken jabbering of Charlie endangers the criminal secrets of Sid, the mad cowboy forces his hand over the babbling Hawtrey's mouth. Hilariously, when Sid removes his hand, Charlie quickly pours another slug down his throat with an expression of indignant glee.

And on the subject of sight gags, take note of the first meeting between Sid James and Peter

Peace is definitely on! Charles Hawtrey, Sally Douglas and Sid James talk it over in *Carry On Cowboy*.

Butterworth. As Sid quietly walks away he ad libs a playful bit of comic business as he pushes Peter's hat over his eyes. The sequence is almost out of shot but remains treasurable filmed antics.

Future creator of *The Rocky Horror Picture Show* and original host of *The Crystal Maze*, Richard O'Brien, crops up as an Indian bare-back rider with Charles Hawtrey's tribe of braves.

Carry On memories

'*Carry On Cowboy* was one of the best films I did in the series - I did enjoy it. I loved the fact that there were moments I could capture that were a little different. There was one scene where it said he was practising with his revolver, so I did two week's rehearsal. It was just a few seconds on screen, where I pull the revolver out of the holster and it twizzles in the air and I grab it in panic. I find I'm holding the barrel and it's pointing at me so I scream and let go of it. It looks like an accident but obviously these are not accidents that you can keep repeating in front of a camera unless you really really practised very hard. I did. I worked for about two weeks just to do that, and every spare moment I was watching what the gun did in mid-air when I pulled it out of the holster. It was worth it - two weeks rehearsal just to capture three seconds on screen - but if it's a laugh and it looks good, it's well worth it'.
Jim Dale

'My one lasting memory of *Carry On Cowboy* was the riding audition. The production team had gathered together around twenty or thirty ponies that they imagined looked like wild mustangs, pintos, painted ponies, call them what you will, the only thing that they had in common was that none of them was really broken in. The test was to ride one of them bare back with no bridle, only a rope halter without a bit, up to point A. Here you were given a bow and arrow, which you rode with to point B, fired at a target from the moving horse and then rode on to the finish. Simple? I rode from the start to point A so well that I received a round of applause from my fellow riders - I took my bow and arrow and rode to point B - as I released my right hand from the rope halter the horse knew I was relying on his goodwill and decided not to give it. With a short, smart little kick I went shooting between his ears and bit the dust, as they say! "Oh, Dear!" cried the first assistant. "Can I try again?" I asked. "Yes" - they all chorused - "Let him try again!". I repeated the test, this time on a different horse. Same routine,

up to point A - fine - take the bow and arrow - fine - ride to point B - release the hold on the halter - and boom - straight between the ears again. A man called 'The Horse Master' smiled the most supercilious smile I had ever seen in my life at me - God! how I hate insult to injury - And he swanned his way over to the animal that had just thrown me and as if to show everyone what a complete and totally useless little shit I was, mounted the beast with style and grace. Boom - He went sailing over the horse, a tickled crowd and a serves you right me. I only did about 3 days' employment on the film, but I did get to watch a lot of filming as I wanted to know everything about the movies I could, and I must say that I was never asked to leave the set, even on days when I had no right to be there what-so-ever, and there were a lot of them! I found it thrilling. Still do!
Richard O'Brien

A Peter Rogers Production

CARRY ON COWBOY

Johnny Finger/The Rumpo Kid **SIDNEY JAMES**
Judge Burke **KENNETH WILLIAMS**
Marshall P. Knutt **JIM DALE**   Big Heap **CHARLES HAWTREY**
Belle **JOAN SIMS**   Doc **PETER BUTTERWORTH**
Little Heap **BERNARD BRESSLAW**
Annie Oakley **ANGELA DOUGLAS**   Sheriff Albert Earp **JON PERTWEE**
Charlie **PERCY HERBERT**   Sam Houston **SYDNEY BROMLEY**
Dolores **EDINA RONAY**   Clerk **LIONEL MURTON**
Curly **PETER GILMORE**   Josh the Undertaker **DAVY KAYE**
Commissioner **ALAN GIFFORD**
Stage Coach Guard **BRIAN RAWLINSON**
Bank Manager **MICHAEL NIGHTINGALE**
Short **SIMON CAIN**   Kitkata **SALLY DOUGLAS**   Mex **CARL McCORD**
Slim **GARRY COLLEANO**
Old Cowhand **ARTHUR LOVEGROVE**   Miss Jones **MARGARET NOLAN**
Blacksmith **TOM CLEGG**
Perkins **LARRY CROSS**   Trapper **BRIAN COBURN**
Dancing Girls **THE BALLET MONTPARNESSE**
Cowhand **HAL GALILI**   Drunk **NORMAN STANLEY**
Mexican Girl **CARMEN DENE**
Minnie **ANDREA ALLEN**   Polly **VICKI SMITH**   Jane **AUDREY WILSON**
Jenny **DONNA WHITE**   Sally **LISA THOMAS**   Bridget **GLORIA WEST**
Stage Coach Driver **GEORGE MOSSMAN**
Rider **RICHARD O'BRIEN**   Pianist **ERIC ROGERS**

Screenplay by **Talbot Rothwell**
Music composed & conducted by **Eric Rogers**
Songs: 'Carry On Cowboy' & 'This is the Night for Love' - music by **Eric Rogers**,
lyrics by **Alan Rogers**
Poster tag-line - 'How the West was lost!!'

Associate Producer **Frank Bevis**   Art Director **Bert Davey**
Editor **Rod Keys**   Director of Photography **Alan Hume B.S.C.**
Camera Operator **Godfrey Godar**
Assistant Director **Peter Bolton**   Unit Manager **Ron Jackson**
Make-up **Geoffrey Rodway**
Sound Editor **Jim Groom**
Sound Recordists **Robert T. MacPhee & Ken Barker**
Hairdressing **Stella Rivers**   Costume Designer **Cynthia Tingey**
Assistant Editor **Jack Gardner**
Master of Horse **Jeremy Taylor**   Continuity **Gladys Goldsmith**
Producer **Peter Rogers**   Director **Gerald Thomas**

A 1965 Anglo Amalgamated film released through Warner-Pathe Distribution Ltd.
'A' Cert. Colour Running time - 95 mins. 8,536ft

CARRY ON SCREAMING!

Without doubt this is one of the series' finest productions, awash with delightfully bad jokes, stunning performances of manic horror and demonstrating the finest directorial display in Thomas' career. While I am biased in that my favourite genres are comedy and horror and I consider Harry H. Corbett one of the most interesting actors of his generation, there is no denying *Screaming*'s place amongst the handful of true classics.

The time was ripe for a bit of comic blood sucking, as even Hammer were on the verge of including corny tag-lines ('You Just Can't Keep A Good Man Down' for *Dracula Has Risen From The Grave*), injecting comic turns from the likes of Roy Kinnear and throwing in a clutch of increasingly scantily-clad temptresses. Like the *Carry Ons*, Hammer became firmly established in the late 1950s by including established television stars (notably Peter Cushing), and building up a reliable collection of interchangeable character actors and a small roster of regular writer/director/technical personnel. Both were made economically and quickly, attracted a widespread audience and quickly became mainstays of the British film industry. Hammer's James Carreras once told Rogers, 'You make the comedy. I'll make the horror'. A *Carry On* debunking of the teeth and claws at Bray Studios was inspired.

Talbot Rothwell tosses in every conceivable biting/vampiric/mad doctor gag in the book and follows the structural blueprint of the standard Hammer mystery house thriller perfectly. In the absence of Sid James, Harry H. Corbett stepped brilliantly into the spotlight as the Holmesian Scotland Yard detective, hot on the trail of ghouls, disappearing women and rather hairy creatures. In a tongue-in-cheek comment on the subject content, Rothwell names the area in which the spooky happenings occur Hocombe wood (pronouced 'Hokum'). Harry contributes a stunning performance of dogged determination, sceptical raised eyebrows and

incompetence and is blessed with the nagging of Joan Sims as a domestic feed for comic business at his Victorian home. His Watson is brought to life by Peter Butterworth. In the first of several outstanding character supports which hover down the cast list but grab most of the best lines, Peter perfectly complements the flamboyant deduction of Corbett.

As with all the best horror pictures, the acting is dead straight - the comic gems coming from misunderstandings and the slow working minds of the British copper on the beat. The threat is real, albeit comedically depicted. Indeed, the film's initial sequence could have come straight from the world of Terence Fisher. The title song, suitably tongue-in-cheek and chillingly witty, matches blood red credits which quiver as a perfectly on-cue female screams in time with the lyrics. The sinister, atmospheric wood, shrouded in mist, with a shadowy tree, bathed in a streaming ray of moonlight, hanging ominously in the foreground is the perfect domain for a strolling Christopher Lee. The first image that wanders into view is Tom Clegg's outstanding monster, shaking the leaves as he passes through the undergrowth, moving out of the world of Hammer and straight into a comical evocation of innuendo-sprinkled fear from Jim Dale and Angela Douglas: 'I didn't mean your icy fingers Albert!'/'Well whose then!?' It is a brilliant piece of transition film-making and sets the scene for arguably the *Carry Ons*' most enjoyable and detailed genre parody.

The interior sets are stunning, with Thomas establishing the ethos of horror through the crumbling brick seen behind flaking paintwork; a small, shadowed window; primitive light encased in cobwebs and the acid stained, experiment-affected floors of the lab - ideally suited to the obsessions of mad Dr Kenneth Williams and his seductive sister, Fenella Fielding. In the finest hour of Fenella's film career, she purrs and giggles pure sexual evil to all and sundry and smoulders around the proceedings in Munsters-style Gothic red velvet.

'Ere, I don't like the look of him - Charles Hawtrey just before being wiped out in *Carry On Screaming!*.

body in the mirror. Convincing himself that he is imagining things, he continues his work, only to turn round and greet the investigating trio of Corbett, Butterworth and Dale. It's all low-brow joys (Peter: 'I am a police detective and I must warn you that I shall take down anything you say!' Charlie: 'Alright. Trousers!'). It's a very brief vignette but one stamped with the Hawtrey mark of genius; his untimely end at the hands of Clegg's lumbering Odbodd highlights the ultimate reality of the blood-soaked plot as a backdrop for the corny gags and farcical performances. Thank heaven for Mr Williamson!

A hilarious montage of classic *Carry On* from the golden age, this film bristles with quotable lines and mesmerising sequences, taking a comic look at every facet of the horror cinema. It tackles an insane, power mad scientist (Williams); a sinisterly seductive temptress (Fielding); a couple of hand-made monsters (Clegg and Cornelius); the towering, Karloffian butler (Bresslaw); a beautiful and helpless heroine (Douglas in the briefest of brief supports); a spooky, cobweb infested mansion; an eerie, misty wood; murders; a plethora of electronic gadgetry; werewolves (two fine manic materializations from Corbett and Dale in homage to the Lon Chaney Jnr/Oliver Reed snarling); a living mummy (a typically named Pharaoh Rubbatiti, played by a completely covered Denis Blake) and a tale of suspenseful deduction pitting good against evil. Sounds like a great way to spend a Saturday night!

Despite the critical acclaim of *Cowboy*, this much superior film failed to enjoy the same popularity with the men from Fleet Street. *The Times* reviewer thought it 'one of the dullest and least spirited of them all' while the cast 'just stand round, say the lines, and listlessly wait for the next laugh'. However, one journalist was instrumental in finding room in the cast for Charles Hawtrey. C.H.B. Williamson wrote a piece in *Today's Cinema* noting that for the forthcoming entry in the *Carry On* series, much respected comic great Charles Hawtrey would be absent from the cast. He expressed his sadness at this and wondered whether the box office returns would be affected by the omission of this vital player. To publicly deny this as simply a rumour and to satisfy panicked distributors and backers, Peter Rogers cast Charles in the minor supporting role of Dan Dann the lavatory man. Originally considered for this part was character player Sydney Bromley (who had scored a hit as Rancher Sam Houston in *Cowboy*), but Hawtrey dominates the small scene in which he features and contributes a memorable cameo turn. The timing at his initial appearance is expert as he cleans his washroom and spies some-

Best performance

In a film so full of great comic creations it is almost impossible to select the pick of the bunch. However, in terms of epitomizing the ghoulish horror and tongue-in-cheek innuendo, Kenneth Williams must have the edge. Cleverly named Dr Watt (due to his electric personality), Kenneth, all ashen face and nervous twitch, steamrolls through the scenario with aplomb. The part gives Williams ample opportunity to go over the top and deliver such deliciously groanworthy lines as, when he discusses driving stakes through people's hearts, 'No, I don't feel like driving tonight', or with the story about Dr Frankenstein and Dr Jekyll stealing his pocket money at school - 'the change did them good!'. Fenella Fielding gleefully highlights the corny jokes, notably counterbalancing Williams' painful pun, 'Fangs ain't what they used to be!', with a despairing 'Spare me!'. It's wonderfully bad dialogue executed with sparkling charm and comic skill. A cultured victim of horrendous greed and black magic, Kenneth is shocked at the sight of a fresh-faced Odbodd clone - 'Oh it's disgusting! Put something on you filthy beast!' - and bemoans his nomadic undead lifestyle ('Oh this is awful, I wish I was dead!' Fenella: 'But Olando, you are dead!'/'What! Oh yes, so I am. What a life!'). The showdown culminates, unhappily, with the demise of the undead Kenneth in his own vat of bubbling toxic material. Grab your chips, remember Kenneth Connor's reference in *Nurse* and Williams' own in *Spying* and join in the choruses of 'Frying tonight!'

Favourite bit

The highlight comes just before Kenneth's memorable first appearance as the bumbling deduction team of Harry H. Corbett, Peter Butterworth and Jim Dale investigate the mysterious 'Bide-a-wee' rest home. The imposing doorway is suitably eerie, complete with a forbidding stone gargoyle. Harry, having knocked gingerly, awaits a response as slow footsteps come closer and closer. As light seeps from inside, a gigantic shadow is cast onto the door and the Bernard Bresslaw homage to Karloff in *The Old Dark House* emerges. Thomas directs the sequence to enhance Bresslaw's already impressive height. The shot of the three investigators craning their necks to see the butler is a classic of visual comedy. Harry enquires, 'Could I see the master of the house?' Bresslaw mutters, 'The master of the house is dead sir!' While Bresslaw continues with his speech, 'He's been dead fifteen years now, but if you come in I'll ask him if he can see you!', Peter Butterworth adds a memorable touch of ad libbed visual clowning as he respectfully removes his hat. Later, as he fidgets and fumbles about Williams' eccentric behaviour, Peter insists that 'there's something not quite right about that man!' as he incorporates the mad doctor's twitching eye. It's an essential counterbalance between the normal and abnormal, full of clever references to *Dr Who* - 'Who's my brother or was, I haven't seen him for ages!' (an in-gag back to Hartnell's training of Williams in *Sergeant*) - and vocal gymnastics with misunderstanding contrasting misunderstanding. It's pure magic.

Did you know?

The basic premise for *Screaming*'s comic structure - the mad man kidnapping young females and encasing them in wax for the ultimate realism in his exhibited models - is the 1933 classic *The Mystery Of The Wax Museum* starring Lionel Atwill. The film was later remade as the 3-D wonder *House Of Wax* starring Vincent Price. It serves as an excellent blueprint for the *Carry On* deconstruction of the haunted cinema.

In the original script the part of Dr Watt was the father of Virula. However, as with Peter Cushing's youthful interpretation of Van Helsing in Hammer's *Dracula*, Kenneth Williams wanted to play the part nearer to his own age. Thus the relationship was changed to brother and sister.

Talbot Rothwell includes a rearranged version of Abbott and Costello's 'Who's on first?' sketch between Corbett and Williams - successfully evoking memories of the Hollywood clowns' brushes with Universal's monsters from *Abbott And Costello Meet Frankenstein* (1948) to *Abbott And Costello Meet The Mummy* (1955) when they sparred with such horror legends as Lugosi, Karloff and Chaney Jr. During *Screaming*'s release, both *The Addams Family* and *The Munsters* were profitably combining laughs with spooks!

Anglo Amalgamated distributed the classic 'Scotland Yard' featurettes hosted by Edgar Lustgarten; one, *Wings of Death* (1961), starred Harry H. Corbett as the Yard's leading light, Superintendent Hammond.

Marty Feldman would contribute a stunning comic turn to a later horror comic masterpiece - Mel Brooks' *Young Frankenstein*.

Frankie Howerd (*The House In Nightmare Park*) and Kenny Everett (*Bloodbath At The House Of Death*) would follow the *Carry Ons*' lead and combine innuendo comedy with horror. The Everett film, co-starring the gloriously evil Vincent Price, was actually condemned by critic Martyn Auty as 'Low-grade *Carry On*'. Ouch!

Carry On director Gerald Thomas provides the endearingly childish jibberings of lovable monster Odbodd Junior and had to 'do the monster voice' for his daughter Samantha for months after before she would go to sleep! Billy Cornelius, who played the creature on screen, takes elements from Boris Karloff's groundbreaking performance of the creature in *Frankenstein* (1931) and contributes a delightfully unaware menacing force.

A national promotion campaign by Plastech Ltd complemented *Screaming*'s release. Rubber monster toys called 'Kreepy Kwivers' could be bought in the foyers of certain ABC cinemas in conjunction with the film - costing the princely sum of 12/6 (62 ½ pence). The immortal tag-line was 'You'll scream with laughter when you buy a Kreepy Kwiver on sale at this cinema!'. If you find one send it on to me!

Screaming's title song was recorded by up-and-coming pop star Boz on Columbia Records. Really dedicated fans could also buy the sheet music.

Screaming was the last film in the series to be distributed by Anglo Amalgamated. With the death of senior partner Stuart Levy in 1966, Nat Cohen took over the company and made known his dislike of the *Carry Ons*. Although they were his most successful commodity, Cohen wanted to promote more high-brow cinema (critics were tending to pan such classics as *A Kind Of Loving* and *Peeping Tom* simply because they came from the same distributor as that of the *Carry Ons*). However, when the company became EMI, Cohen paid tribute to the series with a reference to *Sergeant* in the David Essex/Ringo Starr film *That'll Be The Day*: during the holiday camp sequences, a tannoy announces *Sergeant* as the film attraction) and later played the low-brow comedy game with the 'Confessions...' series, big screen versions of *Steptoe & Son*, *Up Pompeii* and other such Frankie Howerd movies as *The House In Nightmare Park*.

For several cinema releases abroad, the film was renamed *Carry On Vampire*.

Hammer horror or what! Jim Dale and Harry H. Corbett briefly play the chills for real in *Carry On Screaming!*

Look out for...

The sarcastic relationship between Jim Dale and Harry H. Corbett is priceless - all funny looks and cutting remarks. The highlight comes near the film's close when the two resurrect memories of Sid James/Kenneth Connor in *What A Carve Up!* and Stan and Ollie in *The Laurel-Hardy Murder Case* by sharing a four poster bed. Sinister snakes and things that go bump in the night interrupt sleep and Corbett is decidedly worried about Jim's sexuality - 'What about me, ah!'/'That's the trouble... I don't know about you!'. Miss the movie at your peril.

Both Jim and Harry incorporate elements of Kenneth Williams' *Hancock's Half Hour* persona. The bumbling detective of Corbett mumbles 'Good evening' on his first meeting with Bernard Bresslaw, and Dale's handsome hero earnestly searches for his missing girlfriend and blurts out 'Stop messin' about!', followed by a giggle of comic awareness.

Take note of the classic Eric Rogers' musical in-joke when he includes a cunning reference to Harry H. Corbett's day job as the nation's favourite rag 'n' bone man by injecting a few bars of the *Steptoe & Son* theme. Coming just after the end of the first batch of episodes in 1965, the joke was fresh. Another touch of gritty 1960s' television is suggested by a quick burst of the *Z-Cars* theme - Holmesian detective coupled with sardonic, contemporary law enforcement.

Carry On memories

'I have only warm memories of my *Carry On* days. Happy times.'
Angela Douglas

'My favourite *Carry On* anecdote concerns Peter Rogers when he was working on his front garden at his home in Iver, Bucks. A lady drove up in a big car and said, "My good man - how much do they pay you for doing the garden?". "Nothing" said Peter, "but I get to sleep with the lady of the house!". The lady drove away quickly. When I was playing the cab driver in *Carry On Screaming!* it was a very wretched night raining elephants. It was a night shot which went on and on. When we were changing in the Dressing Room Jim Dale said, as a joke, "We ought to go on strike!". I got home about 6am and the phone went - it was Jim Dale and he said, "What did I say in the dressing room, Norman?" I actually said I couldn't remember exactly but it was something about - "I was looking round for Noah's ark and we ought to go on strike for excess watch!". "What's wrong?" I said, "Well" said Jim, "when I got home there was a message to ring my agent - I did so and he was livid". He said "What are you doing trying to call the actors out on strike!" I said I was making a joke about Noah's ark and making water! but he said "That's not what I heard - Peter Rogers is at home waiting by his telephone for you to apologise." Anyway, I said to Jim - "Well you can quote me that it was a joke!". I didn't work on a *Carry On* for Peter Rogers for over ten years - until *Carry On Emmannuelle!*'
Norman Mitchell

A Peter Rogers Production

CARRY ON SCREAMING!

Detective Sergeant Sidney Bung **HARRY H. CORBETT**
Doctor Olando Watt **KENNETH WILLIAMS**
Albert Potter **JIM DALE** Dan Dann **CHARLES HAWTREY**
Emily Bung **JOAN SIMS**
Valeria Watt **FENELLA FIELDING**
Detective Constable Slobotham **PETER BUTTERWORTH**
Sockett **BERNARD BRESSLAW** Doris Mann **ANGELA DOUGLAS**
Dr Fettle **JON PERTWEE** Odbodd **TOM CLEGG**
Odbodd Jnr. **BILLY CORNELIUS** Cabby **NORMAN MITCHELL**
Vivian the Window Dresser **MICHAEL WARD**
Mr. Jones the Shop Manager **FRANK THORNTON**
Desk Sergeant **FRANK FORSYTH** Policeman **ANTHONY SAGAR**
Girl **SALLY DOUGLAS**
Mrs. Parker **MARIANNE STONE** Rubbatiti **DENIS BLAKE**

Screenplay by **Talbot Rothwell**
Music composed & conducted by **Eric Rogers**
Song: 'Carry On Screaming' by **Myles Rudge & Ted Dick**
Sung by **Anon**...or is it Jim Dale - I'm not telling!!

Associate Producer **Frank Bevis** Art Director **Bert Davey**
Director of Photography **Alan Hume B.S.C.**
Editor **Rod Keys** Camera Operator **Godfrey Godar**
Assistant Director **Peter Bolton**
Sound Editor **Arthur Ridout** Sound Recordists **C.C. Stevens & Ken Barker**
Make-up **Geoff Rodway**
Unit Manager **Ron Jackson** Hairdresser **Stella Rivers**
Costume Designer **Emma Selby-Walker**
Continuity **Penny Daniels** Producer **Peter Rogers**
Director **Gerald Thomas**

A 1966 Anglo Amalgamated film released
through the Warner-Pathe Distribution Ltd.
'A' Cert. Colour Running time - 97 mins. 8,746ft

CARRY ON
...DON'T LOSE YOUR HEAD

With the death of Stuart Levy in 1966, the atmosphere at Anglo Amalgamated radically altered as Nat Cohen took command. Despite Cohen's already apparent dislike of the series, Rogers considered the time ripe for a change anyway. It was a matter of days before this hugely successful film producer struck a deal with the almighty Rank Organisation. However, there was a price to pay. While Rank were more than keen to get into the act of promoting these money-spinning comedies, the *Carry On* series was widely associated with the rival company by both the general public and the industry. Thus it was that the *Carry On* series Rank took on lost the all important 'Carry On' prefix. It was a situation that lasted for just two films and both these productions were quickly re-released with the *Carry On* title sloppily tacked on the front. The box-office takings soared the second time around.

Although the title may have been changed to protect the innocent, all concerned with *Don't Lose Your Head* were in fully-geared *Carry On* mood: the cast was awash with team favourites, the script was bristling with Rothwellian gems and Thomas' direction was a spirited homage to the flamboyant swashbuckling of Flynn and Granger. While Rank hoped for the best with this nameless comedy team, Sid, his black fingernail and the gang threw themselves into the action adventure with gusto: Kenneth Williams' flamboyant cry of 'Carry On Chopping' sets the tone of the piece with one drop of the guillotine.

A beautifully constructed period piece, thanks largely to lavish stately home location shooting and particularly high production values, the film is a rip-roaring romp through the French revolution and the cinematic legacy of Leslie Howard. As with the best *Carry Ons*, the film's main perspective is from the ideal of English righteousness and bravery. The French, all pompous elitism and dogged low life (including a quite superb Laurel & Hardyesque couple of bumbling villains from Kenneth Williams and

Peter Butterworth), bicker and moan about the landed gentry while enjoying the life of Riley themselves. The scenario, French aristos having their heads chopped off for the glory of the country, arouses the interest of a couple of foppish dandies from the stiff upper-lipped land of gallantry and fun - England. Michael Ward's whimpering servant breaks down in front of his master and sobs an explanation of the French situation, and the mincing English lords (Sid James and Jim Dale) listen with wide-mouthed anguish. A plan is brewing and when Ward informs the duo that women are getting the chop as well ('I say, that's not cricket!'/'Damned of a waste, to boot!') the time is right for the British invasion. With the prancing Ward out of the way, James and Dale drop their contempt and become their stereotyped *Carry On* selves - Sid all gruff and ready to go and Jim happy to follow and assist.

That's the plot of this fast moving and fun historical, with the good British pitted against the cunning, French. The action changes from the British battling the French on their home terrain to England, with Williams *et al* approaching Sid at his mansion. Finally it's all back to France for the dramatic climax in Williams' luxurious mansion as his 'beautiful things' are quickly smashed and destroyed! With hardly the most vexing plot in the world, the film is simply an excuse to pay a tribute to a thousand sword fights and damsels in distress rescued, as the *Carry On* style takes a sideways glance at the genre.

On the way, Sid and the good guys pick up the camp nobleman of Charles Hawtrey - gleefully embarking on a crusade of rapier battles - while the French have the seductive figure ('there's room for a few lodgers there!') of Joan Sims, bubbling and giggling as the uneducated sex pot in a world of perfect manners. Sid's ultimate macho man finds the perfect damsel in distress in the shape of French actress Dany Robin (veteran of *Le Silence Est D'Or* (1946), *Histoire D'Amour* (1952) and *Waltz Of The Toreadors* (1962) with Peter Sellers), projecting a wisp of romantic charm and subtle acting style which blends with James' 'cor blimey' hero to perfection - false teeth in lockets and all!

It's a colourful, rip-roaring historical romp through the French revolution, complete with a handful of prime Rothwell situations and manic comic creations. The whole radiates confidence in the style that all involved knew to be a winning formula and, although in terms of the series' history this was a vitally important make-or-break production, the team settle into their low-brow comic mode perfectly. If Rank were worried, then it didn't affect the performers on screen. The new distributors accepted that the regular team actors were essential for the continuation of the series' popularity, and quickly grasped the obvious sign that the nameless band of clowns needed the tried-and-tested *Carry On* title to fully get back on course. Peter Rogers never lost his head.

Best performance

Without doubt it's the all-conquering return of Sid James, as he bombards through the Rothwell scenario and completely steals the scenes with a delightfully dual-edged performance. In his persona as English lord Sir Rodney Ffing ('with two f's'), Sid minces and camps around with beauty spot and powdered wig, dancing with Jim Dale and successfully projecting an image of outrageous effeminacy to Williams and the French intruders. It is a stunning character study of English eccentricity.

However, for the Sid connoisseur, there is the roguish and dashing figure of The Black Fingernail - the familiar chuckling, womanizing Sid of old. Playing outside the film's narrative and directly addressing the audience, Sid links the viewer with the tongue-in-cheek adventure story on screen, gleefully looking into the crowd as if to let on that this is just a bunch of familiar and welcome actors larking about at Pinewood Studios. Sid's energetic and enterprising central performance is a touch of warm, good-hearted fun which embraces farcical disguise (including Sid's dreaded drag), sarcastic, bubbling innuendo and stirring sword play. The legendary pistol duel at dawn contrasts Williams' arrogant snobbish figure of French authority with Sid's tongue-in-cheek dandy. Simply pretending to be totally unable to follow the easiest of instructions, James follows behind the marching Williams. When Kenneth turns to be confronted by 'That ffing!', Sid mumbles, 'I say, you're a bit close aren't you?!' It's all inspired stuff and Sid's the boy to watch. If you're on his side, you have the cheerful camp of Hawtrey, the boyish energy of Dale and the spirit of Errol Flynn behind you. Far behind mind you!

Favourite bit

The film's highlight comes with the obsessive beheading sessions organized by those marvellous partners in crime Kenneth Williams and Peter Butterworth in the style of a barbers queue (with Peter cheerfully yelling 'And the next one s'il vous plait!'/'Short back and side, not too much off the top!'). Charles Hawtrey is one nobleman that our heroes (James and Dale) must save from the chop and a host of derring-do escapades ensue. The pair are masterfully disguised as a country bumpkin street trader (Jim - complete with stock of toy guillotines and aristo dolls with fully detachable heads!) and a dignified insurance salesman (Sid - in dark sombre suit and glasses) - 'It's a very good policy your grace. It covers accidental death by drowning, shooting, stabbing, poisoning, hanging...'. Charles: 'Beheading?'/'Ah, no. Well we can't take too many risks you know!' Having successfully organized the subterfuge, Sid cleverly tricks Williams into beheading his chief executioner (Leon Greene), leading to a quick inclusion of one of Betty Box's biggest hits - 'Is there a doctor in the house!?' Full of brilliantly timed performances, treasurable dialogue and an atmosphere of feel-good vulgarity, the sequence is one for the archives. While the super sensitive and ill-informed Tim Pulleine, in *The Movie*, wrote 'the scenes involving Charles Hawtrey going to the guillotine are not so much in poor taste than beyond any kind of taste at all', this comic retelling of the infamous victims of Madame Le Guillotine forms an essential Rothwellian situation.

Did you know?

Don't Lose Your Head publicity material included a puzzle maze block asking the taxing question, 'Can you help Sidney James, Kenneth Williams, Joan Sims, Charles Hawtrey, Jim Dale and Dany Robin escape from the Guillotine?'

When she filmed *Head*, Dany Robin was the proud owner of five crocodiles, Potapot, Razmotte, Moussa, Noiro and Blanco, which she kept at her home just outside Paris. Her menagerie also included a badger, a donkey, a monkey, pigs, stags and horses - surely putting Bardot in the shade! The actress died in 1995 from injuires sustained after a fire at her home.

This was the 25th film from the Rogers/Thomas partnership which spanned back to 1956's *Circus Friends*.

For location work Rogers decamped from Pinewood to Waddesdon Manor, six miles from Aylesbury,

Peter Butterworth and Kenneth Williams, ever the rebels, are just about to disobey the title's advice - *Carry On ...Don't Lose Your Head*.

The Haydn symphony which Dany Robin plays in the film is accompanied by a chorus of 'Yeah! Yeah! Yeah!' from the 1963 Beatles hit 'She Loves You'. The greatest hits album *Oldies but Goldies* was riding high in the charts during *Head*'s release.

Carry On memories

'Can't think of anything very amusing that happened on the *Carry On* sets to me - we were all too busy learning our lines and laughing at Kenny Williams' antics. They were a joy to work on. Very happy times.'
Marianne Stone

'*Carry On...Don't Lose Your Head* had a gag in, that Sid and I thought of. That was when Charlie Hawtrey was about to have his head chopped off. We suggested that the messenger run up and say, "I have a urgent message for you my Lord" and Charlie say, "Drop it in the basket - I'll read it later!".'
Jim Dale

Buckinghamshire. The house was originally built for the Rothschild family and made its film debut here as Kenneth Williams' mansion. It was the only genuine French design chateau in Great Britain.

Look out for...

Charles Hawtrey's entrance is an inspired piece of Thomas direction, with infectious giggling coming from behind a huge book as his name is called for the joys of the guillotine. Ever-faithful assistant Peter Butterworth wanders over to sort out the situation and his angered address leads to Hawtrey's sparkling expression of pure enjoyment which emerges from behind the volume. It's a magic piece of visual clowning played out by the two most gifted technical screen comedians in the team.

Also to enjoy is another prime piece of Charles Hawtrey comedy when his compulsive liar and all-round loud mouth desperately tries to impress a clutch of seductive young things. Boasting about his exploits in France he explains about the numbers he has killed, 'Oh, six, seven!'/'Six or seven. What a bloody sight it must have been!'/'Oh my dear, if my sword hadn't broke it would have been a bloody sight more!'. Yes I know, a corny old gag, but it's those groanworthy chestnuts, delivered by masters like Hawtrey, that make this film one of the best.

A Peter Rogers Production

CARRY ON... DON'T LOSE YOUR HEAD

Sir Rodney Ffing/The Black Fingernail **SIDNEY JAMES**
Citizen Camembert **KENNETH WILLIAMS**
Lord Darcy de Pue **JIM DALE**   Duc de Pommfrit **CHARLES HAWTREY**
Desiree Dubarry **JOAN SIMS**
Citizen Bidet **PETER BUTTERWORTH**   Jacqueline **DANY ROBIN**
Robespierre **PETER GILMORE**
Landlady **MARIANNE STONE**   Henri **MICHAEL WARD**
Malabonce **LEON GREENE**
Guard **HUGH FUTCHER**   Captain of Soldiers **RICHARD SHAW**
Sergeant **DAVID DAVENPORT**
1st Lady **JENNIFER CLULOW**   2nd Lady **VALERIE VAN OST**
3rd Lady **JACQUELINE PEARCE**
Messenger **NIKKI VAN DER ZYL**   Rake **JULIAN ORCHARD**
Lady Binder **ELSPETH MARCH**
Bald Headed Dowager **JOAN INGRAM**
'What Locket?' Man **MICHAEL NIGHTINGALE**
Princess Stephanie **DIANA MacNAMARA**   Little Man **RONNIE BRODY**
Soldier **BILLY CORNELIUS**   Narrator **PATRICK ALLEN**
Girls **MONICA DIETRICH   ANNA WILLOUGHBY   PENNY KEEN
JUNE COOPER   CHRISTINE PRYOR   KAREN YOUNG**

Screenplay by **Talbot Rothwell**
Music composed & conducted by **Eric Rogers**
Song: 'Don't Lose Your Head' by **Bill Martin & Phil Coulter**
Executed by **The Michael Sammes Singers**
Poster tag-line - 'Carry On laughing until you have hysterics....
But Don't Lose Your Head'

Production Manager **Jack Swinburne**
Director of Photography **Alan Hume B.S.C.**   Editor **Rod Keys**
Art Director **Lionel Couch**   Camera Operator **Jimmy Devis**
Assistant Director **Jack Causey**
Sound Editor **W. Nelson**
Sound Recordists **Dudley Messenger & Ken Barker**
Continuity **Rita Davison**   Make-up **Geoffrey Rodway**
Hairdressing **Stella Rivers**   Costume Designer **Emma Selby-Walker**
Choreographer **Terry Gilbert**   Master of Horse **Jeremy Taylor**
Producer **Peter Rogers**
Director **Gerald Thomas**

A 1966 Rank Organisation Release 'A' Cert.
Colour Running time - 90 mins. 8,100ft

CARRY ON
...FOLLOW THAT CAMEL

Again resurrecting the *Carry On* ethos without the title initially in place, this is a spirited dry run for Rothwell's next historical parody, tackling Edwardian restraint (the film is set in 1906) and giving a memorable comic slant on the PC Wren tale, *Beau Geste*. Rank promoted the film as boasting the regular *Carry On* line-up but were still rather uneasy about embracing the series. Rogers and Thomas gathered together a handpicked selection of favourite team members to play the supporting roles while the central comic icon is brilliantly brought to life by vaudeville legend Phil Silvers.

The central role was originally written with the series' leading light, Sid James, in mind, but a minor heart attack kept Sid out of action. In view of Rank's hopes to catapult the series into the international market, pressure was put on Rogers for an American star name for the lead role. Unlike several British movies of the late 1960s, which developed an entire idea and Americanized the scenario for the Hollywood guest, Rothwell simply built up Silvers' part with Bilko-like witticisms and set it down within the standard *Carry On* framework. Silvers' comic style and working experience blended well with the resident Pinewood players - the vaudeville reliance on bodily function gags and cross-talk banter was simply a variation on the British music-hall style. Naturally Sid James is missed, but the clever idea of incorporating a totally individual type of comedic persona was an inspired gamble. The fact that Silvers was cast neither really helped or hindered the film's British business but, more importantly, failed to ignite the series in America once again. However, this matters little: in retrospect the film remains an essential example of the vintage historical comedies.

The bulk of corny Rothwell one-liners are given the Phil Silvers treatment, and he also has the task of playing away from the film's action and looking directly into camera (such as after Joan Sims' sexually charged remarks, 'I have a good ass, no!'). The characterizations surrounding Silvers' basic comic creation are mostly believable and detailed cameos of foreign eccentricity (Sims as the sassy, exotic cafe owner; Bernard Bresslaw, snarling and roaring in the background as the tyrannical Sheikh; Anita Harris as a dusky, seductive dancer; Kenneth Williams turning in an assured portrayal of Germanic determination). As in *Cowboy*, Charles Hawtrey minces around as his usual bumbling self, contrasting with the strict anarchy of Williams ('Pull those bloomers down, pull them down!'/'Herr Commandant, not so loud. Any one listening outside the fort will wonder what's going on in here!'). Angela Douglas, turning in an assured picture of English rose refinement, finds out the facts of life *en route*, and gets embroiled in the dark and shady world of Sheikh Bresslaw. The contrast is dramatically effective, with the well-orchestrated seduction scene complemented by Eric Rogers' musical joke: the inclusion of a snatch from

Phil Silvers plays Nocker playing Bilko playing *Carry On* **- a stunning victorious shot from** *Carry On... Follow That Camel*.

The ultimate *Boy's Own* hero - Jim Dale cracks another one for six in *Carry On... Follow That Camel*.

'Do not trust him Gentle Maiden'. The major link with the pure Englishness of *Carry On* comedy is captured in a fabulous partnership of upper-class hero (Jim Dale) and ever-faithful servant (Peter Butterworth). This enables Rothwell to inject huge elements of tongue-in-cheek English japes and put-downs (all pompous class system and sexual unease), while a fruitful teaming of the bumbling British and the boastful 'Bilko' creates some of the film's most inspired sequences.

Both these Rank entries were later officially included in the series, and there was no doubt in anybody's mind that the French revolution romp and the sun-scorched adventure were *Carry Ons* in heart, mind and spirit. The fun was still there, Phil Silvers proved the perfect guest star and all was right with the world - or was it just a mirage?

Best performance

Standing as a fixed image of English correctness against the rough-and-ready attitude of desert life is the splendid lead performance from the ever-reliable Jim Dale. Peaking in the *Carry Ons* with this fresh-faced and honest figure, Jim strolls with confidence through the dodgy deals of Silvers and the tempting seductions of sex, money and false honour. Partnered by a stunning support performance from Peter Butterworth, he tackles the dangers and primitiveness of Foreign Legion life with dignified awareness and perfect manners. The dialogue in Bresslaw's harem is a notable case, with Dale's bumbling panic and Silvers' wide-eyed delight - 'Well, I'm leaving!'/'What are you, nuts!' - as a dumb-founded

Butterworth looks on. However, while in the face of physical danger, Jim is the ultimate *Boy's Own* hero. While his nervous jittering enhances his seduction scene with Anita Harris, the sequences with Bernard Bresslaw include elements of his almost straight hero of *Cleo* - Bresslaw: 'Quiet, you miserable camel droppings!' Jim is the ultimate good sport, and the cricket sequences that top and tail the film are treasurable moments of feel-good comedy. The role is hilarious, touching, inspiring and played to perfection by Jim in a multi-faceted, wittily delivered central role - 'BO to you, too!'.

Favourite bit

Naturally the favourite sequence includes a totally on-form vignette from Jim Dale, in the sparkling company of Phil Silvers, Bernard Bresslaw and Peter Butterworth in the Sheikh's desert settlement. In a scene awash with memorable lines and tongue-in-cheek satire, Phil's cunning coward is more than happy to save himself and sacrifice his men, while the steely confidence of Jim Dale is more than a match for Bresslaw's evil villain. There are enough corny jokes and knowing looks to make this perfect *Carry On* fare. Bresslaw: 'The infidels will all perish when the second crescent of the moon enters the third phase of Orion'. Silvers: 'When is that?'/'Tuesday!'. The innuendo-geared humour even invades the cut-throat threats of Bresslaw's merciless Sheikh: 'Perhaps a little torture will help you to remember. You have until nightfall to come to your senses - if not they will come off, one by one!' Dale: 'I suppose he means our ears!' Silvers: 'That's my boy, always thinking of the higher things!' It is an excellent piece of cross-talking comic banter, delivered with po-faced sincerity and split-second timing.

Did you know?

When it became clear to Peter Rogers that Sid James was unavailable and that an American talent might be best as replacement, the initial name cited was Woody Allen. Having made his acting/writing film debut with *What's New Pussycat?* in 1965 and creating a cache with the 1960s' hip people, Allen would have made interesting casting to say the least.

During the making of *Camel*, Phil Silvers was going through a particularly difficult time in his private life, coupled with the fact that he was losing his sight. Silvers was wearing contact lenses as well as his familiar glasses to improve his eye-sight. As he lost these on many occasions during shooting, it was a common sight to see Silvers, Dale and Butterworth on hands and knees searching through the sands at Camber!

Clockwise:

Bernard Bresslaw's Karloffian butler gives an eerie welcome to Peter Butterworth, Jim Dale and Harry H. Corbett in *Carry On Screaming!*

'The horse – he couldn't have been!!' Kenneth Williams and Peter Butterworth don't believe it in *Carry On...Don't Lose Your Head*

Larry Taylor drives his point home as Jim Dale, Anita Harris, Peter Butterworth and Phil Silvers look on – *Carry On...Follow That Camel*

This is my desert. A stunning portrait of Bernard Bresslaw – *Carry On...Follow That Camel*

Many of the *Carry On* cast felt ill at ease with the importation of Phil Silvers, particularly Kenneth Williams, who quickly became irritated with the comedian's unending stories and insistence on using idiot boards during filming. After Kenneth voiced his dislike of acting opposite an unprofessional performer, Phil arrived on set the following day having learnt his lines. Williams was touched and the two became tolerant of each other for the rest of the production. However, for Bernard Bresslaw it was a honour to work with this legendary American clown, and he spent many happy hours listening to Phil's stories of Hollywood and Broadway during the Pinewood breaks and lunch times. Jim Dale and Peter Butterworth also made concerted efforts to welcome their star. Silvers had already successfully worked with Peter Butterworth in the 1966 Richard Lester filming of *A Funny thing Happened On the Way To The Forum*.

Like all the *Carry On* genre parodies, the film is awash with cinematic in-jokes and references. Kenneth Williams' crew-cut and monocled German is modelled on Hollywood legend Erich Von Stroheim, while Anita Harris' Corktip will remind film buffs of Claudette Colbert's 'Cigarette' in the 1936 Ronald Colman picture, *Under Two Flags*. Bernard Bresslaw, all flowing robes and sinister snarls, is a direct parody of Anthony Quinn in *Lawrence Of Arabia*.

The flamboyant worshipping display of Bresslaw and his followers every time somebody utters 'Mustapha Leek' led to the cast and crew quickly adopting the phrase when they got the call of nature!

The location shooting at Camber Sands and Rye in Sussex took three weeks, the longest period away from Pinewood Studios in the series' history. All Peter Rogers needed was a couple of fake palm trees and one camel - named Sheena - who came from Chessington Zoo and had to have training in walking on sand after a lifetime in captivity.

Despite the Rank Organisation's reluctance to incorporate the *Carry On* title in their first two films with Peter Rogers, the posters captured the essence of the earlier films with caricatured images of the regulars and clear links with the *Carry On* name via the taglines. For the 1966 release, the poster boasted 'Carry On Laughing until you have hysterics but... Don't Lose Your Head' and for *Camel*, 'Bilko joins the Carry On legion'. They were always part of the series.

Look out for...

Note the return of Vincent Ball, previously seen as the hulking P.T. instructor in *Cruising*. Suitably enough he crops up in *Camel* as a ship's officer, eagerly helping the delectable Angela Douglas with her port-hole!

A lads' night out! Phil Silvers, Jim Dale and Peter Butterworth sample some forbidden pleasures in *Carry On... Follow That Camel*.

The film includes the first appearance in the series from Julian Holloway, son of Stanley Holloway, making his mark as a cheeky British Rail ticket collector who also enjoys a few moments with Miss Douglas. Dirty swine!

Note the gloriously British slant on the burning heat of the desert, with Charles Hawtrey's joyful evocation of the British seaside holiday with the organization of a sandcastle competition. The atmosphere of happy days at Brighton and Blackpool is further developed with the gang's sun-crazed rendition of 'We do like to be beside the seaside!'.

There's a great piece of ad-libbed comedy involving the film's chief assets - Jim Dale and Peter Butterworth. Jim, having caught his leg in the harness of the camel he was riding, was dangling from the beast in need of assistance. Peter, seeing natural comedy in the making, rushed into shot and started shooing the beast away with his umbrella.

Kenneth Williams gleefully hams it up with Shakespearian passion as he grabs a skull which he believes is his beloved Angela Douglas - 'Alas, poor Jane, I knew her well!'

Rejoice in a belated return to the film for Charles Hawtrey, staggering through the desert sands to the aid of an under-siege Silvers and gang. With relish, Hawtrey flamboyantly cries, 'Ooh! Just in the nick!'. Classic!

Carry On memories

'Peter Butterworth and I did a lovely bit of business in Carry On... Follow That Camel - that's when I'm supposed to slide down the neck of a camel. Well I did, but I think I fell sideways by accident and the bloody camel started to bite me. Peter came rushing in with his umbrella, beating hell out of this camel. That shows just what Peter was like, it wasn't that he was coming to my rescue, it was just the makings of a wonderful comedic moment that Peter realized could happen if he rushed in with his umbrella. He wasn't expected to - it wasn't in the script, but he suddenly realized - this was magic, this was comedy and let's not stop the camera, just keep the camera rolling and let's see what happens. Jim Dale might get his leg bitten off but it's going to be funny while it happens! He was marvellous.'
Jim Dale

'The only anecdote which might be of interest was about the filming of Carry On...Follow That Camel. Given the subject matter, everyone anticipated a delightful location in the Mediterranean. However, they discovered that they were going to Camber Sands!! Angela Douglas told me that Peter was so cold after the shooting of him buried in sand up to his neck, that he had to be wrapped in blankets and given brandy - a far cry from the hot desert sun!'.
Janet Brown

A Peter Rogers Production

CARRY ON... FOLLOW THAT CAMEL

Sergeant Ernie Nocker **PHIL SILVERS** Bertram Oliphant 'BO' West **JIM DALE**
Simpson **PETER BUTTERWORTH** Commandant Burger **KENNETH WILLIAMS**
Captain Le Pice **CHARLES HAWTREY** Zig-Zig **JOAN SIMS**
Lady Jane Ponsonby **ANGELA DOUGLAS**
Sheikh Abdul Abulbul **BERNARD BRESSLAW**
Corktip **ANITA HARRIS** Corporal Clotski **JOHN BLUTHAL**
Captain Bagshaw **PETER GILMORE** Sir Cyril Ponsonby **WILLIAM MERVYN**
Ticket Collector **JULIAN HOLLOWAY**
Hotel Manager **DAVID GLOVER** Riff **LARRY TAYLOR**
Raff **WILLIAM HURNDELL**
Doctor **JULIAN ORCHARD** Ship's Officer **VINCENT BALL**
Lawrence **PETER JESSON**
Nightingale the Butler **MICHAEL NIGHTINGALE**
Riffs at Abdul's Tent **RICHARD MONTEZ**
FRANK SINGUINEAU SIMON CAIN
Hotel Gentleman **HAROLD KASKET** Bowler **EDMUND PEGGE**
Harem Girls **CAROL SLOAN GINA GIANELLI**
DOMINIQUE DON ANNE SCOTT PATSY SNELL
ZORENAH OSBORNE MARGOT MAXINE
SALLY DOUGLAS ANGIE GRANT GINA WARWICK
KAREN YOUNG HELGA JONES

Screenplay by **Talbot Rothwell**
Music composed & conducted by **Eric Rogers**
Poster tag-line - 'Bilko joins the Carry On legion!'

Production Manager **Jack Swinburne**
Director of Photography **Alan Hume B.S.C.**
Editor **Alfred Roome B.G.F.E.** Art Director **A. Vetchinsky**
Camera Operator **Alan Hall**
Assistant Director **David Bracknell** Continuity **Joy Mercer**
Assistant Editor **Jack Gardner**
Make-up **Geoffrey Rodway**
Sound Recordists **Dudley Messenger & Ken Barker**
Hairdresser **Stella Rivers** Costume Designer **Emma Selby-Walker**
Dubbing Editor **Wally Nelson** Location Manager **Terry Clegg**
Producer **Peter Rogers** Director **Gerald Thomas**

A 1967 Rank Organisation Release 'A' Cert.
Colour Running time - 95 mins. 8,550ft

CARRY ON DOCTOR

Back to life, back to reality, as the history books are put back on the shelf, Sid James and Barbara Windsor return to the *Carry On* fold and Talbot Rothwell structures the ultimate in-joke infested homage to Norman Hudis. With the fullest roster of team members ever assembled (only Kenneth Connor is missing), all the stereotyped characters firmly in place and the first rip-roaring, flamboyantly uncontrolled star turn from that priceless prince of the comedic art, Frankie Howerd, the recipe for one of the most beloved and enjoyable of British comedies is complete.

It's full of low-brow humour aimed at the nether regions, phantom pregnancies and bedpans, horrendous visitors (Joan Sims' timid assistant to Frankie) and sexy nurses in the shape of bubbly Barbara Windsor (in a series return after over three years) and a wide-eyed Anita Harris (in her second and last appearance). The handsome doctor who causes Anita's pulse to race is the ideal vehicle for Jim Dale - all gangling limbs and charming romantics as his Dr Kilmore combines slapstick with Richard Chamberlain's Kildare personality. His manic 'roof top drama' involving Thomas dutch angles and sexual misunderstanding is a highlight, while his coy pursuit of the nurses is practised on his skeleton - kissing the bony hand and spitting out a mouthful of dust with perfect timing.

It is the eccentricities of the hospital environment that cause the most merriment, with the roguish man-of-the-world of Sid James (suitably cast as a bedridden patient following his recent, real-life heart attack during the making of *George and the Dragon*, and keen to return to the films in any sized role) smoking under the bedclothes, drinking whiskey and over-heating the thermometer at the first meeting with Nurse Windsor. Peter Butterworth, as the representative for the everyman audience, tellingly called Smith, moans and groans at his wife's insistence at bringing the hated grapes but revels in the army-like community of the men's ward. Charles Hawtrey whimpers and whines throughout the proceedings with his morning sickness and pre-natal classes (highlighted by Eric Rogers' inclusion of a moment of 'The Ballet of the Chicks in their Shells' from Mussorgsky's *Pictures from an Exhibition*), while Bernard Bresslaw incorporates his *Army Game* hulking lug persona for the first time after a run of crumbling/terrifying villains. Hattie Jacques injects a touch of love-struck compassion into her over-powering tyrant of a Matron and Kenneth Williams, minces around in a daze with flowers and hallucinations ('Lucy who?'), giggles about his cutting profession ('Yes, get the old butcher's apron off, ah!'), forges a suspicious patient/doctor duologue with Sid ('I mean with a temperature 106 you're dead!'/'Well don't just stand there, bury me!') and establishes a legendary love/hate relationship with Jacques that would continue, on and off, through several further series entries.

As a backdrop to this huge collection of comic individuals, Rothwell builds up a loose but effective plot which includes corruption in high places, the ousting of likable doctor, Jim Dale, the reinstatement of likable doctor, Jim Dale, the demotion of unlikable doctor, Kenneth Williams, and a happy ending for the battling patients. It's flimsy but enjoyable, kick-started by a totally on-form collection of fine comic actors and using the homage to *Nurse* as its textual backbone.

Doctor is the most confident and conclusive tribute to the series' past - the most entertaining and brilliantly timed example being, of course, Frankie Howerd's resurrection of the immortal daffodil sequence. As Frankie lies face down in absolute agony, delectable nurse, Valerie Van Ost, strolls in with a vase full of daffodils from ever-loving Joan Sims. Wickedly walking over to Frankie's bedside, she plucks out a single flower and leans towards him. The bedridden Howerd screams out, 'Oh no you don't. I saw that film!' Van Ost: 'I just thought you might like to smell it!' Howerd: 'Yes, well

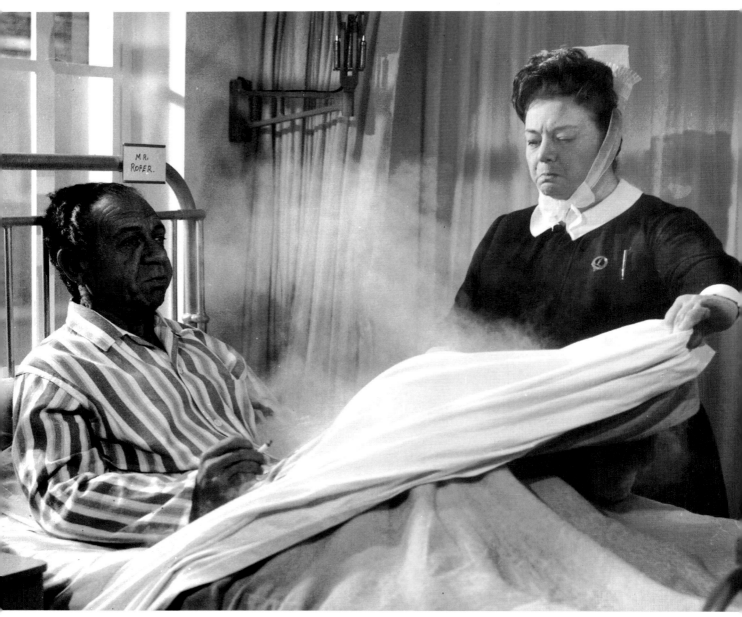

Sid James has a quick one much to Matron Hattie Jacques' displeasure in *Carry On Doctor*.

you've got to be careful - they fill you full of everything!'. The daffodil and memories of *Nurse* even invade the film's opening credits, which include alternative titles for the first time in the series, featuring, in this case, two *Nurse* geared gags: *Nurse Carries On Again* and *Death of a Daffodil*. The casting of Hattie Jacques resurrects strong memories of *Nurse's* formidable Matron, June Jago crops up in the familiar guise of hospital sister (having featured in the medical sequence in *Regardless*) and that great character man, Harry Locke, returns to the *Carry Ons* for the first time since *Nurse* as the jovial porter. Charles Hawtrey is again bedridden and outside the friendly community of the men's ward, while Howerd, James, Bresslaw and Williams play out a manic celebration of Leslie Phillips' amateur operation in *Nurse*. Rothwell creates the finest exercise in medical

Carrying On and his cast of experienced farceurs milk the situation more than dry - it's a non-stop crusade through the middle of the National Health Service with the throttle out. Get well soon!

Best performance

Surrounded by an outstanding, near complete cast of Carry Oners is a debuting Frankie Howerd who ooahs and ahhs for all he's worth. The finest stand-up comic of his generation, Frankie fits perfectly into the flamboyant innuendo of the series and camps with sheer delight. Revelling in his cowardice and hypochondria and awash with groanworthy lines - 'What is mind no matter, what is matter? Never mind!' - this charlatan faith healer is quickly encased within the NHS and suffers every indignity known to man. Cleverly structured as Frankie's usual comic persona within the standard *Carry On* frame-work, his character's stubborness and self-aware comments allow the regular team members to gain plenty of comic mileage from his predicament. Doctor Williams creates the misunderstood illusion of Frankie's impending death, Charlie Hawtrey's mild mannered acceptance of his false pregnancy causes splendid raised Howerd eyebrows, shocked Jim Dale loses his medical instrument ('my thing's caught'/'I beg your pardon!') and the reluctant marriage to deaf and bumbling Joan Sims provide some of the film's finest moments. The marriage from his hospital bed, with a delightful cameo from Peter Jones as a vicar as deaf as the bride, causes manic laughter and anxious disbelief. Frankie's subjection to the early rigours of awful hospital tea, a faceful of water and earth-shattering cleaning machines, makes for a brilliantly timed social document of the overbearing rituals of medical care. Howerd is allowed to play outside the narrative structure, waving to the audience at the close, and thus exposes the film as a film.

Favourite bit

One of the funniest cross-talking sequences in *Carry On* history is created in the initial meeting between Frankie Howerd and Sid James. Having gained near legendary proportions it gets a belly laugh every time. Sid: 'What they got you in for then, something nasty?' Frankie: 'No, not really, just a pain in the back.'/'Last bloke in that bed had the same thing.'/'Did he?'/'Right up to the end.'/'Oh, that's cheering... Ooh! I'll say one thing for them, it's a nice warm bed.'/'Should be, they only took him out half an hour ago!'. Keep a straight face if you can!

Did you know?

When Peter Rogers was planning *Doctor*, he approached John Davis, the head of the Rank Organisation, to clear his use of the title as Rogers' wife Betty Box was still churning out the *Doctor* comedies. Rogers and Betty Box came to a mutual understanding, with Peter giving his wife a percentage of *Doctor's* box office takings. In fact, the nearest the *Carry Ons* ever got to the *Doctor* series style was *Cruising*, where the manic camp and all-out innuendo was contrasted with an injection of the coy romantics and mild comic banter typical of *Doctor at Sea* (1955).

Doctor was the first film in the series to make it big in Canada, leading to the rare dubbing of a *Carry On* into French. France itself never warmed to *Carry On* innuendo and halfhearted attempts at distributing the films there had been limited to subtitled copies.

Future sitcom favourite Penelope Keith is credited with the *Doctor* supporting role of 'Plain Nurse'. However, she must have been cut from the final print for I have yet to spot her through countless screenings of the film.

Frankie Howerd was initially uneasy about accepting this major star turn role in a *Carry On* and declined the part. Kenneth Williams, who was unhappy with his supporting role, was offered the plum part of Francis Bigger and accepted. Eventually, Kenneth began to get cold feet and dropped out of the film. Frankie reconsidered the part, took it and finally Williams agreed to take on the role of Dr Tinkle.

Although Rothwell had built up Kenneth Williams' manic campness in *Spying*, Williams' role in *Doctor* was the first inclusion of the wild flamboyance that would mark all his subsequent *Carry On* performances. In 1967, with the legalization of homosexuality and Williams' own mincing in *Round the Horne*, Rothwell could safely bless the *Carry Ons* with Williams and Hawtrey in fine 'screaming queen' mode.

Look out for...

A spirited hate/hate partnership between Kenneth Williams and Peter Butterworth is forged in just two sequences. Initially, Kenneth delights in informing the hapless Butterworth about his forthcoming operation. 'But won't it hurt?'/'Yes it will hurt, Mr Smith and I want it to hurt. Perhaps next time you consider having a lump you'll think twice about it!' However, the audience's representative gets his own back as Peter lets the manic doctor drop into an ice cold bath. Although Peter's revenge is short-lived, his joyful and sardonic regret is priceless.

Note Kenneth Williams' one lapse into 'snide' mode when, as Hattie Jacques removes the bandages of a certain patient to reveal nothing, Ken mutters: 'Oh! I still don't like the look of him!'.

A moment of ad-libbed apology occurs for Hattie's Matron Lavinia in the bedroom seduction of the madly panicking Kenneth Williams. As Hattie pushes Kenneth on to the bed he accidentally bangs his nose on hers. For a split second the two are out of character and after a blurted word of comfort from Kenneth the tongue-in-cheek romantics continue.

As well as the myriad of salutes to *Nurse*, Rothwell includes a memorable homage to the Betty Box/Ralph Thomas *Doctor* series with the imposing portrait of James Robertson Justice as the tyrannical

Sir Lancelot Spratt situated between the lifts in *Doctor's* hospital. In fact, the eagle-eyed viewer will see that the portrait's inscription reads 'Sir James R. Justice - Founder'. Justice's booming persona had been seen in *Doctor in Clover* with Leslie Phillips and Arthur Haynes, on general release the year before.

Look for a couple of fine supporting turns from *Till Death Us Do Part* star Dandy Nichols as Sid's nagging wife - 'What do you expect if you put yourself down as a hansom cab lamp fitter' - and *Sykes* and *Please, Sir!* favourite Derek Guyler in a dithering cameo as a surgeon: perfect *Carry On* eccentrics.

Listen out for another one of Eric Rogers' musical jokes when, during the hoax operation on Kenneth Williams, Bernard Bresslaw explains he used to be a barber. The soundtrack includes a few bars of Rossini's *The Barber of Seville*.

Carry On memories

'When I made *Carry On Doctor*, one of the cast was Joan Sims. She played a character who was deaf and to whom I was married at the end of the film - the ceremony performed by a deaf vicar. This took place on the very last day of shooting - and when Joan and I got together for the scene we both, suddenly and inexplicably, started to laugh... and laugh... and laugh. There was no special reason for it... there was some mad chemistry at work - so we just stood there, hooting. Since laughter is infectious, the director and crew joined in... People came from other sets to discover what was happening - and they joined in! The place was a shrieking chaos.'
Frankie Howerd

'I have stimulating memories of acting with Sid James, Hattie Jacques and Barbara Windsor. My fondest memory is of playing Charles Hawtrey's pregnant wife. I had the baby - he had the labour pains!'
Gwendolyn Watts

A Peter Rogers Production

CARRY ON DOCTOR

or 'Nurse Carries On or 'Death Of A Daffodil'
or 'Life Is A Four Letter Ward'
or 'A Bedpanorama Of Hospital Life'

Francis Bigger **FRANKIE HOWERD**   Dr. Kenneth Tinkle **KENNETH WILLIAMS**
Charlie Roper **SIDNEY JAMES**   Mr. Barron **CHARLES HAWTREY**
Dr. Jim Kilmore **JIM DALE**
Matron **HATTIE JACQUES**   Mr. Smith **PETER BUTTERWORTH**
Ken Biddle **BERNARD BRESSLAW**
Nurse Sandra May **BARBARA WINDSOR**   Chloe Gibson **JOAN SIMS**
Nurse Clarke **ANITA HARRIS**
Sister Hoggett **JUNE JAGO**   Sir Edmund Burke **DEREK FRANCIS**
Mrs. Roper **DANDY NICHOLS**
Chaplain **PETER JONES**   Surgeon Hardcastle **DEREK GUYLER**
Mrs. Barron **GWENDOLYN WATTS**
Mavis **DILYS LAYE**   Henry **PETER GILMORE**   Sam **HARRY LOCKE**
Mum **MARIANNE STONE**
Mrs. Smith **JEAN ST. CLAIR**   Nurse Parkin **VALERIE VAN OST**
Fred **JULIAN ORCHARD**
Man from Cox & Carter **BRIAN WILDE**   Patient **LUCY GRIFFITHS**
Patient **PAT COOMBS**
Wash Orderly **GERTAN KLAUBER**   Simmons **JULIAN HOLLOWAY**
Nurse in Bath **JENNY WHITE**
Nurse **HELEN FORD**   Night Porter **GORDON ROLLINGS**
Tea Orderly **SIMON CAIN**
Women's Ward Nurse **CHERYL MOLINEAUX**
Female Instructor **ALEXANDRA DANE**
Grandad **BART ALLISON**   Nurse **JANE MURDOCH**
Small Boy **STEPHEN GARLICK**   Mr Wrigley **?**
Narrator **PATRICK ALLEN**

Screenplay by **Talbot Rothwell**
Music composed & conducted by **Eric Rogers**

Production Manager **Jack Swinburne**   Art Director **Cedric Dawe**
Editor **Alfred Roome** B.G.F.E.
Director of Photography **Alan Hume** B.S.C.   Assistant Editor **Jack Gardner**
Continuity **Joy Mercer** Assistant Director **Terry Clegg**
Camera Operator **Jim Bawden**   Make-up **Geoffrey Rodway**
Sound Recordists **Dudley Messenger & Ken Barker**
Hairdressing **Stella Rivers**
Dubbing Editor **David Campling**   Costume Designer **Yvonne Caffin**
Title Sketches by **'Larry'**
Producer **Peter Rogers**   Director **Gerald Thomas**

A 1967 Rank Organisation Release   'A' Cert.
Colour Running time - 94 mins. 8,432ft

CARRY ON

...UP THE KHYBER

This is Talbot Rothwell's most assured historical parody, brimming over with memorable one-liners, set pieces and larger-than-life performances; a glorious tribute to the British spirit played out by a clutch of *Carry On* favourites giving definitive interpretations of their usual characterizations. The one *Carry On* that almost gets its foot in the door as a classic of respectable British cinema, this is the film that gets fans begging for more. While the thin dividing line between fans and dissenters is always apparent, *Up The Khyber* is a film that crosses the boundaries. As such, it is fitting that it remained the favourite entry for both Peter Rogers and Gerald Thomas - along with the next entry - although the fact that the two films topped the box-office takings for 1968-9 could be a strong reason for their affection.

The series, now a national institution, couldn't put a foot wrong and for a period of five years regularly attracted hoards of admiring followers back into the cinema. No other facet of British film was as popular. This film was a surefire winner from the outset and presented Sid James with the plum role of Sir Sidney Ruff-Diamond KCB, OBE, AC/DC, BBC, ITV, 'available for private parties' - the first *Carry On* to cast Sid literally as Sid for a groundbreaking performance of comic flair. Sid is quite superb throughout the film, bumbling around in his cushy, royal patronized position as the Englishman in India during the lavish but declining days of Victoria's imperial rule and engaging the local peasants with a jolly attitude of British, God-on-our-side righteousness.

The essential opposition of Sid with Kenneth Williams reaches its peak in *Up The Khyber*. Williams, as the cynically grinning and awfully well mannered Indian ruler, is a memorable character study of repressed royalty which Kenneth encrusts with touches of 'snide' superciliousness ('The British are used to cuts!') and self-loving arrogance. Williams is in total over-acting mode for the majority of the film, continually stepping out of character (notably

a sly look into camera during the Sims 'sari' joke) and turning on the pantomime villainy at the drop of a turban. However, this contemporary edge is vital to Williams' characterization, and makes his under-played 'white flag' speech even more powerful and threatening. Despite Sid's response and Williams' final camp defeat, the Khasi remains one of *Carry On*'s most important creations.

This is the ultimate battle of the *Carry On* giants; sparks are flying all over the place but British stiff upper-lipped naivety will always win the day. Naturally, the ethos of Kipling is gloriously embraced and debunked following years of filmic attempts at romanticizing the spirit of the British in India. Indeed, Kipling had not only been romanticized, but Americanized and made tuneful with the 1967 Disney classic *The Jungle Book*. This was a colourful, all-singing, all-dancing celebration of a long lost era, but at Pinewood, Rothwell had seen a continual attempt to up hold a myth and the decaying might

Game, set and match to the Brits! Julian Holloway, Sid James, Joan Sims, Peter Butterworth, Angela Douglas and Roy Castle in the earthshattering *Carry On... Up The Khyber*.

A stunning portrait of Charles Hawtrey doing his bit for England in *Carry On... Up The Khyber*.

of British power. In tandem with this was the ever-increasing threat of losing our valued national identity in the European community, while many commonwealth states were fighting for, and winning, independence. It was a time for change and a time for reflection - the British being British, the best reflection was an absurdly comic, but seriously articulate, *Carry On*. Pantomime heroes and pantomime villains could battle it out - where the only barrier between 'them' and 'us' is a wooden gate.

The film includes the most celebrated and cherished sequence of images in the series' history, the climactic attack on the British embassy which is beautifully directed, edited with style by Alfred Roome and played by a collection of fine actors (notably Sid James and Peter Butterworth) at breakneck speed. It is a neat encapsulation of the film's portrayal of the British way of life standing head and shoulders above the rest of the world, despite its comic look at shortcomings and bumbling attitudes. The villains Williams and an impressively out-of-control Bernard Bresslaw (who enjoys a classic early sequence with Charlie Hawtrey and has the time of his *Carry On* life as fur-clad warrior of unassuming strength) scream and plot to perfection, as well as being blessed with prime sexually-geared Rothwell names; Rhandi Lal and Bunghit Din. In complete contrast to Williams, Bresslaw plays his Indian baddie perfectly straight. The sheer power of the actor gives his performance an edge of total control. In one throwaway gesture, Bresslaw parts the harem girls to greet the pseudo-chiefs - it is an act of casual force that informs the role with truth. However, he is allowed one totally comedic moment with a contemporary script amendment - 'That will teach them to ban turbans on the buses!'. It is the crowning glory of his *Carry On* career.

British phlegm is displayed when, as the building crumbles round their heads, the British saviours carry on talking. Only Peter Butterworth is the typical everyman panicker as he reacts to situations with ever-widening eyes, notably in discussion about a fellow missionary. Joan Sims: 'He went down very well with the natives'. Peter: 'Oh did he?' Sid: 'Yeah, they ate him!'. It's all priceless stuff with Sid, wining, dining, womanizing and laughing his way through the scenario. Roy Castle, in a tailor-made role for the absent Jim Dale, turns on the stilted English romantics for his endearing hero, while the laughs are deliciously delivered by Charles Hawtrey, keeping his dangler warm and losing his underpants in a move which establishes the hackneyed but enjoyable plot.

Again, as with most of the movies, the plot is merely the smallest of pegs on which to hang the various essential performances and familiar jokes. However, Rothwell's treatment of old chestnuts creates a fast-moving, totally hilarious film which includes every lavatorial name reference in the book (Private Widdle/Khasi of Kalabar/the settlement of Jacksey). Terry Scott, promoted from Sergeant in the first film to Sergeant-Major here, gives an assured character performance as a hard-boiled, tough skinned, bawling and over-bearing figure of military might. The pride of British power - the trio of James, Castle and Scott - approach the manic dictator of Williams to persuade him that the dreaded 'devils in skirts' wear nothing under their kilts - Scott's hard man image is destroyed by his admission to wearing silk knickers. Castle bumbles and grins with Dale-like nerves in front of Angela Douglas while Sid's almighty figure, clad in white, battles without success to keep the British name clear of abuse. At least one timeless *Carry On* exchange is the result - Kenneth: 'May the benevolence of the God Shevou bring blessing on your home'. Sid: 'And on

yours.'/'And may his wisdom bring success in all your undertakings.'/'And in yours.'/'And may his radiance light up your life.'/'And up yours'. The epitome of obvious *Carry On* humour, it's the sort of dialogue that viewers can chant along to, but the simple fact is that it works every time. A rooting, tooting, action-packed, laughter-filled package of pure *Carry On*, this film is quite rightly up there with the classics. The best of British.

Best performance

Although not making his first appearance until halfway through the film, that comic master, Peter Butterworth, provides the best performance. He initially appears in an Indian market-place flogging his religious ideals, memorably thanking a small boy for his contribution of a banana skin before spotting the dubious article and bawling him out. He's a man of peace with a contradictory attitude of lust and sexual awareness (being lured by a sexy young girl, Dominique Don, and trapped by Roy Castle into joining a 'military punch-up'; entering into the spirit of Bresslaw's harem and joyfully going through the 'my job is to save fallen women' gag!). He steals the dining room sequence with a persona of manic jittering and some classic lines ('Marvellous! Can't wait to leave!'/'Mad! That's the fakir's head, they've killed him!' Sid: 'Well that's dashed unsporting'/'Unsporting!'/'Yes, it's the closed season for Fakirs.'/'I don't believe it, I don't believe it!'/'No, it's true - here... April 1st to September 30th.'/'Of course!'). In this 1968 look at Britain's Victorian might, Butterworth is the

Peter Butterworth is collecting on behalf of the mission in *Carry On... Up The Khyber* while Alexandra Dane is more than willing and able - 'No, they are mine!'

ultimate contemporary interloper, failing to grasp this display of British nonchalance and injecting twentieth-century attitudes of self-preservation, cowardice and disbelief at the manic and out-moded stance of those around him. Peter gives a legendary performance throughout - and it was always a very brave comedy star that tried to play against him and keep at least some laughs to themselves. As with several of his best *Carry On* assignments, Butterworth includes a couple of unscripted sight gags, firstly during the harem sequence as he submerges in the pool to escape the wrath of Bresslaw, and secondly, just before the climactic dinner party. With a quick wink skywards he embraces the Sid James ethos of God-on-our-side invincibility - not in terms of patriotic protection but, again, simply self-protection, with God looking after His chosen 'brothers'. Peter grasps the role with both hands and runs through the film in the perfect mix of bemusement, cowardice, frustration, sexual eagerness and bemused patriotism. Fittingly the last line is his, and as the war-torn Residency falls to bits, the Union Jack pops up with the slogan 'I'm backing Britain'. The sublime Butterworth looks directly into camera and grins, 'Of course, they're all raving mad you know!' It is a finale touched with manic excellence. Nice one Peter!

Favourite bit

No, I'm not going to pick the obvious and choose the almighty, classic-beyond-belief sequence in the dining room! Instead, it's a marvellous piece of work from that best performer Peter Butterworth. Trapped with fellow Brits, Charles Hawtrey, Terry Scott and Roy Castle, the lads are beginning to go to pieces. Ever the reliable officer, Roy Castle tries to calm down his men: 'Now, now, now, now, steady chaps, try and keep calm. We've been in tighter spots than this!' Peter: 'Here we go, he's going to ask us to keep a stiff upper lip next!' / 'I was about to say remember we're British.' / 'I beg your pardon Captain'. / 'Then I was going to say keep a stiff upper lip'. / 'Well I'm not standing around here waiting for mine to stiffen!'. Peter's timing is superb and the farcical facial expression of this bumbling genius is enough to renew your faith in the human spirit!

Did you know?

This was an historic moment in the series, the furthest distance travelled from Pinewood Studios for a location shoot - Snowdonia to simulate the Khyber Pass of the Karakoram mountains of 1890s' India. Once the *Carry On* team had decamped, Gregory Peck and his crew moved into the area to film *The Most Dangerous Man in the World* - set in China!

Those timid people at The Rank Organisation got cold feet about the film's title, believing it insulted the military. They pleaded with Peter Rogers to change it to *Carry On The Regiment*. Please!

Look out for...

There's a stunning cameo from Peter Gilmore as Charles Hawtrey's dying comrade-in-arms. He encapsulates the spirit of Keith Douglas' poetry and a stiff upper lip attitude, then quickly reverting to a seriously terrified soldier and a bombastic, angered figure. Hawtrey is given a rare subdued moment as he grieves for his dead friend, regretting his honest words and contributing a touching vignette. However, Rothwell gleefully defuses the moment by letting Gilmore have the last comic word - a fine minor supporting turn.

The finest support, however, comes from that priceless comic, Cardew Robinson, deconstructing the patriotic ideals and historical comedy with a brilliantly timed performance as the Fakir - full of corny gags, lustful thoughts for Alexandra Dane and a wonderful dead-pan relationship with Williams and Bresslaw. He makes a fine farewell during the classic dining room sequence.

As Kenneth and his men mount the final attack, Sid James is approached. His response is a perfectly timed, 'You wish to see me?' as he shoots the burpa. Before the camera shot is changed for the image of Sid's close-up with the dialogue, you can see Sid mouth the line on the previous camera set-up.

Gerald Thomas executes an inspired juxtaposition shot as Peter Butterworth's mad 'strawberry mousse' mock clarinet playing cuts to a military piper.

The film's credits, again blessed with memorable 'Larry' cartoons, include an Eric Rogers musical joke. The plot's central debate about whether underpants are worn under Sid's soldiers' kilts or not leads to the basic musical theme being a variation of 'Cock O' the North'. What do you expect!

While Sid James dictates his informal note to Queen Victoria, Eric Rogers includes the 'Letter Song' from Tchaikovsky's *Eugene Onegin* in the score.

A brilliant contemporary evocation invades the historical parody during the James/Sims dialogue by the polo field. A certain royal personage is suggested as Sid congratulates a fine shot: 'Well played Philip! That boy will go far... if he makes the right marriage!'

Carry On memories

'My favourite moment of *Carry On... Up The Khyber* was the famous eating scene. We all had to continue eating and chatting completely oblivious of the explosions going on all around us. The food was real - boiled potatoes and ham. As the place slowly disintegrated and debris fell into our food, we pushed it around our plates and tried to avoid actually "eating" any. The scene continued for what seemed an eternity, and this being a filming technique where the actors never actually played to the camera, no-one had noticed the crew's practical joke. We carried on pushing the food around which now included Fuller's earth powder (not harmful but equally not appetising). Eventually we HAD to put some of the revolting concoction in our mouths. This made our serene acting even more difficult. Finally, Sid James broke the silence by emitting one word - "B****RDS!". The director had given the cameramen and crew the wink. They had stopped the cameras but no-one had said "Cut". They all quietly sneaked away and left us to it!'

Roy Castle

'My memories of *Carry On... Up The Khyber* are all happy ones with a few exceptions. One was the fact that I had to cover, or rather be covered in thick brown make-up from top to toe. Apart from where the loin cloth covered! This meant that at the end of the day's shooting I had to sit in a hot bath in order to scrub it off. This took quite some time and, of course, the water got colder. Eventually when I was no longer "The Fakir" the bath in which I sat was full of thick cold chocolate! The Fakir was also called upon to lie on a bed of nails. Now although these nails were tipped with leather they still felt quite sharp. For days after the film finished I could drink a glass of water and spray the lawn at the same time! In my final scene the top is taken off the silver dish which is supposed to reveal the meat course which The Governor (Sid James) and his party are about to enjoy. Instead they find the head of The Fakir with an apple in his mouth. This he spits out and says, "For my next trick!". To get into position I had to bend down under the table, put my head through a hole in the dish and then have the salad etc set round my head! I then had to remain bent in a very uncomfortable position while the scene was lit and finally shot. One episode sticks in my mind very vividly. On a very cold day which I had spent shivering in my loin cloth and thin robe on an exterior in the studio, I crawled back to my dressing room with chattering teeth and got stuck straight into the Scotch bottle. I got my chocolate off and then started on the Scotch again. The next thing I remembered was waking up on the floor of the room. The time was 4 am! Everyone had gone home and the studio was locked! Yes, I had some funny experiences on the *Khyber* and I would not have missed them for the world.'

Cardew Robinson

A Peter Rogers Production

CARRY ON... UP THE KHYBER

or 'The British Position In India'

Sir Sidney Ruff-Diamond **SIDNEY JAMES**
The Khasi of Kalabar **KENNETH WILLIAMS**
Private Jimmy Widdle **CHARLES HAWTREY**   Captain Keene **ROY CASTLE**
Lady Joan Ruff-Diamond **JOAN SIMS**   Bunghit Din **BERNARD BRESSLAW**
Brother Belcher **PETER BUTTERWORTH**   Sgt. Major MacNutt **TERRY SCOTT**
Princess Jelhi **ANGELA DOUGLAS**   The Fakir **CARDEW ROBINSON**
Pte. Ginger Hale **PETER GILMORE**
Major Shorthouse **JULIAN HOLLOWAY**   Stinghi **LEON THAU**
Chindi **MICHAEL MELLINGER**
Busti **ALEXANDRA DANE**   MacNutt's Lure **DOMINIQUE DON**
Major Domo **DEREK SYDNEY**
Bunghit's Servant **DAVID SPENSER**   Sporran Soldier **JOHNNY BRIGGS**
Bagpipe Soldier **SIMON CAIN**   Burpa Guard **STEVEN SCOTT**
Burpa at Door-grid **LARRY TAYLOR**
Burpa in Crowd **PATRICK WESTWOOD**   Burpa on Rooftop **JOHN HALLAM**
The Khasi's Wives **WANDA VENTHAM LIZ GOLD VICKI WOOLF**
ANNE SCOTT BARBARA EVANS LISA NOBLE EVE EDEN
TAMSIN MacDONALD KATHERINA HOLDEN
Hospitality Girls **VALERIE LEON CARMEN DENE JUNE COOPER**
JOSEPHINE BLAIN VICKI MURDEN KAREN YOUNG ANGIE GRANT
SUE VAUGHAN
Narrator **PATRICK ALLEN**

Screenplay by **Talbot Rothwell**
Music composed & conducted by **Eric Rogers**
Poster tag-line - 'Enlist in the Carry On army and see the world - of laughter!'

Art Director **A. Vetchinsky**   Production Manager **Jack Swinburne**
Editor **Alfred Roome**
Director of Photography **Ernest Steward B.S.C.**   Assistant Editor **Jack Gardner**
Continuity **Yvonne Richards**   Camera Operator **James Bawden**
Assistant Director **Peter Weingreen**
Sound Recordists **Robert T. MacPhee & Ken Barker**
Make-up **Geoffrey Rodway**
Hairdressing **Stella Rivers**   Costume Designer **Emma Selby-Walker**
Title Sketches by **'Larry'**   Dubbing Editor **Colin Miller**
Khyber Location Director of Photography **H.A.R. Thompson**
Camera Operator **Neil Binney**
Producer **Peter Rogers**   Director **Gerald Thomas**

A 1968 Rank Organisation Release 'A' Cert.
Colour Running time - 88 mins. 7,903ft

CARRY ON
CAMPING

Criticism is futile in the light of such hilarious innuendo, laid thick with confidence and talent! While *Up The Khyber* captured the heart of a nation, this one captured the whole body, and remains the definitive essay in saucy contemporary humour and a comic social document of the British way of life. Apart from all that, it's very funny as well, which helps a great deal. And, if only for the truly ground-breaking sequence of Barbara Windsor doing exercises, this film has become part of the nation's cultural heritage.

As with *Doctor*, in particular, there is no plot to speak of - it is simply a collection of familiar eccentrics going on a camping holiday. That, as they say, is it, but when you have Sid James and Bernard Bresslaw moaning about the weather and the crummy tents, and chatting up the local talent, that's all you really need. Sid - in definitive form - partners the ambling Bresslaw in deteriorating relationships

with Joan Sims and Dilys Laye. Not all at once you understand, for this is 1969, but even then, Sid was less than happy with the prospect of just snogging at the pictures. He is a man's man who hits on the idea of a nudist holiday to loosen up the women.

At the same time, snooty headmaster of a girls' school, Kenneth Williams, and school matron, Hattie Jacques (who else?) are organizing a trip back to nature for their over-sized and over-sexed girls - who include amongst their number a particularly over-sized and over-sexed Barbara Windsor. The coy references to the beauty of nature and the girls that 'just can't get enough of it!' leads to a myriad of sexual misunderstanding between Jacques and Williams, while the dainty girls in their charge are going at it like nine pins on the park bench.

The middle-class businessman brigade is represented by a pin-striped Terry Scott, who is quickly out of his suit and into country gear for yet another

A *Carry On Camping* line up with Julian Holloway, Terry Scott, Betty Marsden, Sid James, Bernard Bresslaw, Hattie Jacques, Dilys Laye and Kenneth Williams.

horrendous camping holiday with nagging wife, Betty Marsden. Meanwhile, on the other side of town, Charles Hawtrey - all legs and salt-cellars - is having a bit of difficulty with Valerie Leon in a tent (no comment!). Charles, who, as Valerie explains, 'kept touching things!' was simply, 'dying to know what it's like in a tent!'. The loner of the group, Hawtrey wanders throughout the countryside (just behind Pinewood Studios to be exact) in search of places to put up his tent and settle for the night.

For the first half hour or so we follow these various misfits through their struggling and hilarious attempts to find the glorious 'Paradise Holiday Camp'. Travelling past a host of corny situations and prime sea-side postcard scenarios, we encounter Charles Hawtrey, a young farm girl and a cow in search of its ideal bull - 'Ooh! couldn't your father do that'/'No it has to be the bull'. Note the stunned look into camera of our friend on screen, Hawtrey. There is Hattie Jacques with the school's name ('Chayste Place') emblazoned across her chest and Kenneth Williams, delighting in discussing the fundamental beauty of the retreating Barbara Windsor before quickly regaining his self-control and spitting out, 'Disgusting!'. Terry Scott, having enjoyed some outlandish flights of fancy while his never-listening wife is packing the camping gear ('another chap came into the office with a pound of opium, then we smoked it and spent the afternoon in a harem'), throws himself into the farce encountering a raging bull and a gun shot in the backside. Terry turns in a trouser-dropping performance, a back-drop to the brand of comic genius represented by Sid's guffawing innuendo and Kenneth's mincing madness.

Naturally, the stories begin to converge: Charlie Hawtrey teams up with Scott and his wife, gets on their nerves and finds refuge with Williams, Jacques and the girls. Sid's party eventually arrives, after momentarily losing their baggage and Dilys Laye's breakfast en route. With the gang all present, it remains for the owner to sort the grain from the chaff and in wanders a pricelessly bumbling support from Peter Butterworth, who gets a laugh on his first entrance by correcting the sign 'All asses must be shown' with a replacement 'P'. In a spirited reworking of the duologue between Chico and Groucho in The Marx Brothers classic A Day at the Races, Peter and Sid haggle over money and the various extra charges for the holiday in paradise. Butterworth's greedy expression when he sees Sid's wad of notes is a classic and his continual financial additions ('Pound!'/'Pound, I knew it - per tent?'/'Or per person, whichever's the greater!') is inspired stuff. You can feel Peter's eagerness to part Sid from his money wafting off the screen.

Once the team are settled safely in the field, Sid and Bernard approach the sexy nymphets of Barbara Windsor and Sandra Caron, Hattie tries to lure Kenneth into her tent, Charles Hawtrey reunites with a less-than-keen Terry Scott and an all-night rave-up in the adjoining field threatens to disrupt several plans for sexual coupling. This is the old guard spirit of Britain fighting the hippie, flower-powered, drug induced, beautiful people of 1969. The battle between enlightened youth and dumbstruck adults leads to a bizarre plot to infiltrate the enemy lines, with Sid, all furry jacket, black wig and John Lennon glasses, leading the gang in an attempt to blow the hippies' minds - or at least their amplifiers! At the end, everybody's happy: the hippies move on to pastures new, with the delectable school girls and the boyish Charlie Hawtrey in tow; Terry Scott gets the lust back into his marriage; Kenneth and Hattie are united on their bike and the initially disappointed Sid and Bernard find love with those substitute sex-pots, Joan Sims and Dilys Laye. It's been a whiz bang cascade through a clutch of loosely linked sketches and comic devices, but the Carry Ons came out on top with a timelessly funny example of the team's work and the biggest money-making film of the year. It was pretty intense though!

Best performance
In the ultimate encapsulation of his persona, the film's best performance is given by Sid James, chuckling and leering in an innuendo-encrusted star turn which steals the limelight. The epitome of the cockney rogue, Sid hides any insecurity or troubles under a bombardment of puns, laughs and seductive banter. His partnership with bumbling Bernard Bresslaw conjures up a typical exchange in the camping shop about going on a nudist holiday: 'Why not, other people do!'/'Maybe, but not people like us'/'What's the matter with us - we got three legs or something!'/'It's not that...when I'm on holiday I like to relax'/'So'/'And when I relax I like to put my hands in my pockets!'/'You can relax with your hands behind your back can't you. Prince Philip does alright doesn't he'/'Not with nothing on he doesn't!'/'How do you know...'. Even after Bernie gets the final laugh line, Sid comes back immediately with a chirpy, knowing reply to steal the scene. Sid is in full flow in this film, innuendo guns ablaze, giving his usual answer, 'Get away!' to every obvious point, guffawing all over the place, beautifully chatting up Barbara Windsor and providing a contrast to Kenneth Williams in a brief but treasurable sequence. It is Sid in vintage form and, thus, unbeatable.

Could we really leave this out! Contemporary *Carry On* in definitive terms with Kenneth Williams, Sandra Caron, Elizabeth Knight, Anna Karen, Barbara Windsor and the girls getting their chests out in *Carry On Camping*.

Favourite bit

Again I'm avoiding the obvious choice of Barbara's bra-popping, and going for a major sequence with King Sid. For those with short attention spans, the scene comes at the very start of the film - all you have to do is sit through the opening credits, easy enough. Suitably set in a cinema, it has Sid, Bernard Bresslaw, Joan Sims and Dilys Laye enjoying the dubious pleasures of a nudist camp movie, one inspired by such classics as the Pamela Green film, *Naked as Nature Intended*. Sid and the gang sit open-mouthed (for differing reasons) as the first flash of nudity in a *Carry On* appears - not, as is often thought, Barbara's exercise scene. As the dignified narration of the film adds innuendo upon innuendo, Sid laughs and 'Cor! blimey's all over the shop, relishing the discomforture of the girls and rejoicing in disturbing the quiet viewing of Michael Nightingale: 'Oh sorry mate. If I'd known that I'd spoken a bit louder!' The scene is full of British cinematic iconography - the phallic ice-lolly, the fat, Hattie Jacques-like member of the audience, the coy reactions to the sexual matters on screen. Sid guffaws and cheers like the confident charmer he is as he revels in the sexually-charged but frustrated atmosphere of a flea-pit cinema - pure *Carry On* magic!

Did you know?

This sunny camping holiday movie was shot in October/November. In one of the most quoted nightmarish memories of Pinewood production, the mud was sprayed green to make it look like grass,

leaves shedding for the autumn were stuck back onto trees and poor Barbara Windsor, clad in hardly anything at all, is seen sinking into the mud on camera. It's a glamorous life!

For the immortal exercise sequence, Barbara's bra was tied to a fishing line, held on to by some old lag at Pinewood and was to be wrenched off at the right moment, Williams yelling, 'Now let's really see those chests come out!' On the first take, Barbara was pulled off her feet into the mud, and put back on her feet ready for take two. Fearful of exposing any part of her anatomy, Barbara was determined to clutch her breasts the moment the bra was flung off. However, once the deed was done and Kenneth shrieks, 'Matron - take them away!', Hattie Jacques grabbed Barbara's arm with obvious results. The take was perfect and in the can. The male reaction, notably Sid's lusty laugh and Terry Scott's dejected denial, makes the sequence a *Carry On* landmark.

Initially Barbara Windsor wanted to play her part with a refined, public school girl voice. Following a successful solo rehearsal during her shower scene, the time came to film the piece, only this time with Sid James in attendance. The surprise at seeing good old Sid at the knot-hole made Barbara blurt out her line in typical cockney style and the moment remained in the film, thus dictating the entire characterization.

Sandra Caron, playing Windsor's friend, Fanny, is the sister of Alma Cogan.

For the first time Bernard Bresslaw incorporates his *The Army Game* catchphrase, 'I Only Arsked!', finally embracing the spectre of Private Popplewell (with a few extra brain cells) for *Carry On* immortality.

Jim Dale was originally considered for the role of the coach driver, Jim Tanner. His unavailability led to the part being radically cut back and taken on by cheeky chappie, Julian Holloway.

Look out for...

There's a superb cynical cameo from semi-regular Brian Oulton as a bemused and befuddled shop assistant dealing with the cheerful Charles Hawtrey. A diamond.

Note the recreation of Laurel and Hardy's classic comic routine - 'two men - one berth' (initially used in *Berth Marks* (1929) and exaggerated, with Hollywood's resident drunk Jack Norton, in 1944's *The Big Noise*). In *Camping*, Charles Hawtrey, Terry Scott and Betty Marsden go through the motions with hilarious results.

In the brief confrontation between Williams and Hawtrey, Charlie offers a pack of Saxa salt for the lift. Saxa used the *Camping* poster in a publicity campaign.

An in-joke concerning Hattie Jacques and Kenneth Williams crops up in her tent. Hattie grabs Kenneth by the cheeks and looks at him more closely as she murmurs: 'Before I came to your school I was Matron at a hospital. There was a doctor there, he was brilliant, he looked just like you. I worshipped him but he ignored it!'. Another gem of intertextuality, as the scenario, again with Jacques and Williams, had occurred in *Doctor* two years earlier.

Despite a real air of 1960s' hippiedom, *Camping*'s final sequence of drug-ridden rock remains totally timeless - the 'rave' phrase and ethos is as relevant to 1990s youth culture as it was in 1969.

Eric Rogers enjoys himself with the film's score, using a jazzed-up arrangement of 'Mow a Meadow' for the opening titles and incorporating a gigantic musical gag by accompanying Hattie Jacques with Saint-Saëns' elephant theme from 'Carnival of the Animals'. This is contrasted with the glamorous school girls' music, a Haydn symphony.

Carry On memories

'I have been thinking about the *Carry On* filming and can only remember them with warmth and laughter, to have been part of that gang was an experience I will treasure all my life. One time particularly sticks in my memory. It was the making of *Carry On Camping* - in a field - at Pinewood - in November. The British weather was particularly wet that year, and as I spent most of my time in shorts and a skimpy sweater, I was also wet 90 per cent of the time. However, for the sequence of our arrival at the "camp", the script called for "rain" - unfortunately ordinary rain doesn't show up on

camera, so fire hoses, manned of course by firemen, were standing by - happily they didn't direct the hoses straight at us, but up in the air, so that it fell down - quite heavy enough thank you, but we collapsed with laughter - especially as my trousers started to shrink on me. So remember when you see someone in a film in the rain - that in all probability there is a fireman just out of shot holding a hose!'
Dilys Laye

A Peter Rogers Production

CARRY ON CAMPING
or 'Let Sleeping Bags Lie'

Sid Boggle **SIDNEY JAMES** Dr Kenneth Soaper **KENNETH WILLIAMS**
Joan Fussey **JOAN SIMS**
Charlie Muggins **CHARLES HAWTREY** Peter Potter **TERRY SCOTT**
Babs **BARBARA WINDSOR** Bernie Lugg **BERNARD BRESSLAW**
Miss Haggerd **HATTIE JACQUES**
Josh Fiddler **PETER BUTTERWORTH** Jim Tanner **JULIAN HOLLOWAY**
Anthea Meeks **DILYS LAYE**
Harriet Potter **BETTY MARSDEN** Sally **TRISHA NOBLE**
Mrs Fussey **AMELIA BAYNTUN**
Store Manager **BRIAN OULTON** Farmer's Daughter **PATRICIA FRANKLIN**
Farmer **DEREK FRANCIS** Man in Cinema **MICHAEL NIGHTINGALE**
Fanny **SANDRA CARON**
Scrawny Man **GEORGE MOON** Pat **VALERIE SHUTE**
Jane **ELIZABETH KNIGHT**
Joy **GEORGINA MOON** Verna **VIVIEN LLOYD** Hilda **JENNIFER PYLE**
Norma **LESLEY DUFF**
Betty **JACKIE POOLE** Hefty Girl **ANNA KAREN**
Girl with Cow **SALLY KEMP**
Store Assistant **VALERIE LEON** Commentator **PETER COCKBURN**
Sally G-String **GILLY GRANT**
Lusty Youths **MICHAEL LOW & MIKE LUCAS**

Screenplay by **Talbot Rothwell**
Music composed & conducted by **Eric Rogers**
Poster tag-line - 'The Carry On team - refusing to let sleeping bags lie!'

Production Manager **Jack Swinburne** Art Director **Lionel Couch**
Editor **Alfred Roome**
Director of Photography **Ernest Steward B.S.C.**
Assistant Editor **Jack Gardner**
Camera Operator **James Bawden** Assistant Director **Jack Causey**
Continuity **Doreen Dernley**
Sound Recordists **Bill Daniels & Ken Barker** Make-up **Geoffrey Rodway**
Hairdresser **Stella Rivers**
Costume Designer **Yvonne Caffin** Dubbing Editor **Colin Miller**
Title Sketches by **'Larry'**
Producer **Peter Rogers** Director **Gerald Thomas**

A 1968 Rank Organisation film released in 1969 'A' Cert.
Colour Running time - 88 mins. 7,920ft

CARRY ON
AGAIN DOCTOR

Back to the bowels and bed-pans with a vengeance for a quick resurrection of the popularity of *Doctor* that saw the final *Carry On* contribution from Jim Dale for over 20 years. Not really a sequel to the Frankie Howerd classic, this film re-addresses medical innuendo via a parallel world of sexy nurses and bumbling doctors. Although the actors did not reprise their old roles, it was a variation on the earlier theme.

Jim Dale is again the romantic lead, chasing after the nurses and catching most of them, while his heart is stolen by delectable model Barbara Windsor (Melody Madder, via Goldie Locks from Maud Boggins). Hattie Jacques recreates her *Carry On* landmark performance as Matron under the new guise of Miss Soaper, incorporating a warmer personality than usual, while Harry Locke returns to the fold for his third and final medical burst of innuendo. Kenneth Williams pops up in his familiar guise as the supercilious doctor, although here he initially projects an air of good-humoured understanding. He sympathizes with Jim's lusty antics, and, in one hilarious misinterpreted sequence, even seeks advice ('I couldn't possibly say what lovely big other things!'). However, as with Tinkle in *Doctor*, it is a threat to his position and the prospect of

financial assistance to establish his own medical clinic that leads to his intervention in Jim's career. Charles Hawtrey, here with an added touch of acidic wit, drops the camp delivery of earlier movies to present a persona more akin to his normal vocal range. In a semi-wicked partnership with Kenneth Williams, he initiates the downfall of the rising star of Jim Dale. Eventually the combined efforts of Williams and Hawtrey (working like a camp and bickering married couple) see Jim shipped off to an exotic medical mission (just turn left outside the Pinewood canteen), and the second half of the film opens out the hospital humour to include witchcraft gags, the Westernization of cockney native Sid James and the comeuppance of the cold-hearted doctor of Williams.

Joan Sims, bubbling in the background as a beauty conscious millionairess who is treated by doctor Williams ('I took her appendix out the other day'. Hawtrey: 'I hope you both had a nice time'), joins forces with medical genius Jim Dale to establish a weight-reducing establishment, thanks to Sid's mystery mixture. Unlike both *Nurse* and *Doctor*, the humour revolves almost exclusively around the medical personnel instead of the hospital patients. Only one *Carry On* favourite appears as a patient - Peter Butterworth in a cameo - but it's a superb sequence with Jim Dale and Peter Gilmore.

The bulk of comic misunderstanding and sexual frustration is given to the ever-watchable Jim Dale, who bumbles, bumps into things, falls over, stages drink induced threats and chats up Barbara Windsor throughout. Rothwell's sublime farcical structure is given the full treatment by the team, now practically on auto-pilot so familiar are the roles and dialogue style. While the initial half of the film sees manic madness in the wards and white-coated antics, the latter part throws up some inspired moments of comic originality, thanks mainly to the arrival of Sid James. He rushes in, chewing up the furniture, paying for taxi rides with cigarettes, drinking whiskey

Fame at last - Jim Dale wipes his plaque with pride in *Carry On Again Doctor*.

Carry On Camping indeed!! Kenneth Williams and Gerald Thomas take a break

Above: Male fantasy becomes nightmare in *Carry On Up the Jungle*. Frankie Howerd, Kenneth Connor and Sid James blissfully await their fate

Right: Harmony for the clients – Sid James and Hattie Jacques put on the style for *Carry On Loving*

with everything and attempting marriage with Hattie Jacques ('Out there they call it a bleeding ceremony'/'Yes it's often called that here as well!') and every other woman (and, indeed, as he finds to his cost, the occasional man), roaming around like the perfect innocent abroad without the innocence and chuckling with typical energy. It's a firecracker of a performance and successfully links the two halves of Rothwell's medical scenario in a rousing finale: Jim gets to marry Barbara Windsor, Sid and Kenneth Williams become partners in the roaringly successful weight-reducing clinic and Charlie Hawtrey seems his usual blissful self.

The film continued the unabated run of commercial success for the series, but things were on the wane and with Jim's absence until 1492, the cast slowly began to crumble. However, good news folks, it took just under ten years.

Best performance

As the figure who creates every classic comedy moment in this almost plotted script, Jim Dale steals the honours despite working opposite particularly fine efforts from Sid James and Kenneth Williams. The entire film is built around Jim's likable bumbler and he creates a handful of outstanding comic vignettes that stand with the best material in the series. The hospital party sequence (which sees the start of Jim's downfall due to Hawtrey spiking his drink with powerful medical alcohol) features a beautifully worked out moment as Dale desperately tries to manoeuvre through the crowd of dancers with a plate of food in each hand. A notable scene with the glorious Valerie Leon brings on some stunned naivety not seen in Jim since the historical comedies, when, as she tells him it's there for him he chuckles, 'Oh... I know it is! - oh the p..p..paper!' - great stuff. The touchingly emotional, failed relationship with Barbara Windsor in the early stages is contrasted by the innuendo-packed sequence when Windsor arrives having fallen during the filming of a commercial. Their first meeting is a classic, full of Hattie Jacques sardonic comments, the innocent sexuality of Barbara, who wears hardly anything but her smile, and Jim's gob-smacked amazement: 'As a matter of interest...what were you advertising?'/ 'Bristol's Bouncing Baby Food!'/'I can see the connection!'. As Barbara innocently asks 'Can you see them!', Jim perfectly blurts out 'Not half!'. It is an outstanding comic turn. With one perfectly-timed 'Cor!', the comic skill of Jim Dale is unquestionable.

Favourite bit

Fittingly, the best moment includes more prime material from Jim Dale, this time opposite the best comic partner he could wish for, Sid James. The scenes set on the windswept Beatific Islands are exercises in pure comedy genius. A team made in heaven, Jim and Sid bounce witty ideals, innuendo and satirical comments with ease. The contrast between refined English gent and rough jungle-wise know-all is irresistible, conjuring up such priceless moments as Sid's overly concerned reaction to the football results via tribal drums, a Queen Victoria jigsaw puzzle with a missing piece and this exchange about the medical mission equipment: Jim: 'mm... it's a good skeleton, did the last doctor leave it here?' Sid: 'That is the last doctor!'

Did you know?

Jim Dale insisted on doing all his own stunts, throwing himself into such dangerous feats as the immortal cascade downstairs on a hospital trolley and jumping into the collapsing hammock on Sid's island. This latter stunt would cause Jim serious and continuous back problems. After his success in America, Jim was justly proud to be made an honorary member of the Hollywood Association of Stunt Men and the experience was rather handy for the Broadway role of a certain P.T. Barnum.

Shakira Baksh, playing the newly thined-down Scrubba, was Miss Guyana in the 1967 Miss World Contest. She later married Michael Caine and appeared with him in John Huston's classic film *The Man Who Would Be King* (1976).

Look out for...

Charles Hawtrey's brief sequence as Lady Puddleton is a masterpiece of over-played camp and quite simply the most treasurable drag performance in *Carry On*. Also note while in male clothing Charles' least convincing incorporation of his expected entrance line 'Oh! Hello!'. Due to the more serious style of his characterization, the line seems forced and out of context - Charlie quickly passes over it to continue his condemnation of Jim Dale's foolishness.

Eric Rogers pops up to play the clarinet in the medical party sequence. Rogers taps into the past glories of the departing Jim Dale by including the title music from Jim's debut *Carry On* (*Cabby*) and the theme 'The Magic of Love' from another vintage hit, *Spying*.

Take note of another Charles Hawtrey look into camera as he listens in on the intercom to the sexually ambiguous but totally innocent discussion between Kenneth Williams and Jim Dale.

Sid James and friend enjoy a laugh in Carry On Again Doctor.

The film marks the *Carry On* debut for valuable supporting actress Patsy Rowlands as Williams' faithful assistant and, finally, as James' faithful and only wife. She would return to appear opposite Kenneth again in *Loving* and thereafter crop up in every movie up to and including *Behind*.

Enjoy a totally wordless but outstanding comic cameo from Wilfrid Brambell, groping the sexy nurse (Elizabeth Knight) and whispering knowing suggestions accompanied by a wicked wink of the eye. Naturally enough, as with Harry H. Corbett's star turn, Eric Rogers includes a snatch of the *Steptoe & Son* theme. During the same train of events, look out for a sparkling one-off turn from Patricia Hayes as the crumbling and forever sickening Mrs Beasley: 'See you tomorrow, ahh!'.

Carry On memories

'Sid James was a joy to work with, he was a very polite gentleman - a lovely man. We played poker a lot during breaks from shooting - he loved a game of cards and I loved it as well. When he was on screen he was the most giving performer, he didn't have to take, he just gave all the time, and it worked. *Carry On Again Doctor* was our major film together, we did some lovely scenes in that. The thing I remember more than anything was when a true pro like Sid breaks up in a scene you're doing for the film because what you're doing he considers funny. I was very proud in some of those films when people like Kenneth and Sid broke up with laughter due to something I was doing. I was thrilled to bits because I was breaking up ten times more in every scene due to what they were doing. I think all of them were brilliant and to be part of the team looking back now is such a joy for me to remember.'
Jim Dale

'Becoming a semi-regular in supporting roles in the *Carry Ons* meant the main stars gradually noticed the same faces cropping up. The one who particularly seemed to take notice was Sid James. Sid was a big gambler and used to tell me, 'You know, I could actually run a book and I could put a price on actor's heads! I could make so and so a short favourite at one time to be cast again'. He could equally say that - 'Oh no, Gerry Thomas won't put up with that another time!'. I was cast as a cab driver opposite Sid in *Carry On Again Doctor* and just before shooting the scene I was very grateful when he said he had me down as a favourite for a return appearance! People used to watch Sid and try and work out what he was doing - some thought it was the crossword puzzle or, more likely, it would be a case of looking at the Gee-gees. But the man had by that time this eye for seeing exactly what was and what wasn't right for these movies. Consequently he made a point of saying, 'Yeah, I knew you would be back!'. People like Sid James, Jim Dale and Barbara Windsor were just delightfully happy people to be with.'
Hugh Futcher

A Peter Rogers Production

CARRY ON AGAIN DOCTOR

or 'Where There's A Pill There's A Way' or 'The Bowels Are Ringing' or 'If You Say It's Your Thermometer I'll Have To Believe You But It's A Funny Place To Put It'

Gladstone Screwer **SIDNEY JAMES**   Dr James Nookey **JIM DALE**
Dr Frederick Carver **KENNETH WILLIAMS**
Dr Ernest Stoppidge **CHARLES HAWTREY**   Mrs Ellen Moore **JOAN SIMS**
Goldie Locks **BARBARA WINDSOR**   Matron **HATTIE JACQUES**
Miss Fosdick **PATSY ROWLANDS**   Shuffling Patient **PETER BUTTERWORTH**
Mr Pullen **WILFRID BRAMBELL**   Nurse Willing **ELIZABETH KNIGHT**
Henry **PETER GILMORE**   Stout Woman **ALEXANDRA DANE**
New Matron **PAT COOMBS**   Lord Paragon **WILLIAM MERVYN**
Mrs. Beasley **PATRICIA HAYES**   Old Lady in Headphones **LUCY GRIFFITHS**
Porter **HARRY LOCKE**   Night Sister **GWENDOLYN WATTS**
Deirdre **VALERIE LEON**   Porter **FRANK SINGUINEAU**
Out-Patients Sister **VALERIE VAN OST**   X-Ray Man **SIMON CAIN**
Hospital Board Member **ELSPETH MARCH**   Nurse **VALERIE SHUTE**
Scrubba **SHAKIRA BAKSH**   Miss Armitage **ANN LANCASTER**
Men's Ward Nurse **GEORGINA SIMPSON**
Bandleader **ERIC ROGERS**   Patient **DONALD BISSETT**
Pump Patient **BOB TODD**   Plump Native Girl **HEATHER EMMANUEL**
Trolley Nurse **YUTTE STENSGAARD**   Waiter **GEORGE RODERICK**
Night Nurse **JENNY COUNSELL**   Stunt Orderly **RUPERT EVANS**
Patient in Plaster **BILLY CORNELIUS**   Cab Driver **HUGH FUTCHER**

Screenplay by **Talbot Rothwell**   Music composed & conducted by **Eric Rogers**
Poster tag-line - 'Poking their diag'noses' into other people's business - in their
latest laughter operation!'

Production Manager **Jack Swinburne**   Art Director **John Blezard**
Editor **Alfred Roome**   Director of Photography **Ernest Steward B.S.C.**
Camera Operator **James Bawden**   Assistant Editor **Jack Gardner**
Continuity **Susanna Merry**   Make-up **Geoffrey Rodway**
Assistant Director **Ivor Powell**   Sound Recordists **Bill Daniels & Ken Barker**
Hairdresser **Stella Rivers**   Costume Designer **Anna Duse**
Dubbing Editor **Colin Miller**
Producer **Peter Rogers**   Director **Gerald Thomas**

A 1969 Rank Organisation Release   'A' Cert.
Colour Running time - 89 mins. 8,010ft

UP THE JUNGLE

A sparkling tribute to the legacy of Tarzan, this film stomps through an aimless but hilarious track in the African wilderness (with vintage wildlife footage interspersed to add reality to the leafy Pinewood set). Frankie Howerd returns in full ney-neying form, while another welcome cast member is Kenneth Connor, making his first *Carry On* film appearance for over five years.

Frankie and Kenneth form the perfect partnership of mincing ornithologists, bickering about the various specimens they encounter and getting sexually aroused at the sight of Joan Sims' 'milky thigh' in the raw heat of the primitive jungle. Frankie turns in a stunning star performance, camping away madly and stopping only momentarily to consult the plot and incorporate a few threads of linking dialogue. It is a *tour de force* of prudish, refined character, struggling through the uncouth environment of the jungle. While his role in *Doctor* allowed him to inject elements of his unique comic persona, Howerd's *Jungle* performance is continually hamming his dialogue for an unseen audience, even incorporating his stunned 'Please Yourself!' when Sid is unimpressed by his witty observations. His facial expressions and brilliantly timed one-liners are perfectly complemented by Connor's little man lost characterization. The latter continually puts his foot in it as he desperately tries to impress the always unimpressed Sims, giggles as he peeps at her through binoculars in the company of a gorilla and wanders around the undergrowth in search of a toilet area!

As with the majority of the classic films, *Jungle* lacks any convincing plot (a search for Sims' long lost son and a rare example of the hugely gifted Oozalum bird). All the film concerns is a troop of British eccentrics fighting their way through the undergrowth. However, when this includes the brilliant sparring of Frankie Howerd and Sid James, the feeble plot is more than enough. Sid is the ultimate bumbling white hunter, tripping over the jungle foliage, shooting various slaves instead of lions,

sneaking off for a quick nip of whiskey at any time and incorporating coy sexual references to Jacki Piper and highly unsubtle sight gags with his rifle to a knowing Joan Sims. Note the resurrection of the 'big one' gag from *Cowboy* and revel in Sid's pseudo-resurrection of Bogart's Charlie Allnutt character.

Also along for this wonderfully hilarious journey is timid and lazy servant, Upsidasi, a blacked-up Bernard Bresslaw. Bresslaw's performance is so beyond the realms of belief that it fails to ring racist alarm bells. He wanders through the film highlighting the stupidity of the Brits while delighting in donning part of a butler's attire when serving dinner, thus highlighing the ethos of traditional British high society. This leads to one of the milestones in *Carry On* comedy: the refined dinner party in the middle of the jungle, all sexual advances, misunderstanding and a dubious snake!

The comic catalyst is the beautifully incompetent Terry Scott as the token Tarzan-type (a cross between Johnny Weissmuller's jungle charm and the childish wonder of Karloff's Frankenstein Monster - note the lake reference), swinging through the air with the greatest of ill-at-ease. A clumsy figure of baby-faced ignorance, Scott mumbles and murmurs at all and sundry, delighting in his sexual awakening opposite Jacki Piper and almost being seduced by his own mother, the over-amorous Joan Sims. Terry injects a fine monosyllabic performance of stunned innocence. As a result of his actions, Frankie, Sid and the gang end up on the natives' menu ('They can't possibly do this to us, after all we are British subjects!'/ 'They got no taste these people - they'll eat anything!': film buffs refer back to Bing Crosby and Bob Hope in *Road to Zanzibar*), escape by the skin of their teeth and get trapped within a fantasy world of female rule. The novelty of regular marriages (with a hilarious ceremony including Sid's delightful signal with a banana - quite!), soon wears off, even for Sid. Again it is Terry Scott who, through his bumbling help, spoils an ideal situation, while a dragged up Bernard Bresslaw (Connor: 'Look at that - if I get her I've had it!) sorts out the situation. The film is a glorious celebration of the British in their Victorian splendour: searching through the wilds of the world in order to gain knowledge and enhance the nation's might. With outstanding lead performances, the ultimate cynical banter between Frankie Howerd and Sid James and a crafted script of non-stop Rothwell innuendo, it's the most fun you can have while trying to avoid elephant droppings!

Best performance

The award goes to someone who has yet to get a mention and who had the unenviable task of trying to better Sid James and Frankie Howerd in tip-top form. It is, of course, the priceless Charles Hawtrey, who stumbles into the action in the last 20 minutes and completely walks away with the honours. While making his initial appearance, fast asleep at Frankie's lecture, Charles gets the full Thomas build-up as a figure of great importance, authority and potency: 'Tonka the Great... King of Lovers... Father of Countless!'. The appearance of Charles, with his perfectly timed line of, what else(!), 'Oh! hello!', is unlikely but totally wonderful, and he cheerfully giggles at the assembled masses. As it turns out, this weedy figure of regal personage is the long-thought dead husband of Joan Sims and thus, the father of none other than Terry Scott. Shocked at the sudden appearance of his beloved, Charlie blurts out, 'Oh my gawd - it's the wife!'. It remains one of the great moments in the series' history. However, the role

doesn't end there, as he has a quiet word with Sims, enjoying a timeless flashback sequence. Initially full of gibberish innocent baby-talk, the acid-tongued Hawtrey begins to dissect the persona of his wife while retaining the endearing speech style: 'Daddy waddy will have to give mumsey wumsey a smacksey wacksey won't he den. Yes he will den - round the chopsey whopsies.' A cynical look and the biting delivery creates a minor league gem. Finally joining the worn out and sex-weary Sid, Frankie and Kenneth, Hawtrey delights in his position as deposed leader and chats with good humour. It looks like Charlie has simply walked off the street, slipped on his costume and had a friendly chat with some old chums he hadn't seen for a few months. Though outside the major context of the film, Hawtrey's performance stands out as the ultimate character study. Not bad for just ten minutes screen time!

Favourite bit

Charles Hawtrey notwithstanding, the highlight must be a joyful duologue between those two masters of innuendo, Sid James and Frankie Howerd. With Sid just having shot another slave, Frankie enquiries about the latter's well-being: 'What on earth's happened to that poor fellow?' Sid: 'Terrible thing, terrible - he was out beating up front, came across this mad elephant you see.'/'Mad elephant!'/'Yea, nothing more dangerous than a mad elephant.'/'Are you sure it was a mad elephant - he's been shot!'/'Yeah, well - have you ever seen a sane elephant using a gun?!'

Did you know?

With the use of the name 'Tarzan' prevented, the working title for the film was *Carry On Jungle Boy*, which would have cause some raised eyebrows today! The film has sometimes been quoted as '*Carry On Up The Congo*' - a great title.

Frankie Howerd's role of Professor Tinkle was originally written for Kenneth Williams. Unable to fit in with the shooting schedule due to a tight working diary writing *The Kenneth Williams Show* with John Law, he declined the major role. However, Peter Rogers, eager to include Kenneth in the film (as Williams had not missed one since *Cabby*), offered the cameo role eventually played by Charles Hawtrey. Disgusted by this very minor part who doesn't appear until the last few scenes, Williams turned it down and kept out of the film all together. Williams took solace in Bill Cotton's belief that 'television is the medium of the future', but was back at Pinewood Studios within six months.

Cor blimey, what a handful! Carry On Up The Jungle monkey business with Sid James and Joan Sims.

Jim Dale was initially offered the Tarzan parody role taken by Terry Scott. However, Jim was now an established comedy actor and respected for both his film and stage work. He considered the grunting and inarticulate part was a step back from his central *Carry On* roles in *Cowboy*, *Screaming* and *Doctor* and told Gerald Thomas that he didn't want to play it.

Ever the true professional, Bernard Bresslaw learnt all his native orders in a genuine African language. However, the plan backfired: on the first day of shooting, the extras stared at him dumbly, all were of Caribbean origin and thus completely confused by his commands. South African Sid James knew the real thing and congratulated him!

Up The Jungle grabbed the basic plot line of female warriors from a B-movie sub genre of 'Primitive Glamour Girl' pictures boasting gems like *Untamed Women* (1952) and *Wild Women of Wongo* (1965).

Look out for...

Nina Baden-Semper, later a principal character in the hit ITV comedy *Love Thy Neighbour*, is the seductive Nosha with Lincoln Webb in Hawtrey's flashback sequence.

Note a superb piece of comic timing with Frankie Howerd and Kenneth Connor. During the tent

mix-up when the boys are after the sexual charms of Sims and Piper in the middle of the night, Frankie ends up with a gorilla and Kenneth finds himself with Terry's jungle boy. Thomas keeps the camera on the tents, so the action inside is unseen. A couple of screams and a quick scramble brings both terrified clowns out simultaneously and, with a crazed look at each other, the two run off in different directions. Great stuff!

When Valerie Leon and the girls capture the Brits, Kenneth Connor resurrects his old *Ray's A Laugh* line 'Oh! Mate!' - albeit in a totally different context!

Carry On memories

'First day of filming on *Carry On Up The Jungle* - first take, first scene, actors inevitably shy and nervous. I, in leather loin cloth as "Tarzan" being lifted from lying to sitting position beside the lagoon by "Jane". Camera rehearsal (no sound). Much laughter from the technicians, which puzzled me, as I didn't think the dialogue was that funny. Only at the end of the scene did I realize that the leather loin cloth was revealing a part of me that was not supposed to be in the scene!'
Terry Scott

Kenneth Connor caught by the Lubi Dubbies in *Carry On Up The Jungle*.

A Peter Rogers Production

CARRY ON UP THE JUNGLE

or 'The African Queens' or 'Stop Beating About The Bush' or 'Show Me Your Waterhole And I'll Show You Mine'

Professor Inigo Tinkle **FRANKIE HOWERD**
Bill Boosey **SIDNEY JAMES**
Walter Bagley - King Tonka **CHARLES HAWTREY**
Lady Evelyn Bagley **JOAN SIMS**
Claude Chumley **KENNETH CONNOR** Upsidasi **BERNARD BRESSLAW**
Cecil the Jungle Boy **TERRY SCOTT** June **JACKI PIPER**
Leda **VALERIE LEON** Gorilla **REUBEN MARTIN**
Nerda **EDWINA CARROLL**
Nosha Chief **DANNY DANIELS** Witch Doctor **YEMI AJIBADI**
Nosha with Girl **LINCOLN WEBB** Pregnant Lubi **HEATHER EMMANUEL**
Gong Lubi **VERNA LUCILLE MacKENZIE**
Lubi Lieutenants **VALERIE MOORE CATHI MARSH**
Girl Nosha **NINA BADEN-SEMPER**
Noshas **ROY STEWART JOHN HAMILTON**
WILLIE JONAH CHRIS KONYILS

Screenplay by **Talbot Rothwell**
Music composed & conducted by **Eric Rogers**
Poster tag-line - 'The Carry On team in Starkest Africa'

Production Manager **Jack Swinburne**
Director of Photography **Ernest Steward B.S.C.**
Editor **Alfred Roome** Art Director **A. Vetchinsky**
Assistant Editor **Jack Gardner**
Camera Operator **James Bawden** Assistant Director **Jack Causey**
Continuity **Josephine Knowles** Make-up **Geoffrey Rodway**
Sound Recordists **Robert T. MacPhee & Ken Barker**
Hairdresser **Stella Rivers** Costume Designer **Courtenay Elliott**
Dubbing Editor **Colin Miller**
Titles **General Screen Enterprises Ltd.**
Producer **Peter Rogers** Director **Gerald Thomas**

A 1969 Rank Organisation film released in 1970 'A' Cert.
Colour Running time - 89 mins. 8,010ft

CARRY ON LOVING

This is the ultimate 'nudge, nudge, wink, wink, say no more' movie, with more coy references to 'it' than any other film in the series, a jump back (or should that be forward!) to contemporary times and one of the legendary money-spinners. The seductive poster images of the gang in bed with various nubile young ladies and the team's first venture into television at this time could have helped the increase in the already huge following of the series.

This virtually plotless movie is simply a collection of knowing sexually-geared comic sketches linked by the dubious Wedded Bliss Agency run by Sid James and Hattie Jacques. They are a suspicious and, in Sid's case, continually unfaithful 'wedded' couple; the marriage is a sham to impress the marriage agency punters and Jacques remains Sophie Plunkett until the film's slapstick finale. Read the fake marriage of Sid and Hattie as the fake computer giving false love to the customers. The film has a happy roster of the usual Carry Oners, who throw themselves into this, the only real trouser-dropping, mixed-up relationship, more-tea-vicar?, farce in the film series.

The manic mugging of the team forms the backbone of the comedy: Kenneth Williams, an unmarried and unknowing guidance counsellor who finds temporary interest from Hattie; Joan Sims, the object of Sid's lust, continually falling for his cunning plans; Terry Scott, linking the established gang with the fresh intake of younger performers, tackles the tongue-in-cheek romantic lead, while the threads are held together by the comic cement of James and Jacques. The gags are very basic, the situation brief but succinct, the direction simple and the Rothwellian construction the briefest of stories in which to incorporate a torrent of one-liners, arched eyebrows, sexual nerves and Sid's guffaws.

Perhaps the most interesting device is the casting of younger comic talents in a sort of parallel of the roles of Sid and the gang. The likes of Richard

O'Callaghan (shy, nervy and bumbling re early Hawtrey, with O'Callaghan even incorporating 'Oh! hello!' as his introductory line) and Julian Holloway (a swinging Sixties icon, cocky and laughing about his sexual conquests like an early Sid James) fly the Carry On flag, while the glamorous ladies like Jacki Piper and the late Imogen Hassall play the relationships and marriage agency scenario for pathos, injecting realism into the comical situations. In an attempt to address younger ideals and, indeed, a younger audience, the film conducts a continual contrast between these two groups of people: outlandish innuendo from the main team and subtle romantic/sexual frustration comedy from the newcomers. Could this have been a new team waiting in the wings? Whatever the reasons behind the casting, the nature of the love story beast dictated a higher than usual quota of young romantics with serious sex on their minds. While Sid and Kenneth steal the honours, there is no denying Richard O'Callaghan's place as the central figure in the scenario.

Bumbling around the outer circle of these sexual goings-on are a handful of other team members, stuck in brief but outstanding comic cameos - notably big Bernie Bresslaw, turning on the snorting and snarling evil for his overtly jealous wrestler. Charles Hawtrey snoops around in a series of awful disguises, having been hired by Hattie to spy on that rogue of rogues, Sid James. A brilliant combination of Sherlock Holmes (cloak/Victorian telephone) and James Bond (Sid, always on to him, dubs him the 'Bombay Bond', referring back to Spying), Hawtrey is given yet another minor league role which he transforms into a third-billed performance. Finally, Peter Butterworth pops up all too briefly in a one scene uncredited gag appearance with Sid James. Dressed in black and doing the old poisoned mushroom joke, Peter is the image of the endearing murderer, helped by the resurrection of Rogers' undertaker theme from Cowboy, and completed with a gentle grin of self satisfaction. Priceless.

Loving is a standard example of the genre: the cast know what they are doing, the jokes come thick and fast and the humour is typically low-grade. However, there is an air of neglect and a lack of originality about the script and playing. All are going through the motions rather than having the usual ball of fun - it's the ultimate auto-pilot *Carry On* and, thus, remains funny without touching the soul. Thankfully it touches the bottom enough times to pull through to the silent slapstick homage climax and, after all is said and done, Imogen Hassall (giving an impressive multi-faceted performance) looks wonderful.

Best performance

Who else can it be but Sid: no frills, no way-out historical slant, no strange costume and no black-hearted villainy, just Sid pure and simple, going through his chuckling hero persona for the umpteenth time in ultimate Max Miller mode. He enjoys a comically fruitful relationship with Hattie Jacques, delves for as many ploys as he can to attract the attentions of Joan Sims, delights in leading Charles Hawtrey a merry dance, has the briefest of opportunities to contrast his cockney charm with Williams' elitism and deals with Bresslaw's wrestling photograph with typical sarcasm: 'Get away - I thought he was a ballet dancer!'. The script calls for no elaborate word play or subtle timing, and Sid, with all systems go, delivers his lines of knowing innuendo with relish. And believe me, it takes genius to get away with some of these truly corny Rothwell gags. Sid was the only man for the job.

Favourite bit

While Sid is the fountain of all sexual knowledge and understanding, Richard O'Callaghan is the definitive figure of naive anxiety. In the absence of any real loggerhead confrontation between Sid and Kenneth Williams, O'Callaghan steps in as the former's perfect comic foil. The opening sequence in Sid's agency is an example of brilliant, linear writing and fine timing. Sid is all knowing innuendo and comic expression as his new client explains his hobbies and sexual requirements. Sid: 'Well we'll just get a few details. Age?' Richard: 'Oh, ah, seventeen I think!'/'Seventeen!'/'Well I thought the younger she was the longer she'll last!'/'No, no, I want your details - your age!'/'Oh, twenty seven.'/'Twenty seven. What are you interested in?'/'Same as most chaps like to do I suppose.'/'And that is?'/'Well I don't know, I've never done it yet!'/'You should try it - it's lovely. Now you see what I'm trying to do is find out what you like to do so I can fix you up with a girl who likes it too.'/'Oh yes, I would like a girl

who likes it too.'/'Yes, it is handy!'. It's a superb piece of banter between the unenlightened and the master.

Did you know?

Richard O'Callaghan is the son of actress Patricia Hayes, who had just completed her *Carry On* contribution in *Again Doctor*. The press critics, tired of the same faces, picked out O'Callaghan's performance for special mention. *The Times* stated that the film, 'benefits from the work of one newcomer, Richard O'Callaghan, who plays the obligatory innocent with absolutely the right single-minded seriousness and apparent unconsciousness of the humour of his own situation'. I think he was quite impressed!

Despite a talent leading to work with The Royal Shakespeare Company, Imogen Hassall never really escaped the glam-girl roles which won her the title of 'Countess of Cleavage'. Although notable in such popular culture classics as the pilot for *The Persuaders* with Roger Moore and Tony Curtis, and the grunt-athon of Hammer's *When Dinosaurs Ruled The Earth* (1969), she became a 'celebrity', often spotted at film premieres, before she committed suicide in 1980.

Note the similarity between the noises Sid's *Loving* machine makes and those of Alec Guinness' chemical concoctions in *The Man in the White Suit*.

Kenneth Williams' performance is almost autobiographical - he plays an unmarried professional character with little interest in the idea of marriage and obsessed about keeping his regimented life in order. When Sid James is reading his card details, the age of Williams' character is given as 43, his real age when Rothwell completed the script in early 1970.

Once *Loving* was in the can, Bernard Bresslaw resurrected his manic wrestler characterization in another film cameo, opposite Frankie Howerd in *Up Pompeii*.

Loving featured supporting roles from *Dad's Army* star James Beck (1929-1973) and part-time Hammer lesbian vampire, Yutte Stensgaard, as Mr and Mrs Roxby. Sadly their scene ended up on the cutting room floor, along with Norman Chappell's performance as Mr Thrush.

The role of James Bedsop was always intended for Charles Hawtrey. However, due to the character's limited screen time and the obvious importance of Hattie Jacques in the film's narrative, Peter Rogers wasn't going to give Hawtrey his usual third billing.

Charles was unwilling to relinquish his position and Rogers (wanting to include the actor in the film) reluctantly gave in. Quite right too!

One of the Rank Organisation's promotional suggestions to cinemas showing *Loving* was to organize a street parade of 13 young ladies in mini-skirts and sweaters, each to be emblazoned with one letter spelling out the film title!

Look out for...

There's a host of unsubtle place names to complement the unsubtle grandeur of the film, notably 'Much Snogging-On-The-Green', 'Rogerham Mansions' and 'Dunham Road'. Rothwell injects one of his rudest gags via the Terry Scott/Imogen Hassall conversation concerning a cat called 'Cooking Fat', while Scott delights in his 'your wife makes love magnificently!' banter with Bishop Derek Francis.

Bill Maynard turns in a stunning supporting role opposite a super snobbish Kenneth Williams. He's full of cockney cynicism and down-to-earth comments, notably concerning a delightful fireside chair bought by his wife, Patricia Franklin: 'I should bloody well think so as well, I mean look at it - I could only get half me arse on it!'

Eric Rogers enhances Charles Hawtrey's man of mystery image by giving him the continual musical backing of Gounod's 'Funeral of a Marionette' - popular as the theme from *Alfred Hitchcock Presents*. The music had been used to highlight the misunderstood sinister purpose of Brian Wilde in *Doctor*.

During the hilarious slapstick finale, note Eric Rogers' apt inclusion of Johann Strauss' 'The Laughing Song' from *Die Fledermaus*, while the romance of Williams and Jacques is enchanced by Robert Schumann's *Traumerei* .

Terry Scott enjoys his biggest film role, tackling an ambitious series of visual gags and demonstrating his comic timing while taking tea at the home of Joan Hickson. The bumbling romantic clods about the finely decorated, antique-filled room with clumsy energy. The farcical romantic setting with the, as yet, unglamorized Imogen Hassall looking on, is complemented by Eric Rogers' inclusion of a Rachmaninov-like piece to evoke memories of the ultimate British love story, *Brief Encounter*.

Loving is not so much a homage as a reworking of Hudis' *Regardless*. The same basic premise - that of an agency run by Sid James - links a collection of (admittedly, more sexually knowing) sketches. Note the misunderstanding at the initial meeting (Liz Fraser and Ian Curry/Jacki Piper and Richard O'Callaghan), the scene where bumbling clumsiness typifies our own reaction (Connor in The Ruby Room/Scott in Hickson's house), the casting of Fred Griffiths as the taxi driver (Kenneth Williams and the chimp/Sid James at the railway station) and the boxing/wrestling element (Tom Clegg battling Charlie Hawtrey/Bernard Bresslaw - with Clegg as his trainer - battling Richard O'Callaghan). *Carry On* revisited.

Indeed, the location at Park Street, Windsor, doubles for both Sid's 'Helping Hands' and 'Wedded Bliss' agencies in *Regardless* and *Loving*.

During the hospital sequence (after O'Callaghan's brush with Bresslaw), Eric Rogers includes a few bars of the *Doctor* theme and Tony Sagar (one of the ambulance drivers in *Nurse*) appears as a patient.

Carry On memories

'I did feel at the time that I was working with a very professional bunch of people - as you know the films were made on a tight budget which made re-takes a luxury. Kenneth Williams was his usual comical self making people laugh off the set as only he could. Charles Hawtrey was an amusing character of course, and I remember at one meeting, smiling and giggling at anything Peter Butterworth said and did. I had worked with him in a television show and I thought then that he was one of the funniest blokes visually that I'd ever seen.'
Bill Pertwee

'I loved making *Carry On Loving* - Bertie Muffet is a wonderful innocent. The fact that he goes off to meet a girl carrying a bag full of model aeroplanes made out of milk bottle tops was inspired comedy. When I opened the bag on set the first day I found that the props men had actually made about ten of

Charming! Sid James shows his contempt for beloved Hattie Jacques in *Carry On Loving*.

these models - I nearly died laughing. He wasn't supposed to go to those lengths for realism! Charles Hawtrey was as eccentric as ever. I had known him for years because my mother, Patricia Hayes, had done *Norman & Henry Bones the Boy Detectives* with him on radio since the 1940s. He always reminded me of a very old hen, with lots of bits of cotton wool stuck to his face - he never seemed to manage to get his make-up off properly. If he'd finish a bit early he'd come back into the studio to see what was going on and there always seemed to be bits of pink make-up and cotton wool - and those big owl-like glasses and a strange hen-like expression on his face. There was a young chap who was doing a University thesis on the *Carry Ons* and he was allowed to come onto the set by Gerald Thomas. If there was a break in filming he would try and talk to people and he came along with Charles Hawtrey and myself to the canteen a couple of times. Charles was delighted to talk about his early films and this student asked him - "And when did you make your first film Mr Hawtrey?". Charles smiled rather coyly and said, "Well, I'm not going to tell you when I made my first movie - but I made my first talkie in 1932!" He was great. I remember Bernard Bresslaw with great affection. A very kind, gentle giant - always in a good mood. I was a newcomer so felt a bit nervous, but Bernard always made me feel welcome. He used to sit doing *The Times* crossword and he'd say, "Do you want to give us a hand?" and sit and chat with me. I appreciated that. I was very upset on one of the last days of filming. I was actually doing a show in London and on a day that I had a matinee it was the day that they choose to do the great bun fight at the end when everybody was going to get plastered with cake and jelly. I couldn't be there so my stand-in was the one on camera. I think there is one shot of me receiving a cake in my face but that was not done on the day. I went on set the following day where there was this extraordinary mess still left behind - all this real cream and jelly they had got from the canteen. I just had to stand there for a close-up of my face receiving a custard pie or something but I missed the actual event.'
Richard O'Callaghan

'I was only ever in one, *Carry On Loving*. I had no dialogue. My part consisted entirely of being caught in various places kissing Valerie Shute. We would check in every few days and be put in a lift, a car or under a table. Gerald Thomas would call for action and we would start snogging. It was a most enjoyable job largely because Valerie had such a charming sense of humour about the whole

'I bet he knows one or two holds!' - Bernard Bresslaw flexes his muscles as Gripper Burke in *Carry On Loving*.

prospect. Otherwise it might have been deeply embarrassing. I was quite young. They paid me £25 per day. It was the sweetest way ever of making a living.'
Mike Grady

A Peter Rogers Production

CARRY ON LOVING

or 'It's Not What You Feel, It's The Way That You Feel It'
or 'Two's Company But Three's Quite Good Fun Too' or 'Love Is A Four Letter Word'
or 'It's Just One Thing On Top Of Another'

Sidney Bliss **SIDNEY JAMES**   Percival Snooper **KENNETH WILLIAMS**
James Bedsop **CHARLES HAWTREY**   Sophie Bliss **HATTIE JACQUES**
Esme Crowfoot **JOAN SIMS**   Gripper Burke **BERNARD BRESSLAW**
Terence Philpot **TERRY SCOTT**   Sally Martin **JACKI PIPER**
Bertie Muffet **RICHARD O'CALLAGHAN**   Jenny Grubb **IMOGEN HASSALL**
Miss Dempsey **PATSY ROWLANDS**   Sinister Client **PETER BUTTERWORTH**
Mrs Grubb **JOAN HICKSON**   Adrian **JULIAN HOLLOWAY**
Gay **JANET MAHONEY**   Aunt Victoria Grubb **ANN WAY**
Mr Dreery **BILL MAYNARD**   Corset Lady **AMELIA BAYNTUN**
Uncle Ernest Grubb **GORDON RICHARDSON**   Trainer **TOM CLEGG**
Woman **LUCY GRIFFITHS**   Girl Lover **VALERIE SHUTE**
Boy Lover **MIKE GRADY**   Man in Hospital **ANTHONY SAGAR**
Lavatory Attendant **HARRY SHACKLOCK**   Bishop **DEREK FRANCIS**
Emily **ALEXANDRA DANE**   Robinson **PHILIP STONE**
Violinist **SONNY FARRAR**   Mrs Dreery **PATRICIA FRANKLIN**
Grandma Grubb **HILDA BARRY**   Pianist **JOSIE BRADLEY**
Grandpa Grubb **BART ALLISON**   Wife **ANNA KAREN**
Aunt Beatrice Grubb **DOROTHEA PHILLIPS**   Husband **LAURI LUPINO LANE**
Barman **BILL PERTWEE**   Wilberforce Grubb **COLIN VANCAO**
Window Dresser **GAVIN REED**   Second **JOE CORNELIUS**
Maitred' Hotel **LEN LOWE**   Taxi Driver **FRED GRIFFITHS**
Henry **RONNIE BRODY**   Bus Conductor **KENNY LYNCH**
Policeman **ROBERT RUSSELL**

Screenplay by **Talbot Rothwell**
Music composed & conducted by **Eric Rogers**
Poster tag-line - 'Doing their bit for laughter!'

Production Manager **Jack Swinburne**   Art Director **Lionel Couch**
Editor **Alfred Roome**   Director of Photography **Ernest Steward B.S.C.**
Assistant Editor **Jack Gardner**   Make-up **Geoffrey Rodway**
Continuity **Josephine Knowles**   Camera Operator **James Bawden**
Assistant Director **David Bracknell**   Hairdresser **Stella Rivers**
Sound Recordists **J.W.N. Daniel & Ken Barker**
Costume Designer **Courtenay Elliott**   Assistant Art Director **William Alexander**
Set Dresser **Peter Howitt**   Dubbing Editor **Marcel Durham**
Titles & Opticals **General Screen Enterprises Ltd.**   Producer **Peter Rogers**
Director **Gerald Thomas**

A 1970 Rank Organisation Release 'A' Cert.
Colour Running time - 88 mins. 7,930ft

CARRY ON HENRY

This rip-roaring return to the glories of British history saw a fruity cast of Carry Oners turning on the regal charm and Tudor manners. With the series coming of age (this was the 21st entry) and the whole ethos of *Carry On* now a valued and celebrated part of the British way of life, this timely salute to that royal rogue, King Henry VIII, couldn't possibly fail. And, indeed, it didn't. Talbot Rothwell crafted a memorable comic slant on the facts (even throwing in Guy Fawkes some 50 years before he was born), revising the serious interpretations that were, at the time, invading both television and cinema.

Anyone other than Sid James is inconceivable in the lead part, and he rants, roars, womanizes and drinks with a relish that epitomizes the film. Despite injecting moments of cold-hearted authority, it is fundamental that Sid the king is still Sid the cockney clown, so out goes any realism (unlike *Cowboy*) and in comes a warm and endearing performance as a lovable rogue who holds the power of life and death. That Rothwell allows Sid to exercise that power prompted some reviewers to question the film's taste. Indeed, the first sequence, as Sid's wife (Patsy Rowlands) goes to the axe, accompanied by the bumbling, tongue-in-cheek commentary of Terry Scott and a shared but quickly dampened bit of comic banter between Sid and Kenneth Williams, was thought distasteful. However, the fact that the contrasting elements of likable Sid and his dreadful deeds span so well is clear testament to the comic energy of James. Throughout the film nobody comes close to bettering his performance, the impressive roster of *Carry On* team members are happy to tackle important supporting roles. Kenneth Williams, in deliciously supercilious mood, minces, camps and moans around the castle, creating new and ever more bizarre taxes ('S.E.T!... Sex Enjoyment Tax!') and preening himself as the major pillar of reliability ('I learnt long ago there is only one man in all England who can be completely trusted... and

that's me!' - note the 'snide' vocals for the last three words). Charles Hawtrey, back with a vengeance after his previous cameo performances, gives his only really outlandishly camp star contribution to the film series - becoming the perfect foppish dandy as he flits around Sid's castle, tasting his food, tasting his wine and eventually tasting his new wife, Joan Sims, who becomes pregnant while Sid is busy with other matters: 'Have you been dallying with the Queen perhaps'/'Certainly not Sire'/'Your hand on it'/'Not even a finger on it!'. Terry Scott forges a sort of Tudor Laurel and Hardy act with Kenneth Williams, and gives a truly outstanding performance as the inarticulate and confused Cardinal whose hands roam all over the place, while Barbara Windsor cheerfully pops up as the refined Queen Bettina who, unsurprisingly, catches the eye of the King. Kenneth Connor grovels, creeps and grimaces as an anti-royalist and Peter Butterworth drops in for a cough, a spit and 18 words.

The roles are stereotyped certainly, but the narrative they occupy brings them credibility. Rothwell follows the style of William Shakespeare and John Webster in construction of scenes and duologues, the incorporation of passage of time (*Henry*'s events span more than a year), certain characterizations (Hawtrey, for example, is pure Osric) and various plot devices to hurry the historical re-telling along. Full of prime performances and groanworthy gags, the film takes the form of a sparkling Restoration comedy with a touch of Shakespearian grandeur.

Best performance

Who else could it be but Sid James? He strolls with regal authority and aplomb through the legacy of a larger-than-life king without putting a foot wrong. Following in the footsteps of Charles Laughton (Alexander Korda's *The Private Life of Henry VIII*), Robert Shaw (Fred Zinnemann's *A Man For All Seasons*) and performances fresh in the mind, such as Keith Michell (Waris Hussein's *Henry VIII and His Six*

Wives/The Six Wives of Henry VIII - BBC TV, 1970) and Richard Burton (Charles Jarrott's *Anne of the Thousand Days*), Sid proves the ideal comic king. Sid incorporates Laughton's memorable eating sequence by flinging chicken legs and various appetizers absent-mindedly over his shoulder ('Carry on eating!') and establishes a look into the private life rather than public duty of the king. Lusty, fun-loving and determined to put official business on hold for any sexual gratification, Sid chases after and loses Barbara's innocent maiden ('it's a great honour. The King has done me.../'No, no, no full stop!') and enjoys a rough and ready encounter with the stunning Margaret Nolan which is quickly curtailed by the arrival of her father (Derek Francis). Sid, always the equivalent of the working-class clown, here takes centre stage as the dramatic monarch. While still retaining cutting comic observation, he also embraces the power of royal authority. However, despite this regal sincerity, King Henry is simply Sid the cockney charmer, desperately trying to get a bit on the side and failing almost every time. It is a towering comic performance and one of which Sid was justly proud and celebrated for. Long live the King!

Favourite bit

Naturally this must concern Sid, and also includes the delectable Barbara Windsor in her favourite *Carry On* role. The chemistry between the two is irresistible and while Barbara is quietly checking up on the marriage laws (quickly reworked by the king) she comes across a vast volume of information. Sid: 'What you reading?' Barbara: '*Ball's Book of English Law*'/'Pardon!'/'It says here that no marriage is legal unless it is performed by a member of the Church!'/'Oh that's just balls... outlook!'. Corny but hilarious, and Sid's delivery is poetry in motion!

Did you know?

The original alternative title was *Anne of a Thousand Lays*, a less-than-subtle tribute to the Burton film *Anne of the Thousand Days*.

Also of note with regard to the Richard Burton film is the cloak that Sid wears in *Henry* - it is the same one that Burton had donned a few months previously.

Henry set a new record for a *Carry On* budget at the time - around £223,000. The budget provided a wonderfully detailed period feel, lush historical sets and another £5,000 worth of Sid guffaws.

Future rock god David Essex gave a minor acting performance in *Henry* as a page boy. Sadly this interesting cameo was rejected from the final print and

Their little cup doth overflow! Terry Scott and Kenneth Williams in *Carry On Henry*.

lost to the cutting room floor. Familiar *Carry On* player, Tony Sagar, appeared briefly as a 'heckler'. *Doctor* actor Brian Wilde was there as a 'warder' and John Clive cropped up as a camp 'dandy', but, sadly, all were absent from the final film.

Henry boasted the series' best poster tag-line: 'A Great Guy with his Chopper!' Superbly designed, out-sized picture postcards, full of brilliant caricatures of the gang, these posters were vital elements in the film's success, brilliantly tapping into the iconography of Donald McGill. The vintage Rothwell historical comedies boasted superbly designed artwork posters, with, notably, those for *Cowboy* and *Head* depicting the regular team members in realistic form. However, the majority of these posters still embraced *Carry On* corn with the inclusion of a comic tag-line: other notable poster gags included, 'Dick Turpin Carries On with his Flintlock Cocked!' (*Dick*) and 'Enlist in the *Carry On* Army and see the World... of Laughter' (*Up The Khyber*) - OK, it wasn't that great!

When Talbot Rothwell first came up with the idea of a *Carry On* treatment of the reign of King Henry VIII in 1966, Peter Rogers envisaged Harry Secombe in the title role. The composing and performing of popular madrigals was to be a major part of the plot and, thus, the singing Goon was thought ideal. However, the madrigals were dropped in favour of

Executive relief for King Sid James in *Carry On Henry*. Barbara Windsor, in her favourite *Carry On* role, does the soothing job.

Sid's inspired leers, though they would later crop up in the 1972 *Carry On Christmas* television show, sung by Butterworth, Connor, Sims, Windsor, Jacques and Douglas. Sid would join the fun when the songs re-appeared in the stage show *Carry On London!*

Look out for...

There's a fabulous running joke with Kenneth Williams, Charles Hawtrey and the torture chamber, with the king's whims and fancies necessitating alterations to Hawtrey's confession at every new development. Williams is camp and manic, Hawtrey camp and endearing, and the sight gags are pure silent comedy - including the immortal resurrection of the water-spouting punctured body. Although performed by Williams in *Follow That Camel*, this, along with Olsen & Johnson's *Hellzapoppin'*, is the ultimate sound homage to the slapstick gag.

Kenneth Williams and Kenneth Connor join forces in a dastardly plot to kill the king: it's a partnership full of knowing looks and perfectly parodied lines of intrigue which culminates in the memorable detached hand sight gag!

Connor's performance is almost completely devoid of comic business, although he does delight in a rare political and contemporary-geared joke: 'The Queen's in labour'/Sid: 'Don't worry - they'll never get back in!'. It's a brief support, but his sheer acting prowess enhances the role. Towards the film's end, the seductive figure of Monika Dietrich glides by Sid who expresses immediate sexual interest, 'Who's that?'/Connor: 'The new lady in waiting Sire... her name is Catherine Howard!'. Although there's an air of comic historical awareness, Connor delivers the line with perfect under-played conviction. With the *Carry On* interruption over, the reign of Henry VIII returns to facts and Connor's minor gem is the ultimate dramatic bridge.

When Joan Sims faints and Kenneth Williams rushes off to call for medical assistance, he lapses into television in-joke territory by incorporating a Scottish accent and crying 'Dr Finlay...', a reference to Barbara Mullen's persona in *Dr Finlay's Casebook* (1959-66).

Carry On memories

'*Carry On Henry* has a particular memory because at the end of 1970 I'd come back from holiday abroad

and was told by my agent that I was getting to do the film, and at the same time I had messages to phone Robert Nesbitt who was producing The Royal Variety Command Show to be attended by The Queen Mother. I was in a sketch with Leslie Crowther and Shirley Burnette and the whole thing was a great success, with Andy Williams, Sammy Davis Jnr, Dionne Warwick and Freddie Starr making a huge impression. It was a tremendous night and I got to bed very late and a bit hung over. I had to turn up for my day's exterior shooting on *Carry On Henry* the next day. I knew the studio date was coming up about two weeks later but I had to do some exterior things involving riding a horse up to Henry's castle to meet Terry Scott playing the Cardinal. I got there decidedly hung over, up to Pinewood and onto the back lot, redressed and retarted with crenellation and a mighty portcullis. I'm seen riding in through the courtyard and dismounting and seeing Terry Scott. I remember one of the times we were rehearsing I looked around and Gerry Thomas shouted, "Stop looking around - it looks as if you're looking for the bloody number of the house!". I was given this horse and warned, "Watch this one because he threw Julian Holloway last week!" and sure enough, if you watch the film, you will see this quite obviously in Julian's limp. That was a most enjoyable day and my part was finished with a one scene interior shoot with Terry Scott filching money in front of Kenneth Williams, who in turn was filching from Sid James. It was a very funny scene and we had a load of laughs!'
Alan Curtis

A Peter Rogers Production

CARRY ON HENRY
or 'Mind My Chopper'

King Henry VIII **SIDNEY JAMES** Thomas Cromwell **KENNETH WILLIAMS**
Sir Roger de Lodgerley **CHARLES HAWTREY**
Queen Marie of Normandy **JOAN SIMS**
Cardinal Wolsey **TERRY SCOTT** Bettina **BARBARA WINDSOR**
Lord Hampton of Wick **KENNETH CONNOR** Sir Thomas **JULIAN HOLLOWAY**
Francis, King of France **PETER GILMORE**
Charles, Earl of Bristol **PETER BUTTERWORTH**
Duc de Poncenay **JULIAN ORCHARD** Bidet **GERTAN KLAUBER**
Major Domo **DAVID DAVENPORT**
Buxom Lass **MARGARET NOLAN** Physician **WILLIAM MERVYN**
1st Plotter **NORMAN CHAPPELL** Farmer **DEREK FRANCIS**
Guy Fawkes **BILL MAYNARD** 2nd Plotter **DOUGLAS RIDLEY**
Torturers **LEON GREENE DAVE PROWSE**
Katherine Howard **MONIKA DIETRICH**
Guard **BILLY CORNELIUS** Serving Maid **MARJIE LAWRENCE**
Queen **PATSY ROWLANDS** Conte di Pisa **ALAN CURTIS**
Royal Tailor **JOHN BLUTHAL** Flunkey **WILLIAM McGUIRK**
Henry's 2nd Wife **JANE CARDEW** Maid **VALERIE SHUTE**
Henry's Courtiers **PETER RIGBY TREVOR ROBERTS & PETER MUNT**
Executioner **MILTON REID**

Screenplay by **Talbot Rothwell**
This film is based on a recently discovered manuscript by one William Cobbler
which reveals the fact that Henry VIII did in fact have two more wives.
Although it was at first thought that Cromwell originated the story, it is now known
to be definitely all Cobbler's... from beginning to end.
Music composed & conducted by **Eric Rogers**
Poster tag-line - 'A Great Guy with his Chopper!'

Production Manager **Jack Swinburne** Art Director **Lionel Couch**
Editor **Alfred Roome**
Director of Photography **Alan Hume B.S.C.** Camera Operator **Derek Browne**
Continuity **Rita Davison** Assistant Editor **Jack Gardner**
Assistant Director **David Bracknell** Make-up **Geoff Rodway**
Sound Recordists **Danny Daniel & Ken Barker** Hairdresser **Stella Rivers**
Set Dresser **Peter Howitt**
Costume Designer **Courtenay Elliott** Costumes **L. & H. Nathan Ltd**
Assistant Art Director **William Alexander** Dubbing Editor **Brian Holland**
Titles **G.S.E. Ltd**
Producer **Peter Rogers** Director **Gerald Thomas**

A 1970 Rank Organisation film released in 1971 'A' Cert.
Colour Running time - 89 mins. 8,046ft

Sid James and Charles Hawtrey discuss where to stick the crown jewels in *Carry On Henry*.

AT YOUR CONVENIENCE

Despite the number of Sids scored and the film's retrospective position as a classic, this was the first sign of impending decline in the series and the major flop during this seemingly indestructible purple patch. Looking back, this film is the ultimate in-joke: an encapsulation of the innuendo style, cascading with lavatorial gags, lavatorial references and, indeed, lavatories. Like a sly comment on the never-ending churned-out Carry On product, this continuous stream of toilets sets up an effective parody. The script is constructed as a comment on the influence of the unions on the film industry - for the curtailed production at W.C. Boggs read the end of the line at Peter Rogers Productions.

Everything in the film is totally over-played and flamboyantly characterized: Sid James laughs at every single chuckleworthy line and Kenneth Williams minces and moans in an uncontrolled picture of the crumbling authority of British business. Charles Hawtrey (complete with dazzling floral shirt) camps with semi-drunken delight and even plays a Mr Coote, Joan Sims flirts and bubbles with sexually-charged energy, Bernard Bresslaw sinks to a new low of moronic stupidity and Hattie Jacques is the definitive subtle housewife. Everything fits into place perfectly and if you're willing to play the game on the terms of tongue-in-cheek parody, then this is arguably the perfect Carry On.

So why was the film so unsuccessful on its first release? Well, the simple answer was uncharacteristic naivety on Peter Rogers' part - the working-class, beer and chips audience who were the films' chief admirers were not so chuffed with the treatment of the unionists as bumbling, idiotic mini-dictators with attitude problems. While I'm Alright Jack (itself a subtle comic variation of the Richard Attenborough drama The Angry Silence), was a huge box-office success, Convenience died a death. However, the Boulting Brothers' satire was a cleverly written social comment on the unionists' problems, giving both management and workers eccentric figures - Terry-Thomas and Peter Sellers. Both had points to make, both put their points across with comically-geared good sense and both are duped by the lone idiot, Ian Carmichael, who wins out and blows the whole corrupted story.

In the Carry On treatment, the work-force is given the ultimate hero in Sid James, although his major success comes with a lucky spell on the horses and the acquisition of wealth. Kenneth Williams represents the established world of British industry, clinging on to authority while facing threats to traditional ideals. Williams' son (Richard O'Callaghan) is the young romantic lead who wins the girl (Jacki Piper) who is also Sid's daughter, thus joining work-force with management. The lightweight villain of the piece is Kenneth Cope's irritating little man of union dreams and constant strikes, full of communist thoughts and petty minded authority. Cope gives a brilliant interpretation of the role but it wasn't the sort of representation that unions enjoyed. Representing a bombastic figure living by regimented union rules, Cope's performance is totally undermined. Despite comic support from a Carry On regular - an eventually wavering Bernard Bresslaw - Cope's manic worker is dominated at home by his over-powering mother (Renee Houston), beaten in love by the upper-class Richard O'Callaghan and let down by his supporting strikers who throw down their banners and take up their spanners. Following the ultimate sexist put-down (from Hugh Futcher), the workers return to the glories of British manufacturing and the old-fashioned ideals of Kenneth Williams. Sid James reluctantly joins the management and Kenneth Cope gets himself a sexy new female worker and enjoys the film's last line and laugh: 'Carry On Working!'. Although this makes the role endearing and effective, Cope's belief in the unionist movement is easily crumbled by the lure of a short skirt. It's a scenario of Tory success, capitalist authority and upper-class power.

The collapse of British industry - Kenneth Williams, Richard O'Callaghan and Sid James in *Carry On At Your Convenience*. Note the subtle toilet-shaped ink well!

Meanwhile, it's also a very funny assessment of the ultimate *Carry On* elements. Talbot Rothwell shoots through every corny gag in the book, while the team delight in overtly stereotyped performances. For those fed up with the continual anxiety at the works, there is a treasurable domestic running gag with Sid James, Hattie Jacques and their budgie. Rothwell, lifting the idea from a contemporary West End comic hit, creates a priceless line in tongue-in-cheek, 1970s' 'women in their place' attitudes towards Hattie's lazy and bumbling antics. Sid, the man's man, drinking, hard-working, and head of the household, wanders in from another strike and takes refuge in his ramshackle home. Hattie's charmingly sentimental attachment to little Joey (complete with musical inclusion of Gilbert & Sullivan's 'Tit Willow'), an irritating budgie, provides Sid the ideal vehicle on which to vent his marital dissatisfaction. 'Fancy that, a bird opening and closing its beak. We'll have to write to the newspapers about that!'/'Well, it's a start - generally he just sits there doing nothing'/'He's a natural mimic, he's copying you!' However, Sid is equally doting on the bird when Hattie is out of ear shot, and his brilliantly timed attempt at getting the bird to talk ('Ta, daddy, ta, daddy... TA!') is a classic. In the end, Hattie plans to work at Sid's factory, any chance of a James/Sims affair goes out the window (note the touching chat

between the two after the day-trip), the factory is back on top and the *Carry On* atmosphere is fully to the fore. The unionists are slapped on the wrist and all's right with the world. Up the workers!

Best performance

Although in a fairly minor role, Kenneth Williams turns on the dignified pomposity and steals the movie with a performance of world-weary awareness. He is sexually ambiguous (although a widower and father), ferociously proud of his family business and flamboyantly camp in his dealings with the sexually-charged but frustrated secretary, Patsy Rowlands. His dependability, acceptance of the declining industry and behaviour during the riproaring drunken bash in the day-trip sequence ('There once was a fellow called Reg, who went with a girl in a hedge. When along came his wife with a big carving knife and cut off his meat and two veg!') brings an endearing quality to the standard Williams authority figure. Played with a more subtle edge than usual, although full of sweet innuendo and disgusted facial expressions, Kenneth is by turns touching, eccentric and teethachingly funny!

Favourite bit

The film's peak comes in the climactic day-trip to Brighton; a symbolic return to the home of Donald

Sid James chatting up his bird in Carry On At Your Convenience.

McGill's postcards, fish 'n' chips, 'Kiss me Quick' hats, naughty weekends and Max Miller. The scene with Sid, Kenneth, Charles and the gang stomping around the West Pier is so right, it's the perfect environment for a clutch of corny gags, sexual misunderstanding and manic attempts on the shooting gallery. There's a fine cameo from Larry Martyn, forging links with the contemporary yob element (with his cry of 'skinheads!') as he watches a drunken Williams and wildly inaccurate Hawtrey fire their weapons and pick up hordes of inflatable Mickey Mouses and Dumbos. It's a fabulous world of seafood (Rowlands: 'I've heard shellfish do very strange things - in a sex way I mean!'/Williams: 'Ooh! Let's watch them for a bit then!'), fun-fair attractions and much welcome bars. You can almost smell the Brighton sea air and fresh fish and the gang are in full swing. In the company of such familiar performers, the day-trip sequence is the ultimate realization of audience empathy in the series. The gang handles the scene to perfection. Kenneth: 'Fortune telling, certainly not, waste of money. Fakes that's all they are, sitting there looking at their crystal... whatisnames.'/Sid: 'Balls!'/'I quite

agree, absolutely ridiculous!'. Book me a room at The Grand right now!

Did you know?

With the public toilet gag in the title meaningless outside Britain, the film was renamed *Carry On Round The Bend* for the majority of foreign export releases.

During publicity for *Henry*, the 22nd film was announced as *Carry On Comrade*, suggesting an overtly communist angle on the unionist plot. In fact, while *Loving* was at the cinema, the *Comrade* project was cited as the 21st *Carry On*, due to be shot from 12 October 1970. *Henry* quickly usurped it.

Such was the lack of public interest in this film that the initial production cost was only recovered in 1976 after major overseas screenings and various television sales. Usually the *Carry Ons* were making a profit after three days on the home cinema circuit.

Following several comments about Sid James chasing schoolgirls in *Camping*, the decision was made to phase out Sid's sexually-charged persona. In *At Your Convenience*, Sid follows the family man image of his hugely successful television role, Sidney Abbott in *Bless This House*, complete with ever-present pipe and homely pullover, an absentminded wife (Hattie Jacques) and wayward daughter (Jacki Piper). After further incorporation of this new Sid in the next film it was back to the woman-chasing rogue of old.

Bill Pertwee had a cameo role as the Manager of the roadhouse which Richard O'Callaghan and Jacki Piper visit. Having served a similar purpose in *Loving*, Pertwee was considered dispensable here and ended up on the cutting room floor.

Look out for...

As well as Bernard Bresslaw's now usual inclusion of his Popplewell catchphrase, 'I Only Arsked!', he also throws in Miriam Karlin's 'Everybody Out!' from *The Rag Trade*. 'Down with 'em!'

Keep an eye open for Julian Holloway, linking the frustrated romantics, Richard O'Callaghan and Jacki Piper to their equally complicated relationship in *Loving*.

Gerald Thomas enjoys a *Psycho* homage during the sequence in 'The Ghost Train'. While O'Callaghan beats the living daylights out of Cope, the camera remains on the imposing image of a skeleton surfacing from his open coffin - a superb montage evocation of Mrs Bates and all that!

The rogues gallery – Terry Scott and Sid James stroll through *Carry On Henry*

Above: A *Carry On Girls* line up, with all the usual suspects

Right: Battle fatigue – Kenneth Connor crawls through to victory in *Carry On Abroad*

Carry On memories

'For *Carry On At Your Convenience* we were in Brighton for about three or four days and as far as I could tell all these films were made on a terrible shoestring. Most of the location work was done on the Pinewood lot. So when we actually got a trip to Brighton most of the regulars were saying - "Oh? Are we actually going to somewhere away from Pinewood!?" They were quite amazed that they had decided to spend some money and go off down to Brighton where we were all put up in hotels. I saw the film about three or four years after we made it and I personally was very embarrassed by what I was doing. It was all so right wing and presenting the unionists as complete asses. I crept out of the cinema hoping nobody recognized me - fortunately they didn't. However, due to regular television showings, I'm still approached now by children pointing at me and saying - "You were Lew Boggs!"'
Richard O'Callaghan

'*Carry On At Your Convenience* was my biggest *Carry On* role with a trip down to Brighton to boot! I've always believed that they weren't sure about the subject matter and therefore there was a certain amount of unrest and re-writing. I suppose it was that thing of having bidets around all over the place - a mention would always get a laugh but you know, we had everything that goes into a bathroom suddenly everywhere on the set!'
Hugh Futcher

A Peter Rogers Production

CARRY ON AT YOUR CONVENIENCE

or 'Down The Spout' or 'Ladies Please Be Seated' or 'Up The Workers' or 'Labour Relations Are The People Who Come To See You When You're Having A Baby'

Sid Plummer **SIDNEY JAMES** W.C. Boggs **KENNETH WILLIAMS**
Charles Coote **CHARLES HAWTREY** Beattie Plummer **HATTIE JACQUES**
Cloe Moore **JOAN SIMS**
Bernie Hulke **BERNARD BRESSLAW** Vic Spanner **KENNETH COPE**
Myrtle Plummer **JACKI PIPER** Lewis Boggs **RICHARD O'CALLAGHAN**
Hortence Withering **PATSY ROWLANDS** Benny **DAVY KAYE**
Fred Moore **BILL MAYNARD** Agatha Spanner **RENEE HOUSTON**
Maud **MARIANNE STONE**
Popsy **MARGARET NOLAN** Willie **GEOFFREY HUGHES**
Ernie **HUGH FUTCHER** Barman **SIMON CAIN** Mrs Spragg **AMELIA BAYNTUN**
Chef **LEON GREENE** Doctor in Film **HARRY TOWB**
Bunny Waitress **SHIRLEY STELFOX** Hotel Manager **PETER BURTON**
Roger **JULIAN HOLLOWAY**
New Girl **ANOUSKA HEMPEL**

Screenplay by **Talbot Rothwell**
Music composed & conducted by **Eric Rogers**
Poster tag-line - 'Flushed with success - the Carry On team carries on round the bend!'

Production Manager **Jack Swinburne** Art Director **Lionel Couch**
Editor **Alfred Roome**
Director of Photography **Ernest Steward B.S.C.**
Camera Operator **James Bawden**
Make-up **Geoffrey Rodway** Continuity **Rita Davidson**
Assistant Director **David Bracknell**
Sound Recordists **Danny Daniel & Ken Barker**
Hairdresser **Stella Rivers** Costume Designer **Courtenay Elliott**
Set Dresser **Peter Howitt**
Assistant Art Director **William Alexander** Dubbing Editor **Brian Holland**
Titles **G.S.E. Ltd.** Processed by **Rank Film Laboratories**
Toilets by **Royal Doulton Sanitary Potteries** Assistant Editor **Jack Gardner**
Producer **Peter Rogers** Director **Gerald Thomas**

A 1971 Rank Organisation Release 'A' Cert.
Colour Running time - 90 mins. 8,100ft

The Brighton factor in definitive terms: Kenneth Williams, Patsy Rowlands, Charles Hawtrey, Marianne Stone, Joan Sims and Sid James on location for *Carry On At Your Convenience*.

CARRY ON MATRON

With the *Carry On* series wounded by failure, it was back to more instantly profitable fare with the next film - the fourth and final major assault on matters medical. Removing any hint of political comment or dubious materialistic ideals, this film was a complete and utter wallow in the low-brow comedy and flamboyant stereotypes of old: all pregnancy gags, sexy nurses and your average sort of tale of an attempted contraceptive pill burglary!

With a more liberally-minded social environment to work in, Rothwell could move away from the coy community of Hudis' late 1950s' world and his own 1960s' comments on dreadful food and randy doctors. In 1972, with the lid whipped off so many taboos, *Carry On* comedy could draw on a myriad of maternity jokes, less sexually naive situations and actual discussions about birth control. In a further development from the cosy atmosphere of the men's ward familiarity of *Nurse*, the patients in this film are even less important than in *Again Doctor*. Although several expectant mums arrive and have their babies (notably Valerie Leon and Madeline Smith - 'it's all bent to one side!'), they are simply the source of a quick one-liner or just a plot device. Only one genuine expectant mother is given any sort of screen time and that's ever-eating, ever-complaining Joan Sims, who spends the film lying in bed, devouring sausages and tomatoes and faking birth pangs to avoid induced labour. It's a fairly minor supporting turn but delivered beautifully, with belittled railway worker Kenneth Connor the ultimate in anxious expectant husbands. Ranting and raving about the wasted time, the problems of childbirth and, even, incorporating a sly jokey moment of pride about starting another strike - a small redemption from the previous movie perhaps!

The central thread of the story, however, concerns the finely tuned plan of robbing the hospital of its pill supply. Heading the operation is, of course, experienced film crook and all-round charmer, Sid

James. Taking on elements from *The Lavender Hill Mob*, *Two Many Crooks* and a score of second feature British crime thrillers, Sid strolls effortlessly through his part, with the merest of raised eyebrows and chuckling comment enough to get his belly laughs. It's a minor role, but still top billed, because he is the seed for the medical misunderstanding and bumbling that carries the film. Besides, his 'Dr Zhivago' is a gem.

Sid's son, Kenneth Cope (all naive sexuality and quiet manners after his unionist rants last time), goes to the limit of depravity for his dad by donning a nurse's uniform and casing the joint; a performance that blends elements of Dale and Cribbins. Naturally, Cope attracts the attention of sex-mad doctor, Terry Scott. Scott, in his last *Carry On*, tackles a role based round the medics of Jim Dale, with Barbara Windsor chasing and the inclusion of the 'fresh as a mountain stream' gag from *Again Doctor*. Meanwhile, having bluffed his way past Gwendolyn Watts on reception ('It's a surreal... real name!'), Cope bumps into sexy nurse Windsor who discovers his true identity, tosses in a tongue-in-cheek reference about being a 'gangster's moll!' and evokes a priceless shocked expression from Sid as the two 'nurses' are caught in a passionate embrace.

The scenes of the gang's robbery plans (other members being Bernard Bresslaw and Bill Maynard), are juxtaposed with various flights of fancy with the three principal authority figures at Finesham hospital: Hattie Jacques as the endearingly cynical Matron, Kenneth Williams as the overtly eye-popping, hypochondriac surgeon and Charles Hawtrey as the absent-minded psychiatrist. This trio of *Carry On* legends simply camp around the hospital, mugging wonderfully to lesser characters and the camera, and have a whale of a time with the ancient comic dialogue. Note the contrast between the Williams in full flow as he tries to seduce Jacques here, and the subtle Williams in his romantic moment with Jill Ireland in *Nurse*. By this stage of the game, any subtle

acting had been flattened by the relentless parade of quick gags and over-blown innuendo. Again, this is just a long string of comic sketches and characterizations, linked by the hospital environment, where Terry Scott can get away with the deaf, pregnant lady gag ('Are you going to bed or what?'/'And you say...What!') and revel in the company of Margaret Nolan in the elderly husband and the lodger scenario ('that's the trouble - she's pregnant too!'). These are jokes which were circulating almost before the gang were born but come up fresh and hilarious with sparkling delivery from a host of fine actors. The bumbling gang of crooks muff the operation but avoid the long arm of the law, Cope and Windsor get together and the on-off romantic relationship between Kenneth Williams and Hattie Jacques that had stretched back to *Doctor* finally ends in wedding bells.

Best performance
Although again restricted to a fairly minor role which only crops up halfway through the film, it is Charles Hawtrey who steals *Matron*. Conjuring up a laugh with his very character name, 'Dr F.A. Goode', Hawtrey's initial sequence with obsessed Kenneth Williams is a treat of spiralling *Carry On* humour. 'I can't do it lying down!'/'Oh dear me, you do have a problem!'... 'Have you ever known of a case of a man turning into a woman!'/'No, but I've heard of

one who turned into a one-way street!' The shared laughter between the two is electric, and a further priceless moment comes when both discover they belong to the same lodge of 'newts'. A supposed rival for the hand of Hattie Jacques, Charles giggles and gurgles with knowing wit as he settles down with Jacques to watch the television: his moments of slapstick fun are expertly delivered. It's a small part certainly, but beautifully marked.

Favourite bit
The highlight is a priceless one-liner between grumpy hospital porter Derek Francis and jovial cockney crook Sid James, who is cheerfully walking through the door when Derek stops him: 'Are you expecting a baby or what?'. With perfect timing Sid mutters, 'Oh, definitely a baby - I don't like whats!'. Please yourself!

Did you know?
Having got Jack Douglas a part in *Matron* after the casting was complete and production costs organized, Douglas' agent couldn't get him a fee for his brief comic turn. However, such was the success of this cameo that Peter Rogers sent Jack a crate of twelve bottles of Dom Perignon champagne!

For the original *Matron* publicity material Jack Douglas was billed as 'Jack Douglas'!

It's a boy! Sid James reveals all in *Carry On Matron* with Kenneth Cope, Bernard Bresslaw, Bill Maynard, Hattie Jacques and Kenneth Williams.

The plot for the medical television drama Charles Hawtrey and Hattie Jacques settle down to watch is taken directly from the classic 1946 Sidney Gilliat film *Green For Danger*. This Alastair Sim comic-thriller marked the film debut of Hattie Jacques as the voice of the sinister German radio announcer!

Marianne Stone appeared as Mrs Putzova but her brief support was cut from the final print - although she is still listed in the credits.

Madeline Smith proved so popular with the gang that Peter Rogers invited her back for a bigger role in *Abroad*. Other commitments prevented her appearing and Sid's young *Bless This House* co-star Sally Geeson climbed aboard.

Look out for...

At the moment of jubilation when Kenneth Connor's baby is born, Eric Rogers includes a burst of Glenn Miller's 'Chattanooga Choo Choo' on the score.

Ernest Steward, distinguished and much respected *Carry On* director of photography, is credited for writing *The Psychology of Jealousy*, the medical book manic surgeon Kenneth Williams consults.

Take note of Rothwell's low-key resurrection of the sign 'All deliveries at the rear' - his maternity hospital gag from *Cabby*.

There's a priceless moment when Sid James discovers a dragged-up Kenneth Cope and Barbara Windsor snogging on the bed. With perfect timing, he staggers out and cries 'Gawd, blimey!'. Sid's charming reaction to a very scantily-clad Gilly Grant in the bath is another touch of genius.

Enjoy the classic *Carry On* debut of Jack Douglas as the bumbling, working-class father, twitching with nervous energy as he asks, 'Could you get me the Guinness Book of Records please!'. The stunned facial expression of Kenneth Connor and Sid's dumbfounded amazement are priceless reaction shots.

West End producer and *Coronation Street* smoothie, Bill Kenwright, gives an over-the-top turn as an anxious reporter.

Sid James, Bernard Bresslaw and Bill Maynard contribute a bizarre, almost surreal, discussion about London bus routes, which is completely out of context with the rest of the production. It remains one of the most natural and joyous moments in the series.

Carry On memories

'While making *Carry On Matron*, one of my favourites was Kenneth Williams. We used to live near each other in St Pancras. We'd meet in the butchers! Oh, there were never stand-ins! Just a lot of standing about. I think the appeal of *Carry On* was their sea-side postcard type humour. All self cleaning jokes! I remember Charles Hawtrey well. We got on after I told him we had both been to Italia Conti School. I found him to be amusing and charming. He had a fund of stories to tell.'
Wendy Richard

A Peter Rogers Production

CARRY ON MATRON

or 'From Here To Maternity' or 'Familiarity Breeds'
or 'Womb At The Top' or 'The Preggar's Opera'

Sid Carter **SIDNEY JAMES** Sir Bernard Cutting **KENNETH WILLIAMS**
Dr Francis A. Goode **CHARLES HAWTREY** Matron **HATTIE JACQUES**
Mrs Tidey **JOAN SIMS**
Ernie Bragg **BERNARD BRESSLAW** Nurse Susan Ball **BARBARA WINDSOR**
Mr Tidey **KENNETH CONNOR** Dr Prodd **TERRY SCOTT**
Cyril Carter **KENNETH COPE**
Sister **JACKI PIPER** Freddy **BILL MAYNARD** Evelyn Banks **PATSY ROWLANDS**
Arthur **DEREK FRANCIS** Mrs Jenkins **AMELIA BAYNTUN**
Jane Darling **VALERIE LEON**
Ambulance Driver **BRIAN OSBORNE** Frances Kemp **GWENDOLYN WATTS**
Miss Smethurst **VALERIE SHUTE** Mrs Tucker **MARGARET NOLAN**
Pearson **MICHAEL NIGHTINGALE** Miss Willing **WENDY RICHARD**
Au pair Girl **ZENA CLIFTON**
Reporter **BILL KENWRIGHT** Mr Darling **ROBIN HUNTER**
Twitching Father **JACK DOUGLAS**
Mrs Pullitt **MADELINE SMITH** Mrs Bentley **JULIET HARMER**
Nurse in Bath **GILLY GRANT**
Shapely Nurse **LINDSAY MARCH** Nurse **LAURA COLLINS**

Screenplay by **Talbot Rothwell**
Music composed & conducted by **Eric Rogers**

Production Manager **Jack Swinburne** Art Director **Lionel Couch**
Editor **Alfred Roome**
Director of Photography **Ernest Steward B.S.C.**
Camera Operator **James Bawden**
Continuity **Joy Mercer** Assistant Director **Bert Batt**
Sound Recordists **Danny Daniel & Ken Barker** Make-up **Geoffrey Rodway**
Hairdresser **Stella Rivers**
Costume Designer **Courtenay Elliott** Assistant Art Director **Peter Lamont**
Dubbing Editor **Peter Best** Titles **G.S.E. Ltd.**
Processed by **Rank Film Laboratories** Assistant Editor **Jack Gardner**
Wardrobe Mistresses **Vi Murray & Maggie Lewin**
Producer **Peter Rogers** Director **Gerald Thomas**

A 1971 Rank Organisation film released in 1972 'A' Cert.
Colour Running time - 87 mins. 7,871ft

CARRY ON ABROAD

They don't come much better than this celebration of the cheap package holiday, with an over-flowing collection of familiar team members, the finest cast of supporting performers in *Carry On* history and a guaranteed laugh-a-second screenplay, incorporating sight gags, knowing references, slapstick, pratfall, a rare touch of subtle satire and bucketfuls of prime innuendo.

All the 1970s' *Carry On* regulars line up for disastrous foreign meals at a crumbling hotel, as Sid James goes through the motions as his usual lovable, sex-obsessed cockney hero, Kenneth Williams is fully over-the-top as the ferociously proud Englishman given the unenviable task of ensuring a fun-packed holiday ('It's probably raining in London!') and Charles Hawtrey (in his last *Carry On* role) giggles and drinks away from the main group while desperately trying to play leap-frog with the young ladies. Barbara Windsor is the ultimate sex-bomb, struggling to force her various underthings into her case, Bernard Bresslaw is meek and mild as the devout monk who sees the light when modernized and humanized by a loving Carol Hawkins, Joan Sims, as Sid's long-suffering and mildly nagging wife ('don't laugh!'), finds a sort of romantic understanding with typical military Officer-type and all-round coward Kenneth Connor, giggling hilariously at Sid's 'Your only child I presume!' comment. Peter Butterworth charges round the half-finished hotel like a mad whirlwind, the model of the flamboyant, excitable foreigner, with his deliciously over-bearing, explosive and fiery wife, Hattie Jacques ('Sure! - with no blooding food and no blooding stuff!'). Arguably the series' most concentrated cascade of funny moments, there is no real hold-up for semi-serious romantics (all have a comic edge and even the Sally Geeson/David Kernan pairing takes about three lines), no lengthy passages of explanation or historical/social comment and absolutely no room for even an ounce of pathos. It is simply corny joke following one-liner, following outrageous comment, following sight gag: laughs all the way and a timely cocked snook at the ever-increasing popularity for economic holidays abroad. While the British seaside industry was suffering from the tempting display of sun, sea and sauciness of the Mediterranean, the ultimate signifiers for glorious days at Brighton were let loose to deconstruct the reality of foreign travel. The English remain English in a far flung foreign place, and disrupt the sleepy native market town by attacking the brothel of Olga Lowe (complete with a Connor/Hawtrey resurrection of Jim Dale's cricket battling technique from *Camel*), eventually ending up in the company of police chief Alan Curtis and jailer Hugh Futcher. Britishness is mocked but beautifully protected by the stiff-upper-lipped dignity of Kenneth Connor, the wayward tongue of disgusted Kenneth Williams and the down-to-earth casualness of Sid James.

While the majority of the team excel themselves as the definitive stereotyped collection of lovable English eccentrics, several guest artistes crop up on board the coach and on the holiday. Notably among these is a fantastic star support from Scottish entertainer, Jimmy Logan, bouncing around the down-trodden holiday-makers with a never-say-die, Scots rogue attitude to fun, sex and having a wonderful time, battling with Sid for the attentions of Barbara Windsor and contrasting superbly with the snooty indignation of Williams: 'Hey son, hey, is this for the dirty weekend?'/'This is the four day trip to Els Bels if that's what you mean!'/'Same difference isn't it!'/'Have you got a ticket?'/'Certainly - I don't expect to get it for nothing - not the holiday anyway!'). Ray Brooks, as Butterworth's son, is a memorable dashing romantic, June Whitfield, the sexually-refined, nagging wife of Kenneth Connor eventually falls under his charms, while newcomers Carol Hawkins and Sally Geeson shine as the latest *Carry On* beauties. The camp and bewildered John Clive and handsome hero David Kernan are seen in fine supporting roles, Derek Francis fusses and moans in charge of his studious monks and Gail Grainger (in the absence of Valerie Leon) is outstanding as the Wunatours Ltd. courier. Back at home, Jack Douglas wey-heys during classic top and tail pub sequences, as he hilariously bumbles, mutters and jokes with a less than impressed Sid James. Memorably crushing the pub grub ('Not for me I've just had dinner!'), spilling his beer ('Get off!') and delighting in the cloth-capped ethos of Alf (which would form the majority of his contributions), it is a classic cameo.

A collection of comic situations, sexual revelations and collapsing holiday plans leads to the boring end of holiday party which is quickly livened up by Sid's injection of a potent sex drug (well, it allows blokes to see through women's clothes - to their underwear at least!). The party goes with a swing, Hattie Jacques does her Spanish bull impersonation, Charlie Hawtrey talks with glee about his hamsters and everybody couples off (including Williams - a rare example of him establishing a serious relationship with a glamour girl, Grainger). The final joyous scene, with all the holiday-makers surging into Sid's pub, filling the drinks with elixir and locking the doors for an all-night party, leaves the audience in the company of comic friends having a great time, and forms the most satisfying close to any *Carry On*. Charlie Hawtrey quickly pops in with 'What a wonderful idea!' and Sid chuckles, 'Oh no, lock all the doors. Time gentlemen please!'; the scene fades to black and the magic is gone forever. *Abroad* is the final prime example of *Carry On* comedy: the gradual decline of the feel-good factor and the exit of Hawtrey at this point dictated that things would never be the same again.

Best performance

Peter Butterworth's glorious return to a major *Carry On* role followed a collection of all-too brief cameo turns. His manic, over-excited, desperate-to-please hotelier gets the laughs at every opportunity, rushing around in a myriad of uniforms and dealing with the British eccentrics with naivety, notably when Williams gives his name as Stuart Farquhar: 'Stupid what?'/'Stuart... Stuart Farquhar!'/Sid: 'I think he was right the first time!' Peter dishes out the boring English food, tries to hold the hotel together and show the guests a good time - it's a hapless task! - and gets a face full of wet cement from Jimmy Logan, bashed over the head by his wild wife Hattie and deals with a dodgy window in Sid's room. This sight gag from Butterworth is pure Buster Keaton and sets up the golden moment when a drunken Sid walks through the window, smashes the pane and laughs, 'They've put the bloody glass in!' as Joan kills herself laughing. While the hotel is

collapsing all around them, Peter is the only stone-cold sober, level-headed one in the place, trying to convince the merry-making Brits to take notice. Every screamed warning is met with tongue-in-cheek comment or innuendo-charged joke - 'I make like little boy in Holland, I sticking thing in!'/Williams: 'Oh - he'll need an awfully large thing!' - with Peter summing up the entire series with his shriek, 'All you English think about is sex!'. In a recreation of the *Up The Khyber* finale, Peter crashes, bashes, falls and bumbles round the disaster area. A towering comic contribution.

Favourite bit

Even before the madcap antics abroad take hold, the finest piece of comic writing and acting occurs in Sid's glorious oldy-worldy pub, complete with a suspicious Joan Sims, an accident-prone and misunderstanding Jack Douglas and a totally irresistible Barbara Windsor. The film starts with the camera panning past a holiday poster of Sid drinking wine, a Spanish guitar, another superimposed image of Sid bullfighting and then one of Sid as the 'Little Mermaid' before stopping on Sid himself. He turns round to face the audience and launches himself into an obvious stream of innuendo with Windsor at the bar: 'Have you got a large one?'/'I've had no complaints so far'/'Seeing is believing!'/'You won't need a magnifying glass. There you are... no, no, no have it on me - if you know what I mean!'/'Oh, you don't have to draw me any diagrams'/'Pity - just going to get me ballpoint out!'. Jack Douglas lets it slip that Barbara and Sid are booked on the same trip and Windsor reaches the peak of comic expression: 'Me... Oh, I thought of going... Why?!' Magic.

Did you know?

Charles Hawtrey's final *Carry On* presents him as a drunken figure, forever staggering round with a bottle in his hand. Charlie was continually drinking during the filming, and this was Rothwell's comment on a weakness which had stretched back to *Cowboy* and was particularly notable during *Convenience*. Several of the gang were eccentrics in real life and Sid's coded messages to his bookies were tolerated as was Hawtrey's drinking. Sadly, by the early 1970s, the drinking habit of this most accomplished of screen comedy actors had started to affect the smooth production timetable at Pinewood. On *Abroad* Rogers let Rothwell construct Hawtrey's character as tipsy for 95 per cent of the time. The problem contributed to Hawtrey's abandonment from the series, although he had the dubious satisfaction of seeing the series he loved making take a quick nose-dive at the box office soon after his departure.

The wet cement Jimmy Logan falls into (twice!) was in fact cold porridge coloured a fetching grey/green.

When released in Germany the film lost its over-all *Carry On* title completely, finding its way to the cinema as simply *A Mad Holiday!*.

Semi-regular Bill Maynard had a supporting role as Fiddler, the manager of Wunatours, but his work ended up on the cutting room floor. His major early sequence also included priceless work from Gail Grainger and Kenneth Williams, as well as the vast majority of Patsy Rowlands' contribution.

Barry Norman delighted in showering tongue-in-cheek praise on the *Carry Ons* and always had a soft spot for them (and no it wasn't The Grimpen Mire!). For *Abroad* he wrote - 'The *Carry On* films either make you laugh or not and to my eternal shame (for I like to think of myself as a sophisticated person) this actually made me laugh three times - mostly, I hasten to add in my own defence, through amazement at the sheer affrontery of the script!'. He later introduced a radio tribute to Sid James in 1976.

Look out for...

Note the less-than-subtle holiday in-joke during the credits which lists the Technical Advisor as a certain Sun Tan Lo Tion.

The shower scene with James and Windsor has become one of the undiminished images of the series - 'You haven't got any soap on that bit!' - the chemistry between the two being caught on screen in definitive terms.

Carry On memories

'I was delighted when offered a part in *Carry On Abroad* and wondered where, in sunny Europe, we would be filming. Alas, the location turned out to be a car park at Pinewood!'
June Whitfield

'*Carry On Abroad* was great fun - everybody was so professional. You didn't get much chance to rehearse so you'd have your script and get called in for the day's shooting. You would nip along to somebody's dressing room and say, "Do you want to go through the lines?", and just do the scene while we were making up. I remember Sid James, Bernard Bresslaw, Kenneth Williams, Charles Hawtrey and all the gang with great affection. They were all so helpful and just got on with the job. I think the films were so popular because it's just

pure, light hearted fun. They were such lovely characters and people could just sit back and forget their problems. I think that's with any comedy - it's very valuable for the human race to be able to have a damn good laugh. It's a kind of healing. The *Carry Ons* are very valuable and I'm proud to have been a small part of it.'
Carol Hawkins

'The only thing I can say about my experience in *Carry On Abroad* is, apart from a stint in Huddersfield Rep, it was without doubt the lowest paid engagement of my career, but at the same time, the happiest. It was literally three weeks of laughter and commencement of a dear friendship with the wonderful Joan Sims and Hattie Jacques.'
David Kernan

'They were determined that the films were going to be money-makers and we didn't waste time. I remember we had one big scene in the interior of an aeroplane - it was one of my scenes - well that had just disappeared! I suppose they suddenly woke up and thought - we don't need that! Every one of the team were very, very strong characters as people - I mean Charlie Hawtrey was a delightful person. He just seemed to wander through the film, I wonder if he ever looked at his lines or if he just walked in, said a few lines and wandered off

Confrontation time with Sid James and Kenneth Williams in *Carry On Abroad*.

again. I had known Peter Butterworth and his dear wife, Janet Brown, for years. I actually made a film with Janet in 1948 called *Flood Tide*. But what a lovely artiste Peter was. Sid James - his background before he hit the *Carry Ons* was exceptional. Joan Sims is someone I've admired for years - she's kept such a high standard in her work. Kenneth Williams was absolutely the most outrageous of all. You see comedy is a very serious business and they had it worked out to an art form. People who get snobbish about the *Carry Ons* don't understand that it's not everybody can play that sort of thing. The key was the director and the cutting - unless there's a quick cut at the right time, unless the camera is very close to you at the right time you don't get the laugh. I was playing in Pantomime at The King's Theatre in Edinburgh and got special invitation to the Scottish premiere of *Carry On Abroad* at the Odeon Cinema, Glasgow. So we rushed along and the manager had asked me to say a few words - anyway this huge cinema had no lights on at all - just a couple of cleaner's lights and no sign of life anywhere. I banged on this side door and a fellow came out and I said "Is the premiere on today?" and he said - "Oh aye, come in Jimmy, the audience are all in, come up to the manager's office." So about twelve of us trooped up to the office for a drink. Anyway, once I had said my piece to the audience we sat down and a sign appeared on the screen explaining that since there would be no interval people should get their ice-creams now! I went off to buy them and when I returned my friend was laughing his head off. He said "I've never been to a premiere before but you don't expect to see one of the stars queueing up for ice-cream!' But once the film started it got a lot of big laughter."'
Jimmy Logan

'Carry On Abroad is the one that people all over the world remember. You know if they're American they say - "You were in *Carry On Abroad* ? Oh, Jesus Christ, we laughed so much!". The only thing I remember particularly about that was the daunting prospect in the cell scene. I had locked them all up, they had created this uproar at Madame Fifi's and as I said to Sid James - "Madame Fifi is my sister!" . They were all sitting there - the whole Carry On team. Apart from dear Hattie Jacques and that lovely bloke Peter Butterworth, everyone was locked up - Kenneth Williams, Sid James, Charles Hawtrey, Kenneth Connor, Barbara Windsor,

Bernard Bresslaw, Joan Sims... they were all there. So I had this U-shaped collection of *Carry On*. I was looking at them with the camera in front of me and they were all behind the camera doing their reaction takes and sending me up gutless! I remember the scene started on a trickle of water because it had been raining outside causing the foundations of the hotel to slide away at the end of the film and Gerald Thomas wanted to set up this fact. We had a trickle of rain and Kenneth Connor would shout out from behind the camera - "Do stop peeing dear boy!". They were all rotten to me but one had to keep a straight face and it was a strong and very funny scene. It was very well lit I remember, because the cameraman used to come to me and say, "That's great, just keep those eyes flashing from underneath that dark shadow of the cap. It looks great!" The film was very good for me and I suppose that scene comes up on your television screens regularly about three times a year - either in repeats of the entire film or the compilation shows.'
Alan Curtis

A Peter Rogers Production

CARRY ON ABROAD
or 'What A Package' or 'It's All In' or 'Swiss Hols In The Snow'

Vic Flange **SIDNEY JAMES** Stuart Farquhar **KENNETH WILLIAMS**
Eustace Tuttle **CHARLES HAWTREY** Cora Flange **JOAN SIMS**
Pepe **PETER BUTTERWORTH**
Stanley Blunt **KENNETH CONNOR** Floella **HATTIE JACQUES**
Brother Bernard **BERNARD BRESSLAW**
Miss Sadie Tomkins **BARBARA WINDSOR**
Bert Conway **JIMMY LOGAN** Evelyn Blunt **JUNE WHITFIELD**
Lily **SALLY GEESON**
Marge **CAROL HAWKINS** Moira **GAIL GRAINGER** Georgio **RAY BROOKS**
Robin **JOHN CLIVE**
Nicholas **DAVID KERNAN** Miss Dobbs **PATSY ROWLANDS**
Brother Martin **DEREK FRANCIS** Harry **JACK DOUGLAS**
Mrs Tuttle **AMEILA BAYNTUN** Police Chief **ALAN CURTIS**
Jailer **HUGH FUTCHER** Postcard Seller **GERTAN KLAUBER**
Stall-Holder **BRIAN OSBORNE** Madame Fifi **OLGA LOWE**

Screenplay by **Talbot Rothwell**
Music composed & conducted by **Eric Rogers**
Poster tag-line - 'The holiday of a Laugh time!'

Production Manager **Jack Swinburne** Art Director **Lionel Couch**
Editor **Alfred Roome**
Director of Photography **Alan Hume B.S.C.** Camera Operator **Jimmy Devis**
Continuity **Joy Mercer**
Assistant Director **David Bracknell**
Sound Recordists **Taffy Haines & Ken Barker**
Make-up **Geoffrey Rodway** Assistant Art Director **Bill Bennison**
Hairdresser **Stella Rivers**
Costume Designer **Courtenay Elliott** Assistant Editor **Jack Gardner**
Technical Advisor **Sun Tan Lo Tion**
Titles **G.S.E. Ltd.** Processed by **Rank Film Laboratories**
Producer **Peter Rogers** Director **Gerald Thomas**

A 1972 Rank Organisation Release 'A' Cert.
Colour Running time - 88mins. 7,928ft

CARRY ON GIRLS

For the 25th *Carry On* and the first without both Williams and Hawtrey, the series returned to its most basic roots: the seaside postcard and a good-hearted if sexist treatment of the female form. *Carry On Girls* conjures up the ultimate in wet and windy, bored and mindless seaside communities, Furcombe. The ever-enterprising Sid dreams up the entertainment-boosting and business-attracting idea of a beauty contest and epitomizes the feel-good innuendo and down-to-earth humour of the series.

It's a very slender premise for a movie, but the battle between the chuckling fun-filled antics of Sid's crooked twister and the bombastic, anti-fun, Northern woman-libber June Whitfield - blessed with the wonderfully pompous name of Augusta Prodworthy - is great. The film establishes two camps (and that's without Williams and Hawtrey!), with Sid's glorious celebration of innuendo versus June's downtrodden troop of campaigners against 'the sexual gratification of a lot of drooling men!'. Naturally the film makes it compulsory to join Sid's team. Both sides have ample opportunity to put their case forward, and in the end, Whitfield's ideals do succeed in ruining the contest. Rothwell presents a blatant stereotype of lesbianism in Patricia Franklin's role as June's second-in-command, as if to highlight this group as the oppposite of the carefree and unambiguous Sid James. Whereas Franklin dresses as a man with serious intentions, Bernard Bresslaw dons a dress to help out Sid James. The script dictates that both are funny, although Rothwell pokes fun at Franklin's dubious persona while rejoicing in Bresslaw's carnivalesque bumbling.

It is clear throughout that the Sid James' ideal is the *Carry On* ideal. Sid is his old cockney criminal type from his days with Tony Hancock and effortlessly carries off his performance. As with *Camping*, Bernard Bresslaw is his reluctant assistant (burdened and then blessed with Valerie Leon as his girlfriend), while the clutch of glamorous contestants is led by

Barbara Windsor in her broadest and most outlandish cockney. The likes of Margaret Nolan (in her most effective and sizable role), Wendy Richard and Angela Grant decorate the proceedings, with the ever steamed-up Peter Butterworth delighting connoisseurs of subtle acting with a dotty support as the hotel's resident frustrated sex maniac. He forms a memorable contrast with the youthful beauty and free-and-easy sexual charms of the bathing beauties as he sits around the lobby, helplessly fidgeting and spying on the girls. Joan Sims turns up on auto-pilot as another battling, nagging, sexually repressive element, and a delightfully dithering Kenneth Connor wheezes and coughs in a masterly performance of incompetent authority.

On a grand level, this is an answer to condemnation of the immoral quality of innuendo comedy; on a more superficial level, it's pure and simple lowbrow comedy dished up by a cast of comic actors going through the motions for the millionth time. There's an air of staleness about some of the

Old pros back in harness: Gerald Thomas and Sid James enjoy some Brighton larks on location for *Carry On Girls*.

Bernard Bresslaw, Sid James and Kenneth Connor play up to their sexual stereotypes for a *Carry On Girls* promotion shot. Laraine Humphreys is caught off guard!

arguably showcases the last example of definitive stereotyped, larger-than-life, seaside postcard humour. In future, the innuendo would become increasingly unsubtle and bare flesh would be as easily accessible as a good Sid James chuckle. It was this loss of the knowing but cheekily-concealed attitude to sex that made the films less endearing, and with *Girls* a more self aware style had begun.

Nevertheless, it's all classic stuff, full of funny one-liners and containing a stunning piece of comic acting from Sid James. There's a fine early sequence in the council board room as Whitfield tries to defend the heavy rain fall rating in the town: 'Personally I think nine inches is quite an average one', to which Sid replies, 'If you think nine inches is an average one, you've been spoilt!' - an example of the more sexually aware innuendo that became typical of later entries, but nobody could get away with dubious one-liners like Sid James. Fittingly, despite the sabotage of his contest, Sid escapes from the ranting mob in the company of Barbara Windsor, riding off on her motor-bike into the sunset. Here's to Sid and save me the one with the 'beautiful beam!'.

Best performance

It's Sid's film, but in terms of comic characterization, Kenneth Connor steals the limelight as the ineffectual little man, desperately grabbing his minor authority. A fascinating cinematic variation on his irritating comic characterization Sydney Mincing from Ted Ray's radio series *Ray's A Laugh*, Kenneth bumbles in his dodgy figure-of-authority role while battling opposite his millstone of a wife, Patsy Rowlands. Continually puffing on her fags, listening to the radio ('I can't remember a time when you had it off!') and dashing to the toilet, she is the complete contrast to Connor's official, proudly smart and dedicated man of power. Having some priceless moments in between the James/Whitfield banter, Connor particularly shines in the domestic sequence in his bath. Delighting in fantasizing about naval operations and World War II sea battles, he is degradingly undermined by Whitfield in full power. His dignified manner in the most undignified of situations is sublime. Getting caught, with Margaret Nolan, with his trousers down and continually humiliated, Kenneth boils and steams at every problem. The final address to the less-than-interested beauty contest audience is a timeless piece, with a nervous rehearsal back stage before delivering a few words as Sid forces him off. It's a touching, emotional and hilarious resurrection of his little man from *Sergeant* and *Constable*, now in befuddled middle age, sexually inadequate and a bemused figure of fun for everybody around him.

sequences, as if all had done this so many times that the fun and games were getting a bit wearing. Indeed, everybody is showing their age and poor old Sid, still guffawing at every gag and chatting up the contestants, looks clearly older. He still had what it takes though and clearly enjoys himself hugely in certain scenes with Barbara Windsor: 'Excuse me'/'Not now sonny!'/'Sonny! You want your eyes tested!'/'Excuse me - I always thought they built the shock absorbers into the bikes!'.

It's a classic case of a bunch of professionals getting on with doing the business: a handful of the scenes are milestones and several of the performances are vintage *Carry On*, notably those of Sid James, Kenneth Connor and Peter Butterworth. But by now Talbot Rothwell was running out of new ways to coyly refer to sex and the nudge, nudge sense of humour was beginning to wane at the box office. Still, it's an essential entry in the series and

Favourite bit

Peter Butterworth, narrowly pipped for the best performance, contributes to the finest comic exchange - with Joan Sims. Aroused by the host of sexy young things around him he pinches a young Wendy Richard from (where else?) Bristol, and giggles, 'Cheeky little thing - I'd like to put her across my knee!'. Joan raises her eyebrow and comments: 'I'm sure you would Admiral!'/'Yes, by jove...what!'. In an instant, the randy old seafarer snaps back to his elderly statesman persona and pompously wanders away. Peter's stunned expression at the sight of Margaret Nolan is one for the scrapbook as well.

Did you know?

Seaside paradise Furcombe is, of course, Brighton - a memorable return to the home of saucy comedy for all exterior shooting. Rothwell had great affection for the place, having been employed as a clerk in Brighton's Town Hall as a young man and idolizing Brighton's favourite son, Max Miller. The classic sequence with a scantily-clad Margaret Nolan, sexually uneasy Robin Askwith and desperately keen Peter Butterworth is filmed on the town's distinctive pebble beach with The Palace Pier clearly visible in the background. The Lover's Walk that Kenneth Connor refers to is almost there as well - there's a Lover's Lane!

Bernard Bresslaw takes on the character name of Terry Scott from *Camping* - Peter Potter.

Robin Askwith, who appears in his only *Carry On*, had just previously filmed *Bless This House* with Sid James for Rogers/Thomas. He replaced Robin Stewart from the original television series and eventually grabbed the leading role in the four *Confessions...* films which would prove the final nail in the *Carry On* coffin. Askwith's bawdy romps, full of nudity and youthful sexual antics, made the coy innuendo of Kenneth Connor and the gang seem old hat. As Verina Glaessner said in her *Monthly Film Bulletin* review of *Confessions of a Pop Performer*, 'Sidney James has found his younger alter ego in the charmless Robin Askwith'.

Gerald Thomas was desperate to include Kenneth Williams in the cast, although the actor kept turning down a leading role in *Girls* due to work commitments with the stage production, *My Fat Friend*. Thomas trimmed the role down to lighten the filming time but Williams was adamant: the role eventually was camped up by Jimmy Logan. In the good old days, Charles Hawtrey would have wandered in for another scene-stealing cameo.

On the film's release, the BBFC almost made this the first *Carry On* to receive an 'AA' certificate. Indeed, *Girls* was the first *Carry On* film that the BBC originally refused to show before the 9pm watershed. Eventually it appeared as prime time Saturday holiday viewing at 6.40pm.

It was important for Barbara Windsor's character to be able to ride a motor-bike (after all, she is called Miss Easy Rider!), but in reality Miss Windsor had never been on one. Determined not to let the gang down, she had a few quick lessons and successfully filmed the final get-away with Sid James. Barbara's nerves are clearly apparent.

Look out for...

The first major supporting role for Jack Douglas, with Rothwell adding a strong characterization to Jack's stage persona of Alf Ippititimus. He enjoys some marvellous vignettes with Sid James and contributes a wonderful sense of absentminded and eccentric fun to the feminist goings-on, 'I'll take bust any time!'. Take note of Jack's beautifully timed reception scene, cleaning the telephone with a naturalistic and cleverly executed twitch and cough - it's fabulous visual comedy.

There's a subtle in-joke concerning The Rank Organisation, when Bernard Bresslaw, running off in mad panic, bumps into Joan Sims who bangs against a gong in her hotel lobby. Less obvious than *Khyber's* reference but clear nevertheless!

Valerie Leon, in her last *Carry On*, resurrects the style of Imogen Hassall from *Loving* by starting the film as a dowdy nag and finishing up as the ultimate beauty contestant (quickly filling in for a less-than-keen Bernie Bresslaw in drag!). Also note Sid's early reference to this plot development when Barbara insists that she looks a lot different in a bikini - with a jovial nod to Bresslaw he replies, 'So does he, but he's not entering!'.

After her couple of cracking slave girls (in *Camel* and *Khyber*), enjoy Angie Grant's major *Carry On* contribution - a brilliant mix of sultry reserve and wide-eyed passion. She would later tackle larger parts in the 1977 sex comedy *What's Up Nurse?*, featuring Peter Butterworth and Jack Douglas, and the 1978 semi-sequel, *What's Up Superdoc?*, starring Christopher Mitchell and Harry H. Corbett.

Sally Geeson returns from *Abroad* and is greeted with a look of warm affection from her *Bless This House* work mate, Sid. Jimmy Logan also crops up as a terribly camp television producer who works well opposite the no-nonsense cynical comedy of Sid ('Hello, Mr Gayboy!'/'Gaybody!') - a role clearly moulded for the absent Charles Hawtrey.

There's some fairly shoddy editing, notably in the initial sequence with Barbara Windsor and Valerie Leon. Penelope Gilliat's comment in *The Movie* that the series was 'cut like a pound of salami' rang true for the only time here.

Carry On memories

'Memories come back. There was always a good working atmosphere I recall; Gerry Thomas and Peter Rogers always had a good team of people they knew. I think this helped a lot. In *Carry On Girls* I recall being bombarded with bags of flour and soot when the women's lib had a go at the beauty contest. We all had to have baths afterwards! It was cold in the mornings when we started, the leg make-up seemed to be made with cold water! In the same movie was a donkey. The inevitable happened when the poor creature was led onto the set. I enjoyed working with Sid James, he was a sweetie. Always the gent! Peter Butterworth was one of my favourite people. I worked with him several times. On one occasion I recall "telling fortunes" with playing cards. I could only remember that the ace of spades inverted meant you were going to a big building to enjoy yourself! Every time I saw Peter after that he would say "I still haven't been to that big building to enjoy myself!"'
Wendy Richard

'It was amazing for me, because on *Carry On Girls* I was up for an award as the most promising newcomer to the film industry - they should have added of pensionable age! I actually lost out to *Day of the Jackal* so I didn't mind too much. I never

worked with such an unselfish crowd as the *Carry On* team and the experience I gained from those films is incalculable. Sid James in particular on that film was marvellous - he would say, that joke would be better coming from your character. Sid was the master.'
Jack Douglas

A Peter Rogers Production

CARRY ON GIRLS

Sidney Fiddler **SIDNEY JAMES** Hope Springs **BARBARA WINDSOR**
Connie Philpotts **JOAN SIMS**
Mayor Frederick Bumble **KENNETH CONNOR**
Peter Potter **BERNARD BRESSLAW**
Admiral **PETER BUTTERWORTH** Augusta Prodworthy **JUNE WHITFIELD**
William **JACK DOUGLAS** Mildred Bumble **PATSY ROWLANDS**
Mrs Dukes **JOAN HICKSON**
Police Inspector **DAVID LODGE** Paula Perkins **VALERIE LEON**
Dawn Brakes **MARGARET NOLAN** Miss Bangor **ANGELA GRANT**
Debra **SALLY GEESON** Ida Downe **WENDY RICHARD**
Cecil Gaybody **JIMMY LOGAN** Alderman Pratt **ARNOLD RIDLEY**
Larry **ROBIN ASKWITH**
Rosemary **PATRICIA FRANKLIN** 'Half a quid' Citizen **BRIAN OSBORNE**
Fire Chief **BILL PERTWEE** Miss Drew **MARIANNE STONE**
Matron **BRENDA COWLING**
Susan Brooks **ZENA CLIFTON** Francis Cake **MAVISE FYSON**
Eileen Denby **LARAINE HUMPHREYS**
Gloria Winch **PAULINE PEART** Mary Parker **CAROLINE WHITAKER**
Julia Oates **BARBARA WISE**
Maureen Darcy **CAROL WYLER** Constable **BILLY CORNELIUS**
Elderly Resident **EDWARD PALMER** City Gent on Tube **MICHAEL NIGHTINGALE**
'There's Fiddler' Citizen **HUGH FUTCHER** Cloakroom Attendant **ELSIE WINSOR**
Stunt Double **NICK HOBBS**

Screenplay by **Talbot Rothwell**
Music composed & conducted by **Eric Rogers**
Poster tag-line - 'When it comes to beauty queens - it's Carry On and bust!'

Production Manager **Roy Goddard** Art Director **Robert Jones**
Director of Photography **Alan Hume B.S.C.**
Editor **Alfred Roome** Camera Operator **Jimmy Devis**
Assistant Director **Jack Causey**
Sound Recordists **Paul Lemare & Ken Barker** Continuity **Marjorie Lavelly**
Make-up **Geoffrey Rodway**
Hairdresser **Stella Rivers** Costume Designer **Courtenay Elliott**
Set Dresser **Kenneth McCallum Tait**
Dubbing Editor **Patrick Foster** Assistant Editors **Jack Gardner & Ken Behrens**
Title Sketches by **'Larry'** Titles **G.S.E. Ltd.** Processed by **Rank Film Laboratories**
Producer **Peter Rogers** Director **Gerald Thomas**

A 1973 Rank Organisation Release through Fox/Rank Distributions Ltd.
'A' Cert. Colour Running time - 88 mins. 7,921ft

DICK

This is a wonderfully fruity celebration of legendary highwayman Dick Turpin and the ultimate low-brow Restoration *Carry On* comedy, wallowing further in near-the-knuckle gags and sexually aware situations, perfectly suited for this historical salute to a time of a very merrie England. A resurrection of the plot line for *Don't Lose Your Head*, this film reunites the battling anti-hero/quiet alter ego of Sid James and the snooty, official but villainous figure of Kenneth Williams. However, this was the last time the two would work together and in a host of important ways this film was the end of an era.

Although he would go on to do television and stage *Carry On* assignments, this was Sid's last film which led to a marked departure from the tried and tested style of the series. The crucial departing talent was, however, writer Talbot Rothwell whose final script this was. Sid dashes and chuckles elaborately through this last example of Rothwellian wit, playing opposite a kind, warm and hard-done-by housekeeper creation from Hattie Jacques - also departing from the films with this entry. Clearly, this was a major watershed and effectively laid the series to rest. Fittingly, the bulk of the original cast members were gleefully reunited for a fond farewell of corny innuendo and murky locations.

Beginning with a finely directed sequence of Turpin riding across the countryside, the film is awash with memorable comic turns and dozens of classic one-liners. It is perhaps a touch lacking in serious adventure and action, as the ageing comic principals were restricted to studio-bound dialogue situations of increasingly awful magnitude. Joining the nostril-flaring elegance of Williams on the law-enforcing side is a marvellous lead role from Jack Douglas - finally tackling some major comic dialogue and playing brilliantly opposite the established series' favourites - while Bernard Bresslaw blasts his top and loses his clothes as the chief of the Bow Street Runners in a flamboyant and quick-tempered

performance. Bresslaw lives the life of the landed gentry with glamour girls on the side, a slightly prim Margaret Nolan for a wife and several attempts at seducing the Parisian-cum-cockney sparrow leader of 'The Birds of Paradise' travelling show - Joan Sims. In an earthy and effective evocation of pub-based entertainment performances, Sims milks her aggressively sexual characterization for all it's worth, particularly opposite the ultimate effeminate figure of Williams. The final major representative of the law enforcing agents is Kenneth Connor, in his smallest *Carry On* role as a dithering and ancient Bow Street Runner, equally interested in enjoying the sexual favours of the local lovelies as capturing the dreaded Turpin.

While Sid James is the perfect lovable Dick Turpin, hiding behind his black cloak and face mask at night, he never loses that full-of-lusty-innuendo laugh. Sid's highway gang also includes the bubbling and beautifully formed figure of Barbara Windsor,

What a way to go! Sid James departs the *Carry On* movies with a playful Barbara Windsor in tow - *Carry On Dick*.

Sid James displays his huge weapon in *Carry On Dick* **- much to the shock of Joan Sims and the delight of Penny Irving.**

flashing her breast for the last time in the series, and seductively stripping off in a reappraisal of the Dany Robin/fake Black Fingernail scene from *Don't Lose Your Head*. Peter Butterworth, muttering and mugging in a very minor role, grabs a few prime opportunities to shine, notably during the night raid of Joan Sims and the girls, and with a fine stunned expression of sincere admiration as Windsor pops out of her blouse. While Peter looks on in awe, Sid gets the laugh: 'Have we got enough out there for a good collection?'/'Oh I'll just pop out and see!'/'You pop out any more, we'll have standing room only.' As that little exchange suggests, the cover that Sid's gang uses is the local church and his much respected position as the peaceful vicar.

The final sequence is a brilliantly orchestrated confrontation between the endearingly crooked Sid and the self-righteously pompous Williams, with James seemingly trapped by the steely-eyed Bresslaw, the bumbling, accident prone Douglas and the crumbling Connor. Eventually Sid gets away with the myriad of good-natured crimes and jolly, schoolboy-ish japes, but it's the end of the trail for Sid as guiding light and the feel-good Rothwellian joy of *Carry On*. Stand and deliver for the last time.

Best performance

Not just out of respect for his final film, but also for the depth and sincerity of his complex dual role, the best performance has to go to Sid James. He incorporates the beloved cockney crook and chuckling persona as the daring part of his characterization to devastating effect while the real beauty of the role lies in the mild-mannered Reverend Flasher. Apart from the flamboyant, innuendo-sodden name, the vicar is a million miles from anything else Sid contributes to the series. Even the Black Fingernail had a foppish camp persona which comically contrasted the rough-and-ready Sid of old. In *Dick*, his vicar is under-played to perfection, and simply reacts with a quiet shake of the head to the bizarre and comically-charged situations around him. In a particularly notable scene, Sid delivers his one and only unaware innuendo joke while discussing the poor condition of his church's musical instrument with Williams and Douglas: 'Well, I'm a mere man like yourself Captain. I would like to get my organ in use again!'. There's no typical Sid James laugh or knowing wink to the audience, just casualness and surprise at Williams' contorted disgust. Following the cleverly organized escape route, Peter Butterworth rides the get-away coach with Sid and Barbara within. Caught by a rival highwayman shouting 'Stand and deliver', Sid pokes his head out and chuckles 'That's just what I was about to do!' with Barbara's cheeky comment 'And about time too!' - what a way to go! A sympathetic edge is injected into the role and the end product is a fittingly muted farewell for Sid - while there are the much welcome flashes of typical Sid innuendo, the Reverend Flasher characterization is a masterpiece of *acting* work.

Favourite bit

The final piece of legendary Rothwell spiral innuendo writing incorporates a brilliant dialogue with Sid James, Kenneth Williams and Jack Douglas - three masters of the timed line. Discussing the secret identity of 'Big Dick Turpin', Williams explains to the man of cloth about the amazing birth mark that the highwayman has, 'if you'll pardon the expression Reverend... on his diddler!'/'Diddler, I don't know what that is'/'Oh, well, perhaps a more familiar word for you would be....'/'Oh! But I fear that won't be of much use to you'/'Why not?'/'Well, so many folk round here keep poultry!'. It's as smutty as *Carry On* could get without going overboard and the gentle, bemused delivery of Sid brings these priceless Rothwell lines a touch of quiet dignity. If hardly Shakespearian, the words sound sweet and hilarious, 'Jack the Woodcutter' and all!

Did you know?

Sid James was almost twice the age of the real Dick Turpin, who was hanged in York in 1739 at the age of 33. At the time of the film's release, Sid had just celebrated his 61st birthday!

South Africa banned *Dick* due to Sid James' depiction of a criminal in vicar's clothing.

Eva Reuber-Staier, playing one of the 'Birds of Paradise', was a former Miss World.

Talbot Rothwell was forced to retire from writing after suffering an attack of nervous energy while typing the first draft of *Dick*'s script. Unable to focus on the keyboard and confused by the whole idea of writing, a visit to the doctor told him he was suffering from nervous exhaustion, eye-strain and overwork. He was ordered to rest and the final version of the film's script was typed by his daughter Jane from his dictation and rough draft. On the completion of this, his final work, he chose to retire quietly.

Look out for...

Jack Douglas is fully launched into the main *Carry On* squad and enjoys several major comic situations built around his persona, notably the almost immortal toilet watching sequence.

Take note of the marvellously realist sets and perfectly chosen country locations. 'The Old Cock Inn' atmosphere is pure eighteenth century and creates a true feel of seedy low-life and criminals on the run.

Marianne Stone turns in her finest *Carry On* cameo as the aged old hag in 'The Old Cock Inn' with an intimate knowledge of Turpin's personality. She enjoys herself in a spirited performance opposite Kenneth Williams and Jack Douglas.

During this inn sequence, Kenneth Williams takes on the vocal characterization of a criminal type (Dandy Desmond) to hide his law-enforcing identity. The vocals he employs are a slight variation from his rustic folk singer 'Rambling Syd Rumpo' from *Round the Horne*.

Kenneth Connor's old duffer persona incorporates the vocal traits of Michael Ripper's ever faithful lift attendant from the *St Trinians* comedies.

Carry On memories

'The one memory I have of the *Carry Ons* was the absolutely marvellous team spirit which was really created by the warmth and absolute generosity of Sid James.'
Bill Maynard

A Peter Rogers Production

CARRY ON DICK

Dick Turpin/The Rev Flasher **SIDNEY JAMES**
Captain Desmond Fancey **KENNETH WILLIAMS**
Harriett **BARBARA WINDSOR** Martha Hoggett **HATTIE JACQUES**
Sir Roger Daley **BERNARD BRESSLAW** Madame Desiree **JOAN SIMS**
Tom **PETER BUTTERWORTH** Constable **KENNETH CONNOR**
Sgt Jock Strapp **JACK DOUGLAS**
Mrs Giles **PATSY ROWLANDS** Bodkin **BILL MAYNARD**
Lady Daley **MARGARET NOLAN**
Isaak the Tailor **JOHN CLIVE** Bullock **DAVID LODGE**
Maggie **MARIANNE STONE**
William **PATRICK DURKIN** Sir Roger's Coachman **SAM KELLY**
Mr Giles **GEORGE MOON**
Squire Trelawney **MICHAEL NIGHTINGALE** Browning **BRIAN OSBORNE**
Rider **ANTHONY BAILEY** Highwaymen **BRIAN COBURN & MAX FAULKER**
Footpads **JEREMY CONNOR & NOSHER POWELL** Lady **JOY HARRINGTON**
Tough Men **LARRY TAYLOR & BILLY CORNELIUS**
'The Birds of Paradise' **LARAINE HUMPHREYS LINDA HOOKS**
PENNY IRVING EVA REUBER-STAIER

Screenplay by **Talbot Rothwell**
Based on a treatment by **Laurie Wyman & George Evans**
Music composed & conducted by **Eric Rogers**
Poster tag-line - 'Dick Turpin carries on with his flintlock cocked!'

Production Manager **Roy Goddard** Art Director **Lionel Couch**
Editor **Alfred Roome**
Director of Photography **Ernest Steward B.S.C.**
Camera Operator **Jimmy Devis** Continuity **Jane Buck**
Assistant Director **David Bracknell**
Sound Recordists **Danny Daniel & Ken Barker**
Make-up **Geoffrey Rodway** Hairdresser **Stella Rivers**
Costume Designer **Courtenay Elliott**
Set Dresser **Charles Bishop** Dubbing Editor **Peter Best**
Master of Horse **Gerry Wain**
Assistant Editor **Jack Gardner** Casting Director **John Owen**
Stills Cameraman **Tom Cadman**
Wardrobe Mistresses **Vi Murray & Maggie Lewis**
Coach & Horses supplied by **George Mossman**
Titles **G.S.E. Ltd.** Processed by **Rank Film Laboratories**
Producer **Peter Rogers** Director **Gerald Thomas**

A 1974 Rank Organisation Release through Fox/Rank Distributions Ltd.
'A' Cert. Colour Running time - 91 mins. 8,201ft

CARRY ON
BEHIND

Although the times were a-changing, this film at least tried to continue the *Carry On* series in the same style as the classic James/Rothwell era, thanks mainly to an innuendo-crammed screenplay by Dave Freeman (who had worked on both the film and TV versions of *Bless This House* and several spin-off television *Carry Ons*). He clearly understood the style of Rothwell's linear comedy: building up innuendo and farce in a sketch format linked by the briefest of storylines.

This is a modern reworking of *Camping*, with all the usual stereotypes in place and a more near-the-knuckle treatment of sex and nudity. It has a completely meaningless title, following on in style from the slightly risqué *Dick*, though Kenneth Williams maintained that the film was so called because of the archaeologist party and other holiday-makers travelling in caravans and carrying their equipment *behind*

them! Quite. *Behind* also boasts a fine cast of regulars - less than usual certainly, but still enough to keep it firmly in the familiar pattern. Kenneth Williams, grabbing centre stage with Sid's departure, minces and whines throughout the piece, giving a performance full of outrageous comments with touches of his youthful 'snide' vocals. Indeed, his last line, 'Stop Messin' About!' remains the major signifier for the good-time *Carry On* feel in the film. Bernard Bresslaw crops up as the ultimate hen-pecked, put-upon husband who falls foul of several comic situations and displeases his wife, Patsy Rowlands, while his mother-in-law, a menacing supporting turn from Joan Sims, joins them on holiday and disrupts the fun. Kenneth Connor, popping up throughout the film as the randy old major who owns the caravan site and Peter Butterworth as the shuffling odd job man give stunning performances - maintaining the continuity of the series with two memorable and battling lead roles. Jack Douglas gives an excellent star performance as his usual jittering self but has a lot more screen time, while newcomer Windsor Davies takes on the impossible, and fills in for the absent Sid James. As it happens he does a very good job of it, charming his meat customers ('Give that to your husband and you're in for a night of romance!'/Marianne Stone: 'Oh, can I do it in the oven?'/'Do it where you like, it's your kitchen!'), chatting up the female campers (notably Carol Hawkins and Sherrie Hewson), chuckling at every slight misfortune, desperately trying to get away with murder while his wife's about and enjoying putting down the authority figure - and thus embracing the ethos of Hudis *Carry On*. Notably on the first meeting with Kenneth Connor: 'Nice vans these'/'Not bad!'/'How long?'/'About fourteen feet!'/'No, no, no. I mean how long are you staying!'/'Depends'/'On what?'/'Whether we get any!'. In a homage to the camping holiday of James and Bresslaw, the team of Davies and Douglas is very effective. Meanwhile the real revelation of *Behind* is a

A quick bang! Elke Sommer gets to grips with Carry On humour as Kenneth Williams gives her a lesson in under-playing - Carry On Behind.

Would you go to this man's confessional?Sid James lets the refined mask slip for *Carry On Dick* publicity

Right: At the court of King Hal – Peter Butterworth and Barbara Windsor show respect in *Carry On Henry*

Below: Down the Pan. Sid James, Joan Sims and Hattie Jacques share a laugh on set during the making of *Carry On At Your Convenience*

fascinating leading performance from Hollywood star Elke Sommer, who brilliantly wanders into the film, tossing fractured English comments into the usual concoction of farce and innuendo ('Hitting it off? What does hitting it off mean? Same as having it off, no!'), and teaming to superb effect with the snooty figure of Kenneth Williams. An international guest star on par with Phil Silvers, Sommer seems amazingly at home with a series she wasn't familiar with, a group of actors who had been together, on and off, for almost 20 years, and a style of comedy she was totally new to. Thankfully, if the continual references to 'having it off', bathing beauties' bums and screaming campness begins to wane, then Sommer's misunderstanding of English innuendo is a welcome burst of fresh ideas.

In the end, of course, everybody goes home happy - the split asunder married couples get back together again, the bickering married couples find renewed happiness, Kenneth Connor makes a successful play for the hired stripper (Jenny Cox) and Kenneth Williams finds himself in the enviable position of camping about in a pit with Elke Sommer. The dialogue is corny, it's true, and the essence of simple-minded, no-nonsense fun and games is beginning to pale, but *Behind*, following a film that saw the farewell of so many important contributors, does stand up very well. It's a final jolly holiday with the gang.

Best performance

The major connection back to the glories of *Camping* is the fascinating eccentric of Peter Butterworth, here as another money-pinching tramp who moans, groans and slobs through the corny gags and outlandish situations with perfect comic timing. Butterworth gives a mature, emotional and touching quality to this basic characterization which is almost too good for the tailender knock-about humour of *Behind*. While delighting in moments of surreal humour and shocked amazement at Williams and Sommer, it is his renewed relationship with wife Joan Sims that makes this performance so powerful. Hiding away in the lower reaches of the credits and not even getting his face on the poster, Peter's contribution is the very heart and soul of the film.

Favourite bit

It's Peter Butterworth again, as archaeologists Kenneth Williams and Elke Sommer scramble about for caravan accommodation. Peter, all shuffling nerves and suspicious glances, listens as these

Steady lads! Elke Sommer gets the pulses of Windsor Davies and Jack Douglas racing in *Carry On Behind*.

figures of academia explain the situation. Butterworth: 'Operations... What kind of operations!'. Williams: 'Somewhere to examine our artefacts'. Sommer: 'Yes, he will be getting them out and I shall be sticking labels on them!'/'You do what you like - it's still twenty quid a week!' Priceless stuff.

Did you know?

The thought of phasing out Sid James from the Carry Ons had arisen in the early 1970s due to a mixture of concern over his public exposure - the films running side by side with his television work in Bless This House - and, more importantly, worries that audiences would feel uncomfortable with a man over 60 chasing teenage girls. However, the role eventually played by Windsor Davies in Behind was in fact written with Sid in mind. He was due to star in the film but an Australian tour with The Mating Game clashed with the shooting dates.

Elke Sommer first came to the notice of Peter Rogers and Gerald Thomas after playing madcap farce in the Peter Sellers classic A Shot in the Dark. Before her Carry On debut, she had appeared in limited roles for Betty Box in Deadlier Than The Male, Percy and Percy's Progress. After joining in the fun of the first male member transplant, Carry Ons were a quiet natural succession! Sommer plays her Behind role with innuendo-encrusted delight - Margaret Dumont's comedic unease with The Marx Brothers meets a watered-down Confessions from a Holiday Camp!

Elke Sommer picked up the top wage packet for any Carry On - £30,000. Equalling the huge sum paid to Phil Silvers for Camel, it was six times the average earnings of Sid James or Kenneth Williams.

In the early sequence in Davies' butcher shop, Jack Douglas gets locked in a freezer. For the desired effect on screen, Jack was covered in frosty-effect plastic, however, the rest of the gang, thinking he got away with it lightly, threw him in a pond!

On the poster for the film, the bottom innuendo of the title is further emblazoned with the registration of the car carrying Williams, Connor et al - it's 13UM!!

Eric Rogers' title theme is a Scott Joplin type rag based around the notes B E and B, the initials of Peter Rogers' wife, Betty Evelyn Box.

The voice of Joan Sims' foul-mouthed mynah bird is provided by Gerald Thomas.

On the film's release, Peter Rogers was quoted as wanting to bring the total of Carry On films to 30. As this was the 27th production, perhaps he was sensing the end which was indeed coming.

Look out for...

Ian Lavender, still at the time that stupid boy on television in Dad's Army, is given the chance to step into the still vacant shoes of Jim Dale as the mumbling young lead. Adrienne Posta, playing Lavender's sexually forthcoming but naive wife, was fresh from low-brow cinematic comic romping with Frankie Howerd in Up Pompeii and Percy with Hywel Bennett. Ian Lavender turns in an effective if limited performance and later cropped up in such classics of subtle film comedy as Confessions of a Pop Performer and Adventures of a Private Eye!

Peter Butterworth throws in an in-gag while dusting off an ARP helmet which he is hoping to re-shape into a convincing Roman artefact for Kenneth Williams. Pleased with his work he smiles and mutters, 'Good enough for Julius Caesar!'. Williams, of course, was the emperor in Cleo.

Note Eric Rogers' introductory theme for Carry On debutant Windsor Davies: Karl Nicolai's 'The Merry Wives of Windsor'.

Keep an eye peeled for two popular comedy glamour girls during the mad-cap, slap-stick, trouser-ripping finale: Diana Darvey from The Benny Hill Show and Georgina Moon, memorable as Erotica in the Frankie Howerd classic Up Pompeii.

Liz Fraser returned to the Carry Ons for the first time since Cabby over 12 years before. Importantly, she is the only glamour girl to develop from sexy, fun-loving young thing in the early films to the battling, nagging wife figure of the seaside postcard, while still, eventually, injecting her married persona with a touch of warmth.

There's a marvellous sequence when Kenneth Williams thinks he has injured himself (Sommer: 'Is Professor of Archaeology! Is bleeding terrible!'/ Davies: 'Never mind his qualifications - is he hurt bad!'). Eventually the hapless Williams ends up in hospital with George Layton and former Miss England, Linda Hooks (having appeared as a Bird of Paradise in Dick and due for a return in the next film). At the time, Layton in a doctor's coat was familiar to audiences from his role as Paul Collier in television's Doctor in the House, Doctor at Large and Doctor in Charge. When he made his Behind cameo, Layton was writing the hit show *Doctor on the Go* starring Robin Nedwell and Geoffrey Davies. 'Here what are you - a vampire!'

Larry Martyn turns in a fine cameo as the bemused maintenance man, shocked at the seductive sight of stripper Jenny Cox. There's also interesting support from Hugh Futcher as an aggressive and slightly displeased chair painter!

Carry On memories

'I returned from India on March 8th, 1975, after a 3 and a half month tour playing Polonius in *Hamlet* for the New Shakespeare Company in association with the British Council. My agent phoned me in a bit of a 'state' as she had a client booked to play the Barman in *Carry On Behind* and he'd got some other offer which involved quite a lot of money. In other words she asked Gerald Thomas if he'd have me to play the tiny part of the barman instead of Chris Gannon. He said, "Yes" - consequently I was booked to film on March 19th 1975 - but we overran so I did TWO days on the film - which was most enjoyable. Everything was great fun and most efficient - most shots were done in one take - Kenneth Williams was being a bit "remote" - Ian Lavender was great fun and ran me back into London at the end of both days and I thoroughly enjoyed myself. That is the total extent of my career in the *Carry On* films! I'm only sorry I didn't do more!'
Kenneth Waller

'My last one was *Carry On Behind* as the painter with Peter Butterworth and the chairs. I remember we had problems with the actual painting of the chairs. I was booked just for a morning's work on that film and I was doing something else on television at the time and was allowed out for the film job. The thing was I simply couldn't get back for

the TV assignment because what was absolutely going to be a half day turned into, believe it or not, three days work on *Carry On Behind*.'
Hugh Futcher

A Peter Rogers Production

CARRY ON BEHIND

Professor Roland Crump **KENNETH WILLIAMS**
Professor Anna Vooshka **ELKE SOMMER**
Arthur Upmore **BERNARD BRESSLAW** Major Leep **KENNETH CONNOR**
Daphne Barnes **JOAN SIMS** Fred Ramsden **WINDSOR DAVIES**
Ernie Bragg **JACK DOUGLAS**
Henry Barnes **PETER BUTTERWORTH** Sandra **CAROL HAWKINS**
Carol **SHERRIE HEWSON**
Sylvia Ramsden **LIZ FRASER** Linda Upmore **PATSY ROWLANDS**
Joe Baxter **IAN LAVENDER**
Norma Baxter **ADRIENNE POSTA** Vera Bragg **PATRICIA FRANKLIN**
Landlord **DAVID LODGE**
Mrs Rowan **MARIANNE STONE** Doctor **GEORGE LAYTON**
Bob **BRIAN OSBORNE** Clive **LARRY DANN** Sally **GEORGINA MOON**
Maureen **DIANA DARVEY** Veronica **JENNY COX**
Electrician **LARRY MARTYN** Nurse **LINDA HOOKS**
Barman **KENNETH WALLER**
Man with Salad **BILLY CORNELIUS** Woman with Salad **MELITA MANGER**
Painter **HUGH FUTCHER** Nudist **HELLI LOUISE JACOBSON**
Student with Ice-cream **JEREMY CONNOR**
Lady in Low-cut Dress **ALEXANDRA DANE**
Projectionist **SAM KELLY** Plasterer **JOHNNY BRIGGS**
Lady with Hat **LUCY GRIFFITHS**
Short-sighted Man **STANLEY McGEAGH** Wife **BRENDA COWLING**
Man in Glasses **SIDNEY JOHNSON** Courting Girl **DRINA PAVLOVIC**
Student **CAROLINE WHITAKER** Man with Water **RAY EDWARDS**

Screenplay by **Dave Freeman**
Music composed & conducted by **Eric Rogers**
Poster tag-line - 'Carry On Behind...with the '76 touch -
The Carry On team...looking
a site for sore thighs!'

Production Manager **Roy Goddard** Art Director **Lionel Couch**
Editor **Alfred Roome** Director of Photography **Ernest Steward B.S.C.**
Camera Operator **Neil Binney**
Make-up **Geoffrey Rodway** Continuity **Marjorie Lavelly**
Sound Recordists **Danny Daniel & Ken Barker**
Hairdresser **Stella Rivers** Costume Designer **Courtenay Elliott**
Set Dresser **Charles Bishop**
Dubbing Editor **Pat Foster** Titles **G.S.E. Ltd.**
Processed by **Rank Film Laboratories**
Assistant Editor **Jack Gardner** Caravans supplied by **CI Caravans**
Producer **Peter Rogers** Director **Gerald Thomas**

A 1975 Rank Organisation release through Fox/Rank Distribution Ltd.
'A' Cert. Colour Running time - 90 mins. 8,139ft

CARRY ON ENGLAND

A major departure from the slap and tickle style of *Carry On* comedy, this film, the first after the death of Sid James, met with a woefully poor reaction from the public and brought the *Carry Ons* to their lowest level. The sexual frustration and innocent banter had been completely abandoned and in its place was a more open-minded attitude to sex. Whereas Sid and the gang laughed and joked about it, the *England* cast is made up of youthful exponents of sex and aged Carry Oners who battle against it. Sadly lacking in a solid team of old favourites, the film had a script (by Jack Seddon & David Pursall) which replaced the non-stop stream of innuendo of the Rothwell era with a more smutty, arrogant form of comedy. The team are stripped of their major comic stereotypes and only a starring role for Kenneth Connor offered a past face any decent screen time.

Here Kenneth moves away from his endearing little man persona to a bombastic, foul-tempered and obsessive military dictator, running his mixed battery of British soldiers like a prison camp. Peter Butterworth, shamefully restricted to a few scenes, makes the most of his cocky put-down to the bumbling Connor, contrasted with his own nervous persona when he is in assistance to the Brigadier. Butterworth, all stiff-upper-lipped mockery and cowardly energy when the bombs start falling, gives a pleasing if ultimately unsatisfactorily brief cameo. Joan Sims is even worse off, presented with the throw-away role of a domineering lovelorn Private with barely ten lines to deliver. Indeed, the only member of the *Carry On* team to remain in anything like their usual comic characterization is the much welcome Jack Douglas, who twitches and jerks around the barracks in several inspired scenes of eccentric comedy. Like a refugee from the earlier films, Douglas acts as a vital bridge between *England* and the rest of the series. Despite limited screen time in comparison with the previous film, Douglas comes out as the most likable and effective *Carry On* turn. And that's it, only four regulars recruited to see through this resurrection of *Sergeant*, although a barking mad, sinisterly grinning and ball-crushing Windsor Davies (injecting his manic creation, Sgt Maj Williams from *It Ain't Half Hot Mum* into the series) partners Connor in several promising comic sequences. Notably there's a fine piece of stunned amazement as Connor orders him to remove his trousers ('But Sir, we has only just met!') while the laughing, sadistic image of military might of Davies does hold the squad together with Hartnell-like authority.

Peter Jones steps into the madness with his only major *Carry On* contribution (following his cameo in *Doctor*). Besieged by a script full of dreadful, and I mean dreadful puns, Peter struggles with lavatorial humour and a collection of painfully unfunny comments, singlehandedly having to put across the worse selection of jokes in *Carry On* history with conviction. Admittedly the jokes are supposed to be

Sergeant revisited - Windsor Davies and Kenneth Connor in *Carry On England*.

corny, and Jones' purpose is to be humoured by the lowly ranks and congratulated for his wit by Peter Butterworth. However, the desired effect of this showcasing of self-aware poor gags is undermined by the fact that the genuine jokes within the film are not much better. That Connor's character is called Captain S. Melly and the troops under him call him 'Smelly' just about sums up the level of wit seen here. The actors, all professional and superb performers, do their utmost to pull through to the end but it's a long slog. The characters are unlikable, the set pieces mistimed and the humour fairly basic throughout.

The major mistake on Peter Rogers' part was to recruit a host of new actors to take on the leading roles, notably Patrick Mower and Judy Geeson who mug, ham and mistime gags with glorious regularity. Untrained in music-hall comic delivery and saddled with loose direction and dreadfully under-written characters, they are unable to let their hair down and enjoy the corniness of the jokes. Indeed, the tango sequence when Mower puts words to the music: 'Get those pants down!'/'Not bloody likely!', has to be the rock bottom for *Carry On*. However, both gamely pull through the film, with Mower's cheerful cockney attitude providing several fine touches of bawdy originality.

Meanwhile, Melvyn Hayes, wandering in for the briefest of support performances, tackles the humour on its own level and has at least one treasurable moment with Windsor Davies. The aggressive Davies orders him to fetch his uniform, and the disgruntled Hayes refuses. Davies gets irate: 'Get it out, lovely boy! Get it out!', to which Melvyn mutters: 'Pardon!'. It's the most basic sort of *Carry On* innuendo to be sure but brilliantly delivered and refreshingly simple. Diane Langton, touted as the 'new Barbara Windsor', contributes an over-exaggerated but enjoyable sex-bomb performance, contrasting the dignified authority of Kenneth Connor with a fine line in easy-going banter.

Clearly there are moments to enjoy and a clutch of the actors are always worth watching, regardless of the poor material. However, in comparison to the classic entries this is too much change, too soon. A new team could not be recruited overnight, and even though the odd familiar face is in the background, the chief exponents of the romantic ideals and comic lines are those youthful characters who lack the grasp of innuendo timing. If you like, Connor takes on the mantle of the anti-fun Augusta Prodworthy, and he is only allowed to emerge into his lovable, bumbling self at the end. For all that, the final rousing attack on the German airplanes overhead does get the old patriotic juices flowing, and

Connor and Davies milk the comic opportunity perfectly: 'Sixpence for everyone you shoot down - two bob if it's a German!'. Peter Jones and Peter Butterworth quickly depart after enlivening the latter stages of the film, and it's left to the over-excited Jack Douglas and the barrack boys and girls to save the day. That and a handful of priceless actors just about saves the film!

Best performance

Despite its totally uncharacteristic feel, the most effective performance must be that of Kenneth Connor, who contributes an amazing picture of military obsession and outraged authority. For Connor the actor it was a welcome break from comic voices and frustrated little men, and he is here given full range with a role on screen 95 per cent of the time, bawling out orders with energetic power. The role is played perfectly straight, and is used as the catalyst for a myriad of jolly japes and authority-baiting by the recruits. It's not so much a farce performance as a serious interpretation of misguided faith. Kenneth injects moments of powerful acting amidst the smutty gags and dung throwing, notably giving a rousing speech and juddering to a Hitler salute. The humour is dampened by Patrick Mower's comeback, but Connor is *acting* with real conviction. Of course, there are priceless moments of typical *Carry On* farce as well, memorably his shocked expression when Windsor Davies informs him he is a ball-squeezer, and the small grin of childish satisfaction at the very end of the movie. However, for the majority of the film, Kenneth is cold, calculated and evil (taking elements from his groundbreaking radio broadcast *The Burnt Offering* and tossing in the manic persona of Otto Preminger from *Stalag 17*). Let's face it, any British officer who has a dog called Hitler isn't the ideal flat-mate! Stomping around the barracks, stopping the recruits getting their ends away, and continually misunderstanding and miscommunicating his orders, Kenneth is a humourless tyrant. It remains Kenneth's most ambitious, complex and, ultimately, uncelebrated contribution to the series.

Favourite bit

While the script is full of mistimed jokes and lacks a constant stream of one-liners and comic situations, there is one sequence which ranks with any of the true landmarks of the series. Naturally, it involves the two finest performances, those of Kenneth Connor and Windsor Davies, who are trying to sort out why the female recruits are topless. 'What the devil's going on here? Why are they all on parade half naked?'/'Because Sir, you said they was to come on parade wearing trousers and that is all!'/'I did not!'/Tricia Newby: 'Oh yes you did Sir!'/'Quiet! Sergeant Major, when I said that's all, I didn't mean that's all, I meant that's all, that's all!'/'That sounds like a lot of alls, Sir!' A brief return to prime glories!

Did you know?

The original idea for Seddon & Pursall's army comedy was a half-hour treatment for the 1975 television series *Carry On Laughing*. When in late 1975 Rogers and Thomas were looking for a new film idea, they approached the two writers and decided to extend the programme to feature-film length. At the time Dave Freeman was planning another *Carry On* which was never completed.

Despite their clear lack of understanding of *Carry On* humour, Seddon & Pursall had a proven track record for film writing, notably penning three of the Margaret Rutherford/Miss Marple films for MGM. Other film writing credits include *The Longest Day*, *The Blue Max* and the classic, pseudo-Marple Terry-Thomas/Eric Sykes black comedy *Kill or Cure* (director George Pollock, composer Ron Goodwin for MGM). With a cast including Dennis Price, Lionel Jeffries and Peter Butterworth it had to be good.

After filming *England*, Diana Langton was asked to step into Barbara Windsor's shoes when she starred in the ITV resurrection of *The Rag Trade*, with ever-present star and fellow *England* sufferer, Peter Jones.

Peter's role of the desperately unfunny Brigadier was originally offered to Kenneth Williams. However,

due to other work commitments during the three-week shooting schedule for the role, Kenneth turned down the film and Peter Jones agreed to go through the motions. During the evenings Peter was in Ludlow, rehearsing Polonius in *Hamlet* - talk about the contrasts of the acting profession!

Despite prominent thanks to the Imperial War Museum for the authentic World War II gun, this film was one of the most expensive of the series, costing over £250,000 to make. The previous average cost had been £200,000 and for *England* no one was on the top regular team member wage packet of £5,000 (usually reserved for Williams and James).

The Rogers/Thomas partnership regularly earned £15,000 for the actual filming and each took a healthy percentage of the profits. A top rock group also invested money in the production of *England* and rumours spread that it was the disbanded Beatles' firm 'Apple'.

England was so poorly received by the public that some cinemas screened it for less than three days. It only recovered its production cost after extensive television sales and international release.

Eric Rogers, having scored the previous 21 films, refused to work on *England* because of Peter Rogers' insistence on cutting back the budget. Instead of the 40-piece orchestra which Eric was used to, the producer would stretch to only 20 musicians. Declining the post, Eric Rogers invited his friend and *Porridge* composer Max Harris to take his place, though he would return for the next film.

Experienced editor, Alfred Roome, had retired at the end of 1975 and Richard Marden took his place.

Carol Hawkins, a fine Carry Oner in *Abroad*, *Behind* and several of the television shows, was offered the featured role played by Tricia Newby in *England*. Carol turned down the role because of its nudity content and sailed into the frantic farce of *Not Now Comrade* with Leslie Phillips, where her stripper persona lost her clothes but never her dignity.

The British Board of Film Censors originally gave *England* an 'AA' certificate, but Rogers, fearful of losing his younger and most loyal audience, made some subtle cuts and got the rating lowered to the more usual 'A'.

Before filming began on the new production, Rogers and Thomas made a rare excursion into the

The master at work: Gerald Thomas advises *Carry On* newcomers Melvyn Hayes and Patrick Mower during the making of *Carry On England*.

cinema and watched a film together - the hugely successful *Confessions of a Driving Instructor* - which prompted the two to inject more risque qualities to the *Carry Ons*. Bad move folks!

Look out for...

Despite the fact that the cameo appearances of Peter Butterworth and Joan Sims seem to have been grafted onto the script in order to include some familiar faces, they do share one memorable comic moment together. The cowardy Butterworth, desperately trying to impress the bemused Peter Jones, agrees to a bit of unarmed combat with Joan's woman of steel. Peter's defeated pleas are priceless!

Julian Holloway turned in his last supporting contribution to the *Carry Ons* and makes it a fitting farewell with a few brief scenes as the bombastic army doctor, prescribing asprins for all the mock illnesses from the troops and quickly swallowing some himself on the sight of Diana Langton. Injecting an air of tongue-in-cheek innuendo with Connor and Davies, Julian is effectively paired with a notable cameo of attractive disbelief from Linda Hooks.

Also of note in the supporting cast are an effective few lines of cynical rebuke from Patricia Franklin as the canteen cook.

The major link with *Sergeant* is Windsor Davies' gleeful display at the training exercise, notably during the swinging on the rope and rifle practice. Davies' well-timed, 'No, no, that it not the way!', throughout the feeble efforts of Mower and co. is very effective.

The stirring opening credits, blessed with Max Harris' patriotic theme and the image of a Union Jack, form an impressive beginning to this proudly British movie. Harris even continues the trend of Rogers' musical gags with a few bars of 'Run, Rabbit, Run' during the bayonet sequence.

Carry On memories

'I only did one *Carry On* film - *Carry On England* - but I was thrilled to be able to say - "I made one of them!" My lasting memory about making *Carry On England* was the way the film was shot! No clever key-hole shots - the director just pointed the camera at the actors and let the "clowns" do the "funnies".'
Melvyn Hayes

'Peter Rogers decided to broaden the style of comedy. I always thought that everything should be left to the imagination. *Carry On England* went just over the edge. It was less like family entertainment. Myself and the other regulars in the film were very concerned during the scene where the girls take their tops off. I had understood that the audience wouldn't see anything and that the camera would pan to Kenneth Connor's comic expression - which is funny. They went too far and the comedy was lost.'
Jack Douglas

A Peter Rogers Production

CARRY ON ENGLAND

Captain S. Melly **KENNETH CONNOR**
Sgt. Maj. 'Tiger' Bloomer **WINDSOR DAVIES**
Sgt. Len Able **PATRICK MOWER** Sgt. Tilly Willing **JUDY GEESON**
Bombadier Ready **JACK DOUGLAS** Brigadier **PETER JONES**
Pte. Alice Easy **DIANE LANGTON** Gunner Shorthouse **MELVYN HAYES**
Major Carstairs **PETER BUTTERWORTH**
Pte. Jennifer Ffoukes-Sharpe **JOAN SIMS** Major Butcher **JULIAN HOLLOWAY**
Captain Bull **DAVID LODGE** Gunner Shaw **LARRY DANN**
Gunner Owen **BRIAN OSBORNE**
Melly's Driver **JOHNNY BRIGGS** Corp. Cook **PATRICIA FRANKLIN**
Nurse **LINDA HOOKS**
Officer **JOHN CARLIN** Freda **VIVIENNE JOHNSON**
Officer **MICHAEL NIGHTINGALE**
Gunner Hiscocks **JEREMY CONNOR** Gunner Parker **RICHARD OLLY**
Gunner Thomas **PETER BANKS** Gunner Drury **RICHARD BARTLETT**
Gunner Childs **BILLY J. MITCHELL**
Gunner Sharpe **PETER QUINCE** Gunner Gale **PAUL TOTHILL**
Pte. Murray **TRICIA NEWBY**
Pte. Evans **LOUISE BURTON** Pte. Edwards **JEANNIE COLLINGS**
Pte. Carter **BARBARA HAMPSHIRE** Pte. Taylor **LINDA REGAN**
A.T.S. **BARBARA ROSENBLAT**

Screenplay by **David Pursall & Jack Seddon**
Music composed & conducted by **Max Harris**
Poster tag-line - 'It's the biggest bang of the war!'

Production Manager **Roy Goddard** Art Director **Lionel Couch**
Editor **Richard Marden**
Director of Photography **Ernest Steward B.S.C.**
Camera Operator **Godfrey Godar**
Wardrobe **Vi Murray & Don Mothersill** Casting Director **John Owen**
Stills Cameraman **Ken Bray**
Make-up **Geoffrey Rodway**
Sound Recordists **Danny Daniel & Gordon McCallum**
Continuity **Marjorie Lavelly** Hairdresser **Stella Rivers**
Costume Designer **Courtenay Elliott**
Set Dresser **Donald Picton** Dubbing Editor **Pat Foster**
Assistant Editor **Jack Gardner**
Assistant Director **Jack Causey** Titles **G.S.E. Ltd.**
Processed by **Rank Film Laboratories**
Our Grateful Thanks Are Due To The Imperial War Museum
For The Loan Of The Gun
Producer **Peter Rogers** Director **Gerald Thomas**

A 1976 Rank Organisation Release through Fox/Rank Distributions Ltd.
'A' Cert. Colour Running time - 89 mins. 8,000ft

THAT'S CARRY ON

Bearing in mind the radical changes to the *Carry On* style introduced in the previous film, this compilation of the innuendo-laden glories of the classic movies was a timely and much welcomed feature-length salute. To use the tag-line of the film's inspiration, *That's Entertainment* - 'Boy, do we need it now!'.

The sequel to this MGM blockbuster had been released just before the *Carry On* treatment, and while Hollywood could boast Fred Astaire and Gene Kelly, Pinewood rejoiced in the company of Kenneth Williams and Barbara Windsor. A fine tribute to the much lamented Sid James and the priceless memories of past *Carry On* glories, the film remains the ultimate *Carry On* compilation, awash with all the true milestones in the series' history. From the classic dining room sequence (*Khyber*), Charlie Hawtrey's bayonet practice (*Sergeant*), shower scenes from both *Constable* and *Abroad* to *Nurse's* daffodil gag and the 'infamy' by-play from *Cleo*, it includes every gem to form the definitive 90-minute package of the series' highlights. Importantly, the linking dialogue by Tony Church is clever, entertaining, risque and accurate. For one of the only times, the number of films is correctly given (28 at the time), the team's crowning glories are praised with fitting innuendo and even the number of Sid's wives as Henry VIII is given as eight (incorporating both Joan Sims and Barbara Windsor, who were additions to his widely credited six!).

For the introductory job, Williams and Windsor were the perfect choice, remaining at the time the best loved Carry Oners, and also having well defined and television exposed comic *personalities* rather than being exclusively actors. Their delivery and confident presentation provides a likable and enjoyable comic partnership, with delightful pieces of spontaneous wit and camping, notably in the introduction of *Screaming's* clips: 'I've been in some dark holes myself in *Carry On Screaming!*'/Windsor: 'Oh, which part did you play?'/'Just a bit part... I did the

biting!'. Kenneth's facial expression and open-mouthed amazement is marvellous. Barbara looks stunning throughout the film, and shines with cheeky humour, affectionate memories of Sid and bucketfuls of corny innuendo.

The films are shown in more-or-less chronological order. However, to wet the appetites of the *Carry On*-starved audiences, the first films covered are the Anglo to Rank cross-over movies: *Head, Camel* and *Doctor*. After a flash of Frankie Howerd wit and mad medical goings-on, the scene fades to black and white, a screaming train shoots into view and that very first classic moment with Bob Monkhouse and Kenneth Connor is remembered. The seven black-and-white films are dealt with together and suddenly it's back to colour for *Cruising, Jack* and a complete run of the movies. Only twice does the chronological sequence alter, firstly with the out-of-context and misused *Convenience* sequence, merely to capture a few lines of unsubtle charm from Sid James to Joan Sims and to heighten the agonizing situation of Kenneth Williams' eagerness to spend a penny. As in Frank Sinatra's introduction of the first MGM compilation, the final segment is given over to a celebration of the best clip. In Hollywood's case it's *An American in Paris*, at Pinewood it's *Carry On... Up The Khyber*.

The only movie missing completely, apart from mention as a statistic, is *England* - certainly not still on general release at the time of *That's Carry On*, but importantly, for various reasons, still very fresh in the audience's memory. Perhaps this is the Rogers/Thomas partnership wiping the slate clean, giving a nod of respect to Sid and establishing the heritage of feel-good *Carry On* for a possible new start - as Kenneth says: 'It's not all over!'. As the best tribute to the series it's a masterpiece; it's also a perfect exercise in how to make a new *Carry On* film with a couple of days' shooting in a projectionist's room and some hasty re-editing of old movies. The newly resurrected series *was* very short-lived, but this compilation was a good try at drumming up declining *Carry On* loyalty.

Best performance

With just two new performances to choose from and with all respect to Barbara Windsor, this is Kenneth Williams' film. Rich with the outrageous delivery and linking style of his successful *International Cabaret* days on television, this is Williams the super cult, delighting in re-living past glories and re-examining the early days of black-and-white mugging and cries of 'Charming!'. Joining in with Barbara to create a tongue-in-cheek, suggested sex scene in the initial, pitch black sequence - 'You wiggle and I'll shove - we're nearly there!', Williams minces and groans with fine timing. The running gag concerning Kenneth's desperate need for relief spans years of old *Carry On* movies, and with his agonized facial expressions, comic disdain and 'little boy' characterization, it is a masterclass in overplaying comic situations to perfection. This is the Williams camp persona of 24 earlier films captured in one roller-coaster performance.

Favourite bit

In terms of patriotic poetry and pride in the *Carry On* ethos, the finest moment comes with Kenneth Williams' heart-felt and sincerely delivered comic monologue on the power of being British at the film's close. He grabs the limelight and despite the shameless running of the credits over his speech, Williams looks deep into the camera with intense feeling and passion: 'That's the trouble with the world today. They haven't the courage to Carry On like that brave few up there. But never fear, they'll always be ordinary, decent men and women ready to step in and fill the ranks... and all the other cinemas throughout this septic isle. Ah, the far flung Dominions and the Majestics and the Regals and the Gaumonts with their great organs coming up out of the floor - the mighty wurlitzers, not to mention the Granadas and the Roxys and the Ionics and the raviollis and the savaloys and the pease pudding. One empire may have gone but another will spring up to take its place, nay twins or even triplets. And we shall Carry On beyond these shores in Thailand and Iceland, in Indistan and Pakistan, in the far away Burmese and the take away Chinese. We shall make them laugh on the beaches and in the Middle East, in the front stalls and up the back, and the back stalls as well! Yes for we are that... that precious few, that happy band that is forever England. I don't speak for one, I speak for all... Give us the fools and we will finish the job. For in a corner of every foreign field we'll leave a little something... which is part of our national heritage!'. Full of flamboyant Churchillian elements and complemented by Eric Rogers' stirring 'Cock O' The North' theme from

Khyber, it is a masterly close to this tongue-in-cheek but sincere celebration of the *Carry Ons*.

Did you know?

This was the final Peter Rogers production distributed by Rank. A co-production between Rank and EMI (Cohen's re-shaped Anglo), this film was poorly received at the box office and followed a couple of poorly patronized *Carry On* movies. Following the final major hit with *Dick*, audience figures began to decline with *Behind*, while *England* was taken off at some cinemas after just three days! While Rogers condemned Rank for treating his films like poor relations with limited distribution and allowing poster designs and advertising for the films to decline in quality, Rank were distressed at the series' failure to attract the audiences. Rank was happy to back a critically condemned series of films while they were making money. When they started to fail at the box office it was time to let go. Peter Rogers took his winning formula to an independent company.

Indeed, for *That's Carry On*, you can see Peter Rogers' point. While every inch an 'A' attraction, the film was quietly released as a support picture to *Golden Rendezvous*, an Alastair Maclean spy film with Richard Harris and John Carradine.

Bresslaw, Silvers, Sims, Williams, James, Jacques, Windsor, Dale and Hawtrey herald the pick of the crop on the *That's Carry On* poster.

The film was tied in with Kenneth Eastaugh's *Carry On Book*, which actually features on the small, B-movie space for *That's Carry On* on the poster. The rest was made up of black-and-white resurrections of past poster caricatures, highlighting the main stars of the series: Charles Hawtrey (*Convenience*), Hattie Jacques (*Loving*), Sid James and Kenneth Williams (both in *Again Doctor*). It was a sad end for the association with Rank which reached back to 1966. Thankfully, a colourful poster for the film was spartanly available with the legend: 'Everyone who's anyone is in it... RIGHT IN IT!'

Look out for...

This is an essential document for any film historian, capturing the essence of *Carry On* in neatly collected chunks. Look out for your all-time favourite bit, it's bound to be there or at least something just as good, as Groucho might say. It also contains the most impressive cast of British comedy actors in any one film - count 'em!

Carry On memories

'I worked as assistant editor on seventeen *Carry On* films and edited *That's Carry On*. It was mainly culled from sections from the other films. In fact, Gerald Thomas and myself sat there for about six weeks looking at every single *Carry On* film - sometimes three a day! The writer was nearly always Talbot Rothwell and, of course, you get these characters coming out with the same jokes picture after picture. It always worked and some of the critics used to say it was all like seaside postcard humour. Every joke had a double meaning so it was up to the individual if they laughed! If they were thinking of the dirty side of things then that was up to them! Just for a laugh, I remember Peter Rogers putting a load of these seaside postcards up the corridors at Pinewood where people put stills up of their films. *That's Carry On* was basically us picking out what we thought were the best sections. In fact we made the mistake of joining them all up before editing and sitting in a theatre one

day to watch it. It was mind-numbing - it lasted six hours! Eventually, we whittled it down and then spent a day and a half shooting in one of the projection boxes at Pinewood with Kenny Williams and Barbara Windsor.'

Jack Gardner

A Peter Rogers Production

THAT'S CARRY ON

Introduced by
KENNETH WILLIAMS & BARBARA WINDSOR

Featuring from the Carry On archives:
ERIC BARKER AMANDA BARRIE SUSAN BEAUMONT JOHN BLUTHAL
BERNARD BRESSLAW
PETER BUTTERWORTH GERALD CAMPION ESMA CANNON TOM CLEGG
ROY CASTLE
CYRIL CHAMBERLAIN JOHN CLIVE KENNETH CONNOR
KENNETH COPE HARRY H. CORBETT BERNARD CRIBBINS JIM DALE
WINDSOR DAVIES ED DEVEREAUX
ANGELA DOUGLAS SALLY DOUGLAS JACK DOUGLAS SHIRLEY EATON
FENELLA FIELDING
PETER GILMORE FRED GRIFFITHS ANITA HARRIS WILLIAM HARTNELL
IMOGEN HASSALL
CHARLES HAWTREY PERCY HERBERT JOAN HICKSON JULIAN HOLLOWAY
FRANKIE HOWERD WILFRID HYDE-WHITE HATTIE JACQUES JUNE JAGO
SIDNEY JAMES
GERTAN KLAUBER ROSALIND KNIGHT DILYS LAYE VALERIE LEON
HARRY LOCKE
JIMMY LOGAN TERENCE LONGDON KENNY LYNCH VICTOR MADDERN
ELSPETH MARCH
BETTY MARSDEN JULIET MILLS WARREN MITCHELL
BOB MONKHOUSE MICHAEL NIGHTINGALE MARGARET NOLAN
RICHARD O'CALLAGHAN JULIAN ORCHARD
BILL OWEN LANCE PERCIVAL LESLIE PHILLIPS JACKI PIPER TED RAY
PATSY ROWLANDS
TONY SAGAR TERRY SCOTT PHIL SILVERS JOAN SIMS
MADELINE SMITH ELKE SOMMER
SUSAN STEPHEN MARIANNE STONE JIMMY THOMPSON
JUNE WHITFIELD
KENNETH WILLIAMS BARBARA WINDSOR

Original Screenplay by **Tony Church**
Archive material by **Talbot Rothwell, Norman Hudis, Sid Colin & Dave Freeman**
Music Arranged by **Eric Rogers**
Poster tag-line - 'Everyone who's anyone is in it...Right in it!!!! -
The best gags from the Carry On series'

Director of Photography **Tony Imi B.S.C.** Editor **Jack Gardner**
Production Manager **Roy Goddard**
Dubbing Editor **Christopher Lancaster**
Sound Recordists **Danny Daniel & Ken Barker**
Titles **G.S.E. Ltd** Producer **Peter Rogers** Director **Gerald Thomas**

A 1977 Rank/EMI film released through the Rank Organisation in 1978 'A' Cert.
Colour/Black & White
Running time - 95 mins. 8,524ft

CARRY ON
EMMANNUELLE

It was back to basics in more ways than one with this, the final film in the linear 20-year run of the original series. It's a return to innocent sexual banter and tongue-in-cheek innuendo; even though sex makes up the bulk of the film's plot it is treated with comic awareness and not smutty leering. Certainly not the immoral comedy that contemporary critics dubbed it, *Emmannuelle* was long unavailable to the general public due to a legal problem over its video certificate rating. The film returns to the tried and tested corny gags and enjoyably larger-than-life performances from its experienced team. When Philip French wrote that the film was 'put together with an almost palpable contempt for its audience. This relentless sequence of badly written, badly timed dirty jokes is surely one of the most morally and aesthetically offensive pictures to emerge from a British studio', I think he missed the point! Although there are several sequences of dreadfully handled innuendo, with some of the coy sexual couplings of Suzanne Danielle and the various big-wigs around London simply unbelievable in their banality, there is enough downbeat humour and spirited playing from the team to keep this film reassuringly in the *Carry On* style.

Kenneth Williams, mincing around the production as a ferociously camp, impotent and flagrantly over-the-top French ambassador, gives a stunning star performance complete with appalling gags and over-played continental angst. It's a performance which goes beyond the boundaries of mere comedy acting and ends up as a parody of a parody of his previous camp personality. It's wonderful stuff and rife with tongue-in-cheek sex references and flashes of Williams' bare bum (a throw back to both *Constable* and *Behind* and, as *Film & Filming* commented, 'a treat for which I'm not sure the cinema audiences are altogether ready!'). Williams goes into overdrive, throwing innuendo-encrusted lines all over the place, resurrecting the snake sequence from *Jungle* and spending the majority of the film in limp-wrist-

ed mode. Only at the close does he successfully re-bed his delicious wife and partake in the joyous fun and games with his old colleagues. Suzanne Danielle is certainly the ideal Emmannuelle and gives an impressive and stylish performance, swaying gracefully through the over-the-top camp and innuendo with a delightfully casual attitude to her flamboyant sexual activities.

However, the real heart of the film is provided by Williams' class-aware, sexually open below-stairs staff. While Danielle gradually sleeps her way across London, the comic sparring and perfectly-timed innuendo from the staff is inspired - not surprising, when they are made up of four *Carry On* survivors from the golden age: Kenneth Connor, Peter Butterworth, Joan Sims and Jack Douglas. Connor, all cockney charm and sexual antics, is the spirit of Sid James haunting the old Pinewood set. Full of patriotic pride, lusty jokes and constant talk about

What a pair! Kenneth Williams in gleeful mood with Suzanne Danielle - a publicity shot for *Carry On Emmannuelle*.

sex, he contrasts brilliantly with the prim and proper dignity of Sims as a po-faced, stern, anti-fun figure who eventually throws herself into sexual enjoyment. Peter Butterworth shuffles around the place in an inspired portrayal of dithering old age, struggling to hear and see the action going on around him, while Jack Douglas gives his finest film performance as the upright figure of authority, Lyons the butler. For the only time in the film series, Douglas moves successfully away from his jittering 'Alf' persona (which is only resurrected briefly during the London Zoo sequence), and presents a straight performance of respectability and comic wit. Introduced with a dead-pan *Hellzapoppin'* reaction to Danielle's line 'I am your mistress', Jack goes into a fine torrent of frustrated self regret and anxious panic. 'Oh my God! I knew she'd catch up with me one day, it's my own fault. Wait a minute, what am I talking about? I haven't got a mistress!' Though finally getting embroiled in the sexual goings-on and low-brow humour of the film, Douglas moves at a sedate and leisurely pace through a memorable leading role. It's a masterpiece of under-played innuendo. There is much comic mileage from Danielle's very foreignness: like Elke Sommer in *Behind*, she continually mispronounces words for innuendo effect - note her continual reference to Jack as Loins! - although the idea lacks the sparkle of the 1975 film simply because Danielle is acting foreign misunderstanding while Sommer was actually living it.

Thus, all the best moments come with the experienced comic banter between the four *Carry On* servants, even when they drag through a lengthy re-examination of their favourite amorous experiences! Sims' story boasts a wordless romance with Victor Maddern in a laundrette and creates a touching, sub-*Brief Encounter* British affair while Connor steals the honours with a memorably seedy tale involving Claire Davenport, Norman Mitchell and a wardrobe. A sequence of relentless smut and awful gags, it ends with Kenneth standing in the collapsed piece of furniture and crying 'Ooooh! me hangers!'. It's that sort of script! Parts are so gloriously awful that they make you shudder, but the performances enhance the sub-Rothwellian innuendo with endearing characters and richly delivered dialogue. The audience knows it's in good company, gamefully playing the game for the last time and having a ball.

Best performance

In a cast full of outstanding comic turns, the finest must be Peter Butterworth's delightful aged boot-boy, Richmond. Staggering around the sexually-orientated antics with an air of eccentric disbelief, Peter desperately tries to get involved in Danielle's sexual

life-style (and, indeed, if the script is to be believed, succeeds!). After a slow start, the film instantly picks up when Joan Sims and Peter Butterworth wander on to set to see what's going on and Peter cups his ear to improve his hearing: the obvious innuendo references about the sexy figure of Suzanne Danielle and things looking up, are well played and memorably repeated by his deaf old bumbler. Although only 59 at the time of filming, Peter staggered with convincing weariness, forming a fine partnership with the ageing but still active Kenneth Connor: 'You for coffee?'/'No thanks, I'm staying here!'. When Peter recalls his war-time experiences, despite the tongue-in-cheek, comic look at the war, his chillingly moved and thoughtful delivery brings a dignified and well-rounded performance to the slap-stick camp of the movie. The flashback sequence, all cinematic snogging and drag humour, has Peter's warm energy and spirited delivery at its centre - creating a fresh-faced squaddie persona, thankful to survive the German advances and rush into a long-term relationship with a shapely French Miss. While the awful gags flow like water and the priceless actors mug with wonderful effect, Peter Butterworth quietly goes through the motions, adding bits of visual humour and ad-libbed movements to his role, notably when Connor asks what's going on and Butterworth tries to act out the sexual carryings-on with subtle mime (Connor gets the added laugh with his 'Here, hold me hat!' thanks to Peter's spirited support). Peter Butterworth steals the film.

Peter Butterworth gamely going through the motions for the last time - *Carry On Emmannuelle*.

Favourite bit

Naturally the highlight of the film concerns all five team members, and stands as one of the most purely concentrated moments of *Carry On* comedy. When Suzanne Danielle arrives home unexpectedly, she expects a warm welcome from husband Williams. Her energetic but unsuccessful seductive techniques lead to a shocked but excited Jack Douglas peering through the bedroom door keyhole. Joan Sims creeps up behind him, attacks him, condemns him and then joins him: it's a world of 'what the butler saw' gags, sexual antics in high places, sexual antics in low places and ageing Carry Oners having a good time. Douglas: 'Oh, Richmond. I think you ought to look at this!'/Sims: 'Do you think he ought to at his age!'/'It might jog his memory'/Butterworth: 'Ah! What am I going to see?'/'Well it certainly won't be *The Muppet Show*/'Is it... is it *Starsky and Hutch?*/'If you ask me it's more like 'Starkers and Crutch!'. Oh, if only all the film could have been so wonderfully corny and typically tongue-in-cheek. The coy innuendo of the British eccentricities is counterbalanced by the sexual antics of Williams and Danielle - 'You've broken it!'/'Oo, la, la, turn over and let me have a look!'/'No, no, not that, my back!' - while the lusty Kenneth Connor joins in for a last-minute belly laugh: 'Snow White meets the incredible shrinking man... I think she's knackered him, ah well, back on the job!'.

Did you know?

Nobody knows why the extra 'n' appears in the leading role's name: 'misspelt as well as misconceived' was critic Derek Malcolm's comment. However, the poster cleverly prints *Emmannuelle* in the typeface for the original film and has *Carry On* in the big, bold, saucy block capitals per usual. Instead of Sylvia Kristel, sitting cross-legged on a wicker chair, the *Carry On* version has Kenneth Williams in the same pose holding a pair of union jack pants!

Following the breakaway from Rank, Peter Rogers found independent backing for *Emmannuelle* from Cleves Investments Ltd. and formed a production company called, suitably enough, Thirtieth Films. It was distributed by Hemdale, who had previously handled the Peter Cook/Dudley Moore/Kenneth Williams comedy *The Hound of the Baskervilles*. Later productions would include the Jim Dale/John Gielgud farce *Scandalous* and the Christopher Lee werewolf flick *The Howling II*.

The perfect *Carry On* glamour girl, Suzanne Danielle, enjoyed a long relationship with *England* star Patrick Mower and starred opposite Cannon & Ball in the 1983 Val Guest film *The Boys in Blue*. The cast also included *Emmannuelle's* Jack Douglas.

Australian writer Lance Peters had enjoyed success as a leading television writer in his own country before moving to London in 1974. Commissioned to write *Emmannuelle*, he followed the innuendo-filled style of Rothwell but injected a lamentable reference to his homeland in the shape of body-builder Harry Hernia, played with painful lacklustre by Howard Nelson.

Though condemned for its pornographic nature, the film has no more flashes of nudity than several previous *Carry Ons*. Apart from several naked rear shots of Suzanne Danielle the film is pretty tame. Barbara Windsor showed about the same in *Again Doctor* and *Henry*, and the nearest *Emmannuelle* gets to any serious coupling is as Suzanne Danielle shows her legs and kisses a few footballers. Unless you are shocked by the sight of a young footballer removing his top then I think the film's a safe family movie. However, it was given an 'AA' certificate and, unlike with *England*, Peter Rogers was not willing to cut material to have the certificate lowered. Importantly, the rating denied access to the *Carry Ons'* crop of young followers (their biggest audience group being the 8-17 year olds) and the film proved disastrously unsuccessful at the box office. While it tried to follow the *Confessions...* pattern of youthful sex, it didn't go far enough to attract the '18' audience. However, it was a bit too far for loyal *Carry On* fans and, thus, fell between two stools.

The seed that caused the film's bad press was probably planted by a widespread but misinformed rumour that Barbara Windsor had walked off the set in disgust. In reality Barbara was never even on set - she had been offered the briefest of guest appearances as the ideal sexual fantasy in dream sequences for Peter Butterworth, Kenneth Connor and Jack Douglas. Unimpressed, Barbara turned down the role and these scenes eventually developed into the favourite amorous adventures flashback sequences. However, the national newspapers seized on the story and branded *Emmannuelle* pornography from the word go. Compared to earlier films, the nudity is more pivotal to the plot, but basically it's just Danielle clasping her breasts in the best Windsor tradition and a quick flash from Tricia Newby to raise Williams' hopes in the company of his doctor (Albert Moses).

The stigma remained, for when Leslie Halliwell discussed *Emmannuelle* in his 1987 book, *Double Take and*

Fade Away, he commented that it 'was so badly made as to be an insult; and so lacking in jokes as to seem in worse taste than the porno movies which it painfully tried to parody'.

Kenneth Williams was dreadfully unhappy about the film's script and continually turned Gerald Thomas' offer down. Several re-writes were undertaken in order to coax Williams into the cast and eventually, out of friendship for the makers, he relented. Kenneth received £6,000 for the film: his highest *Carry On* wage packet. *Emmannuelle*'s complete budget was in excess of £320,000.

A businessman as well as a film-maker, Peter Rogers had always maintained that once the films started to lose money that would be the end of it. True to his word, he pulled the plug after this entry, though rumours of the 31st film began almost immediately.

Look out for...

Kenneth Connor slyly embraces the original source for the parody when he discusses sexual antics with the gang and tells Suzanne Danielle that 'One day they'll be queueing up for the film rights of yours!'. The initial aeroplane seduction scene is a direct parody from the 1974 *Emmanuelle* original.

Larry Dann takes on the mantle of the bumbling romantic lead typical of Jim Dale, but injects a more vindictive streak which dictates he plays away from the main core community spirit. The role of his mother provides a brief but treasurable few scenes for an over-protective Beryl Reid.

The opening Bee-Gees parody, 'Love Crazy' was written by Kenny Lynch and performed by Masterplan. A clever, innuendo-based opening song, it was released as a single by Satril but enjoyed no chart success.

During Tricia Newby's taxing role as the nurse, Eric Rogers resurrects the Jenny Cox stripper theme from *Behind*.

Eric Barker gives a wordless cameo of sexual frustration as a bumbling old Army General, resurrecting memories of sparring with Williams and Connor in 1958's *Sergeant*. A further link to the first movie is the editor, Peter Boita, whose only *Carry On* film credits were the first and the thirtieth.

Henry McGee turns in a superb comic cameo as the pseudo-David Frost television interviewer, Harold Hump ('Hello, good evening, good night and welcome'), who finally succumbs to the charms of Suzanne Danielle on air. The spirited reaction of Kenneth Connor is outstanding.

Carry On memories

'I was delighted with my straight role in *Carry On Emmanuelle* - it was a valuable acting lesson! Suzanne Danielle was delightful to work with in that - we got on awfully well. We had one scene when I handed her the phone. I'd got the phone wire twisted round my neck so when she took the phone from me and reached back into the bed I was pulled towards her! I was tied up so I actually went right into her breast and Gerry Thomas said, "Keep it in" - so we did!'
Jack Douglas

Cleves Investments Ltd. Presents A Peter Rogers Production
A Gerald Thomas Film

CARRY ON EMMANNUELLE

Emile Prevert **KENNETH WILLIAMS**   Emmanuelle Prevert **SUZANNE DANIELLE**
Leyland **KENNETH CONNOR**   Lyons **JACK DOUGLAS**   Mrs Dangle **JOAN SIMS**
Richmond **PETER BUTTERWORTH**   Theodore Valentine **LARRY DANN**
Mrs Valentine **BERYL REID**   Nurse in Surgery **TRICIA NEWBY**
Doctor **ALBERT MOSES**   Harold Hump **HENRY McGEE**
Harry Hernia **HOWARD NELSON**   Blonde in Pub **CLAIRE DAVENPORT**
BBC Newcaster **TIM BRINTON**   ITN Newscaster **CORBETT WOODALL**
Prime Minister **ROBERT DORNING**   US Ambassador **BRUCE BOA**
Ancient General **ERIC BARKER**
Man in Laundrette **VICTOR MADDERN**   'Drunken Sailor' **NORMAN MITCHELL**
Admiral of the Fleet **JACK LYNN**   Police Commissioner **MICHAEL NIGHTINGALE**
Lord Chief Justice **LLEWELLYN REES**   Arabian Official **STEVE PLYTAS**
Cynical Lady **JOAN BENHAM**   Nurse in Hospital **MARIANNE MASKELL**
Girl at Zoo **LOUISE BURTON**   Emigration Officer **DINO SHAFFEK**
Customs Officer **DAVID HART**   German Soldier **GERTAN KLAUBER**
Sentry **MALCOLM JOHNS**   French Parson **JOHN CARLIN**
Featuring **GUY WARD**   **JAMES FAGAN**   **JOHN HALLETT**
DEBORAH BRAYSHAW   **SUZANNA EAST**   **BRUCE WYLLIE**
PHILLIP CLIFTON   **STANLEY McGEAGH**   **NEVILLE WARE**
NICK WHITE   **JANE NORMAN**   **BILL HUTCHINSON**

Original Screenplay by **Lance Peters**
Music composed & conducted by **Eric Rogers**
Song: 'Love Crazy' by **Kenny Lynch**
Sung by **Masterplan**
Poster tag-line - 'When it comes to foreign affairs it's...Carry On Emmanuelle'

Director of Photography **Alan Hume B.S.C.**   Editor **Peter Boita**
Art Director **Jack Shampan**
Production Manager **Roy Goddard G.F.P.E.**   Camera Operator **Godfrey Godar**
Make-up **Robin Grantham**
Executive Producer for Cleves Investment Ltd. **Donald Langdon**
Assistant Directors **Gregory Dark & Mike Higgins**
Sound Recordists **Danny Daniel & Otto Snel**   Continuity **Marjorie Lavelly**
Wardrobe **Margaret Lewin**   Stills Cameraman **Ken Bray**
Hairdresser **Betty Sheriff**
Costume Designer **Courtenay Elliott**   Set Dresser **John Hoesli**
Assistant Editor **Jack Gardner**
Dubbing Editor **Peter Best**   Titles & Opticals **G.S.E. Ltd.**
Processed by **Technicolor Ltd.**
Producer **Peter Rogers**   Director **Gerald Thomas**

A 1978 Hemdale Release 'AA' Cert. Colour Running time - 88 mins. 7,916ft

CARRY ON
COLUMBUS

In the 14 years since *Emmannuelle*, far too many *Carry On* regulars had joined old Sid in the green room upstairs. This was the one chance I had of watching the filming of a *Carry On* at Pinewood (being just 7 years old when the thirtieth film was made!), and despite containing heaps of rubbish and many miscast performers, *Columbus* isn't as awful as it could have been. Not quite, at least!

Following in the footsteps of a series which had reached international cult status, this film had far too much to live up to. All the old stereotypes are kept intact, corny gags are tossed around like tasty *hors d'oeuvres* and informed series fans will spot several resurrections of past glories: the snake charmer sequence (*Spying*), the soaking from the skies (*Henry*), the primitive native settlement (*Up The Jungle*), the low-life bar with drugged drink (*Follow That Camel*). However, the only major on-screen link with those halcyon days is the stunning title performance from a hugely welcome Jim Dale, strolling through the action and awful jokes with a confidence and timing far superior to anything else in the picture. Indeed, Jim is the only original Carry Oner to get any sort of look-in, with the only other fully-fledged member of the team to jump aboard the sinking ship being Jack Douglas. Shamelessly relegated to one decent joke and a few bemused looks, Douglas struggles to make any impact. Frankie Howerd was cast as the forlorn King of Spain, but the role was more cramped than camp, and seemingly interchangeable with any past *Carry On* type. The part was eventually blessed with the raffish sarcasm of Leslie Phillips. The role amounted to very little, but Leslie, returning after an amazing 32 years, injected some priceless timing and bemused sighs to milk maximum comic effect. He is partnered by his girlfriend from *Nurse*, June Whitfield, and the two have a couple of scenes which redeem the dross between. Whitfield: 'I have seen his testimonials!'/Phillips: 'Yes I'm sure you have!'. Meanwhile, Bernard Cribbins crops up in a major supporting turn to resurrect some glorious

memories with old co-star Jim Dale. Despite being hampered by a totally unfunny role, Cribbins brings a wonderful touch of easy-going cheerfulness to the movie and the early scenes with Dale create moments of pure *Carry On* enjoyment. Suddenly the film comes to life with vintage exchanges and totally convincing *Carry On* turns: the two-hander with Dale and Cribbins discussing 'the sea of gloom' and the arrangement for preparation, are priceless. Jon Pertwee, chucked into the adventure for a quick cough and a funny facial expression, is seemingly tacked on to add another familiar face, while poor old Peter Gilmore strolls in for one line and quickly strolls out again. And that, as they say, is it - just seven past stars of the series making a return. However, even though the majority of these have

The new world - Sara Crowe joins *Carry On* legend Jim Dale for some reheated innu-endo - a cracking publicity shot for *Carry On Columbus*.

minor parts with little narrative importance, their professionalism and knowledge of how to play low-brow comedy shines through every frame.

The script, full of holes as many of the movies were but bristling with some truly terrible jokes, was penned by experienced *Carry On* writer Dave Freeman. The best gags are culled from Rothwell's films or Freeman's past successes *Carry On Again Christmas* (Jim Dale's buried treasure speech just before his attempted execution) and *Carry On Laughing* (Sara Crowe displaying her concealed femininity under hypnosis). The rest is pretty feeble and untypical stuff: you certainly don't expect the Spanish Inquisition even if it is 1492 and Spain. The black-hooded religious nuts have a terrible sequence of embarrassingly unfunny chanting, while the one priceless moment concerning this particular narrative thread comes from the Jewish Bernard Cribbins refusing the ham sandwich because it's got no mustard on it. It's not earth-shatteringly hilarious, but Bernie's timid delivery and Jim Dale's quick response stands out as a *Carry On* beacon of light.

Naturally, like the previous films, *Columbus* looked to contemporary television stars, and, thus, to a fresh crop of younger talents, unfamiliar with the music-hall style of comedy. While the golden days had comic *actors* who had served their apprenticeship through stage and radio, the new film recruited

Rik Mayall flares his nostrils and over flows with Williamsisms in a *Carry On Columbus* publicity photograph. Did anything really change?

politically correct *comedians* with attitude. Without doubt, the talent boasted by *Columbus* is outstanding and the new cast, with respect and affection for the corny days of James' guffaws and Williams' camp, threw themselves into their roles. Paying tribute to the old team system, Sara Crowe strikes the perfect pitch of Barbara Windsor's sexuality, incorporating a wonderful recreation of the latter's harem dance from *Spying* and counterbalancing it with a fresh slant on Juliet Mills' performance from *Jack*. Camping through the film with deliciously self-aware bad jokes and fluttering eye-lids, her performance is good *Carry On* fun, while Alexei Sayle turns in an endearing nod to the hulking bumblings of Bresslaw. Both Rebecca Lacey (in a minor Windsor-esque flirt) and Daniel Peacock (a gritty criminal-type) provide well-acted and interesting character studies. Don Henderson injects sea-faring realism into his role, creating a delightful bit of suspicious by-play with Jim Dale.

The sad fact is that these performances are all but smothered by appallingly developed characterizations and a rather unhelpful lack of decent jokes. In the main, *Columbus* plays like a well-budgeted fans' convention film celebration of the series: the heart's in the right place but, despite the involvement of Rogers and Thomas, the whole thing lacks the magic touch of experience. Instead, it has the feel of the stereotyped view of *Carry On*: the new jokes are all school-boy smut and base innuendo, lacking the clever spirals of humour of Rothwell's work; the performances are totally over-the-top, lacking any warmth or emotion and the editing is sloppy and incoherent. Maureen Lipman wanders around in the background, tackling the nagging Joan Sims persona, but with a terribly underwritten role and outlandish and irritating facial contortions which make you want to sling a brick at the screen. Peter Richardson walks through his leading role in a trance and mistimes promising (albeit obvious) innuendo with alarming regularity ('And did he give you one!' delivered like a serious question!), while the romance with Holly Aird is mind-numbing banality. Nigel Planer's characterless delivery of a few lines in the first scene lacks the spark of comic originality of his *Young Ones* days. Clearly these are wonderful actors who are both professional and experienced: indeed, Planer and Richardson created the most inventive string of movie parodies of the last decade with *The Comic Strip*, while Lipman remains perhaps our most accomplished comic actress. Here, seemingly restricted by the *Carry On* style, they flounder on the shores of a witless script and uninspired presentation. All in all, it's a shameless waste of talent.

The Best of Times – Valerie Leon offers her services to a more than eager Charles Hawtrey
in *Carry On...Up the Khyber*

Above: 'Not before a meal...' Joan Sims is ready, willing and able in a classic *Carry On...Up the Khyber* pose

Right: Patriotic glory as Sid James wipes out the foreign johnnie in *Carry On...Up the Khyber*

Despite the bad elements, and there are many, the film does rejoice in several gems of Carry On comedy allowing the die-hard follower to give a big thumbs up. Of the new cast members, Julian Clary steals the limelight in a staggering resurrection of Charles Hawtrey camp, mincing throughout the sea-faring goings-on with a carefree casualness and a range of delightfully coloured costumes that Hawtrey would have killed for. He even includes 'Oh! hello!' as his opening line. Rich in glorious innuendo and delivering the lines with just the right degree of a knowing wink to the audience and total conviction in the dodgy story-line, Clary creates at least one masterpiece during the deserted galleon feast. Tucking in with birdish delicacy ('Full as an egg!') and enjoying some wonderfully coarse innuendo ('Could do with something hot inside me!'), he finally jumps into a spontaneous flamenco dance which is all too brief. Keith Allen, a superb comedian and an always watchable actor, grabs the memorial Peter Butterworth role with spirited relish and captures the essence of Carry On in a complex and beautifully played supporting part. Wandering around the ship threatening to renew his poisoning antics in his position as ship's cook, he injects his performance with a perfectly rounded characterization which informs even the most mundane and deadeningly unfunny lines with neat detail and endearing style. His cry of 'No, no, no - I was trying to kill the rats!' is a classic. Take my word for it! And finally, there is the gloriously flamboyant Rik Mayall, storming through the first sequence in flagrant Kenneth Williams mode, nostrils flaring all over the place and ever-widening eyes bringing lustre to the creaky old gags. In a superb duologue with Sara Crowe ('I want you to keep an eye on his doings!'... 'Be assured, I shall get my hands on it!'), that first sequence is a heart-warming demonstration that Carry On could still be alive and well with performers born after the series had began in 1958.

Indeed, contrary to most of the critics, I believe the first half of the film is littered with treasurable moments and clever sight gags from the experienced and hugely talented cast. It's a case of true pros grinning, bearing it and pulling a few moments of wonderfully low comedy out of the rubbish. The scenes on board ship with Jim Dale, Bernard Cribbins and Peter Richardson are relaxed, informal, well-acted and funny. The tongue-in-cheek homosexual references from Clary brilliantly contrast with the sour-faced Richard Wilson and even the under-employed Maureen Lipman grabs a few laughs. However, once the all-important destination of America is reached, that's about it. While critics reached for superlatives for the American cross-talk banter of Larry Miller and Charles Fleischer, the Carry On follower reached for the Khyber video. There's no doubt that the joke of the Brooklyn street-wise Indians having more brains than the supposed conquerors is promising. However the anti-Brit gags and continual incorporation of Americanisms replace the corny British gags of the early part of the movie with unsubtle digs at the British eccentrics. Unlike the tongue-in-cheek leg pulling of our idiosyncrasies in Rothwell's work where the Union Jack ruled and American natives turned out to be led by Charles Hawtrey, Columbus goes too far, leaving the supposed hero of Jim Dale a complete idiot. The magic just vanishes in the new world: Jim's out-of-character squashing of a huge, albeit fake, spider; the unconvincing and under-funded parody of Indiana Jones; the bemused reaction to tobacco. It's all a load of balls in more ways than one. In the end, Dale is fooled by fool's gold, but in a totally confusing ending (if you're as thick as I am and don't get it on the first two viewings - that Spanish Inquisition person who confiscates the fake gold from Phillips is Peter Richardson) the problem is resolved and Jim gets his girl.

It was a very brave try to breath new life into a series which had long since passed its peak, and whose firmly established team of comedy greats was largely spilt asunder. For fans it was one more film to enjoy and contained enough pleasant moments to make you glad it was made, but it must be said that the project was ill-conceived and made for all the wrong reasons. It was the end to a glorious comic collective that had spanned 34 years and remains a final salute to a British institution which suffered major losses in 1993. Jump on aboard for the last Carry On and leave all hope behind!

Best performance
It doesn't take a genius to work out that the film belongs completely to a powerhouse central performance from Jim Dale. On screen almost all the time, he creates a stunning piece of work from limited resources - the sign of a true film star. It's a performance full of notable sight gags, well delivered jokes with no redeeming features and energetic action injected into a film which would have sunk without him. Without doubt it's a true five Sid performance in a clear one Sid film. Though working beautifully with old colleagues like Bernard Cribbins, the key to Jim's success is his relaxed and effective work with the newcomers. He coaxes a dull but competent supporting turn from Peter Richardson and delights in some fine old world innuendo with Julian Clary and Keith Allen: 'Welfare Officer... take that man's ball off!'/'Which one!'. It's childish stuff but inspired. Jim, being the trooper that he is, injects

self-aware glee and knowing winks to the audience as he goes from one bad gag to another. Sparring with glamorous model, Sara Stockbridge when she reveals her future assignment, 'Michelangelo wants to do me up on the ceiling!', with a winning grin and twinkle in the eyes, Jim comes back with, 'Well you mind you hang onto something while you're up there!'. It's a lesson in playing low-comedy with affection and style. He delights in moments of all-embracing adventure, with wonderfully detailed tales of sea-faring fun and flamboyant efforts to drum up interest (plugging a host of freaks in an echo of his *Barnum* triumph helped by some suitable circus music on the soundtrack). While ending up with royal egg on his face, he still wins the day and gets the girl. Incorporating Kenneth Connor's military impatience and Sid's laugh, Jim embraces his position as the James of the 1990s *Carry On*. Rip-roaring through inferior material and having a whale of a time, he single-handedly holds the entire project together and provides a treasurable performance which must rank with the series' best. Sit back and enjoy!

Favourite bit

For me, the highlight comes very early and, inevitably, from Jim Dale. No Dave Freeman corn is needed as Jim delights in a priceless bit of sight humour. Struggling to lay out a map on his desk, he reaches for the weight and lets go of the map, reaches again and lets go again and then tries to hold the weight with his chin and bring it down on the map. Naturally the map rolls once more. Finally the weight is successfully placed on the map as the other side rolls back. It's Jim's first appearance and all's right with the *Carry On* world. Thank God it wasn't cut out.

Did you know?

On the first day of filming a *Carry On*, Gerald Thomas and Peter Rogers always shared a pot of caviar, while Rogers and the cast presented Thomas with a small gift - from an army doll for *Sergeant* to a ship in a bottle for *Columbus*. Other gems included a cowboy doll (*Cowboy*), a heart-shaped cushion (*Loving*), a King Henry doll (*Henry*) and a photo of Suzanne Danielle in a gold frame (*Emmannuelle*).

Adrian Edmondson was one of the new cast members mentioned in the press. However, he didn't join fellow 'Young Ones' Mayall, Planer and Sayle in the fun and games of *Columbus*. *The Young Ones* writer and *Carry On* fan, Ben Elton, was also rumoured to be keen to get a role.

The editor does a very confusing job of *Columbus* and, at the instructions of producer John Goldstone, cut out hoards of material with the *Carry On* greats. A lengthy discussion on board ship with Jim Dale and Bernard Cribbins was cut to ribbons while a minor but entertaining cameo from Jon Pertwee was almost completely curtailed. Pertwee, staggering through with aged bumbling, had a scene when he was married to some young thing by T.P. McKenna's Archbishop. The scene was cut, McKenna was completely removed from the film and audiences had to suffer unfunny romantic dialogue rather than precious moments from a fine veteran Carry Oner.

The historic first meeting between *Carry On* greats Jim Dale and Jack Douglas forms one of the film's most memorable moments. The cunning Dale dishing out payment to the bumbling Douglas leads to a few gems of confused innuendo. However, the sequence was cut in half and ruined. After Jack is fooled with his money, he turned on the old 'Alf' persona and started jittering and twitching - with the obvious result of the money being spilt all over the floor. Still shaking and bumbling, Douglas staggered out of the room as the camera remained on Jim's bemused expression. The sound effect of the splash as Douglas falls overboard came from outside the cabin and Jim simply raised his eyebrows and continued working. It could have been one of the best moments in the film and, indeed, Jack Douglas considered it the best scene of his *Carry On* career. Sadly the men with power thought otherwise!

Major *Carry On* fan and all-round movie nut, Jonathan Ross had agreed to make a gag-appearance in the film. Sadly he had other working commitments on the one-day shoot for his scene and couldn't feature - he was due to play the bemused hairdresser customer who has his ear cut off by Alexei Sayle! The role was subsequently played by David Boyce.

In a television interview with Jonathan Ross in January 1991, Sara Stockbridge happily admitted to wishing to appear in a *Carry On* film. Magic was in the air, as future *Columbus* cohort Jim Dale was a fellow guest.

In the press publicity for *Columbus*, superb *Carry On* newcomer, Keith Allen said, 'I grew out of adolescence with three ambitions, to make a hit record, be on *Top of the Pops* and appear in a *Carry On* film.'

Sara Crowe married Jim Dale's son, Toby, during the making of the film. The two had met on set while

Toby was acting as his dad's double and performing his part of a hooded Spanish inquisitor, along with Bill's son James Pertwee and writer, Dave Freeman.

Producer John Goldstone, who had been responsible for the legendary comic masterpiece *Monty Python's Life of Brian*, angered *Carry On* fans by insisting that even if the likes of Sid James, Kenneth Williams and Hattie Jacques had still been alive they would have been 'too old' to have been cast!

Goldstone had, in fact, worked with Williams when he struggled with innuendo comedy as the producer of Peter Cook's *The Hound of the Baskervilles*. Goldstone's director was ex-Andy Warhol cohort and *Carry On* fan, Paul Morrissey.

All the original survivors of the team had been approached to support Jim Dale's performance. However, in the event only Jack Douglas accepted his cameo role while the others were otherwise engaged. Joan Sims was filming *On The Up*, both Barbara Windsor and Bernard Bresslaw were Carrying On in Blackpool and Terry Scott was too ill to journey to Pinewood Studios. Kenneth Connor probably spoke for them all: 'I want to be remembered as a *Carry On* principal not a bit-player!'.

It's almost impossible to believe, but Jim Dale was, in fact, second choice for the lead role of Columbus! Goldstone's original choice, Robbie Coltrane, had turned down the part.

Carry On Columbus watches and T-shirts formed part of the mass market advertising campaign for the film.

Harry Enfield, a known *Carry On* follower and co-creator of *Carry On Banging*, was offered the supporting role of Bart Columbus before Peter Richardson. Distressed at the offical attempt to resurrect the films after so many of the original cast had died, Harry turned down the part. But what a team Dale and Enfield would have made.

While The King of Spain was originally offered to Frankie Howerd, Peter Rogers had planned to partner Frankie with Joan Sims as the Queen. When this casting proved impossible, Bernard Bresslaw and Barbara Windsor were approached. Neither would play ball either.

The sequence where Jim Dale and Bernard Cribbins arrive at America was filmed at Frensham Pond. Thirty years earlier, Gerald Thomas had used the same boat, the same location and the same star -

Bernard Cribbins - in a sequence with Kenneth Williams for *Jack*.

Columbus cost an amazing £2.5 million to make - most of which went on the splendid boat set and the colourful parade of costumes. Sadly, as Rogers used to say, 'You don't laugh at the scenery!' - people still didn't. The trouble was they didn't laugh at the script very much either! However, it was a success, thanks to the *Carry On* name, and made £1.6 million at the box office. That was double the money the two other 500th anniversary celebration films, *Christopher Columbus - The Discovery* and *1492* made, and their combined budget was £45 million! With successful video sales and sky movie screenings, *Carry On Columbus* was a commercial blockbuster.

Look out for...
The opening credits, blessed with stirring *Carry On*-esque music from Python composer John Du Prez, are a stunning start (complete with in-gags like *Curry On House*). As I was at the premiere screening, sat with Jim Dale and Gerald Thomas and cheered along with them at the first movie for 14 years, it's a set of titles which can always send a shiver down my spine. Happy memories.

The closing credits are worth hanging around for as well. Despite bad reaction from some die-hard fans, the rap song 'Carry On Columbus' is outstanding, combining references to Americanisms (Marilyn Monroe/Little Richard/Cadillac) with spirited chanting in the style of the Vangelis 1492 score. Brilliant. Written and produced by ex-Sex Pistols manager and rock icon, Malcolm McLaren, along with Lee Gorman, the song was recorded by Forbidden Planet with featured vocals from Jayne Collins and Debbie Holmes.

Enjoy the first image of the film as the Rank gong gag from *Khyber* is resurrected. It's a touching link to past days of charm, fun and feel-good *Carry On*.

Also during this initial scene with Rik Mayall, look out for a scruffy Tony Slattery, recreating memories of Ian Wilson's messenger from *Cleo*. While Wilson comes 'hot-foot from Rome', the smoking soles of Slattery have made a similar dash from Lisbon.

There's a gloriously patriotic moment as Jim Dale tries to convince Martin Clunes that a map of the British Isles is, in fact, an illustration of Italy - all chest-swelling pride and stirring use of 'Rule Britannia' on the soundtrack. Vintage *Carry On*.

A brilliant still which illustrates the successful mix of old and new comic talents for *Carry On Columbus*. Bemused veteran Bernard Cribbins joins stunned newcomers Julian Clary and Keith Allen.

Jack Douglas claims just one classic piece of dialogue, working with the gorgeous Rebecca Lacey. While Jack looks over board, Rebecca approaches this signifier for glory *Carry On* days. 'Hello Marco - what are you looking at?'/'Sharks - Man-eating sharks, this sea's full of them. You mind you don't fall in!'/'Goodness, you don't think they'll eat me whole!'/'No, I'm told they spit that bit out!'. With Sid's 'nine inches' line from *Girls* it ranks as the most risqué gag which the gang get away with. It also got the biggest laugh of the entire film at the cinema showings. Note the *Jaws* theme music.

Carry On memories

'Many years had gone by since my last appearance in a *Carry On* film at Pinewood. If my memory serves me right it was *Carry On Screaming!* where I played a mad Professor who grew "something nasty from a thumb". I cannot tell you how pleased I was to be warmly embraced by Gerry Thomas and welcomed home with the somewhat ominous codicil, "You are one of the few left!" I was also delighted to be made welcome by the original producer, Peter Rogers who, though a veteran, keeps an experienced production eye on things. The lighting cameraman was still the same and I therefore felt very much at home. The sets and costumes were magnificent, as was the cast. As soon as I arrived in make-up who should I meet but my old friend Jim Dale, Maureen Lipman and

the famous classical actor T.P. McKenna who was playing a one-day cameo as the Archbishop who was to marry me. As in all my appearances in *Carry On* films, I was engaged in a cameo role myself. I was sorry to leave at the end of a very nostalgic and happy day.'
Jon Pertwee

'I played Diego the Prison Officer in *Carry On Columbus* and in many ways it's like Kenneth Williams. I could almost hear him saying the lines in my head. It's sort of a middle sized part - I mean I pop in and out all the time, but it's the sort of thing Kenneth Williams could have done before breakfast. It was sad walking around the studio looking at the old posters of things like *Carry On Cleo* with Sid James and Kenneth Williams. I'm sure the corridors are full of ghosts!'
Julian Clary

'God knows what I'm doing in this - I thought you would tell me! The plot is some Spanish lady who's marrying her daughter off to a rich doddery old man and the daughter falls in love with Columbus' brother or young mate or something! I'm sort of an ogress who's in it for the money - and I end up sailing to the West Indies with Columbus. My first day was a bit tricky because I spoke the first line so it was all very nerve-wrecking. All these people are out there and, of course,

you don't rehearse on a film - you just turn up and perform. I actually rang the writer and said, "I'm a bit worried about this part. I really don't know what to do with it because I'm not allowed to have a Spanish accent!". He rang back and said, "Have you thought of having a fan!" Great *Carry On* philosophy - if in doubt hold something.'
Maureen Lipman

'I think there's a worry that the target audience had only ever seen the re-runs on TV and is therefore expecting those dead people to be in it. We'll have to see really. I mean it was a clever idea of theirs to recruit talent outside of the variety ghetto - people like me, Keith Allen, Peter Richardson

and Julian Clary are the closest to the likes of Sid James and the others.'
Alexei Sayle

'My last work for Peter Rogers had been *Carry On Emmannuelle* with Claire Davenport - a lovely 20 stone lady in her underwear... you got good value - and Kenneth Connor. Years later I met Gerald Thomas in Poland Street and he said "Norman, what are you doing?" and I said "Not working for you!". He replied, "You will be - we're doing *Carry On Columbus* and there are lots of parts in it for you." That's right - I never heard another word! That's show biz - but they were very good to me and you can't always win!'
Norman Mitchell

Island World Presents A Comedy House Production . In association with Peter Rogers Productions.
A Gerald Thomas Film

CARRY ON COLUMBUS

Christopher Columbus **JIM DALE**   Mordecai Mendoza **BERNARD CRIBBINS**
Bart Columbus **PETER RICHARDSON**   Countess Esmeralda **MAUREEN LIPMAN**
Achmed **ALEXEI SAYLE**   The Sultan **RIK MAYALL**   Fatima **SARA CROWE**
Don Juan Diego **JULIAN CLARY**   Pepi the Poisoner **KEITH ALLEN**
King Ferdinand **LESLIE PHILLIPS**
Don Juan Felipe **RICHARD WILSON**   Chiquita **REBECCA LACEY**
Duke of Costa Brava **JON PERTWEE**   Queen Isabella **JUNE WHITFIELD**
The Wazir **NIGEL PLANER**   The Chief **LARRY MILLER**
Marco the Cereal Killer **JACK DOUGLAS**   Genghis **ANDREW BAILEY**
Wang **BURT KWOUK**   Ginger **PHILIP HERBERT**
Baba the Messenger **TONY SLATTERY**   Martin **MARTIN CLUNES**
Customer with Ear **DAVID BOYCE**   Nina the Model **SARA STOCKBRIDGE**
Maria **HOLLY AIRD**   Torquemada **JAMES FAULKNER**
Inquisitor with Ham Sandwiches **DON MACLEAN**
Inquisitors **DAVE FREEMAN DUNCAN DUFF JONATHAN TAFLER**
JAMES PERTWEE TOBY DALE MICHAEL HOBBS
Cardinal **PETER GRANT**   Countess Joanna **SU DOUGLAS**
Manservant **JOHN ANTROBUS**   Meg **LYNDA BARON**
Sam **ALLAN CORDUNER**   Fayid **NEJDET SALIH**   Mark **MARK ARDEN**
Abdullah **SILVESTRE TOBIAS**   Tonto the Torch **DANNY PEACOCK**
The Bosun **DON HENDERSON**   Cecil the Torturer **HAROLD BERENS**
Governor of the Canaries **PETER GILMORE**
Captain Perez **MARC SINDEN**   Pontiac **CHARLES FLEISCHER**
Hubba **CHRIS LANGHAM**   Poco Hontas **REED MARTIN**
Ha Ha **PRUDENCE SOLOMON**   The Shaman **PETER GORDENO**

Screenplay by **Dave Freeman**   Additional Material by **John Antrobus**
Music composed by **John Du Prez**   Recorded at **The Hit Factory**
Mixer - **Mike Ross Trevor**   Song 'Carry On Columbus'
Written and Produced by **Malcolm McLaren & Lee Gorman**
Performed by **Jayne Collins & Debbie Holmes**
Published by **Chrysalis Music/Warner Chappell Music/Island World Music**
Poster tag-line - 'Up your anchor for a well crewed voyage!'

Production Supervisor **Joyce Herlihy**   Costume Designer **Phoebe De Gaye**
Editor **Chris Blunden**
Production Designer **Harry Pottle**   Director of Photography **Alan Hume B.S.C.**
Casting **Jane Arnell**
Dance Staging **Peter Gordeno**   Production Co-ordinator **Lorraine Fennell**
Art Director **Peter Childs**   Script Supervisor **Maggie Unsworth**
Assistant Directors **Gareth Tandy Terry Bamber & Becky Harris**
Assistant to John Goldstone **Lisa Bonnichon**
Assistant to Rogers/Thomas **Audrey Skinner**
Accounts **Bob Blues Gordon Davis & Jacky Holding**
Art Director **Peter Childs**
Set Decorator **Denise Exshaw**   Assistant Art Director **Edward Ambrose**
Scenic Artist **Ted Mitchell**
Production Buyer **Brian Winterborn**   Boat Consultant **David Raine**

Camera Operator **Martin Hume**
Camera Focus **Simon Hume**   Clapper Loader **Sean Connor**
Camera Grip **Colin Manning**
Art Department Assistant **Peter Francis**   Gaffer Electrican **Denis Brock**
Best Boy **Billy Poccetty**
Sound Recordist **Chris Munro**   Sound Maintainance **Graham Nieder**
Chief Dubbing Editor **Otto Snel**
Dubbing Mixers **Kevin Taylor & Michael Carter**
Assistant Editor **Steve Maguire**
Dialogue Editor **Alan Paley**   Stunt Double **Paul Jennings**
Assistant Dialogue Editor **Andrew Melhuish**
Footsteps Editor **Richard Hiscott**
Wardrobe **Ken Crouch   Sue Honeyborne   Jane Lewis & Jo Korer**
Dubbing Editor **Peter Horrocks**   2nd Assistant Editor **Natalie Baker**
Stunt Arranger **Jason White**
Assistant Dubbing Editor **Christine Newell**
Make-up **Sarah Monzani & Amanda Knight**
Hairdresser **Sue Love & Sarah Love**   Unit Nurse **Nicky Gregory**
Production Runner **Stuart Gladstone**
Floor Runner **Natasha Goldstone**   Unit Publicist **Ann Tasker**
Casting Assistant **Gina Jay**
Special Effects by **Effects Associates**   Title Design **Gillie Potter**
Stillsman **Keith Hamshere**
Property Master **Charles Torbett**
Costumes supplied by **Angels & Bermans**
Construction Manager **Ken Pattenden**   Chargehand Carpenter **Bill Hearn**
Chargehand Rigger **Les Beaver**   Chargehand Painter **Michael Gunner**
Chargehand Plasterer **Ken Barley**   Stand-by Props **Philip McDonald**
Stand-by Carpenter **David Williams**   Stand-by Painter **Peter Mounsey**
Stand-by Rigger **Gordon Humphrey**   Stand-by Stagehand **Leonard Serpant**
Unit Drivers **Keith Horsley & Brian Baverstock**
Colour by **Rank Film Laboratories**
Originated on **Eastman Colour Film from Kodak**
Lighting services by **Michael Samuelson Lighting**
Stills processing by **Pinewood Studios**
Cameras supplied by **Camera Associates**
Titles & Opticals **General Screen Enterprises**
Title Backgrounds **C & P Graphics Enterprises**
Insurance Arranged by **Rollins Burdick Hunter Limited**
Production Legal Services **Marriott Harrison**
Completion Guarantee furnished by **The Completion Bond Company**
Prosthetics (Ear) **Aaron Sherman**
Computer Services **Sargent-Disc Limited, London**   Glasses by **Onspec**
All Hair Products supplied by **Paul Mitchell Systems**

Thanks to THE SPANISH TOURIST OFFICE
Executive Producer **Peter Rogers**   Producer **John Goldstone**
Director **Gerald Thomas**

A 1992 Island World Release 'PG' Cert. Colour Running time - 91 mins. 8,176 feet

'Matron!' 'Cor!' 'O...

'Charmin...

'Stop messin' about!'

CARRY ON TELEVISION & STAGE

Hello!'

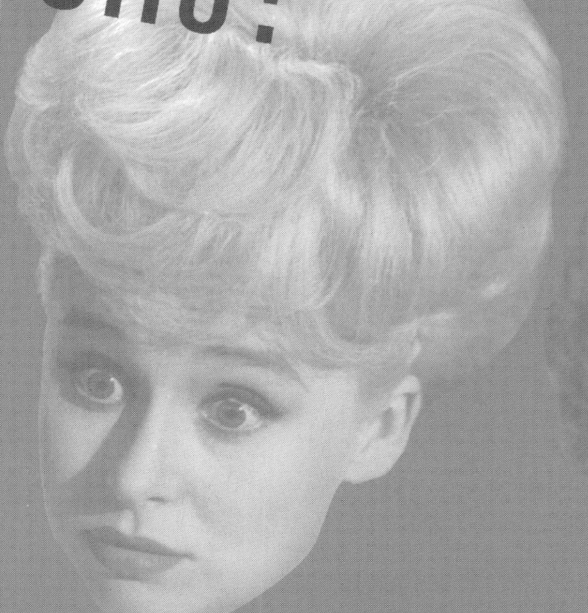

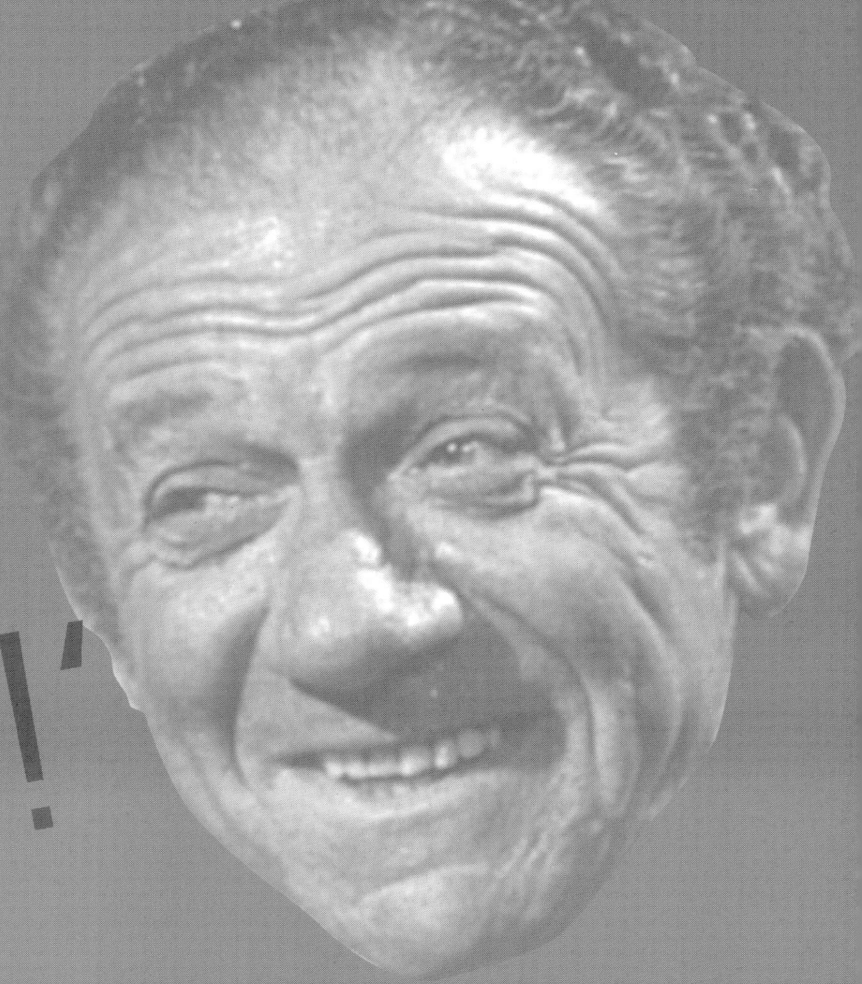

Get Away!'

'Matron!'　'Oh! Hello!'

TELEVISION

CUT!　'Charming!'

'Stop messin' about!'　Get Away!'

CARRY ON CHRISTMAS

Starring
SID JAMES as Ebenezer Scrooge
TERRY SCOTT - Dr Frank N. Stein, Convent Girl, Mr Barrett &
Baggie the Ugly Sister
CHARLES HAWTREY - Spirit of Christmas Past, Angel,
Convent Girl & Buttons
HATTIE JACQUES - Elizabeth Barrett, Nun & Bemused passer-by
BARBARA WINDSOR - Cinderella, Fanny & Spirit of Christmas Present
BERNARD BRESSLAW - Bob Cratchit, Frankenstein's Monster,
Spirit of Christmas Future, Convent Girl, Town Crier & Policeman
PETER BUTTERWORTH - Dracula, Street Beggar,
Convent Girl & Haggie the other Ugly Sister
With Special Guest
FRANKIE HOWERD - Robert Browning & Fairy Godmother

Screenplay by **Talbot Rothwell**

Comedy Consultant **Gerald Thomas**　Choir Routine staged by **Ralph Tobert**
Designer **Roger Allan**　Producer **Peter Eton**　Director **Ronnie Baxter**
By arrangement with **Peter Rogers** - Creator and Producer of the *Carry On* series.

Broadcast Christmas Eve, 1969 - 9.15pm　Thames Television Production
Colour　Running time - 50 mins.

It was always inevitable that the *Carry Ons* would
spread their wings and take on other aspects of the
entertainment industry. Following their most finan-
cially successful year at the box office, with *Khyber*
and *Camping* taking more money than any other films
in Britain for 1969, ITV producer Peter Eton
approached Rogers and Thomas for permission to
mount a *Carry On* television special. Broadcast on
Christmas Eve 1969, it began a series of four shows
which, Morecambe & Wise-like, became essential
viewing for British families gathered around their
TVs with a glass in one hand, a mince pie in the
other and a jolly paper hat plonked on their heads.

This first Christmas spectacular is, by far, the best
of all the spin-off *Carry Ons*, thanks mainly to a wonderfully on-form Talbot Rothwell script and a huge
percentage of valued team members. Making the
basic premise an innuendo-sodden tribute to 'The
Father of the Traditional Christmas', Charles
Dickens, Rothwell creates a marvellously irreverent
re-telling of *A Christmas Carol* and successfully mixes
in elements of 'poet's corner', Hammer horror films
and pantomime to forge the ultimate Christmas
comedy. It's all corny gags, drag scenes and spot-on
timing, delivered in front of a live audience and
thus, allowing such experienced ad libbing and
music-hall talents as Frankie Howerd, Peter
Butterworth and Charles Hawtrey to have the time of
their lives. For the first time, these comic talents
escape the restriction of scripted dialogue and let fly
with outrageous in-jokes, corpsing and pleading
looks to the audience. Sid James, the perfect comic
Scrooge, moans and groans his way through the
piece, incorporating his usual Sid laugh at everybody else's misfortune and poverty. Chuckling as he
wanders into view, he delightfully looks into camera
and sneers, 'I'm a nasty piece of work ain't I!'. With
a cold-hearted streak, moaning and humbugging all
over the place, Sid's crooked old miser is given the
same endearing edge as his villainous *Cleo* persona:
injecting lusty laughter at the glamour girls around
him and hoarding cash with a spirited relish which
creates a stunning central performance.

Sid is ably supported by a host of *Carry On*
favourites who, in true Rogers' repertory fashion,
gallop through an assortment of characterizations.

Sid, always the miserable Scrooge, gets embroiled in various plot-lines with a collection of flamboyantly played comic turns from the likes of Barbara Windsor, Bernard Bresslaw and Hattie Jacques. Second billing for the show goes to regular television farceur Terry Scott, who jumps up the billing for a *Carry On* due to his TV track record, while Frankie Howerd, stumbling into the fray for a couple of priceless cameos, simply stops the show at one point and goes into his stand-up routine.

Sid is the fixed point in a changing narrative, following the strict restraint of Dickens with just the odd leering look and piece of fruity innuendo to keep it ticking along. Bernie Bresslaw makes a totally sympathetic and hulking Bob Cratchit and the initial scene recreates the atmosphere of Dickensian London to comic perfection. The real fun comes when Charlie Hawtrey, suspended from a wire, pops in as a Christmas fairy (what else!) and grants Bresslaw's wish. Gloriously played with self-aware knowing looks and in-gags about the fact that this is just make-believe after all (Hawtrey's cry to the stage hand to lift him out of shot), this is *Carry On* comedy firing on all cylinders and makes fabulous television.

The Scrooge story-line is complemented by various visits from the obligatory Christmas ghosts, who show Sid visions that Dickens never dreamt of! Charlie Hawtrey crops up first, moaning and groaning in a comic variation on Marley's ghost - camping and ad-libbing opposite the totally stunned and bemused Sid who simply sits back and lets Hawtrey get on with it ('I say! - how much longer do I have to stand here moaning and clanging?'). A fine comic turn, Charlie's sniggering spirit, continually chuckling at his own spooky absurdity, leads into the first sketch within the Scrooge story, dealing with a doctor to whom Sid had refused a financial loan. The doctor being Terry Scott's Frank N. Stein, it enables Rothwell to resurrect memories of *Screaming* and throw in some ripe gags. Peter Butterworth wanders in as a friendly Count Dracula: cue comic mayhem. Scott and Butterworth pay little regard to the script, and the two panto pros go into a tongue-in-cheek sequence of corpsing, ad libbing and knowing expressions. It's pure magic. Into this montage of terrible jokes comes the sexually obsessed creature of Barbara Windsor and the lumbering and over affectionate monster of Bernard Bresslaw - the by-play between Scott and Butterworth about the missing piece of the monster is one for the classic archive.

Meanwhile it's on to Barbara Windsor's highly sexed ghost who tells the sad story of failed and ever more failing poet Robert Browning (a stunning turn from Frankie Howerd) and the love of his life

(Hattie Jacques). A boisterous drawing room melodrama with Scott hamming and Howerd camping, it's the cue for Bresslaw's peace and love ghost ('Greetings and salutations Daddio!') who delights Sid with an over-blown presentation of *Cinderella*. Again it's Peter Butterworth and Terry Scott treating subtle acting like a dirty word and giving full-blown interpretations of their ugly sisters. Frankie drops in for some splendid Hawtrey ribbing and a fine line in Mae West-like fairy wit, while Barbara Windsor suffers from some painfully dreadful but memorable Rothwell rhyme and Sid redeems himself by awakening and offering his fortune to Hattie Jacques.

A break-neck crusade through a clutch of outstanding Christmas institutions, given the Midas Rothwellian touch and blessed with an unsurpassable cast, this was the highlight of *Carry On* television and, naturally led to further entries in the series. Do your best to dig out this long forgotten gem and have yourself a merry little Christmas. It should be essential yule-tide material along with Bing Crosby and The Queen's Speech!

Best performance

While being mainly restricted to second in command roles in the film series, Terry Scott steps firmly into the limelight with his two Christmas television shows. Excellent throughout, it is in Rothwell's wonderfully constructed horror sequence that Terry

Ticket for the recording of 1969's *Carry On Christmas*, with realistic sketches of the entire cast. Note Hawtrey and Butterworth's poses from *Screaming* and Jacques and Bresslaw from the *Camping* poster.

shines. His Dr Frank N. Stein, obsessed with creating life and finding the missing component for Bresslaw's physique, growls and roars around his lab, chewing the furniture with over-acting and milking every last drop of fun from the situation. He has a wonderfully hammed partnership with Butterworth's Dracula. Gleefully throwing himself into a totally unconvincing werewolf persona, Terry grins and giggles with risque pleasure over the secret piece of human anatomy he handles, 'It's a beauty!'. Faced with the flamboyant sexual energy of monster Windsor - all black leather and wild blonde hair screaming, 'Recharge Fanny!' - Terry comes back with a very risque gag, even by Rothwell's standards: 'No, we're having none of that nonsense tonight!'. It's a sublime piece of work.

Favourite bit

In 50 minutes of television time so full of priceless moments, it is hard to select the finest, but the honour must go to Frankie Howerd who falls down the chimney during a particularly heart-felt Hattie Jacques speech. Frankie, adjusting his wig and bemoaning 'Ah! greetings!' to the audience, simply walks into the spotlight and takes over. Treating the script like some sort of inferior guideline which deserves to be ignored, he launches himself into a collection of painful puns and in-jokes. Realizing what he's there for, he looks to Hattie and gets back on track. In an outstanding moment of comic timing he explains her misfortune and urges the audience to look at her. The camera quickly flips to Jacques and then back to Howerd who laughs with disbelief, 'That was a quick look wasn't it? What, are you saving film!'. Delighting in the risque dialogue he looks into camera and chuckles 'I should get the kids to bed now, it's hotting up now!' and, while in mid-stream of comic business with Hattie, Howerd starts to corpse. Struggling to deliver his lines Frankie giggles - 'I'm laughing and I'm in it!!'. It's the performance of a true professional.

Did you know?

Such was the popularity of the *Carry On* gang that the 1969 Christmas special pulled in record viewing figures of 8.1 million - the most watched ITV show for the Christmas season.

Bernard Bresslaw's perfect interpretation of Frankenstein's monster was his chance to prove himself in the part at last. In 1957 he had auditioned for the role in the Hammer horror film *The Curse of Frankenstein*. Failing to win the part because he was, in his own words, 'too 'orrible!', he saw the role go to Christopher Lee.

Carry On Christmas was made back-to-back with the early 1970 release *Up The Jungle*, with most of the film's cast, including guest star Frankie Howerd, wandering into the television experiment. This explains why some publicity photographs of Sid James and television face, Barbara Windsor, on the Pinewood jungle set, were in circulation. During her rehearsals for *Christmas*, Windsor donned a safari outfit and posed with Sid's Bill Boosey persona.

Look out for...

Sid James greets Barbara Windsor as The Ghost of Christmas Present with typical glee. When she tells him of the plight of that poor poet Browning, Sid muffs his line, 'He's dead lousy not poor!' and injects a stunned chuckle to mask the mistake.

There's a particularly amazing drag sequence with Peter Butterworth, Terry Scott, Bernard Bresslaw and Charles Hawtrey as little girls with Hattie Jacques' religious authority figure. It's almost beyond belief and Hawtrey ad libs shamelessly! Great stuff.

CARRY ON AGAIN CHRISTMAS
or 'Carry On Long John'
or 'I'm Worried About Jim Hawkins'

Long John Silver **SIDNEY JAMES** Squire Treyhornay **TERRY SCOTT**
Old Blind Pew, Night Watchman & Nipper the Flipper **CHARLES HAWTREY**
Dr Livershake **KENNETH CONNOR** Jim Hawkins **BARBARA WINDSOR**
Rollicky Bill **BERNARD BRESSLAW** Ben Gunn & Ship mate **BOB TODD**
Kate **WENDY RICHARD**

Screenplay by **Dave Freeman & Sid Colin**

Comedy Consultant **Gerald Thomas** Designer **Roger Allan**
Executive Producer **Peter Eton** Director/Producer **Alan Tarrant**
By arrangement with **Peter Rogers** - Creator and producer of the *Carry On* series

Broadcast Christmas Eve, 1970 - 9.10pm Thames Television Production
Black & White Running time - 50 mins.

After the huge success of 1969's television special, 1970 saw Sid James and the gang mounting a seasonal sequel. Strangely, considering the popularity of the first show, this programme was filmed in black and white for a broadcast on Christmas Eve. At the time all channels were experimenting with colour transmissions, with notable events like tennis at Wimbledon and Jon Pertwee's first season of *Doctor Who* getting the extra budget for colour transmission. The second *Carry On* special was hit by the same technician's strike that hit *Bless This House* and thus is the final Carry On filmed in black and white.

Without doubt it pales in comparison with the 1969 show, due mainly to an inferior script from

Sid Colin and Dave Freeman. The cast is once again top notch but most of the comic situations are lacking in original sparkle (many of which would be resurrected by Freeman over 20 years after for his *Columbus* script - notably the Sid James mock hanging ploy 'I'm ready for heaven'/Scott: 'Where is it!'/'Up there somewhere - I'll sit on a cloud and play me harp!'. Jim Dale later had a good crack at it). It's all very much standard *Carry On* fare, but the superior cast - particularly Sid James, Charles Hawtrey and Terry Scott - forge some memorable comic turns and establish an effective and particularly earthy style of humour for television at the time. The cast ham, camp, mince and ad lib for all they're worth, trying to capture some moments of comic greatness within a rather weary framework.

With the ultimate Christmas story having been the source of Rothwell's masterly touch, Colin and Freeman looked for another family audience tale to deconstruct. They struck upon Robert Louis Stevenson's rip-roaring adventure story *Treasure Island* and conveniently set it around Christmas Eve; it was a Christmas television favourite anyway, due to Robert Newton's wonderfully, bleary eyed, over-blown performance for Walt Disney in 1950. The *Carry On* team grabbed the seasonal fun and games and created a scenario of non-stop innuendo and childish smut. The gags may be weak and obvious but the delivery is inspired throughout.

Naturally, Sid James tackles the central role, roaring and growling with flamboyant energy as he pursues Flint's hidden treasure. With vocal delivery dipped in whiskey and a convincing persona who strolls through the film with barely a gag, Sid's comedy comes from the bizarre supporting figures around him. A narrative story rather than the loosely connected sketch format of the 1969 effort, this has some plum roles for a host of familiar Carry Oners and second billing goes again to Terry Scott. As in Rothwell's earlier Christmas show, Scott is superb, clearly showing that his medium was the cosy, restricted environment of television and, more importantly, the presence of a live audience. A marvellous historical persona of lusty sexuality and law-abiding authority, he injects a myriad of farcical facial reactions when faced with the busty Miss Windsor and is memorably contrasted with the dithering old doctor, Kenneth Connor. The latter injects a fine line in aged innuendo (to Barbara: 'What a fine strapping fellow you've grown up to be!') and fruitless sexual ambition. Barbara Windsor, the most unconvincing Jim Hawkins in recorded history, wanders through the seedy pub atmosphere looking stunning, with prominent assets and giggling persona. At times Barbara seems so nonplussed

by the dialogue she is delivering, she practically gives up and just laughs at the banality of some of her jokes - 'I was terrified, for a minute I thought it was coming out!' - relax, it's only a Christmas ghost! Taking a deep breath, playing the unsubtle cross-dressing humour with relish and enjoying the company of a camp Hawtrey, this is Barbara Windsor in definitive *Carry On* terms. Charles Hawtrey enjoys not one but three supporting roles, making a memorable Blind Pew, complete with little jig, and minces with rare delight during the latter part of the production. Toss in an over-the-top turn from Bob Todd as a manically crazed Ben Gunn (in a sort of cross between Peter Butterworth and Jon Pertwee) and a gaggle of scantily-clad *Carry On* sex-pots and you have a fine, if not classic, example of the series.

Light years away from the quality of the films the team were making at the time, this does contain at least some great performances, notably from Windsor and Scott. Indeed, it's a great show just to put on, relax, empty your mind and prepare for the Christmas onslaught. If you can imagine *Carry On Columbus* at half the length and with the classic *Carry On* cast it so badly needed, then you almost have *Again Christmas* in a nutshell. It's a ball without it all!

Best performance
No, it's not Sid this time: he's great, but Charles Hawtrey's wonderfully camp cabin boy just about steals his march. Perhaps his most overtly effeminate screen performance, Hawtrey is the prefect foil for Sid's gruff and hard-edged pirate. All their best scenes are together and Charles relishes the truly corny Freeman/Colin dialogue, memorably looking to the audience for sympathy and laughing at the risque camp comments. Sid: 'We've already got a cabin boy. You'll have to be something else - how do you fancy the cook?'/Charlie: 'Well, I'll have to look at him first!'. Caught up in the shady world of ship intrigue and whispered rumours of mutiny, Hawtrey bumps into Pirate Sid and explains the garbled message he's just received. Bemused, Sid roars, 'What the hell are you talking about?' as Charlie answers, 'I haven't the faintest idea!'. In the hands of a lesser actor it would be nothing: enhanced by that simple touch of Hawtrey genius, it's everything.

Favourite bit
The highlight comes before the real narrative begins and even before casting has been decided. Sid James wanders on as Long John Silver, ahhing and a'roaring. However, all the other male team members in the cast stagger on in Long John guise, hoping for the plum part, much to the distress of Sid ('And who the hell are you!' to Kenneth Connor!).

Hawtrey makes a wonderfully effete Silver: 'I travelled quite a bit - and I'm known throughout the Spanish main...'/Sid: 'As a noisy, loud-mouthed twit!'. Terry Scott's outrageous claim, 'my purpose is quite clear, no coarse or vulgar gags I'll crack!' is answered by Sid: 'Well, then you're in the wrong mob here!'. It's a surreal piece of rhyming innuendo that makes for classic television. Almost Pythonesque in its approach, it benefits from an outstanding cast of now departed comic greats.

Did you know?

1969 had Frankie and the gang deconstructing Dickens, 1970 boasted a black-and-white Sid galloping through *Treasure Island*, but 1971, in the wake of *Carry On At Your Convenience*, had no new Christmas carryings on at all. Instead the 1969 show enjoyed a repeat on 20 December. However, in the usual Christmas Eve slot, Sid James and Kenneth Connor kept the flag flying with *All This and Christmas Too!*.

Look out for...

Linda Regan, who years later would crop up as one of the ATS girls in *England*, is briefly glimpsed on Sid's treasure island as one of Bob Todd's sexy young companions. Keep your eyes peeled for a young Carol Hawkins as well!

There's a pleasant little exchange between Terry Scott and Sid outside the old tavern: begging for money Sid explains, 'I'm Flint!'/Scott: 'Well I'm skint - Merry Christmas!'. The most obvious comic technique of cheerful rhyming put-down, it's inspired stuff.

CARRY ON CHRISTMAS
or 'Carry On Stuffing'

Starring
HATTIE JACQUES - Fiona Clodhopper, Miss Harriet,
Miss Molly Coddles & The Fairy Godmother
JOAN SIMS - Lady Rhoda Cockhorse,
Miss Esmerelda, Princess Yo-Yo & Clodhopper's Mother-in-Law
BARBARA WINDSOR - Milk Maiden, Eve, Maid,
Miss Clodhopper & Aladdin
KENNETH CONNOR - Club Chairman, Lt. Bangham/Insp. Knicker,
General Clodhopper & Hanky Poo
PETER BUTTERWORTH - Captain Alastair Dripping, Sir Francis Fiddler,
Admiral Rene & Widow Holinone
with
NORMAN ROSSINGTON - Valet, Tardy dinner guest & Genie of the Lamp
JACK DOUGLAS - Mr Firkin, Adam,
Ringworm the Butler/Charles Burke & The Demon King
BRIAN OULTON - Oriental Orator
BILLY CORNELIUS - Waiter   **VALERIE LEON** - Serving Wench
VALERIE STANTON - Demon King's Vision

Screenplay by **Talbot Rothwell & Dave Freeman**

Designer **Tony Borer**   Costumes **Frank Van Raay**

Executive Producer **Peter Rogers**
Producer **Gerald Thomas**   Director **Ronnie Baxter**

Broadcast 20 December 1972 - 8pm   Thames Television Production
Colour   Running time - 50 mins.

A collection of Christmas tales based around an eighteenth century feast, this special remains a decidedly hit and miss affair: full of Rothwellian genius, Freeman originality and tons of rubbish from both. Some of the sequences are so rambling and lacking in coherence that one pleads for a Sid chuckle. However, with a prime cast of *Carry On* legends giving sterling work - notably Kenneth Connor and Peter Butterworth - there is much to enjoy in the programme.

With a huge majority of male players out of the show, the jokes and comic banter is more fairly spilt between the stars and the three ladies get some priceless material. Barbara Windsor shines with glamour, notably in the initial 'Garden of Eden' tale ('How do you know if you're never had it!'), while Joan Sims effortlessly rises above the poor material of 'The Sailor's Story' to give a miniature rendition of Victorian melodrama. Hattie Jacques, through a number of subtly enlivened character studies, finally goes out in a burst of smut as the bemused and disgusted Fairy Godmother in the show's pantomime.

It's hardly Shakespeare, then again it's hardly vintage Talbot Rothwell either with the opening credits more akin to Benny Hill than Brighton beach. The camera pans past the name of our luxurious location, 'Turnit Inn' (be honest!), and up come Butterworth and Connor in a horse-drawn coach. Put in a wiggling Barbara Windsor in a pull-away dress and a quick blow on Connor's horn(!), and the realm of Hill's Angels and cheap laughs comes bounding in.

A collection of visual humour vignettes follows (with Butterworth getting Douglas' flu brush up his backside, Connor getting Jacques' bed-pan up his back side and Valerie Leon getting up everybody's back side). It spans well, but the speed-up camera technique and Jack Douglas' camp announcer soon begin to pall. However, once the guests are settled around the table and the masterly Kenneth Connor introduces the meal and the stories, it's fun and games aplenty - if not all the time!

'The Last Out-Post' resurrects *Jungle*'s celebrated tropic bird and *Khyber*'s dining room sequence, even allowing Butterworth to repeat his cowardice act: 'The natives are revolting!'. The dialogue is pretty awful but the cast is top-notch and several moments are treasurable, including Peter's seduction of Barbara Windsor as her father, Connor, bursts in and disturbs them ('Remember your position!'/'Thank you, Sir!' - as he grabs Windsor once more). Again it's Connor and Butterworth that enliven the haunted house mystery, with Kenneth particularly outstanding as a straight-faced picture of dignified law-enforcement, reverting to his cheeky giggle as he follows Barbara into a cupboard with the immortal exit line, 'Knickers off for Christmas!'. Jack Douglas is in there moaning and groaning as an ashen-faced villain (as Connor reveals, 'Allow me to show you his coconuts!'), but it goes on a bit and is punctured with delicious delight. Connor: 'In England we only go in there to wash our hands!'/Butterworth: 'Curious, in France we wash our hands in a hand basin!'... Jacques: 'What are you doing Lieutenant?'/Connor with his nautical Sexton: 'Nothing Mam, merely showing her my instrument!'/'Your what!'.

The linking sequences delight in Jack Douglas turning on the 'Alf' persona with some wicked and unfinished limericks, while canned laughter backs the 'filmed' visuals and Valerie Leon, as the perfect waitress, wanders around in the lowest of low cut dresses, much to Connor's pleasure. As a final Christmas salute, the gang take part in a risque pantomime for our amusement and amazement. Long before Jim Davidson and Mike Reid, the Carry Oners deconstructed panto with a self-aware sexuality. As Hattie explains the idea of men playing women and vice versa, Peter Butterworth looks stunned and comments, 'That sounds very queer!'. All well-versed in the art of pantomime, the cast seem to be having a whale of a time as Butterworth drags up as the dame, Connor is quite superb as the slinky chinaman and Windsor, outstanding in more ways than one, is Principal Boy.

The dialogue isn't brilliant, but then again what do you want at Christmas time? Art?! It's rather like watching a local amateur dramatic production with some very promising actors in the company! As a Carry On, this feast of fun does lack that vital spark; however, as a fun-filled celebration of innuendo, comic greats and over-excess for yule-tide, this is hard to beat. The gang, if not all here, certainly are all there, and delight in a number of comic situations which remain classics of Carry On. Pass the figgy pud and let your hair down.

Best performance

Perhaps the hardest job in the Carry On canon, for all the players are given about the same amount of things to do and all are outstanding. However, for a valuable record of one of this country's best and most respected pantomime dames, the reward goes to Peter Butterworth in the panto section. Capturing his wide-eyed and lovable grotesques to perfection, this show injects some ribald comments and cheeky

raised eyebrows into his usual children's audience performance. Bemoaning the sexually charged antics of his son (Barbara Windsor) and always on about the permissive society, the merest mention of money for his/her sexual favours leads to a change of heart: 'Why didn't you mention this before!'. Performed in rhyme throughout and blessed with sterling support from Kenneth Connor, it could only end on one note. An off-key one, as they join forces to sing about their favourite fish for supper - 'There's A Plaice For Us!'.

Favourite bit

Peter Butterworth, in another guise, also introduces the highlight as his musical boffin uncovers some long-lost Elizabethan madrigals concerning the exploits of King Henry VIII. A glorious retread of Sid's Henry and later incorporated into Carry On London!, these ballads are priceless Freeman material and are delivered with straight-faced dignity by Kenneth Connor, brilliantly singing 'Balls, balls, banquets and balls!' in particular. All the Carry Oners present are involved, with Peter Butterworth tossing in ad libbed facial reactions to the lyrics 'a trust fund immediately', and Jack Douglas crosses his eyes and looks the part to a tee. However, Barbara Windsor gets the best lyrics during the Hampton Court number: 'There we beheld his Majesty/ Standing at the window for all to see/Oh, how his royal subjects fought/ For a glimpse of King Harry with his Hampton Court!' It's certainly not Doris Day, but it's magic!

Did you know?

This was the show that saw the departure of Charles Hawtrey from the Carry On team. Gerald Thomas had cast him in several major roles in the special and offered him second billing. Hawtrey, fully aware that Sid James, Kenneth Williams and, more importantly in terms of television, Terry Scott, were not in the show, demanded top billing for the first time in Carry On history. Thomas was adamant that Hattie Jacques was getting top billing, despite a fairly limited contribution. Hawtrey continually turned down Thomas' offer of second billing and finally explained that he would be taking lunch at Bourne & Hollingsworth if Gerald wished to talk to him further. Thomas was obviously keen to include Hawtrey in the cast but would not give in to his request. Thomas phoned the department store, spoke to Hawtrey and, again, offered him second billing. Hawtrey thought for a moment, muttered 'No!' and hung up: he was never seen in Carry On land again. Looking back one can see Charles' point: after all he was regularly enjoying third billing in the movies and third billing in the specials. With all three of those artistes above him (James, Williams, Scott) not involved in the 1972 show, logic suggests that Hawtrey would lead the pack. Indeed, in terms of Hawtrey and Jacques, she hadn't been above him since *Cabby* almost 10 years before and in the latest movie - *Abroad* - Hawtrey was third and she was eleventh (under guests Jimmy Logan and June Whitfield). However, billing was not an issue with the *Carry On* controllers and Hawtrey had pushed once too often. He was out and the script was quickly re-worked. Having allowed for Hawtrey's camp persona in each story, the characters were changed to suit the style of Norman Rossington while Brian Oulton stepped in at the last minute for a brief cameo during the panto.

Charles Hawtrey was clearly involved in the project until the last moment - he appears emerging from a Christmas pudding with 1972 TV special team members, Butterworth, Douglas, Connor, Jacques, Sims and Windsor, in the M. Terry cartoon promoting the show in the *TV Times* for Christmas 1972.

Fairy Godmother was Hattie Jacques' favourite acting part and she relishes in the idea of doing a *Carry On* variation on the theme. Clearly she grabs her performance with both hands.

Look out for...

The imposing Gothic atmosphere of 'The Sailor's Story' comes complete with Hattie Jacques' barnstorming harridan of a housekeeper. The gags are on the dodgy side but the team would never let such a comic situation dwindle away.

Enjoy Norman Rossington's Hawtreyesque Genie, highlighting the whole thing as a stage production while also highlighting Barbara Windsor's unmanly physique with, 'Well, you've got to have boobs in any show!'. The critics loved that one and celebrated the show as smutty, cheap but very funny.

Carry On memories

'Although I had known Tolly Rothwell for a number of years and we had often spoken of collaborating on something, we never actually sat down and wrote anything together. Tolly was not in the best of health after his years in a Prisoner of War camp and although he started to write the 1972 *Carry On Christmas* special he became ill and was unable to finish it. I took over from him which is why we have a shared credit. I remember writing the script under severe difficulties. I was suffering a bad attack of sinus trouble which gave me a

combined toothache and ear-ache. In the middle of the script there was a power cut and I finished it with two candles stuck on my typewriter. Just as I got to the end a candle fell over and set light to the script! I think this was when the miners went on strike - I felt like joining them!'
Dave Freeman

'Charlie Hawtrey was supposed to be in the 1972 show but he threw a moody. Sid wasn't going to be in it and Charles didn't want to take second billing to Hattie Jacques, because alphabetically he thought he should be top. He went off to Bourne & Hollingsworth to have something to eat and he said, "If they want to talk to me I'll be having Brown Windsor at the Restaurant!" There was no such thing as billing really, it depended on what you were doing. Charles let Gerald Thomas down badly just two days before filming and so he was never used again which was a great shame because he was my favourite actor in the team.'
Barbara Windsor

WHAT A CARRY ON!

Introduced by SHAW TAYLOR

Starring
SIDNEY JAMES   BARBARA WINDSOR
KENNETH CONNOR   PETER BUTTERWORTH
BERNARD BRESSLAW   JACK DOUGLAS

Programme Associate **Tony Hawes**   Director/Producer **Alan Tarrant**

Broadcast 4 October 1973 9pm   ATV Network Production
Colour Running time - 50 mins.

Basically a filmed record of highlights from the first West End night of the legendary stage revue *Carry On London!*, this televised special remains valuable documentation of this historic branch of the series. The television presentation, *What A Carry On!*, was hosted by *Police 5* icon Shaw Taylor and featured abridged versions of the Rothwell comedy sketches and musical numbers. Featuring exclusive interview footage with the show's cast - Sid James, Barbara Windsor, Kenneth Connor, Peter Butterworth, Bernard Bresslaw and Jack Douglas - the new material was interspersed with vintage footage from the *Carry On* films. A Thursday evening had never been more fun! A timely plug for the November release of the new film, *Carry On Girls*, and various comments from the celebrity audience rounded off a priceless piece of television. Although no match for the obvious thrill of seeing the show live, this gallop through the best bits is pure gold dust.

CARRY ON CHRISTMAS

Starring

SIDNEY JAMES - Mr Belcher the Store Santa Claus, Seed Pod,
Sir Henry, Sgt. Ball & Robin Hood
JOAN SIMS - Bishop's wife, Adele, Virginia's Mum, Salvation Army lady,
Traffic Warden, Maid Marian, Ballet dancer & Senna Pod
BARBARA WINDSOR - Virginia, Crompet the Pit cavegirl, Fifi, Lady Fanny,
Ballet dancer & Lady Frances of Bristol
KENNETH CONNOR - Mr Sibley the Store Manager, Bishop, Anthro Pod,
Pte. Parkin, Will Scarlet & Ballet dancer
PETER BUTTERWORTH - Caveman carol singer, Ancient gent, dart player,
German soldier, Friar Tuck & Ballet dancer
BERNARD BRESSLAW - Bean Podkin the Cave Teenager, Captain Ffing-Burgh,
Dart player, Merry man, Police Officer & Ballet dancer
JACK DOUGLAS - Caveman carol singer, Crapper the Butler, German soldier,
Alan-A-Dale & Ballet dancer
JULIAN HOLLOWAY - Angle leader & Captain Rhodes
LARAINE HUMPHREYS - Bed Customer

Screenplay by **Talbot Rothwell**

Choreographer **Terry Gilbert**   Music Associate **Norman Stevens**
Designer **Allan Cameron**   Executive Producer **Peter Rogers**
Producer **Gerald Thomas**   Director **Ronald Fouracre**

Broadcast Christmas Eve 1973 - 9pm   Thames Television Production
Colour   Running time - 50 mins.

A sparkling return to form for the *Carry Ons* on Christmas television saw the much welcome presence of a chuckling and totally on-form Sid James. With a script completely in the hands of Talbot Rothwell and an outstanding supporting cast, mostly culled from the stage show cast, this programme remains a classic example of 1970s' *Carry On*. It was the last totally original Christmas special and captures the glorious essence of innuendo and larger-than-life performances.

As with the first Christmas show, this is a collection of comic sketches linked by Sid James - in this case in the guise of a department store Father Christmas. Giving a performance of concentrated leers and knowing winks, Sid creates the ultimate guide through a bizarre collection of Christmases past. As with all these television ventures, the scripts borrow heavily from the more familiar film entries, and a number of performances from the gang are moulded round past successes (notably Sid James in eighteenth century form/*Don't Lose Your Head* and German soldier Peter Butterworth/*Abroad*).

The first excursion into history takes the team back to prehistoric times, with a resurrection of Rothwell's masterpiece, *Cleo*. Full of nearer-the-knuckle innuendo (gags based around playing with yourself et al!), this vignette begins with a beautiful bit of sight humour from Peter Butterworth and Jack Douglas. Joan Sims moans and sighs throughout as Senna Pod, taking over from where Sheila Hancock left off. Kenneth Connor is a delight as an aged variation on Hengist Pod (here playing Anthro Pod!) 'How long have I been asleep?'/Sims: 'Since October!'/Bresslaw: 'We almost buried you twice!'

and Sid James, all wild hair and giggles, simply barges in and steals the scene, as well as the sexy cave-girl of Barbara Windsor! It's all smut, mugging to the camera, aged innuendo and pure joy.

However, Sid the Santa leads us on to the second section where subtle humour and straight-faced dignity is the name of the game. With Bernard Bresslaw mincing around the drawing room and Jack Douglas wey-heying with aplomb, it remains for Sid's serene nobleman to inject knowing comments and underplayed ideals. Instead of the usual raucous chuckle, lines like 'My wife loves it you know!' are greeted with a wry raised eyebrow. The bulk of the scenario, dealing with Barbara Windsor's over-flowing delight in a game of 'Postman's Knock' with Julian Holloway, is just saucy enough to get Connor and Butterworth to throw in *Carry On* comments, while the rest of the gang keep the lid on all-out innuendo. It does end with a classic exchange between James and Connor when it is discovered that Holloway has relieved himself in the garden! Kenneth: 'It's not so terrible really, to write your name in the snow.'/Sid: 'I agree - but it wasn't his handwriting!'.

Then it's fast forward to the batteleweary First World War adventures of the British tommies, Sid James, Kenneth Connor and Bernard Bresslaw. A wonderful collection of Rothwellian banter and barrel-scraping innuendo, there are enough pauses for sentiment and pondering to make this a respectful and very funny tribute to the troops. Sid turns on the usual rasping chortle and down-to-earth speech, while Bernie Bresslaw is all stiff-upper-lipped dignity. Kenneth Connor, joyfully scooping corned beef out of a tin and chuckling with elements from his early Hudis characterizations, steals the scene with moments of sincere pathos and some precise carol renditions: his sudden realization that it's Christmas Eve creates a charming atmosphere of soldiers away from the glories of the traditional British Christmas. Throw in a memorable word-slip over his character name from Sid, a couple of flamboyant French ladies - Joan Sims and Barbara Windsor (Joan: 'We are not 'fraid, Captain!'/Sid: 'No, just a bit worn round the edges!') - and German figures of war in the shape of Peter Butterworth and Jack Douglas and you have an instant *Carry On* classic.

After sketches set in 2001BC, 1759 and 1917, there is a jump back in history to a plum role for Sid - that of Robin Hood in 1192 - rounding off this Christmas gem with a rip-roaring crusade through Rothwellian gags and priceless comic turns. Bounding into the local grassy knoll, Sid is an aged Robin, continually explaining that 'there's plenty of twang left in my bow!', thus pre-empting Sean

Connery in Dick Lester's *Robin and Marian*. With the perfect *Carry On* Friar Tuck in Peter Butterworth and Kenneth Connor's whimpering Brummie Will Scarlet, Sid gallops through the sketch, backed by a wonderfully awful collection of ditties from Jack Douglas (Sid: 'Oh shut up!'), a *Screaming*-like harridan from Joan Sims and Barbara Windsor from Bristol (As Sid says, 'Where else!'), popping out of her clothes and getting to grips with Robin as the merry men gather round. In a show when Robin's arrow droops and Sid looks into camera with - 'It's always the same in bloody Nottingham!' - things are always worth watching.

It's an echo of the times when the Carry Oners were still mainly all in action, Talbot Rothwell could scrape a few more worthwhile gags off the wall and Sid James could embody the spirit of Christmas with giggling style. Get the beers out, finish the roasted peanuts, chuck on the paper hat and sit back with Sid and the gang. Seasonal laughter guaranteed.

Best performance

Sid James, as the personification of festive cheer, links the show with comic elegance injected with the exact amount of unsubtle *Carry On* style, combining the typical Sid persona with touches of Will Rogers-like philosophy into camera. Clad in his Santa outfit (complete with fur-trimmed knickers!), Sid enjoys memorable encounters with the gang - notably Barbara Windsor and Joan Sims as sexually forward daughter and worried mum. Sid's reaction to Windsor's flamboyant teenager is a treasure - 'Yeah! well you're making it hard for me!'- and sees Sid the rogue in definitive terms. However, this is contrasted with moments of pathos and delight in the spirit of Christmas as he introduces the manic ballet-dancing sequence. A few lines in the local pub, with moaning and groaning darts players Bresslaw and Butterworth, draws out some brilliant work from the players while Sid's hard-done by, lack of Christmas spirit disbelief is a masterclass of comic genius made easy. This is Sid's show and he makes the perfect Santa Claus - what more could the average bloke in the street want under his Christmas tree than the list of items that Sid would surely require! As the credits roll and the gang climb onto a horse-drawn sleigh, Sid cheerfully looks around, chuckles with the team and waves goodbye to the viewing audience. It's a magic moment.

Favourite bit

The first scene cannot be bettered despite the approaching wave of classic historical innuendo. A slick Kenneth Connor escorts the new girl through the store and bumps into Sid chomping a sausage sandwich while working. It is a classic encounter between the righteousness of the working-class man and the officialdom of Connor's anti-fun manager. Dismayed at this dubious item of food, Connor demands its removal. Sid just moans about his wife, 'Do you know, last night when I got into bed I made one reasonable request. What do you think she said?'/'Put that wretched thing away!'/'How did you know!'/'Mr Belcher!'/'Yeah!'/'I would prefer that you did not eat whilst you are on the job.'/'She said that an' all!'. Complete with a moment of cheerful fun as Sid's Santa beard begins to slip off, this is a piece of obvious Rothwell gagging performed by two of the best innuendo-mongers in the business.

Did you know?

Such was the success of the First World War sketch that Talbot Rothwell planned a full-length feature *Carry On* based around the idea. *Dick* was just in pre-production and Rothwell would not write another *Carry On*. However, the scenario was re-worked and resurrected by *Carry On* fan Ben Elton and Richard Curtis with the 1989 classic *Blackadder Goes Forth*.

Although this was the last completely original *Carry On* special for Christmas, the tradition did continue until the Christmas before Sid's death. For 1974, audiences were treated to a repeat of the 1972 'Stuffing' show and for 1975, the 1973 classic received a welcome repeat. The shows were not seen again until their belated video release in 1992.

The rehearsals for this 1973 Christmas classic took place at The Serbian Community Centre, London, while the gang's popularity led to Sid James and Barbara Windsor taking centre stage as the cover stars for the festive *TV Times*.

Look out for...

During the eighteenth-century drawing room Christmas, Joan Sims huffs and puffs with outlandish pomposity in a brilliant inclusion of Dame Edith Evans' acting eccentricities.

At the close of the caveman section, Sid leers over Barbara Windsor and addresses the television audience. Linking into the conventions of commercial television he chuckles, 'Well, there you are. You've had your first bit, now I'm going to have mine!'.

Sid gets the show's biggest laugh during the wartime Christmas. Approached by Germans Peter Butterworth and Jack Douglas, Sid remains on guard. Peering into the British trench the Germans

Above: Leslie Phillips, June Whitfield, Barbara Windsor and Jack Douglas celebrate their late colleagues in The British Comedy Society's Hall of Fame, Pinewood Studios, 26 April 1998

Right: Finalist in the greatest photo ever taken competition!! Peter Rogers surrounded by his loyal *Carry On London!* cast – Barbara Windsor, Jack Douglas, Sid James, Bernard Bresslaw, Peter Butterworth and Kenneth Connor

The God-like Sid James and his dirty habit!! Fun on the set of *Carry On Camping*

A honeymoon trip to Pluritania. Barbara Windsor and Sid James in *The Prisoner of Spenda*.

shout down, Butterworth: 'We are wishing you Merry Christmas!'/Douglas: 'And peace on you!'/Sid: 'Not from up there mate!'. The studio audience's reaction lasts for seconds, making Sid pause before continuing the script.

CARRY ON LAUGHING

As the ITC Video label shouted, 'not to be confused with the movie compilation series, these made for TV sitcoms are a unique *Carry On* experience.' This was another brave experiment on Peter Rogers' part. Branching away from the film series was all well and good - the Christmas specials had become an institution while the stage farce was packing them in. But to try and recapture the spirit of the film series as an actual television series was different. Rogers realized that the cinema entries were gradually losing popularity: 1975's *Behind* was the start of the end.

However, he also knew that his earlier films were still hugely popular. The place where that popularity was at its peak was on television, with classics like *Teacher* and *Cabby* enjoying record audience figures. Thus in late 1974 and early 1975, two lots of 25-minute chunks of *Carry On* were filmed at ATV's Elstree Studios for broadcasting in 1975 on LWT, with series one going out on Saturdays and the peace of Sunday evenings being shattered by series two. Boasting some fine writers and almost all the regular *Carry On* team members, these vary from the excellent to the downright awful. In the end they didn't quite make the grade.

Peter Rogers, interviewed in 1977, explained that the series hadn't achieved what he set out to do:

namely, to save the flagging *Carry On* film ship - which by 1977 was sunk bar its mast - and also to introduce audiences to new faces who would be incorporated into the film series. Both Melvyn Hayes and Diane Langton made appearances in *Carry On Laughing* shows just before the filming of *England*, as did supporting performers, Vivienne Johnson and John Carlin. These comic adventures do contain some hilarious and historical elements, and while not classics, have enough Sid chuckles, Barbara giggles and Butterworth eccentricity to please even the most fussy of fans.

THE PRISONER OF SPENDA

Prince Rupert/Arnold Basket **SID JAMES**
Vera Basket/The Grand Duchess Ingrid of Coronia **BARBARA WINDSOR**
Count Yerackers **PETER BUTTERWORTH**
Madame Olga **JOAN SIMS**
Nickoff **KENNETH CONNOR**
Colonel Yackoff **JACK DOUGLAS**
Duke Boris **DAVID LODGE**   Tzana **DIANE LANGTON**
Major **RUPERT EVANS**   Waiter **RONNIE BRODY**

Screenplay by **Dave Freeman**
Music by **Richard Tattersall & John Marshall**

Graphics **George Wallder**   Animator **Len Lewis**   Designer **Stanley Mills**
Executive Producer **Peter Rogers**
Producer **Gerald Thomas**   Director **Alan Tarrant**

Broadcast 4 January 1975 - 8.45pm   ATV Network Production
Colour   Running time - 21 mins.

The first four shows in the series boasted the majestic presence of Sid James, and this first episode has six Sids for the price of one: two leading roles and four other gag appearances (wordless cameos as a chef, a sea-dog, a camp dandy and a stern-faced businessman). The script is, admittedly, full of truly awful puns and one-liners, but the cast, a healthy roster of six regular Carry Oners, milks the situation for all it's worth. A sparkling parody of *The Prisoner of Zenda* (get away!), the characterizations are hardly more than ciphers for a torrent of corny humour. However, certain performances do stand out from the rest, and with a cast like this who's complaining?

Sid is splendid in both his roles, watering down his chuckling rogue to something akin to Sidney Abbott for his British holiday-maker and injecting elements of pathos and dignity for his regal persona. Barbara Windsor gives one of her most comically assured and entertaining screen performances, while Kenneth Connor is simply superb as a briefly seen but totally memorable grinning saboteur. Peter Butterworth and Jack Douglas take on the roles of David Niven and Lewis Stone from the classic Ronald Colman interpretation, with Douglas turning on the jitters throughout, falling into things and collapsing (as David Lodge says, 'He often goes off in the warm weather!'). Butterworth is his usual outstanding self, working closely with Sid James and gaining comic mileage from his name, Count Yerackers - as Sid blurts out: 'Count me what!'.

The whole thing boils down to a tatty and sloppily written television farce which is instantly redeemed by a collection of actors far superior to their material. The likes of Joan Sims, barking out her lines as a seductive Russian, belong in dramatic environments. Connor and Butterworth contribute character studies of such depth and beauty that one longs to see them have more air time. These brief characters are enhanced and enlivened by thoughtful performances and an affection for the series, complementing the central roles of Sid James and Barbara Windsor with three-dimensional aids and enemies.

Freeman's script is never anything more than workman-like and it doesn't need to be. Importantly, this episode tries to recapture the spirit of the films in microcosm, giving a host of team members the chance to shine. In some ways it doesn't quite work, with seven or eight comic personalities all trying to make the most of a bare 20 minutes of script. As the series developed, each show would be built around one or two star turns with the others simply backing them up with the odd line (sometimes very odd line!). As a slice of television history and a rare piece of original carrying on with a prime cast, *The Prisoner of Spenda* is invaluable.

Best performance

Although up against a host of outstanding character-izations, the moments of pure *Carry On* fun come from Barbara Windsor as the slightly naive, slightly saucy wife of Sid James. She appears relaxed with her role, confident with the gags and at ease with the cast. Bubbling over with giggling glamour and grinning sexual energy, Barbara injects moments of pathos, frustration, adoration, fear and plain and simple innuendo into her role. Discussing the holiday location she mutters, 'I'm told it's quite small but very beautiful!', brilliantly feeding Sid the line for the laugh: 'What is?!'. Reacting to the innuendo lines around her, Barbara's English lass abroad persona can highlight the double meaning commands these foreign strangers inadvertently come out with. While the bumbling Douglas talks about precaution for the honeymoon Barbara explodes: 'I beg your pardon!', while she has a delicious sequence of frustrated angst when she needs the Ladies room. 'Oh Arnold, do something'. Sid begins to pour a drink, 'Oh, don't do that!' - it's classic stuff.

Favourite bit

The short-sighted Sid James, trying to fight like his regal lookalike, staggers and stumbles around the castle, poking everything in sight. Seeing the blurred figure of a little boy statue, he stabs it and water starts pouring out. With perfect timing and shocked dismay Sid mutters, 'You filthy swine!'. Cracks me up every time!

Did you know?

This first episode of *Carry On Laughing* was complemented by a colourful caricature cover by Arnaldo Putzu for *TV Times* (4-10 Jan, 1975), with the caption 'Happiness is ITV and a New Year *Carry On*'. The design featured Peter Butterworth driving a Rolls-Royce with Barbara Windsor reclining on the wing and Joan Sims laughing in the back. Sid James (shown in his *The Prisoner of Spenda* persona) was a passenger, as were Kenneth Connor and Jack Douglas (both from *One in the Eye for Harold*), while David Lodge (*The Baron Outlook*) scowled in the background.

With this major excursion into television, many of the regulars thought the film series had come to an end. However, Sid James was relieved to disclose in a *TV Times* interview on the set of *The Prisoner of Spenda* that, 'we hear we're doing yet another film some time in 1975', although, as it turned out, Sid would be absent from the cast.

Look out for...

Kenneth Connor enjoys a memorable opening sequence with Sid James. As he lists the items foreign visitors can not bring into the country, the objects get more and more outlandish, eventually reaching Milliganesque proportions. The idea was in fact similar to a moment from the John Cleese/ Graham Chapman script *Rent-A-Dick*, and who delivered the scenario in that movie but Spike Milligan.

As always, Peter Butterworth injects moments of ad libbed visual humour into his basic characterization. A moment to treasure is when he hides behind a potted plant in the restaurant and quickly grabs a puff on his cigarette before bringing his cloak across his face.

Also in the restaurant sequence, a heavily disguised Kenneth Connor comes in as the waiter with a fake moustache. Mid-way through his delivery, the moustache begins to fall off and eventually Kenneth lifts it off completely as he makes his exit. Sid is clearly as amused as the audience.

The final sword fight has elements of *Don't Lose Your Head* while Kenneth Connor's cowardly fighting brings memories of Rothwell's masterpiece, *Cleo*.

THE BARON OUTLOOK

Baron Hubert **SID JAMES**   Lady Isobel **JOAN SIMS**
Marie **BARBARA WINDSOR**
Sir William **KENNETH CONNOR** Friar Roger **PETER BUTTERWORTH**
Rosie **LINDA HOOKS** Griselda **DIANE LANGTON**
Sir Simon de Montfort **DAVID LODGE** Ethelbert **JOHN CARLIN**
Soldier **JOHN LEVENE** Gaston **BRIAN OSBORNE** Herald **ANTHONY TRENT**

Screenplay by **Dave Freeman**
Music by **Richie Tattersall & John Marshall**

Graphics **George Wallder**   Animator **Len Lewis**   Designer **Ray White**
Executive Producer **Peter Rogers**   Producer **Gerald Thomas**
Director **Alan Tarrant**

Broadcast 11 January 1975 - 8.45pm - ATV Network Production
Colour   Running time - 24 mins.

This is a rip-roaring historical romp with Sid in tip-top form surrounded by a plum collection of regular Carry Oners. This is the contemporary, chuckling, nagged-to-death Sid of domestic sitcom dropped into a historical scenario. Joan Sims turns on the over-bearing authority once more and makes poor old Sid's life a misery while the typical Freeman plot of female masquerading as man leads a short-haired Barbara Windsor to pose as a French nobleman - providing a fine moment of visual comedy when a wasp gets down her armour. As with Sara Crowe in *Columbus*, her feminity is finally revealed - much to the pleasure of those red-blooded males in the castle. 'Once I was known as Europe's greatest Knight!'/'You play your cards right mate you still could be!'.

There's some priceless support from Kenneth Connor and Peter Butterworth, who enhance another couple of comic eccentrics and milk some excellent moments from feebly developed characterizations. Connor is superb as the wheezing, bumbling old buffer based around his *Dick*-persona, continually clad in his beloved armour and frying chips in the huge vat of boiling oil. Peter Butterworth is outstanding as the sex-mad, bemused and totally bewildered Friar, shuffling throughout the draughty old castle with a lusty devotion to the local fair maidens and an obsessive quest for scientific knowledge.

The plot is practically non-existent (David Lodge inspecting the kingdom's castles with Windsor's captive soldier in tow); the dialogue, nothing more than competent; and the historical details sketchy to say the least. However, as an example of 1970s' *Carry On*, this show is extremely pleasing to view: full of choice star turns from a handful of magical clowns and dripping with wonderfully bad one-liners and stunned facial expressions. Sid is brilliantly down-to-earth, offering the supercilious Lodge a hearty meal of turkey and muttering, 'I know what he wants... stuffing!', while Butterworth's passions overflow with the delightful glamour girls who were always on hand for these *Carry On* extravaganzas, before being interrupted by Sid and his guest. With typically obvious innuendo dialogue and timing of sheer perfection, Peter blurts out, 'I was just about to get it out when you entered!'. The humour is the most basic smut but the actors involved make the whole project enjoyable and fun. It's hardly vintage stuff but there's enough to satisfy the connoisseur innuendo-monger.

Best performance

Sid James steals the show - all confident chuckles, weary bemusement and delight in the company he keeps. Clad in a huge red hat and bedraggled nobleman's clobber, Sid ambles throughout the action (what there is of it!) with superb comic put-downs and innuendo-encrusted comments. He is the ultimate hard-done-by ne'er-do-well, spiritedly opposing the figure of authority from David Lodge, battling his nagging wife and quietly shaking his head with disbelief at the antics of Connor and Butterworth. Sexually aroused by the final bursting out of Barbara Windsor and chuckling and grinning with vintage Sid elements, he even leads the gang in a brief rendition of 'Greensleeves'. It's suitably reworked for the *Carry On* style: Sid joyfully shouts out, 'All together now!', as Kenneth Connor starts playing the spoons and Peter Butterworth provides accompaniment on bellows! It's all go for Sid.

Favourite bit

Sid again, with his fair lady Joan Sims. As the pair bemoan the decline of their food and home comforts, Sid expresses disgust at the taste of the milk. Joan bitterly complains that it's the bad weather which makes it turn. Sid is not convinced. 'It doesn't turn it into bloody water does it!'.

Look out for...

John Levene, popular as companion Sergeant Benton opposite Jon Pertwee on *Doctor Who*, crops up briefly in a scene with Barbara Windsor.

Keep your eyes peeled for Linda Hooks, looking as lovely as ever, and successfully helping dear old Peter Butterworth to live up to his name of Friar Roger.

In the early scenes with Barbara Windsor and Brian Osborne, note the use of stock sequences for the battling troops - they're taken from Laurence Olivier's 1945 classic, *Henry V*.

THE SOBBING CAVALIER

Lovelace **SID JAMES**   Sir Jethro Houndsbotham **JACK DOUGLAS**
Sarah **BARBARA WINDSOR**   Lady Kate Houndsbotham **JOAN SIMS**
Oliver Cromwell **PETER BUTTERWORTH**
Colonel **DAVID LODGE**   Cavalier **BRIAN OSBORNE**   Captain **BERNARD HOLLEY**

Screenplay by **Dave Freeman**
Music composed by **Richard Tattersall & John Marshall**

Graphics **George Wallder**   Animator **Len Lewis**   Designer **Richard Lake**
Executive Producer **Peter Rogers**
Producer **Gerald Thomas**   Director **Alan Tarrant**

Broadcast 18 January 1975 - 8.45pm   ATV Network Production
Colour   Running time - 23 mins.

This is the most successful attempt at presenting the *Carry On* film atmosphere in a 20-minute format. All the favourite comic types are included, the gags are fresh innuendo cleverly worked into the story-line and the acting is superb. Relying on elegant acting and serious history played for laughs rather than a barrage of one-liners and farcical performances, this re-working of Cromwellian England sees two stunning performances from Sid James and Jack Douglas. Jittering throughout with nerves and panicked energy, Jack is flustered by the imposing threats from the royalists and the roundheads: 'Bloody hell fire, they've got me both ways!'. Joan Sims nags away in the background, Barbara Windsor loses her clothes

(almost a pre-requisite by this stage of the game) and David Lodge growls a few priceless put downs. Peter Butterworth is stunning as Oliver Cromwell, while Sid can simply be Sid - chuckling at the glamour girls, battling the bad guys, battling his brother-in-law and embracing the audience with a warm personality and a winning wink. Without doubt, this is Sid James' last truly great contribution to *Carry On* comedy.

Basically this is *The Baron Outlook* re-done in different costumes, but here the comedy flows with originality and confidence, the playing is excellent throughout and Freeman's gags don't hold up the narrative. There's just enough wonderful, barrel-scraping innuendo to get Douglas and James sparring, while the good gags, when they come along, really hit home. Once, even, the glories of vintage Rothwell are evoked in a three-way exchange concerning conflicting ideas of Sid washing himself and seducing Miss Windsor. Joan: 'He could have it in the kitchen'/Jack: 'He only wants a bath!'/Sid: 'You speak for yourself!'. The comic ball is bounced between the three and it's great to watch. In the end everything works out for the best, with Sid getting a laugh from Barbara Windsor as he chuckles, 'I've got something down here I want in the oven!' and pulls out a chicken. It's the humour that works, the humour we want and the humour that Sid could play with his eyes shut.

Best performance

In fact, the finest acting turn contains no funny lines at all and raises laughs only by the fear he engenders in others: it's Peter Butterworth's outstanding interpretation of Oliver Cromwell. Clad in black and strolling round the castle with a suspicious, mischievous grin on his face, he is a straight-laced, anti-fun figure of comic evil. Peter grabs the role with relish and creates a mini masterpiece out of it. In an intense and incisive character study, his mock kindness and control on his temper presents itself brilliantly during the climatic trial sequence with a dragged up Sid James. It is a scene of subtle gags and beautiful under-playing: a far cry from much of the over-the-top mugging that marks out *Carry On Laughing* as a ham's paradise.

Favourite bit

It's a brief exchange between Sid James and Jack Douglas. As the battle-weary Sid arrives at the window he complains of wounds and starvation. The ever unsympathetic Jack goes away, comes back and hands Sid some objects: 'there's a walnut and a bandage now hop it!'. It's classic Freeman *Carry On*.

ORGY AND BESS

Sir Francis Drake **SID JAMES**   Queen Elizabeth I **HATTIE JACQUES**
King Philip **KENNETH CONNOR**   Lady Miranda **BARBARA WINDSOR**
Lord Essex & Master of the Rolls **JACK DOUGLAS**   Todd **VICTOR MADDERN**
Quaker Reporter **McDONALD HOBLEY**   Crew Member **BRIAN OSBORNE**
Sir Walter Raleigh **JOHN CARLIN**   Lord Burleigh **NORMAN CHAPPELL**

Screenplay by **Barry Cryer & Dick Vosburgh**
Music composed by **Richie Tattersall & John Marshall**

Graphics **George Wallder**   Animator **Len Lewis**   Designer **Richard Lake**
Executive Producer **Peter Rogers**   Producer **Gerald Thomas**
Director **Alan Tarrant**

Broadcast 25 January 1975 - 8.45pm ATV Network Production
Colour Running time - 23 mins.

A historic *Carry On* in more ways than one: it celebrates the glories of Elizabeth I and life at the royal court, but in terms of the series itself, this show includes the final appearances of Sid James and Hattie Jacques. Though the pair officially bowed out after *Dick*, this was the last *Carry On per se* for both, and despite the groanworthy script, the old magic is still apparent as they trundle through the same old innuendo and farcical comments. If there's rather too much camping about from John Carlin and Norman Chappell, one perfectly timed chuckle from Sid is enough to bring the colour back to your cheeks. Hattie is also on tip-top form, milking her virginal reputation and sexual frustration for all it's worth, with Kenneth Connor quite stunning as the King of Spain. Clicking his heels, spouting Spanish rubbish and rolling his dialogue into mouthfuls of continental love, Connor pops up only twice although he enjoys a round of applause on his exit and leaves an indelible mark. Barbara Windsor pops up and pops out, while Jack Douglas enjoys not one but two (count 'em) roles, contributing a typical Alf-like persona as well as a splendid straight turn as Lord Essex. Delivering his lines with dignified relish, Jack injects moments of treacherous, anti-royal and, even worse, anti-Sid dialogue, while slotting in some truly wonderful innuendos. Cryer and Vosburgh settle into that all-out *Carry On* style perfectly, including some very risque gems - Douglas on Windsor: 'They say she has welcome inscribed on her chamber!' - while tapping into Rothwellian incorporation of contemporary knowledge (the Elizabeth and Philip match/television news techniques). Popular song titles are used for corny and effective in-jokes, the team are all on sparkling form, the terrible gags come thick and fast, the screenplay is rich in typical *Carry On* exchanges and Sid laughs like never before. It's a funny if uneven affair and a priceless record of the end of an era.

Best performance

'Not me you fool!'. As the final Sid contribution, it has to be his definitive Sir Francis Drake, taking over where Terence Morgan left off! Throughout, he over-plays his guffawing laugh, never lets a cheap tag-line go by, meets Hattie with a cheerful click of the heels and 'Hello Bess - getting much!', and always comes up on top. Seducing Hattie Jacques, succumbing to the charms of Barbara Windsor and fighting camp ideals and authority figures, Sid is the epitome of *Carry On* manhood. Enjoying a brief sequence on board ship with Victor Maddern, Sid immediately brings *Orgy and Bess* into the realms of greatness as he discusses the Queen. A sailor shouts out, 'A vast behind', and Sid mumbles, 'I know she has but she's still the Queen!'. Again, it's obvious humour but done poetically. As Hattie winds up the tale with 'let there be bunting and frolics!', Sid gets literally the last laugh with, 'Try saying that after a couple of drinks!'. With a final perfectly timed guffaw into camera, that's it: a golden moment to be sure.

Favourite bit

Inevitably, the best moment comes from the partnership of Sid and Hattie. It's one of Barry Cryer's most treasurable lines of dialogue and one even Talbot Rothwell would have been proud of. Hattie: 'You scintillate!'/Sid: 'I sin after eight as well!'. Excellent.

Did you know?

Sadly, a couple of interesting performances were cut out of *Orgy and Bess*. That distinguished thespian Simon Callow crops up in the credits but was cut out of the narrative, while Richard Wattis filmed a comic cameo which was cut shortly before the show was broadcast. It was Wattis' final assignment, as he died just a few weeks later.

Orgy and Bess, along with *The Nine Old Cobblers*, was selected as the *creme de la creme* of *Carry On Laughing* series one. The two shows enjoyed a repeat screening in the weeks immediately after the second series was broadcast.

Look out for...

Enjoy Victor Maddern's scruffy old sea-dog, lapsing into Churchillian tones to express his distress. Sid, looking bemused, sighs, 'Thank you Richard Burton!'. It's an in-joke shared between the two actors from their time on *Carry On Cleo*.

Respected announcer and broadcaster McDonald Hobley has a brief linking sequence as an Elizabethan reporter.

Admiral Clanger makes a discovery: a vintage Peter Butterworth eccentric from *The Case of the Screaming Winkles.*

'I remember Richard Wattis who had a speech, accompanied by patriotic music, swearing never to bend the knee to the Spanish dog. At that point, a cannon ball came through the window and he immediately switched to singing "Granada, I'm falling under your spell". It was a vintage cast - Sid, Hattie, Ken Connor and Barbara Windsor. It was great fun!'

Barry Cryer

ONE IN THE EYE FOR HAROLD

Ethelred **JACK DOUGLAS** Athelstan **KENNETH CONNOR** Else **JOAN SIMS**
Isolde **DIANE LANGTON** William the Conqueror **DAVID LODGE**
Nellie **LINDA HOOKS** King Harold **NORMAN CHAPPELL**
Old Hag **PATSY SMART** Egbert **JOHN CARLIN**
Herald **BRIAN OSBORNE** Messenger **PAUL JESSON**
Black Cowl **JEROLD WELLS**
Pikemen **BILLY CORNELIUS** & **NOSHER POWELL**

Screenplay by **Lew Schwarz**
Music composed by **Richie Tattersall & John Marshall**

Graphics **George Wallder** Animator **Len Lewis** Designer **Ray White**
Executive Producer **Peter Rogers**
Producer **Gerald Thomas** Director **Alan Tarrant**

Broadcast 1 February 1975 - 8.45pm ATV Network Production Running time - 24 mins.

Carry On memories

'No, I am afraid I only ended up on the cutting room floor of *Orgy and Bess* (an episode of *Carry On Laughing*), one of the most tragi-comic episodes of my career - my first television, I alerted family and friends to glue themselves to the television when it came up and there I wasn't until the credits! I don't think I have terribly much to tell you about it. It was one of Barry Cryer's very funniest scripts, the title alone is a masterpiece but the various exchanges; "I got a little epistle last night"/"I know you did. I carried you home!" and "Could I play you something on my virginals?" (Barbara Windsor)/"You have some left?" (Sid James) and finally the really immortal exchange between Sir Francis Drake and Queen Elizabeth I (Sid & Hattie); "Shall we go back to my place or shall we go to your gaff by the river?" (Sid)/"Hampton Court?" (Hattie)/"No, I always walk this way!" (Sid), will remain with me forever. All I really remember about the cast is that they didn't rehearse very much because they all seemed to be on the phone to their stockbrokers all the time. Accordingly when we came to record it they all seemed extremely nervous which surprised me a great deal. Kenneth Connor was rather brilliant as the Spanish Ambassador but seemed to be nursing a deep grudge against the world at large. He asked me what I had just been doing. I told him, I'd been doing two plays by Brecht at The Traverse. He said, "Well this isn't Brecht - it's better!"'

Simon Callow

As the first episode in the series without Sid James, this show had a lot to live up to. Bearing in mind that it also saw the absence of such regulars as Peter Butterworth and Barbara Windsor, the comedy had to be more heavily given over to just a couple of central characters. As it happened, this experiment worked brilliantly and established the style for later entries. A sort of *Funny Thing Happened on the Way to the Battle of Hastings*, this show partners Jack Douglas and Kenneth Connor bravely lugging a secret weapon across the country to King Harold's troops. While enjoying a huge dose of typical *Carry On* innuendo, the script also pauses for moments of Goonish surrealism, including the Mukkinese Battlehorn played by Norman Chappell and, aptly, David Lodge, reliving some Sellers memories with a Clouseau-like French accent and mock English crown with a mini-Union Jack perched on it. Joan Sims pops up very briefly as a French seducer but is quickly tricked and disposed of by Kenneth Connor and his gun powder. Almost the entire show is played out in a state of love/hate cross-talking banter between Douglas and Connor, and very funny it is too. There's lots of comic mileage milked from the continual reference to the secret weapon as the 'you know what!', while Jack, relishing his 'Alf' jitters and manic twitching, chats up buxom Diane Langton and laughs heartily in the true style of *Carry On*. Douglas, as a newer member of the team, was often given the most lewd and leering lines of dialogue and injected them with spirited good humour. Here he shouts after the departing Langton: 'I'll be coming up your way in a minute!'. For 1975 this was pretty hot stuff; one can only presume that the men in power at ITV were less aware of the gags than the film censors! Contrasting with Connor's man of peace, Douglas ad libs and plays the 'Cor!' with mighty innuendo as he approaches Langton's serving wench. However, as Connor states, 'It does not arise in the monastery!'/'No, I'm sure it doesn't!'. The playing between the two stars earns this particular entry its extra Sid and lets the 20 odd minutes pass with good cheer and laughter.

Best performance
Kenneth Connor begins the show as a worldly, calm man of God; hurled out of his monastery he suddenly transforms into a bumbling mess, complete with Hengist Pod vocals from *Cleo*. Alternating between bumbling fool, naive religious authority figure and clever fighter, Kenneth enjoys a scene with Joan Sims ('Ah! Miss Unimportant!') and even includes his old Hudis catchphrase - 'Missus!'. It's at times a subtle performance but one of all-out innu-endo. It's outstanding stuff.

Look out for...
The war is reworked as a football match, with Norman Chappell and John Carlin shouting instruc-tions and bickering on the side-lines.

The final moment of history faking, the covering up of Harold's accidental death, is typical *Carry On* histrionics with Douglas blurting out: 'Bung an arrow in his eye and let's scarper!'.

THE NINE OLD COBBLERS

Lord Peter Flimsy **JACK DOUGLAS**
Punter **KENNETH CONNOR**
Maisie **BARBARA WINDSOR**
Amelia Forbush **JOAN SIMS**
Inspector Bungler **DAVID LODGE**
Charlie **VICTOR MADDERN**
Miss Dawkins **PATSY ROWLANDS**
Vicar **JOHN CARLIN**
Pianist **SAM HARDING**

Screenplay by **Dave Freeman**
Music by **Richie Tattersall & John Marshall**

Graphics **George Wallder**   Animator **Len Lewis**
Film Cameraman **Jack Atchelor**
Designer **Richard Lake**   Executive Producer **Peter Rogers**
Producer **Gerald Thomas**
Director **Alan Tarrant**

Broadcast 8 February 1975 - 8.45pm   ATV Network Production
Colour   Running time - 24 mins.

THE CASE OF THE SCREAMING WINKLES

Lord Peter Flimsy **JACK DOUGLAS**   Punter **KENNETH CONNOR**
Mrs MacFlute **JOAN SIMS**   Admiral Clanger **PETER BUTTERWORTH**
Inspector Bungler **DAVID LODGE**   Nurse Millie Teazel **SHERRIE HEWSON**
Potter **NORMAN CHAPPELL**   Madame Petra **MARIANNE STONE**
Major Merridick **JOHN CARLIN**   Charwallah Charlie **MELVYN HAYES**
Colonel Postwick **MICHAEL NIGHTINGALE**

Screenplay by **Dave Freeman**
Music by **Richie Tattersall & John Marshall**

Graphics **George Wallder**   Animator **Len Lewis**
Cameras **Mike Whitcutt**   Lighting **Pete Dyson**
Vision Control **Gerry Taylor**   Sound **Len Penfold**   Vision Mixer **Felicity Maton**
VTR Editor **Peter Charles**   Wardrobe **James Dark**
Make-up **Sheila Mann**   Designer **Lewis Logan**
Executive Producer **Peter Rogers**   Producer **Gerald Thomas**
Director **Alan Tarrant**

Broadcast 2 November 1975 - 7.25pm   ATV Network Production
Colour   Running time - 24 mins.

THE CASE OF THE COUGHING PARROT

Lord Peter Flimsy **JACK DOUGLAS**   Punter **KENNETH CONNOR**
Dr. Janis Crunbitt **JOAN SIMS**   Inspector Bungler **DAVID LODGE**
Irma Klein **SHERRIE HEWSON**   Lost Property Attendant **PETER BUTTERWORTH**
Ambulance Driver **NORMAN CHAPPELL**   Harry **BRIAN OSBORNE**
Norman **JOHNNY BRIGGS**   Freda Filey **VIVIENNE JOHNSON**

Screenplay by **Dave Freeman**
Music by **Richie Tattersall & John Marshall**

Graphics **George Wallder**   Animator **Len Lewis**   Cameras **Mike Whitcutt**
Lighting **Pete Dyson**
Vision Control **Gerry Taylor**   Vision Mixer **Felicity Maton**   Sound **Len Penfold**
VTR Editor **Peter Charles**   Wardrobe **James Dark**   Make-up **Sheila Mann**
Designer **Lewis Logan**
Executive Producer **Peter Rogers**   Producer **Gerald Thomas**
Director **Alan Tarrant**

Broadcast 23 November 1975 - 7.25pm   ATV Network Production
Colour   Running time - 24 mins.

In many ways the crowning glory of *Carry On Laughing* and quite arguably the finest piece of post-Sid James *Carry On* filmed, these three detective adventures are blessed with some of Dave Freeman's most wonder-fully appalling jokes which are delivered with straight-faced sincerity by the crime-busting duo at their centre. In a perfect example of the series' attempt at building the comedy around a smaller number of main characters, Jack Douglas and Kenneth Connor wander through a world of mad murderers, morning tea, flying daggers, peering through keyholes and outlandish clues.

Narratively speaking, it is influenced by the cosy 1920s' world of Lord Peter Wimsey mysteries, while Freeman's deconstruction of the detective genre wal-lows in everything from Sherlock Holmes-like London mists to Batman-like painfully contrived clues concealed in riddles. It's a world of Agatha Christie dignity: all vicars, sinister tea parties and country village community. The crimes are unbeliev-

Kenneth Connor, David Lodge and Jack Douglas enjoy a laugh on the set of Dave Freeman's classic *The Case of the Coughing Parrot*.

came up to me and asked if I could hold it for him!'. Down at The Nine Old Cobblers (something about the name of a bell which rings when murder is done - though precious few seem to be bothered), Barbara Windsor ('Just given old Charlie his oats!') wobbles and giggles her way through a supporting role as the perfect landlady/barmaid, while Victor Maddern pops in for a few rustic mutters and a quick sup of ale. There's a superb naval resurrection of Butterworth's old sea-dog from *Girls* in *The Case of the Screaming Winkles*, helped out by a dewy-eyed bimbo persona from Sherrie Hewson ('I don't like the look of him!'/'I never damn well did!') and a magical climactic sequence in a fun-fair. The devil in *The Ghost Train* signals something other than campy evil after Butterworth's attack. Freeman's obsession with corny, childish innuendo is well satisfied, while a clutch of cleverly worked out riddles and clues are enjoyably bad.

As ever, in dealing with situations made-up from groanworthy one-liners, Freeman also indulges his love of alliterative comedy (found in definitive terms with Jim Dale's tongue-twisting speech in *Columbus*). Some of the exchanges between Jack Douglas and Kenneth Connor - 'A nibble on the Nile Delta'/'Hannibal on the Nile...'; when discussing a damp helmet, 'Is it pith?'/'No it's merely condensation!' (both from *The Case of the Coughing Parrot*); 'Clanger... Clanger... That rings a bell!'/'So I believe M'Lord!' (*The Case of the Screaming Winkles*) - are wonderfully dreadful and the whole series has an air of tongue-in-cheek splendour that signals the best, feel-good atmosphere of the classic film adventures. Almost feature length in quantity, with tight script editing and another mystery sewn into the story these shows could have been moulded into an acceptable full-blown *Carry On* film. However, as it is, they remain a flash of originality and inspiration that failed to rescue the series from the inevitable close. However, the adventures of Flimsy and Punter do capture some priceless moments from a series in rapid decline.

ably bizarre, the characterizations simply selected from the stock *Carry On* file and the dialogue at times awe-inspiring in its banality. However, the performances of Douglas and Connor are flawless throughout: they play the humour with reverence and allow the outlandish characters of Barbara Windsor, Joan Sims and Peter Butterworth to bounce innuendo, smut and childish japes around in the background.

The beauty of these shows is that how ever absurd the scenario gets, the detectives are totally commited to discovering the culprits. What's more, these shows are fun and very funny. There's a pleasant, historically-accurate feel about the mist-swirling streets of London and the lush home counties luxury of the old manor houses. David Lodge stomps through the proceedings as the typically thick and bumbling, Lestrade-like, Inspector, while the crimes themselves are so strange that they serve merely as a long list of weird and wonderful clues and opportunities for straight-laced comic deductions from Connor and Douglas. It works so well because here are two competent detective brains suddenly let loose in a world of knickers gags, glamour girls and second-hand innuendo.

The Coughing Parrot scenario is perhaps the most enjoyable, blessed with an endearing infected bird and wonderfully strange goings-on based around the low-life by the London docks. Joan Sims is involved in the manic plot of stolen artefacts as some sort of Margaret Rutherford-like museum curator with the best Pharaoh name since *Screaming*, and the perfectly formed figure of Vivienne Johnson tosses in a few half-baked Windsorisms: 'A gent

Best performance

Without doubt these are Jack Douglas' shows and he brings a touch of dignified comic acting technique to form his finest contribution to the history of *Carry On*. Monocled and well-spoken, with just the merest hint of 'Alf' jittering, Jack strolls through the strange happenings and horrific murders with a casual, sophisticated style. Working to sheer perfection with cohort Connor, Jack delights in moments of surreal stupidity and happily listens to the wise advice of his servant. The opening scene in the first adventure (*The Nine Old Cobblers*) is typical, with Douglas musing over the crossword clue concerning four letters beginning with 'C' which differentiate a male chicken from a female chicken. With assured confidence, Connor answers 'Crow, m'lord!' and, as the audience join in for the beautifully timed punchline, Jack pauses, thinks and asks the question: 'Do you have a rubber?!'. It's this obvious, well-worn sort of humour, played with conviction worthy of Shakespearian verse, that marks this unique comic partnership as a gem of *Carry On*. Jack could even indulge his love of ad lib opposite that master Connor, notably in the *Winkles* story, as he removes a clue from its shell and Jack laughs, looks at Kenneth and mutters: 'Fiendishly clever!'. It wasn't in the script - it's just two actors enjoying themselves in front of an audience. What more do you want!

Favourite bit

The highlight of the series comes in *The Case of the Coughing Parrot* with the briefest of brief contributions from Peter Butterworth who plays off Connor and Douglas to perfection. As a shy, timid and nervously frustrated old eccentric at the Lost Property Office, Butterworth explains his problems and bemoans his fate. Questioned by Connor about this strange coughing bird, he is quizzed as to whether he has had it handed in. With skill and timing beyond the material, Butterworth mutters, 'Can you describe it! - I've got fifteen!'. Totally unaware of the madness of the situation, he bumbles and moans about his lot and almost single-handedly wins the entire set of three shows its extra Sid rating! Superb.

Look out for...

Joan Sims bashes out 'Syncopated Rhythm' on the drums in *The Nine Old Cobblers*.

Look out for a 1990s *Coronation Street* duo, Johnny Briggs and Sherrie Hewson, in *The Case of the Coughing Parrot*. Briggs had been serving his apprenticeship as a small-part Carry Oner since *Khyber*, while Sherrie Hewson had just filmed the 27th cinema release, *Behind*, before this particular episode was broadcast.

In *The Case of the Coughing Parrot*, Kenneth Connor rounds off his performance of quiet restraint with a burst of hilarious *Carry On* mugging as he chokes and coughs due to the infected parrot - just in case people were taking his acting too seriously!

Carry On memories

'I loved the role of Lord Flimsy. What Gerald Thomas cleverly decided was that on television in a shorter format you couldn't duplicate what he had done in 26 movies at that time. So what he decid-ed was that Sid would star in that one, Barbara would star in that one and so on - this was the branch of the series that I was given top billing on. It gave another insight to *Carry On* and it was lovely for me. I was very proud of those shows. I am delighted that they are now available on video - releases for which I did the voice-over on the advert.'
Jack Douglas

UNDER THE ROUND TABLE

King Arthur **KENNETH CONNOR**   Lady Guinevere **JOAN SIMS**
Merlin **PETER BUTTERWORTH**   Sir Pureheart **BERNARD BRESSLAW**
Sir Gay **JACK DOUGLAS**   Black Knight **OSCAR JAMES**
Sir Osis **VICTOR MADDERN**   Sir William **NORMAN CHAPPELL**
Lady Ermintrude **VALERIE WALSH**   Man-At-Arms **BILLY CORNELIUS**
Minstrel **DESMOND McNAMARA**   Shortest Knight **RONNIE BRODY**
Trumpeter **BRIAN CAPRON**   Knight **BRIAN OSBORNE**

Screenplay by **Lew Schwarz**
Music composed by **Richie Tattersall**, **John Marshall** & **Max Harris**

Graphics **George Wallder**   Animator **Len Lewis**
Cameras **Mike Whitcutt**   Sound **Len Penfold**
Lighting **Pete Dyson**   Vision Control **Jim Reeves**   Vision Mixer **Carole Legg**
VTR Editor **Peter Charles**   Wardrobe **James Dark**   Make-up **Sheila Mann**
Designer **Brian Holgate**
Executive Producer **Peter Rogers**   Producer **Gerald Thomas**
Director **Alan Tarrant**

Broadcast 26 October 1975 - 7.25pm   ATV Network Production
Colour Running time - 25 mins.

SHORT KNIGHT, LONG DAZE

King Arthur **KENNETH CONNOR**   Lady Guinevere **JOAN SIMS**
Merlin **PETER BUTTERWORTH**
Sir Lancelot **BERNARD BRESSLAW**   Sir Gay **JACK DOUGLAS**
Mabel **SUSAN SKIPPER**
Sir William **NORMAN CHAPPELL**   Herald **BRIAN OSBORNE**
Minstrel **DESMOND McNAMARA**
Man-At-Arms **BILLY CORNELIUS**   Trumpeter **BRIAN CAPRON**

Screenplay by **Lew Schwarz**
Music composed by **Richie Tattersall**, **John Marshall** & **Max Harris**

Graphics **George Wallder**   Animator **Len Lewis**
Cameras **Mike Whitcutt**   Sound **Len Penfold**
Lighting **Pete Dyson**   Vision Control **Jim Reeves**   Vision Mixer **Carole Legg**
VTR Editor **Peter Charles**   Wardrobe **James Dark**   Make-up **Sheila Mann**
Designer **Brian Holgate**
Executive Producer **Peter Rogers**   Producer **Gerald Thomas**
Director **Alan Tarrant**

Broadcast 16 November 1975 - 7.25pm   ATV Network Production
Colour Running time - 24 mins.

One Sid rating for a couple of shows which barely have one good gag between them. Based around the legendary King Arthur, these tales cover almost exactly the same ground and rely heavily on the utterly hilarious word-play between knight and night - careful or your sides may split! Arthur is

Kenneth Connor enjoys some horseplay on location for _Short Knight, Long Daze_.

blessed with a superb seedy picture of middle aged incompetence from Kenneth Connor who couldn't give a bad performance if he tried. Struggling desperately against a script of single entendres linked by misconceived camp and farcical medieval domestic banter, Connor's role is a fine beacon of past glories.

The tales tell of Arthur and his Knights of the Round Table, introducing a new member into the throng. Both times it is Bernard Bresslaw - only his accent changes to differentiate between the shows. Endearingly, the second episode, _Short Knight, Long Daze_, includes a George Formbyesque wanderer, continually chuckling and crying out 'Don't worry Missus - he won't feel a thing!', while _Under the Round Table_ presents Bresslaw as a dignified but incompetent powerhouse. Joan Sims, all sexual frustration and marital angst, barely gets a look in and her dialogue is so banal that it hardly affects the narrative. However, she does manage to inject a couple of delightful moments: notably with the Formbyisms opposite Bresslaw - 'Am I champion'/'You are that lad!' - and her lusty exhaustion after a sex-filled time with the braver Bresslaw: 'What a knight!'. Told you it was funny! Peter Butterworth is wonderful as the bumbling old Merlin and there are several sexy turns from the likes of Valerie Walsh and Susan Skipper. In the absence of both Kenneth Williams and Charles Hawtrey from these televisual feasts, the effeminate humour was given to either Bresslaw or Douglas. Here it's Jack Douglas' turn and he delivers the painfully deadening camp humour ('They wouldn't give you the rust off their baldricks!') with an air of uncomfortable bemusement. Mincing around in a blonde wig and bouncing gags off the regal Kenneth Connor, he fails to gel but does at least present one golden _Carry On_ moment. Hearing

the noise of horses approaching in the distance Douglas explains to the King that it's, 'Old Merlin playing with his coconuts again!'/'Silly old man - he can hardly see as it is!'. A moment of _Carry On_ originality amidst dire scripting. The medieval comedy is fun merely due to the actors involved: the jokes are seriously bad and almost remove the will to live. If it wasn't for Connor and Butterworth you might as well go and pull out your own Excalibur.

Best performance
Peter Butterworth just about steals the shows with a dithering picture of confused old age and magical powers. Delighting in the awful gags and the company of friend Kenneth Connor, Peter happily overplays the humour and ad libs with relish. Injecting elements of Moore-Marriott's old Harbottle from _Oh, Mr Porter_, he talks to Connor through a hatch in his door and runs through the complicated ritual of making an appointment. 'I can't let you in here unless you say the secret password!'/'The secret password!'/'You said that very nicely - Come in!'. Dealing with a stuffed chicken, Peter grabs it by the throat and threatens, 'I'll do the talking!', and momentarily makes Joan Sims stop in mid-sentence as he mutters on about not blowing on his crystal ball. Clearly Peter, having read the script, decided to spruce up the action with some throwaway lines that no-one wanted to throw away. It's a masterclass in rising above your material to present a complex, multi-layered comic character study.

Favourite bit
My favourite moment comes at the end of _Short Knight, Long Daze_. As the royal subjects converge on Kenneth Connor, with Peter Butterworth using the opportunity to stare into camera with a manic comic look, Schwarz includes his most inventive line of dialogue. Desperately trying to justify his position, Connor regales the crowd with kingly tones: 'I am your King - give me loyalty! I am your ruler - give me your obedience!', finally succumbing to nerves and jittering, 'I'm an old man - give me ten yards start!'. It's priceless Shakespearian deconstruction and Connor delivers the gag to perfection.

Did you know?
During the filming of _Carry On Cleo_, Jim Dale suggested the idea of a _Carry On Camelot_ to Peter Rogers, with Sid James taking the role of King Arthur. At the time, Rogers turned it down because it was a subject which did not interest him. Over 10 years later, Jim's original idea is resurrected here. Jim Dale himself went on to enjoy a medieval romp in the 1979 Disney adventure _The Spaceman and King Arthur_.

Although uninterested in the idea during the golden days of 1964, with the appearance of these two shows on television in 1975, Gerald Thomas expressed a sincere interest in making a full-length feature *Carry On* out of the Kenneth Connor/King Arthur scenario. It was initially planned as the 28th movie until a certain Second World War script presented itself.

AND IN MY LADY'S CHAMBER

Sir Harry Bulger-Plunger **KENNETH CONNOR**
Baroness Lottie Von Titsenhausen **BARBARA WINDSOR**
Clodson **JACK DOUGLAS**   Mrs Breeches **JOAN SIMS**
Silas **PETER BUTTERWORTH**   Starkers **BERNARD BRESSLAW**
Virginia **SHERRIE HEWSON**   Willie **ANDREW RAY**
Lilly **CAROL HAWKINS**   Teeny **VIVIENNE JOHNSON**

Written by **Lew Schwarz**
Music composed by **Richie Tattershall, John Marshall & Max Harris**

Graphics **George Wallder**   Cameras **Mike Whitcutt**   Sound **Len Penfold**
Lighting **Pete Dyson**
Wardrobe **James Dark**   Make-up **Sheila Mann**   Vision Control **Jim Reeves**
Vision Mixer **Mary Forrest**   VTR Editor **Peter Charles**   Designer **Anthony Waller**
Executive Producer **Peter Rogers**
Producer **Gerald Thomas**   Director **Alan Tarrant**

Broadcast 9 November 1975 - 7.25pm ATV Network Production
Colour   Running time - 25 mins.

WHO NEEDS KITCHENER?

Sir Harry Bulger-Plunger **KENNETH CONNOR**
Baroness Lottie Von Titsenhausen **BARBARA WINDSOR**
Clodson **JACK DOUGLAS**   Mrs Breeches **JOAN SIMS**
Klanger **BERNARD BRESSLAW**   Willie **ANDREW RAY**
Virginia **SHERRIE HEWSON**   Lilly **CAROL HAWKINS**
Teeny **VIVIENNE JOHNSON**   Newsboy **BRIAN OSBORNE**

Written by **Lew Schwarz**
Music composed by **Richie Tattershall & John Marshall**

Graphics **George Wallder**   Cameras **Mike Whitcutt**   Sound **Len Penfold**
Lighting **Pete Dyson**
Wardrobe **James Dark**   Make-up **Sheila Mann**   Vision Control **Jim Reeves**
Vision Mixer **Mary Forrest**   VTR Editor **Peter Charles**   Designer **Anthony Waller**
Executive Producer **Peter Rogers**
Producer **Gerald Thomas**   Director **Alan Tarrant**

Broadcast 30 November 1975 - 7.25pm ATV Network Production
Colour   Running time - 25 mins.

This is an amazing attempt to contrast the smutty glories of *Carry On* with the refined restraint of *Upstairs, Downstairs*. No-one plays for subtlety, just for all out trouser-dropping farce as the refined lifestyle of the landed gentry is deconstructed and debunked. As with its more serious predecessor, the most interesting characters come from downstairs with Jack Douglas' impeccable Gordon Jackson parody and the likes of Joan Sims, Carol Hawkins and Vivienne Johnson mugging around opposite the refrained home owners. The humour is practically non-existent at times, although huge bursts of unsubtle

innuendo come forth at odd moments - notably when Kenneth Connor and Barbara Windsor get together. As with the King Arthur episodes, the two story-lines are almost impossible to separate, both dealing with a strange and well endowed new footman in the household, Bernard Bresslaw in both cases. There is clumsy comedy based round the newfangled things in the modern home and the absentminded dithering of Connor as Douglas struggles to help him understand telegrams and telephones. Sherrie Hewson is quite splendid as Connor's frightfully well-spoken daughter, while Barbara Windsor is the model of unsubtle cockney cheer, bursting out of her dress and sending up her persona shamelessly while remaining unwilling to partake in the offical *Carry On* movie for 1975. Barbara is totally over-thetop and the chief delight of the shows is the outrageous sexual suggestions that get Connor's bloodpressure sky high: 'I just love the sound of it!'.

And in my Lady's Chamber boasts no story-line to speak of: welcoming Connor's son fresh from safari but spiralling into a Whitehall farce scenario of *Loving*-like bed-hopping, drugged champagne and various sexual couplings. The acting is manic, Jack Douglas injects 'Alf' twitches into his butler persona and everybody has a ball. Lacking any real comic coherence, the cast more than make up for any shortcomings, and there's at least one delightfully dodgy line. As Barbara Windsor closes the show and pulls the sex beast Bresslaw into her room, she coos, 'I've got a damp patch as well!'. How did they get away with that gag? The second episode is more of the same, although here we have the threat of war, moments of half-baked political satire with Sherrie

Carol Hawkins, Bernard Bresslaw, Joan Sims, Jack Douglas, Vivienne Johnson, Peter Butterworth, Barbara Windsor, Kenneth Connor, Andrew Ray and Sherrie Hewson in a publicity shot for *And in my Lady's Chamber*.

Jack Douglas and Kenneth Connor in *And in my Lady's Chamber.*

Carry On humour - notably Douglas twitching - these sequences achieve the basic requirement for subtle digging at the straight-laced world of *Upstairs, Downstairs.*

Did you know?
Former child star, Andrew Ray is the son of *Teacher's* Ted Ray and the brother of *Constable's* Robin Ray.

Look out for...
Peter Butterworth pops up all too briefly as the super-refined Captain Silas Carshaw in the first episode, turning on the military man power and slick charmer to impress Sherrie Hewson. Enjoying only a few lines of dialogue, Peter grins and bumbles with perfection.

Hewson's involvement with the Suffragettes and a totally obvious German spy, Bresslaw, trying to be inconspicuous with lines like, 'You have my word as an English gentlebloke!'. Barbara is once again the tart with a heart and loads of money, seducing hordes of military men and seeing this particular branch of the series out with a plug for a past Broadway success, *Oh! What A Lovely War!*. This comic scenario would be resurrected over 10 years later as the more subtle comic-drama of *You Rang M'Lord*, featuring Windsor in several episodes, while lovers of really low-brow British comedy should refer to the 1976 Diana Dors sex comedy *Keep It Up Downstairs*. Here the cast of *Carry On* regulars have a fair bash but to little effect.

Best performance
Joan Sims, without doubt one of our foremost actresses, spent a lifetime in supporting roles opposite Sid James and Kenneth Williams. She always gave a flawless performance and these shows present her with an outstanding role which successfully takes over the comedy. Although a comic treatment of Angela Baddeley's serious performance, Joan enjoys mainly straight dialogue delivered with a comic, gruff and hearty persona. Laughing at the stiff-upper-lipped manners of Douglas and delighting in the rough and ready approach of Bernard Bresslaw, Sims controls the kitchen with a feel-good attitude which dominates the show.

Favourite bit
As a result of Joan's marvellous contribution, the best sequences are those downstairs, and, in particular, those moments of comic banter between Cook Sims and Butler Douglas. Injected with traces of

LAMP-POSTS OF THE EMPIRE

Lady Mary Airey-Fairey **BARBARA WINDSOR**   Stanley **KENNETH CONNOR**
Elephant Dick Darcy **JACK DOUGLAS**
Dr Pavingstone **BERNARD BRESSLAW**
Lord Gropefinger **PETER BUTTERWORTH**   Witchdoctor **OSCAR JAMES**
Mabel the Gorilla **REUBEN MARTIN**
Native **WAYNE BROWNE**
Man on Park Bench **NORMAN CHAPPELL**
Old Man At Club **JOHN CARLIN**
Neighbouring Man At Club **MICHAEL NIGHTINGALE**

Screenplay by **Lew Schwarz**
Music composed by **Richie Tattersall & John Marshall**

Graphics **George Wallder**   Animator **Len Lewis**
Cameras **Mike Whitcutt**   Sound **Len Penfold**
Wardrobe **James Dark**   Make-up **Sheila Mann**   Lighting **Pete Dyson**
Vision Control **John Crane**   Vision Mixer **Mary Forrest**
VTR Editor **John Hawkins**   Designer **Michael Bailey**
Executive Producer **Peter Rogers**
Producer **Gerald Thomas**   Director **Alan Tarrant**

Broadcast 7 December 1975 - 7.25pm   ATV Network Production
Colour   Running time - 24 mins.

For the 13th and final *Carry On Laughing* show, the gang resurrected the ethos of *Carry On Up The Jungle* and contrasted it with a flamboyantly, tongue-in-cheek, *Boy's Own*-styled adventure story. A sort of Donald McGill meets Michael Palin's *Ripping Yarns* if you like! It's all very entertaining stuff with a top-drawer cast of major *Carry On* talent led by Barbara Windsor, Kenneth Connor and Jack Douglas. Windsor, all refined dignity and lusty sexuality, gets the best gags and delivers them with self-aware grace. Kenneth Connor, tapping into his old Norman Hudis, giggling, 'ho,ho', youthful hero persona, tackles his central role well but overplays his hand on the 'Dr Pavingstone' running gag. One reference to the fact that this is merely a play and the people in it merely players would be funny, but after three repeats of the same frustrated cry of, 'that's my line', the idea begins to fade. Having said that, Connor sparkles in the jungle environment, contributing a quite splendid magic act with his own whistling accompanying his amazing feats. Jack Douglas - marvellous in this ultimate *Carry On* incorporation of his 'Alf' persona - bumbles and falls all over the place. The beauty of his creation is his confidence and self-assurance contrasted with his obvious stupidity and clumsy persona. Crashing into the scene *à la* Tarzan and jittering and twitching throughout the jungle, Douglas contributes a unique style of comic expression. If all else fails, he has the typical absurd character name of 'Elephant Dick' and as Kenneth Connor comments to Barbara Windsor: 'They don't call him Elephant Dick for nothing do they!'/'Well, they do actually!'. Peter Butterworth and Bernard Bresslaw are on hand with some memorable comic support: all eccentric quirks and innuendo-encrusted dialogue. The mini-variety show, complete with scantily-clad Miss Windsor, Douglas' pidgin English cooing and by-play with manic witch-doctor, Oscar James, makes for a merry carry on up the jungle again. It lacks the solid central comic power of Sid James, but as a half hour effort, this is one of the best in the series. *Carry On Laughing* was an experiment which didn't achieve its objective, but it did bring another six hours of *Carry On* to the eager fan. As a social document for the mid-1970s' view on sexism, comedy and the British way of life, these shows are perfect pieces of reference. Besides that, when the wind's in the right place, there are plenty of laughs to be had as well.

Best performance

As the object of the search, Bernard Bresslaw brings a lovely touch of bewildered calm to his role of Dr Pavingstone. Shocked at Douglas' belief that he's cracking up ('Who's mind's gone!'), Bresslaw is all eye-popping amazement and embittered moans. The victim of witchcraft, he enjoys some priceless banter with the sexually over-active Barbara Windsor and is initially shocked by her appearance. Displaying her pink boots, Barbara mentions her pink underwear. Connor brilliantly comments, 'Steady on girl - it'll take him a week to get over the boots!'. Lacking any intrinsically funny lines himself, Bernie milks the comic situation of his absurd ideas and actions to create a beauty of a performance.

Favourite bit

The love/hate banter between Jack Douglas and Barbara Windsor remains constant throughout the jungle trek and provides some fine comic moments. Barbara complains about Elephant Dick's appalling

navigation skills - he even loses the porters on the first day! Douglas, in a feeble defence, explains that loads of people lose their porters on the first day, but as Barbara bitterly points out, 'Not in Victoria Station!'.

Did you know?

Mabel, the mad gorilla that Kenneth Connor meets in this episode, is played by Reuben Martin. He served the same purpose in the 1970 classic *Up The Jungle*, again opposite Connor.

Look out for...

There are references to two fine comic double acts. When Kenneth Connor's magic show begins to collapse due to the witchdoctor, Kenneth shouts out , 'What do you think of it so far!' to which the voodoo artefact answers 'Rubbish!'. Stunned, Kenneth emerges from within the story and explains, 'So that's where they got it from!'. And, of course, before Eric and Ern we had Laurel and Hardy. Once all the team are affected by the witchcraft-induced tails, Barbara puts on her Ollie pose and mutters, 'blown it again - didn't you Stanley!'.

A PETER ROGERS AND GERALD THOMAS PRODUCTION

CARRY ON LAUGHING'S CHRISTMAS CLASSICS

Introduced by
KENNETH WILLIAMS & BARBARA WINDSOR

Featuring the work of
**BERNARD BRESSLAW PETER BUTTERWORTH SANDRA CARON ROY CASTLE
KENNETH CONNOR JIM DALE LARRY DANN WINDSOR DAVIES
JACK DOUGLAS SALLY GEESON ANITA HARRIS CAROL HAWKINS
CHARLES HAWTREY SHERRIE HEWSON JULIAN HOLLOWAY
FRANKIE HOWERD HATTIE JACQUES SID JAMES VALERIE LEON
JULIAN ORCHARD PATSY ROWLANDS TERRY SCOTT JOAN SIMS
KENNETH WILLIAMS & BARBARA WINDSOR**

From
*Carry On Doctor, Carry On... Up The Khyber, Carry On Camping, Carry On Again Doctor,
Carry On Up The Jungle, Carry On Henry, Carry On Abroad, Carry On Dick* and
Carry On Behind.

Created by **Peter Rogers & Gerald Thomas**
Original Material by **Talbot Rothwell & Dave Freeman**
Music by **Eric Rogers**

Designer **Bill Laslett** Production Assistant **Caroline Hahn**
Editor **Jack Gardner** Producer **Gerald Thomas** Director **David Clark**

Broadcast 22 December 1983 - 7.30pm Thames Television Production
Colour Running time - 24 mins.

Or a case of *That's Carry On* for people with short attention spans! That feature-length compilation had led to the ITV smash hit series *Carry On Laughing* in 1981, a slapdash affair with bits and pieces of classic *Carry On* tossed in like the proverbial salad. However, the huge ratings figures promoted an extra special Christmas episode. At the end of the third season, hard cash was put up front, Gerald Thomas was roped in to organize the show and a couple of *Carry On* survivors were dragged into the studio. They had done it before so why not have them do it again?

Thus it was that Kenneth Williams and Barbara Windsor pulled out some tired old innuendos to link choice clips from *Carry On* days past. Seemingly ad libbed and certainly unrehearsed, the linking sequences are full of ripe corny comments and tongue-in-cheek sexuality. Barbara: 'I was just thinking - all these years and I've never had it!' Williams: 'You've... never had it. Nev...never had it! Never had what!'/'A white Christmas!'/'Oh right! Yes, a white Christmas - yes, ooh, you had me worried there for a minute!'. Beginning with a stirring and out of tune rendition of the Irving Berlin classic as shots from movies like *Dick* and *Henry* are depicted as cards on a tree, the show includes some great treasures. There's the Frankie/Sid duologue from *Doctor*, Barbara and Jim sharing a medical anatomy discussion in *Again Doctor*, the glassless window scenario from *Abroad* and an edited highlights presentation of the dining room sequence from *Khyber*. It's fun, cheering and short. The final image of Williams as a fairy on top of the tree is a winning one and the affectionate Christmas good wishes from our hosts is heart-warming and evocative. It was a fond look at happy, never to be re-captured days: Ken's looking older, the laughs are still in the air, camp is rife and Christmas pleasure is ensured. It was the fifth and final Yuletide *Carry On*.

Carry On memories

'Those compilations were made originally because at the time a gentleman called Philip Jones, head of Thames television light entertainment, had seen *That's Carry On* on television and thought it would be a good idea to do some half hour compilations. They were quite difficult to do because it wasn't just lifting a scene out and joining it on, the scenes were recut to try and bring them up to a more modern-day pace. I didn't have the original trims to go back to. Often it was a question of replaying music, cutting bits out of the music by taking bars out and trying to smooth things over. We didn't record music - just rearrange the original material. I'm sure if my old mate Eric Rogers had been alive he'd strangle me at times after what I've done to his music!'
Jack Gardner

'That was a very emotional show to do. Kenny and myself got together for a few hours to record our linking scenes and, of course, Sid had gone, Peter had gone and Hattie had gone. We got very tearful during recording.'
Barbara Windsor

A Hat Trick Production for Channel Four

NORBERT SMITH - A LIFE
CARRY ON BANGING

Sir Norbert Smith **HARRY ENFIELD**   Greenham Guard **JACK DOUGLAS**
Greenham Women's Leader **BARBARA WINDSOR**
Greenham Officer **KENNETH CONNOR**
Greenham Girls **BRIDGET BRAMMALL LYNNE BREARE AMANDA BROWN**
FRANCES GEARY TRACEY-ANN MORRIS VANESSA MORGAN JUSTINE PAGE
CHARLOTTE PLEAT EMMA-JANE REED & SUE WAYMAN

Written by **Harry Enfield & Geoffrey Perkins**
Music by **David Firman**

Casting Director **Rebecca Howard**   Lighting Cameraman **John Rosenbury**
Editor **Alan Mackay** Sound Editor **Deborah Shorrocks**
Location Manager **Kathy Fisher**   Research **Jane Bigger**
Costume Designer **Sharon Lewis**   Make-up Designer **Jenny Shircore**
Designer **Graeme Story** Production Manager **Mary Bell**
Executive Producer **Denise O'Donoghue**
Producer **Geoffrey Perkins**   Director **Geoff Posner**

Broadcast 3 November 1989 - 10.30pm   Channel Four Television
Colour Running time - 52 mins ('Carry On Banging' section - 3 mins).

It was over 10 years since the last *Carry On* film had hit the big screen and a collection of young comedians and entertainers had become a front-line fan club of the old style of Sid James and Talbot Rothwell. One of the key figures in this movement was Harry Enfield who loved the old *Carry On* movies. When in 1989 he joined forces with Melvyn Bragg to present a parody of the British film industry, the *Carry Ons* were a natural inclusion.

Despite this being very much unofficial *Carry On* and, indeed, using the style for parody rather than for an offical continuation of the series, the Enfield celebration was a masterpiece of concentrated innuendo. Although the sequence is a very minor part of the programme (amounting to no more than three minutes in a featurette length television special) the *Carry On* tribute comes near the close of the show and remains the highlight. Thanks mainly to sympathetic handling, Harry Enfield succeeded in coaxing back three of the original cast to join in the fun and games: Kenneth Connor, Barbara Windsor and Jack Douglas. The basic premise for the supposed feature is a tongue-in-cheek attempt to milk *Carry On* comedy from the anti-nuclear campaigners of the 1960s. In terms of the career of Norbert Smith, this *Carry On* was made around 1980.

The sequence begins brilliantly, with tense and serious music complementing an aged Enfield in battle dress guarding the Aldermaston gates. The old soldier walks up to a similarly sombre Jack Douglas and the *Carry On* style bursts onto the screen as Barbara Windsor jumps out from the back of an army truck and attacks the military power with cheeky comments and a bevy of forthright female followers. Full of memories of powerful females from *Doctor* and *Girls*, Barbara's over-sexed figure goes into parody over-drive, with CND stickers on her low-cut jumper. Leading a gaggle of scantily-clad *Carry On* cliched Greenham Common women, the old 1970s' style is captured perfectly. Into the throng stumbles Kenneth Connor, and the dialogue, although risque, follows the pattern of the later *Carry Ons*. With jokes built around mass debates and erections, the show creates some magical Rothwellian gags and, indeed, if the series had continued unabated after *Emmannuelle* it is conceivable that this is the sort of material that would have emerged. *Carry On Banging* could have been a four Sid movie.

Best performance

Although it was over a decade since he last carried on, Kenneth Connor still shines with comic genius. Resurrecting his persona from *England*, Connor barks his commands to the hapless Douglas and Enfield while desperately trying to calm down the wild sexually-geared panic of Windsor and her girls. In a few brief lines Connor brings the military innuendo to a head and delights in a few farcical looks and stunned explanations. It's a masterpiece of timing and the last Connor contribution to a comedy style he had enhanced for a 30-year period.

Favourite bit

Harry Enfield, clearly having the time of his life with a bunch of comic heroes, throws himself fully into the style and creates an immediate rapport with the old Carry Oners. To Kenneth Connor's friendly attempts at calming down Windsor's fears, he suggests a big discussion (the mass debate gag crops up). This dubious comment, Connor barks at his men, but Enfield tries to explain: 'I meant we could thrash it about out in the open, Sir!'/Connor: 'That's what I thought you meant!'. Classic stuff.

Did you know...

Harry Enfield admitted in a *TV Times* interview that although the show featured parodies of Ealing comedy, Will Hay, Cliff Richard movies, kitchen sink drama and Hollywood musicals, his favourite day of filming for *Norbert Smith - A Life* was the *Carry On* comic tribute.

Enfield approached Barbara Windsor to star in this brief snippet of *Carry On*. Initially she refused but Enfield was insistent. Windsor, a huge fan of Enfield's comedy, finally agreed and he asked her if she could rope in Frankie Howerd. Frankie was approached but illness kept him out of the fun. However, Barbara talked over the project with veterans Kenneth Connor and Jack Douglas and rounded up a cast for a prime evocation of the classic *Carry On* style.

Look out for...

Note the brilliant pseudo-Eric Rogers musical score from David Firman as Barbara Windsor pops out of the truck and the immortal title 'Carry On Banging' appears in typical seaside postcard lettering.

Carry On memories

'Harry Enfield started asking about the *Carry Ons*, like *Carry On Camping*, and how we'd done it in terrible weather, freezing cold and icy! Well, the day we actually did the scene for *Norbert Smith* it went down to 2 degrees and it was just falling down with sleet and snow. I had all these young girls around me. My life had gone back twenty years, except I was now fifty years old. It was just unreal, because there were all these young girls moaning and groaning, screaming "We're cold! We want our agents!". They were moaning about unions and here was Miss Windsor still doing it as though it was *Carry On Camping* all over again!'
Barbara Windsor

'Matron!' 'Oh! Hello!' 'Cor!' 'Charming!' 'Stop messin' about!' 'Get Away!'

Louis Benjamin Presents
The Peter Rogers Production

CARRY ON LONDON!

Starring
SIDNEY JAMES   BARBARA WINDSOR   KENNETH CONNOR
PETER BUTTERWORTH   BERNARD BRESSLAW   JACK DOUGLAS

Act 1
Overture!
Orchestra under the direction of **RICHARD HOLMES**
Round-About Victoria!!! The Dancing Girls & Boys
SIDNEY JAMES   BARBARA WINDSOR   KENNETH CONNOR
PETER BUTTERWORTH   BERNARD BRESSLAW   JACK DOUGLAS
What A Carry On! **SIDNEY JAMES   BARBARA WINDSOR   KENNETH CONNOR**
JACK DOUGLAS   PETER BUTTERWORTH   BERNARD BRESSLAW
GEORGE TRUZZI & BILLY TASKER
Carry On Girls **TRUDI VAN DOORN**
The Carry On Showgirls   The Dancing Girls & Boys
Introducing **LES QUATRE ROSETTI**
Emergency Ward 99 and a Bit
Dr Hacker **PETER BUTTERWORTH**   Dr Ram **KENNETH CONNOR**
Nurse Booby **BARBARA WINDSOR**   Matron **BERNARD BRESSLAW**
Dr McAndrew **SIDNEY JAMES**   The Patient **JACK DOUGLAS**
Deauville 1900 **The Showgirls**
The Dancing Girls & Boys   Les Silhouettes
Elizabethan Madrigals **SIDNEY JAMES   BARBARA WINDSOR   KENNETH CONNOR**
PETER BUTTERWORTH   BERNARD BRESSLAW   JACK DOUGLAS
London Night Out **The Showgirls & Boys**
Curtain Time At The Royal Standard Music Hall
Programme..Miss Lottie Collins **TRUDI VAN DOORN**
Our Worthy Manager **JACK DOUGLAS**
Miss BARBARA WINDSOR
The Glamazons
Our Patriotic Tableaux......The British Empire. A Tribute To Our Gallant Soldiers

Act 2
Carry On London **TRUDI VAN DOORN**
The Dancing Girls & Boys   The Showgirls
Hello Dollies Introducing **The New Dolly's**
Be Prepared The Scoutmaster **SIDNEY JAMES** Scout Badcock **BERNARD BRESSLAW**
Scout Muggeridge **JACK DOUGLAS**   Scout Pennimore **KENNETH CONNOR**
Barbara **BARBARA WINDSOR**   Ethel **PETER BUTTERWORTH**
The Girls & Boys introduce singing star **LYNN ROGERS**
...and now 'The Maestro' **SIDNEY JAMES**
Cleopatra's Palace on the Nile **The Dancing Girls & Boys**
The Carry On Showgirls

Cleopatra's Boudoir Cleopatra (Queen of the Nile) **BARBARA WINDSOR**
Abdul (a Hefty, Dusky Eunuch) **BERNARD BRESSLAW**
Grabatiti (High Priest) **PETER BUTTERWORTH**
Mark Antony (Lend me your ears) **KENNETH CONNOR**
Caesar (Rome's Godfather) **SIDNEY JAMES**
Titus Atticus (Captain of the Guard) **JACK DOUGLAS**
Smile **SIDNEY JAMES   BARBARA WINDSOR**
KENNETH CONNOR   PETER BUTTERWORTH
BERNARD BRESSLAW   JACK DOUGLAS & The Full Company

Written by **Talbot Rothwell, Dave Freeman**
& Eric Merriman
Additional material by **Ian Grant**
Orchestra directed by **Richard Holmes**
Based on the Carry On films
as directed by **Gerald Thomas**

Choreography **Tommy Shaw**   Designer **Tod Kingman**
Painted by **Tod Kingman Ltd.**
Costumes designed & made by **R St. John Roper Ltd.**
Special Period Costumes by **Bermans Ltd.**
Film Sequences by **World Background Ltd.**
Electrical Equipment by **Rank Strand Electric Ltd.**
Special Properties by **Peter Pullen**
Wigs by **Simon Wigs Studios**   Shoes by **Anello & Davide Ltd.**
Manager & Stage Director **Alan West**   Wardrobe Mistress **Eve Barnes**

Assistant Choreographer & Ballet Mistress **Lynette Leishman**
Executive Producer **Albert J Knight**   Comedy Director **Bill Roberton**

Performed at The Victoria Palace, London 4 October 1973 - March 1975
1st Night. 7pm   Then. 6.15pm/8.45pm Previewed at The Birmingham Hippodrome
14 September 1973 - 29 September 1973 Fri. 14 Sept. 8pm   Sat. 15 Sept.
6.15pm/8.45pm w/c 17 Sept. Mon, Tues, Thurs, Fri. 8pm
w/c 24 Sept. Wed & Sat. 6.15pm/8.45pm Seats 75p-£6

If a successful film series could make successful television, then why not a hit stage show? This was the reasoning of Peter Rogers, who grabbed the idea of bringing the spontaneous wit of his talented comic cast into the West End for a burst of good old music hall innuendo. Under the watchful eye of theatrical impresario, Louis Benjamin, Rogers collected his star cast of Sid James, Barbara Windsor, Kenneth Connor, Peter Butterworth, Bernard Bresslaw and Jack Douglas, all fresh from creating cinematic

A flagon of ale and all's right with the world – *Carry On Henry* with
Sid James and Julian Holloway

Tarzan Lives – Terry Scott plays his *Carry On Up the Jungle* jungle boy straight –
for his studio portrait at least!!

Dan Dann interrogated at his convenience – Charles Hawtrey and Harry H. Corbett get down to it in *Carry On Screaming*!

Carry On Again Doctor. Another lonely Saturday night for Doctor Jim

Salute – Peter Butterworth turns on the charm for *Carry On Abroad*'s Brits on the razzle

mayhem in *Carry On Girls*. As the poster screamed, 'At last! They're CARRYING ON... LIVE! on STAGE'. The idea was inspired and a sure-fire hit, and was tried out at the Birmingham Hippodrome during September 1973. It was a huge success, and the cast and crew moved down south and straight into the old home of The Crazy Gang, The Victoria Palace. Setting up residence in October 1973, the show lasted for 18 months and became one of the most profitable and talked-about revue shows in theatrical history. The logical successors to the mad-cap antics of Bud Flanagan and the boys, Sid James and the Carry Oners created a huge public response and dictated that *Dick*, released mid-run, would be the last truly successful box-office hit in the film series.

A rag-bag of sketches, stand-up routines, song and dance and speciality acts, the *Carry On* show resurrected the spirit of variety. However, it was the innuendo-encrusted, mini *Carry On* film-like sketches from the pen of Talbot Rothwell that brought the crowd rushing in for more. Starring all six regulars in a series of sketches, these concentrated bursts of *Carry On* were contrasted with comic songs, straight songs and other bits and pieces. As a show it was supposedly very slap-dash but nobody really seemed to care. The fact was that for the first time you could actually pay and see Sid James doing his *Carry On* chuckling in person. Accept no substitutes!

All the favourite elements of *Carry On* were there, including a manic hospital sketch entitled 'Emergency Ward 99 and a bit' in tribute to the defunct ATV series, *Emergency Ward 10*, which had been pulled from the air in 1967. In the absence of Hattie Jacques, a dragged-up Bernard Bresslaw did the honours as Matron, while a flamboyant Jack Douglas was the subject of comic operations from doctors Peter Butterworth and Sid James.

Historical *Carry On*, *Henry* in particular, was resurrected with 'Elizabethan Madrigals', a musical celebration with uplifting songs performed by the gang and lifted by Dave Freeman from his own Christmas special of 1972. Live on stage Sid and the team rejoiced in such unforgettable ballads as 'Balls, balls, banquets and balls!' which brought the house down every time!

Carry On Cleo was re-evaluated as 'Cleopatra's Boudoir' and, at last, allowed Barbara Windsor to interpret the Queen of the Nile, with Sid's chuckling Julius Caesar stealing the laughs. Peter Butterworth as the amazingly named and wonderfully outrageous Grabatiti was in delightful form.

Sid James took centre stage for a few words, while Jack Douglas - the only real comedian of the group - grabbed the chance to impress in his 'Alf' version of Leonard Sach's outlandish introductions of *The Good*

Old Days. The show was the stuff dreams are made of! Just about makes me wish I was ten years older so I would have had the chance to see it.

Did you know?
Remarkably little was changed from the Birmingham preview season, though the second musical number titled 'What A Carry On!' in the West End started life as 'Over To You!'. The Trudi Van Doorn solo 'Carry On Loving' became 'Carry On London' in the capital and the final number headlining Sid in 'Fine Feathers' changed to a celebration with the entire cast in the heart-warming farewell song, 'Smile'.

Talbot Rothwell was commissioned to write all the material for the show but ill health dictated that only the hospital, camping and Cleopatra sketches were his work. Dave Freeman wrote the 'Elizabethan Madrigals', while Grant and Merriman wrote the other musical numbers.

The tribute to 'The Royal Standard Music Hall' featured Barbara Windsor and the gang in celebration of the good old days of variety. The Royal Standard Music Hall stood from 1910 until 1963 and was pulled down only to be rebuilt as The Victoria Palace!

Sid James was keen to keep Jack Douglas out of the stage show due to the latter's strong training in live theatre. Unlike the rest of the cast, Sid saw Jack as strictly a comedian and not an actor. Fearful of Douglas' ad libs and banter with the audience, Sid struck a deal with the comic. However, once when the audience were particularly encouraging, Jack began wandering from the script and bouncing new gags and comic by-play off that other accomplished

'Be Prepared' - Jack Douglas, Peter Butterworth, Bernard Bresslaw, Sid James, Barbara Windsor and Kenneth Connor in a montage from *Carry On London!*

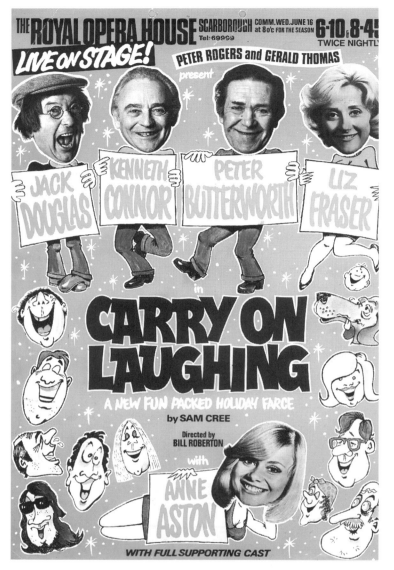

Poster for the 1976 stage hit, *Carry On Laughing*.

Once those who wanted to leave had left, the cast, true professionals, carried on the gags regardless.

Carry On London! director, Bill Roberton, is the brother of Jack Douglas.

Rehearsals for *Carry On London!* took place at The West End Great Synagogue.

ATV recorded the entire show for their edited television presentation *What A Carry On!*.

Carry On London! was the most expensive revue show to that date: the costume budget alone was £50,000.

During March 1974, Barbara Windsor was absent from the show for three weeks due to exhaustion. Her understudy Anita Kaye successfully stepped in.

Don Robinson
In Association with Peter Rogers and Gerald Thomas
Presents

CARRY ON LAUGHING
WITH 'THE SLIMMING FACTORY'

Jack Hardy **JACK DOUGLAS**   Major Chambers **KENNETH CONNOR**
Willie Strokes **PETER BUTTERWORTH**
Milly **LIZ FRASER**   Candy Maple **ANNE ASTON**
Mrs Babbington **BEAU DANIELLS**
Albert Waterman (Milly's Lover) **DANNY O'DEA**
Alice Pringle **BARBARA SUMNER**   Hilde **LINDA HOOKS**

The action takes place in The Get-U-Fit Health Farm
Act 1   Sc. 1 - Monday morning   Sc. 2 - Wednesday morning
Act 2   Sc. 1 - Thursday afternoon   Sc. 2 - Thursday night

Written by **Sam Cree**

Designer **Saxon Lucas**   Theatre & General Manager **John Palmer**
Company & Stage Manager **Tommy Layton**   Deputy Stage Manager **Sue Smith**
Assistant Stage Manager & Sound Control **Alan Bone**
Wardrobe Mistress **Judi Tillotson**   Telephone kindly loaned by **G.P.O.**
Sporting equipment supplied by **B & J.M. Jungeling Ltd.**
Scenery Constructed & Painted by **Northern Scenery Services Ltd.**
Hair Styles **Mr Paul, Marshall House, Scarborough**   Director **Bill Roberton**

Performed at The Royal Opera House, Scarborough
16 June - September 1976 1st Night. 8pm. Then. 6.10pm/8.45pm

worker of an audience - Kenneth Connor. Sid just stood on stage in shock - unable to continue the sketch and unwilling to stray from the script. Jack quickly returned to the words of Talbot Rothwell and the incident was never repeated.

An early morning live appearance on Pete Murray's *Open House* radio show dictated that the team stay in a hotel the night before the broadcast.

Sid James had begged Barbara Windsor to appear in the show after her initial refusal to take part. Driving her down to location shooting for *Girls in Brighton*, Sid explained that the show would not go on without her and, thus, she changed her mind and journeyed to Birmingham with the gang for September.

During the successful London run at The Victoria Palace, an IRA bomb-scare occurred in the theatre.

A brave attempt at continuing the *Carry On* legacy in the immediate wake of Sid James' death in April 1976, *Carry On Laughing* delighted the summer season audiences at Scarborough for that year, playing at The Royal Opera House - where else! Unlike the legendary *Carry On London!*, this show was a straight, no frills stage farce which basked in the *Carry On* glow with outrageous innuendo and a small clutch of original players. While a huge majority of the team either had other working commitments or were unwilling to return to *Carry On* following Sid's death, a fine cast including Jack Douglas, Peter Butterworth and Kenneth Connor decided to play ball. Also aboard for the fun was Liz Fraser, having just returned to the series with her featured role in *Behind*, while lower down the stage cast list was the glamorous Linda Hooks who had previously appeared in three of the films and a couple of the *Carry On Laughing* shows on television.

The basic plot was a trouser-dropping, marital problems, 'more tea, vicar?' farce set in an outlandish health spa. Top-billed Jack Douglas wandered through the fast-moving but uninspired plot, while the true honours were stolen by the shuffling Peter Butterworth as the gloriously named Willie Strokes!

Mike Hughes for Liver Promotions Ltd. Presents

WOT A CARRY ON IN BLACKPOOL

Starring
Leading Man **BERNARD BRESSLAW**   Leading Lady **BARBARA WINDSOR**
Juvenile Lead **ANDREW GRAINGER**   Light Comedy Relief **RICHARD GAUNTLETT**
The Merry Maids **JACQUELINE DUNNLEY RACHEL WOOLRICH**
MELANIE HOLLOWAY NATALIE HOLTOM
The Jolly Juveniles **JONATHON BLAZER JULIAN ESSEX SPURRIER**

Act 1
Arrival 'You're Got To Carry On'
BARBARA WINDSOR, BERNARD BRESSLAW & Full Company
'Phone Home' **BARBARA WINDSOR**
'At The Digs' **BERNARD BRESSLAW, ANDREW GRAINGER &**
RICHARD GAUNTLETT
Rehearsals 'T'aint Nobody's Business If I Do'
BARBARA WINDSOR & The Jolly Juveniles
'Speciality' **RICHARD GAUNTLETT**
'Tricky Business' **BERNARD BRESSLAW &**
BARBARA WINDSOR
Out of Town 'Old Fashioned Girl' **The Merry Maids & The Jolly Juveniles**
'Slippin' Around The Corner' **ANDREW GRAINGER**
& RACHEL WOOLRICH
'Blackpool's Own Darby and Joan'
BERNARD BRESSLAW & BARBARA WINDSOR
'Slippin' Around The Corner to The Rose & Crown' **Full Company**

Act 2
It's Show Time 'Get Happy' **BARBARA WINDSOR**
& Company
'Out Of Their Minds' **BARBARA WINDSOR & BERNARD BRESSLAW**
London Medley 'Vultures For Culture' **The Company**
'Chelsea Party' **BARBARA WINDSOR, BERNARD BRESSLAW,**
ANDREW GRAINGER, RACHEL WOOLRICH & RICHARD GAUNTLETT
'Convent Garden' **BARBARA WINDSOR & ANDREW GRAINGER**
'Speciality' **RICHARD GAUNTLETT**
Just Go To The Movies 'Charlie Chaplin' **BARBARA WINDSOR**
'Nelson Eddy' **RICHARD GAUNTLETT**
'Frankenstein's Monster' **BERNARD BRESSLAW**
'Betty Grable' **BARBARA WINDSOR**
Wot A Carry On **Full Company**
'Mum Interrupts' **BARBARA WINDSOR**
Finale 'One Step' **Full Company**

Written by **Barry Cryer & Dick Vosburgh**
The Orchestra under the direction of **Tim Parkin**
Synthesisers **Peter Lingwood**   Bass Guitar **John Saunders**
Drums **Dave Tyas**

Directed & Devised by **Tudor Davies**   Choreography **Paul Robinson**
Set Design **Gareth Bowen**
Costume Designer **Kathryn Waters**   Sound Design **Clement Rawling**
Music Associate **Phil Phillips** Company Stage Manager **James Skeggs**

Stage Manager **Sharon Curtis**   Wardrobe Mistress **Heidi Wynter**
Lighting Design **Graham McLusky**
Additional Orchestrations **Phil Phillips & Colin Fretcher**
Assistant Stage Manager **Fiona Cheese-Hayward**
Production Electrican **James Long**
Production Sound Operator **Adrian Watts**
Production Carpenters **Drew Taylor & Phil Lawson**
Orchestral Management **London Music Associates**
Sound System **Mac**   Electrical Equipment **White Light North**
Computer & Synthesiser Programming **Tim Parkin**
Press Representative **Clifford Elson**   *For First Leisure*
General Manager **Peter Walters**
Deputy General Manager **Eileen Rawcliffe**
Stage Staff **Keith Faulkner Ian Sayle & Glen Ewen**
From an original idea by Associate Producer/Production Manager **Martin Witts**

Performed on The North Pier, Blackpool 22 May 1992 - 27 June 1992 6pm/8.30pm
26 July 1992 - 25 October 1992 Sundays only 5pm/7-30pm Seats - £4.75-£6.75

While Peter Rogers and Gerald Thomas were gainfully trying to turn Young Ones into Carry Oners at Pinewood, preparations were being made for a feel-good, traditional *Carry On* by the sea. With the smell of fish 'n' chips wafting on the breeze and the lusty innuendo blue on the horizon, the name was officially adopted for a right royal *Carry On in Blackpool*. For the first time you could enjoy a fresh fish supper, eat your fill of candy floss, have a quick ride on the dodgems and delight in watching Bernard Bresslaw and Barbara Windsor live on stage - all on the same day!

It was also the first time that a new generation of *Carry On* followers (myself included) could savour the pleasures of stage *Carry On*. In an attempt to resurrect those glorious days of *Carry On London!*, the show was structured as a revue comprising comic sketches, song and dance and solo variety spots. Written by Barry Cryer and Dick Vosburgh, with a keen ear for *Carry On* dialogue, the production was based around the exploits of a 1940s' repertory theatre company by the sea. Perfect for the carefree, bright and breezy style of *Carry On*, it allowed for a huge amount of sketches built around seaside postcard topics and humour.

Blessed with an accomplished cast of mainly young newcomers, the production's chief joy, of course, was the spirited reunion of Bernard Bresslaw and Barbara Windsor. Having last carried on together in 1975's *Carry On Laughing* series, this was a glorious return to fond memories, corny gags and slapstick humour. Barbara appeared on stage by rushing down the central aisle, crying out 'Cor! What A Carry On!' and it was like nothing had changed. The jokes were back where they belonged: in front of a working-class audience of holidaymakers out for a good laugh. We got it! Through a galaxy of bizarre characterizations and groanworthy gags, the two *Carry On* survivors did their stuff to huge cheers and belly laughs. Bernard camped about as an overpowering and over-sexed Blackpool landlady, while Barbara delighted the crowds with a eye-watering speciality act with a huge balloon and enjoyed

herself hugely in a glittering and very effective tribute to Betty Grable. Barbara also contributed a tumbling Charlie Chaplin turn to the Hollywood section of the show.

Naturally, it was when the two stars were together that the good old days simply rushed back, when as two aged, bath-chaired old codgers by the sea, Bresslaw and Windsor discussed past times and frustrated futures. When I saw the show, the two were delightfully ad libbing about 'banging' back stage and the corny gags got even worse through these two old pros' banter. A delightfully incompetent magic act, with Bernie looking for volunteers in the audience as a mystic Barbarella(!) reads people's minds with blatantly obvious trickery, was a classic. However, the real risque stuff poured out during a magical heckling sequence when the two stars hurled abuse at a straight-laced stage melodrama (you could almost hear Frankie Howerd shout 'Get the kids to bed!') with the straight-laced Rachel Woolrich giving an excellent foil performance. Ripe innuendo and farcical expressions were directed to the audience in this last true stand of the *Carry On* style. While Jim Dale was gamely struggling against the Spanish Inquisition and the Freeman jokes, Barbara Windsor and Bernard Bresslaw were having a ball in Blackpool playing to their most dedicated audience - coachloads of *Carry On* fans! It was an experience I wouldn't want to have missed... and I'm glad I didn't!

Best performance

Without doubt the finest turn came from Bernard Bresslaw during the Hollywood tribute. Resurrecting his powerhouse image of the Frankenstein Monster from 1969's *Carry On Christmas*, this hulking, lumber-ing frame staggered onto stage surrounded in eerie stage fog. An imposing presence of manic evil, Bresslaw stood staring into the audience for a split second before whipping a ukelele from behind his shoulder and giving us a George Formbyesque creature. Bemoaning his unlucky record with girls, Bresslaw replaced the Karloffian menace immediately, and allowed his ashen face to light up with comic Blackpool memories and cheerful cries of 'Turned Out Nice Again!'. It was a stunning effect and pure gold *Carry On*.

Favourite bit

A show capturing the essence of *Carry On* comedy is full of favourite bits, but purely from a personal and emotional point of view, the best moment must have been the finale. For the last time, there were Bernard Bresslaw and Barbara Windsor running over the same, weary old gags from some twenty years previously - delighting in their awfulness and joyfully celebrating the legacy of the series. Sid would have been proud.

Did you know?

Apart from penning the *Carry On Laughing* show *Orgy and Bess* with Barry Cryer, Dick Vosburgh had contributed ideas and brief snippets of dialogue to *Nurse, Regardless* and that other Kenneth Connor/Peter Rogers gem, *Watch Your Stern*.

The show proved so successful in Blackpool that plans were mooted for a UK tour of the production during July, August and September 1992. The idea was shelved but thankfully the laughs continued at Blackpool on Sundays only.

Poster for the 1992 seaside extravaganza, *Wot A Carry On in Blackpool*.

'Matron!' 'Cor!' 'O

'Charmin

'Stop messin' about!'

CARRY ON

EXTRAS

'Hello!'

'Get Away!'

'Matron!' 'Oh! Hello!' 'Cor!' 'Charming!' 'Stop messin' about!' 'Get Away!'

CARRY ON CHRONOLOGY

1913

Sid James born Sidney Joel Cohen in Johannesburg, South Africa, 6 May - starred in 19 *Carry On* films, 8 television shows and 1 stage production.

1914

Peter Rogers, producer, script contributor, music contributor and all-round driving force behind the *Carry On* series, born in Rochester, Kent, 20 February. Charles Hawtrey born George Frederick Joffree Hawtree, Hounslow, 30 November - starred in 23 *Carry On* films and 2 television shows.

1916

Talbot Rothwell born in Bromley, Kent – thought up his first corny gag at the age of four after returning from an unsuccessful day at the pond, 'No newts is good newts!', a reference resurrected for *Matron*. Rothwell's initial work for Peter Rogers, later called *Carry On Jack*, took him three months to write, while *Cabby* took just two weeks. He was in perfect *Carry On* mode for over a decade.

1917

Frankie Howerd born Francis Alick Howerd, 6 March – starred in 2 *Carry On* films and 1 television show.

1918

Kenneth Connor born 6 June – starred in 17 *Carry On* films, 17 television shows and 2 stage productions.

1919

Peter Butterworth born in Bramhall, Cheshire, 4 February – starred in 16 *Carry On* films, 13 television shows and 2 stage productions.

1920

Gerald Thomas born in Hull, 10 December.

1921

Music men Eric Rogers and Bruce Montgomery born.

1923

Original *Carry On* writer Norman Hudis born.

1924

Hattie Josephine Jacques born in Sandgate, Kent, 7 February - starred in 14 *Carry On* films and 3 television shows.

1926

Kenneth Charles Williams born in London, 22 February - starred in 26 *Carry On* films and 1 television show.

1927

Jack Douglas born Jack Roberton in Newcastle-upon-Tyne, 26 April - starred in 8 *Carry On* films, 16 television shows and 2 stage productions. Terry Scott born John Owen Scott in Watford, 4 May - starred in 7 *Carry On* films and 2 television shows.

1930

Joan Sims born in Laindon, Essex, 9 May - starred in 24 *Carry On* films and 13 television shows.

1934

Bernard Bresslaw born in London's East End, 25 February - starred in 14 *Carry On* films, 9 television shows and 2 stage productions.

1935

Jim Dale born James Smith on 15 August - starred in 11 *Carry On* films.

1937

Barbara Windsor born Barbara Ann Deeks in Shoreditch, 6 August - starred in 10 *Carry On* films, 14 television shows and 2 stage productions.

1946

Gerald Thomas begins work at Denham Studios.

1949

Peter Rogers produces his first feature film - *Marry Me!*

1956

Circus Friends, the first Peter Rogers/Gerald Thomas film released. A Children's Film Foundation production, it starred Carol White and Alan Coleshill.
On 11 November, Hattie Jacques first appeared in *Hancock's Half Hour* on BBC radio. The episode was entitled 'The New Secretary' and marked the first teaming of the core *Carry On* stars: Sid James, Kenneth Williams and Hattie Jacques. Meanwhile, Charles Hawtrey and Kenneth Connor were assisting Ted Ray in *Ray's A Laugh*.

1957

Peter Rogers and Gerald Thomas release the John Mills thriller *The Vicious Circle* and *Time Lock* (later paired in some American cinemas with the Edward D. Wood Jr gem *Plan 9 From Outer Space*). Their production company, 'Insignia', later to become 'Adder' during the early Rothwell *Carry On* era, was based at 19 Bolton Street, W1. G.H.W. Productions were involved in *Cruising*, the first three *Carry Ons* appeared through the B&D Film Corporation and *Screaming's* production home was Ethrio, before eventually, the mere mention of the names Rogers/Thomas became an instant signifer for classic comedy.
The first episode of the ITV situation comedy *The Army Game* is broadcast on 19 June. Val Guest's comedy *Carry On Admiral* (aka *The Ship was Loaded*, based on the play *Off the Record* by Ian Hay and Stephen King-Hall) released in April.
Stuart Levy at Anglo feels a title change for *The Bull Boys* is needed and Peter Rogers considers writers Spike Milligan, Eric Sykes, John Antrobus, Ray Galton and Alan Simpson to work on a treatment.

1958

The Duke Wore Jeans starring Tommy Steele marked the first Gerald Thomas (director), Peter Rogers (producer) and Norman Hudis (writer) film release. Rogers/Thomas release two more dramatic films,

Chain of Events and *The Solitary Child*, via their production company.
Carry On Sergeant. Starring Kenneth Williams, Charles Hawtrey, Kenneth Connor, Hattie Jacques and Terry Scott. Filmed from 24 March to 2 May at Pinewood Studios and on location at Queen's Barracks, Guildford, Surrey. Released, August.
Carry On Nurse. Starring Kenneth Williams, Kenneth Connor, Charles Hawtrey, Hattie Jacques and Joan Sims. Filmed from 3 November to 12 December at Pinewood Studios.

1959

March - *Nurse* released.
Carry On Teacher. Starring Kenneth Williams, Kenneth Connor, Charles Hawtrey, Joan Sims and Hattie Jacques. Filming began in March at Pinewood Studios and on location at Drayton Secondary School, Ealing. Released, August.
Rogers/Thomas release *Please Turn Over* starring Ted Ray, Lionel Jeffries, Jean Kent, Leslie Phillips and Julia Lockwood, while featuring *Carry On* regulars Charles Hawtrey and Joan Sims. Norman Hudis wrote the screenplay from Basil Thomas' West End hit, *Book of the Month*.
Carry On Constable. Starring Sid James, Kenneth Williams, Charles Hawtrey, Kenneth Connor, Hattie Jacques and Joan Sims. Filmed on location in the streets of Ealing from 9-20 November and at Pinewood Studios from 23 November to 18 December.

1960

February - *Constable* released.
Watch Your Stern emerges from the Rogers/Thomas/Hudis stable with the tag-line 'the latest and funniest of a great line of British comedy hits'. *Carry On* faces Kenneth Connor, Sid James, Joan Sims, Hattie Jacques, Leslie Phillips and Eric Barker joined Spike Milligan, Eric Sykes and Noel Purcell in the cast. It was Sykes' only film for Peter Rogers, he would later be interviewed for the ITV show, *What A Carry On!* expressing a desire to make a *Carry On*.
No Kidding marked a semi-serious comic outing for Rogers/Thomas, with a Norman Hudis/Robin Estridge script based on Verity Anderson's *Beware of Children*. Carry Oners Leslie Phillips, June Jago, Irene Handl, Joan Hickson and Brian Rawlinson joined Geraldine McEwan, Noel Purcell and Julia Lockwood. The 1960-61 ABC television situation comedy *Our House* delighted in capitalizing on the popularity of *Carry On*. The cast included early team members Charles Hawtrey, Joan Sims and Hattie Jacques, as well as future *Carry On* great, Bernard Bresslaw. Norman Hudis wrote the first batch of scripts.

Carry On Regardless. Starring Sid James, Kenneth Williams, Kenneth Connor, Charles Hawtrey, Joan Sims and Hattie Jacques. Filmed from 28 November - 17 January 1961 at Pinewood Studios and on location on the corner of Park Street, Windsor.

1961
March - *Regardless* released.

What A Carry On! was the title for a *Carry On* film which was halted before Norman Hudis had began work on the script. An army comedy starring Jimmy Jewel and Ben Warris had come out under this title some 10 years before.

Carry On Smoking, a Norman Hudis scripted *Carry On* film concerning the training of firemen (or *Carry On Sergeant* in different uniforms!) was set for filming with the whole gang but was abandoned in case its release coincided with a real-life fire tragedy.

Peter Rogers and Gerald Thomas release *Raising the Wind* starring a regular crop of *Carry On* stars: Leslie Phillips, Sid James, Kenneth Williams, Liz Fraser and Eric Barker. James Robertson Justice barked out some prime Bruce Montgomery musical commands while Jim Dale made his Rogers/Thomas debut as a timid trombonist opposite Williams in full camp flight. The C.M. Pennington-Richards comedy *Dentist on the Job* is released in Europe as *Carry On TV,* cashing in on its vintage *Carry On* cast of Bob Monkhouse, Kenneth Connor, Eric Barker, Shirley Eaton and Charles Hawtrey.

1962
Carry On Cruising. Starring Sid James, Kenneth Williams and Kenneth Connor. Filmed from 8 January to 16

Sid James and Kenneth Williams meet on equal terms for the first time in Carry On Cruising.

ANGLO AMALGAMATED present
A PETER ROGERS PRODUCTION
"CARRY ON CRUISING"
In Eastmancolour starring
DNEY JAMES - KENNETH CONNOR - LIZ FRASER
NNETH WILLIAMS - DILYS LAYE - ESMA CANNON

February at Pinewood Studios. Released, April. For the first time you could see official carrying on in glorious Eastman Colour.

Carry On Flying, a Norman Hudis scripted *Carry On* film concerning the manic exploits of a group of young RAF recruits, was ready for shooting but abandoned. *Carry On Spaceman,* a Norman Hudis attempt to cash in on the space race with a *Carry On* based around a group of raw recruit astronauts, had a script ready for shooting but was abandoned. Later, Denis Gifford would produce a screenplay for *Carry On Spaceman* which also went unproduced.

Anglo releases the Norman Hudis scripted *Twice Round The Daffodils,* the Rogers/Thomas straight filming of Cargill & Beale's *Carry On Nurse* inspiration, *Ring For Catty.* Juliet Mills, Donald Sinden and Ronald Lewis star, with Kenneth Williams and Joan Sims keeping the *Carry On* flag flying. *The Iron Maiden* also appeared, starring Michael Craig, Anne Helm, Alan Hale Jr, *Jack's* Cecil Parker and a huge traction engine. A sort of retread of *Genevieve* with a dash of *Nearly a Nasty Accident,* Gerald Thomas injected Carry Oner Joan Sims and future Carry Oner Jim Dale into the cast. Series regulars Brian Oulton, Brian Rawlinson, Judith Furse and Michael Nightingale gave their usual flawless support, while Noel Purcell, Sam Kydd and the Eric Rogers score kept the pace brisk.

1963
Donald McGill (1875-1963) Father of the seaside postcard.

Carry On Cabby. Starring Sid James, Hattie Jacques, Kenneth Connor, Charles Hawtrey and Jim Dale. Filmed from 25 March to 7 May at Pinewood Studios and on location in Windsor. Released, June.

Talbot Rothwell's hero and music hall legend Max Miller (1895-1963) died at his Brighton home on 7 May at the age of 68 - the pure gold of British music hall and the country's finest stand-up comedian.

Carry On Jack. Starring Kenneth Williams, Charles Hawtrey and Jim Dale. Filmed from 2 September to 26 October at Pinewood Studios and on location at Frensham Pond. Released, November.

Another Rogers/Thomas fringe *Carry On, Nurse On Wheels,* again starring Juliet Mills, is released by Anglo. Scripted by Norman Hudis it features support from Noel Purcell, Derek Guyler, Joan Sims and Jim Dale.

Carry On farewells

Mario Fabrizi (1925-1963)... *Cruising.*

1964
Carry On Spying. Starring Kenneth Williams, Barbara Windsor, Charles Hawtrey and Jim Dale. Filmed from 8 February to 13 March at Pinewood Studios. Released, June. The Edgar Wallace classic *Who Was*

Maddox? is the support picture.

Carry On Cleo. Starring Sid James, Kenneth Williams, Kenneth Connor, Charles Hawtrey, Joan Sims and Jim Dale. Filmed from 13 July - 28 August at Pinewood Studios. Released November. With *Jack* still on general release in early 1964, the faithful *Carry On* fan could enjoy three movies in one year.

1965

Carry On Cowboy. Starring Sid James, Kenneth Williams, Charles Hawtrey, Jim Dale, Joan Sims, Peter Butterworth and Bernard Bresslaw. Filmed from 12 July to 3 September at Pinewood Studios and on location at Chobham Common, Surrey and Black Park, Fulmer, Buckinghamshire. Released, November. Rogers and Thomas also released their last non-*Carry On* entry for seven years - the sparkling Talbot Rothwell crime comedy *The Big Job*. The film was based on a weary old plot, filmed in vintage terms as *A Fire Has Been Arranged* starring Bud Flanagan, Chesney Allen, Alastair Sim and Robb Wilton, and Peter Rogers assembled a prime cast. Carry Oners Sid James, Jim Dale, Joan Sims and Lance Percival were joined by Dick Emery, Sylvia Syms and the latest *Carry On* glamour girl, Edina Ronay.

Carry On farewells
Freddie Mills (1922-1965)... *Constable* and *Regardless*.

1966

Carry On Screaming!. Starring Kenneth Williams, Jim Dale, Peter Butterworth, Charles Hawtrey, Joan Sims and Bernard Bresslaw. Filmed from 10 January to 25 February at Pinewood Studios and on location in Windsor, Berkshire and Fulmer, Buckinghamshire. Released, August.

Stuart Levy, Head of Anglo Amalgamated died. He had been credited for borrowing the *Carry On* title from Val Guest's *Carry On Admiral*, and his death spelt the end of the Anglo *Carry On* era.

Carry On... Don't Lose Your Head. Starring Sid James, Kenneth Williams, Charles Hawtrey, Jim Dale, Peter Butterworth and Joan Sims. Filmed from 12 September to 28 October at Pinewood Studios and on location at Waddesdon Manor, Clandon Park and Clivedon. Released, December.

1967

Carry On... Follow That Camel. Starring Jim Dale, Peter Butterworth, Kenneth Williams, Charles Hawtrey, Joan Sims and Bernard Bresslaw. Filmed from 1 May to 23 June at Pinewood Studios and on location at Rye and Camber Sands, Sussex. Released, September.

Carry On Doctor. Starring Frankie Howerd, Kenneth Williams, Sid James, Charles Hawtrey, Jim Dale, Barbara Windsor, Hattie Jacques, Bernard Bresslaw,

Peter Butterworth and Joan Sims. Filmed from 11 September to 20 October at Pinewood Studios and on location in Maidenhead. Released, December.

Carry On farewells
Jerry Desmonde (1908-1967)... *Regardless.*

1968

Carry On... Up The Khyber. Starring Sid James, Kenneth Williams, Charles Hawtrey, Peter Butterworth, Joan Sims, Bernard Bresslaw and Terry Scott. Filmed from 8 April to 31 May at Pinewood Studios and on location in North Wales. Released, September.

Carry On Camping. Starring Sid James, Kenneth Williams, Charles Hawtrey, Joan Sims, Bernard Bresslaw, Peter Butterworth, Barbara Windsor, Hattie Jacques and Terry Scott. Filmed from 7 October to 22 November at Pinewood Studios.

Don't Lose Your Head and *Follow That Camel* re-released with the *Carry On* prefix.

1969

February - *Camping* released.

Carry On Again Doctor. Starring Jim Dale, Sid James, Kenneth Williams, Charles Hawtrey, Hattie Jacques, Joan Sims, Barbara Windsor and Peter Butterworth. Filmed from 17 March to 2 May at Pinewood Studios and on location in Maidenhead. Released, August.

Carry On Up The Jungle. Starring Frankie Howerd, Sid James, Charles Hawtrey, Kenneth Connor, Joan Sims, Terry Scott and Bernard Bresslaw. Filmed from 13 October to 21 November at Pinewood Studios.

Carry On Christmas. Starring Sid James, Terry Scott, Charles Hawtrey, Hattie Jacques, Barbara Windsor,

Crash! Bang! Wallop! What a picture - a wedding photo at Pinewood with Sid James, Joan Sims, Peter Rogers, Gerald Thomas, Barbara Windsor, Charles Hawtrey, Kenneth Williams, Hattie Jacques and Jim Dale - *Carry On Again Doctor*.

Peter Butterworth, Bernard Bresslaw and Frankie Howerd. Recorded Sunday, 14 December at the Thames Television Studios, Teddington Lock and broadcast Christmas Eve.
Carry On farewells
Howard Marion Crawford (1914-1969)... *Regardless.*

1970

March - *Up The Jungle* released. *Mister Jerico*, starring Herbert Lom, is the support picture.
Carry On Loving. Starring Sid James, Kenneth Williams, Charles Hawtrey, Hattie Jacques, Terry Scott, Joan Sims, Bernard Bresslaw and Peter Butterworth. Filmed from 6 April to 15 May at Pinewood Studios and on location in Windsor and on the corner of Park Street, Windsor. Released, September.
Carry On Henry. Starring Sid James, Kenneth Williams, Charles Hawtrey, Joan Sims, Barbara Windsor, Terry Scott, Kenneth Connor and Peter Butterworth. Filmed from 12 October to 27 November at Pinewood Studios and on location at Windsor Great Park and the Long Walk at Windsor Castle.
Carry On Again Christmas. Starring Sid James, Terry Scott, Charles Hawtrey, Barbara Windsor, Kenneth Connor and Bernard Bresslaw. Broadcast Christmas Eve.
Carry On fan John Lennon pays homage to Charles Hawtrey on The Beatles' last released, penultimately recorded, album, *Let it Be*, introducing the first track, 'Two of Us', with 'I ain't dig a pygmy by Charles Hawtrey and the deaf aids. Phase 1 in which Doris gets her oats!'
Carry On farewells
Ann Lancaster (1920-1970) ... *Again Doctor.*

1971

February - *Henry* released.
Carry On At Your Convenience. Starring Sid James, Kenneth Williams, Charles Hawtrey, Hattie Jacques, Bernard Bresslaw and Joan Sims. Filmed from 22 March to 7 May at Pinewood Studios and on location in Brighton. Released, December.
Tongue-in-cheek suggestion from Eric & Ernie on *The Morecambe & Wise Show* to make *Carry On Ern*.
Peter Rogers produced and wrote the music for the Joan Collins/Tom Bell science-fiction romance *Quest for Love*. Directed by Ralph Thomas, it boasted supporting turns from Denholm Elliott and Laurence Naismith.
Music For Pleasure release 'Oh! What A Carry On!' (MFP MONO 1416) featuring recordings by Kenneth Williams, Jim Dale, Kenneth Connor, Frankie Howerd, Bernard Bresslaw, Joan Sims, Barbara Windsor and Dora Bryan.
Carry On Matron. Starring Sid James, Kenneth Williams, Charles Hawtrey, Hattie Jacques, Joan Sims, Bernard

Bresslaw, Terry Scott, Barbara Windsor, Kenneth Connor and Jack Douglas. Filmed from 11 October to 26 November at Pinewood Studios.
Carry On farewells
E.V.H. Emmett (1902-1971)... *Cleo.*
Cecil Parker (1897-1971)... *Jack.*
Kynaston Reeves (1893-1971)... *Regardless.*
Denis Shaw (1921-1971)... *Regardless.*

1972

Carry On Abroad. Starring Sid James, Kenneth Williams, Charles Hawtrey, Joan Sims, Peter Butterworth, Kenneth Connor, Barbara Windsor, Hattie Jacques, Bernard Bresslaw and Jack Douglas. Filmed from 17 April to 26 May at Pinewood Studios and on location at Slough, Berkshire.
May - *Matron* released.
December - *Abroad* released.
Peter Rogers and Gerald Thomas present the film version of *Bless This House*, based on the hugely popular Sid James ITV situation comedy which had started in 1971. Dave Freeman wrote the screenplay and Sid was joined by fellow Carry Oners Peter Butterworth, Terry Scott and June Whitfield. It was blessed with the tagline, 'The Greatest Family Comedy team now on the Big Screen!', although Robin Stewart was replaced by Robin Askwith.
Sid James hosted a half-hour television compilation of *Carry On* clips for the Australian television station HSV7 Melbourne, surprisingly entitled, *Carry On Sid*.
Carry On Christmas. Starring Hattie Jacques, Joan Sims, Kenneth Connor, Barbara Windsor, Peter Butterworth and Jack Douglas. Broadcast 20 December.
Carry On farewells
Esma Cannon (1896-1972)... *Constable, Regardless, Cruising* and *Cabby.*

1973

Carry On Girls. Starring Sid James, Barbara Windsor, Joan Sims, Kenneth Connor, Bernard Bresslaw, Peter Butterworth and Jack Douglas. Filmed from 16 April to 25 May at Pinewood Studios and on location in Brighton and Slough.
Carry On London!. Starring Sid James, Barbara Windsor, Peter Butterworth, Kenneth Connor, Bernard Bresslaw and Jack Douglas. Stage revue which enjoyed a preview season at the Birmingham Hippodrome during September and opened in the West End at the Victoria Palace on 4 October. Sid released a single, 'Our House'/'She's Gone' (Pye 7N 45281), to complement the show.
What A Carry On!, a filmed record of highlights from *Carry On London!*, broadcast on ITV, 4 October.
November - *Girls* released.
Carry On Christmas. Starring Sid James, Joan Sims,

Barbara Windsor, Kenneth Connor, Peter Butterworth, Bernard Bresslaw and Jack Douglas. Broadcast Christmas Eve.
Carry On farewells
Cyril Raymond (1897-1973)... *Regardless*.
Tony Sagar (1920-1973)... *Sergeant, Nurse, Regardless, Cruising, Screaming and Loving*.
Jean St Clair (?-1973)... *Doctor*.
George Woodbridge (1907-1973)... *Jack*.

1974

Carry On Dick. Starring Sid James, Kenneth Williams, Barbara Windsor, Hattie Jacques, Joan Sims, Bernard Bresslaw, Peter Butterworth, Kenneth Connor and Jack Douglas. Filmed from 4 March to 11 April at Pinewood Studios and on location in nearby country-side and woods around Iver Heath. Released, July.
Carry On farewells
Cyril Chamberlain (1909-1974)... *Sergeant, Nurse, Teacher, Constable, Regardless, Cruising and Cabby*.
Judith Furse (1912-1974)... *Regardless, Cabby and Spying*.

1975

Barbara Windsor took her one-woman revue show, *Carry On Barbara* round Australia and New Zealand.
Carry On Laughing. 1st series.
The Prisoner of Spenda - starring Sid James, Barbara Windsor, Joan Sims, Jack Douglas, Kenneth Connor and Peter Butterworth. Broadcast 4 January.
The Baron Outlook - starring Sid James, Barbara Windsor, Joan Sims, Peter Butterworth and Kenneth Connor. Broadcast 11 January.
The Sobbing Cavalier - starring Sid James, Barbara Windsor, Joan Sims, Peter Butterworth and Jack Douglas. Broadcast 18 January.
Orgy and Bess - starring Sid James, Hattie Jacques, Barbara Windsor, Kenneth Connor and Jack Douglas. Broadcast 25 January.
One in the Eye For Harold - starring Kenneth Connor, Jack Douglas and Joan Sims. Broadcast 1 February.
The Nine Old Cobblers - starring Jack Douglas, Kenneth Connor, Joan Sims and Barbara Windsor. Broadcast 8 February.
Carry On Behind. Starring Kenneth Williams, Kenneth Connor, Joan Sims, Bernard Bresslaw, Jack Douglas and Peter Butterworth. Filmed from 10 March to 18 April at Pinewood Studios and on location in Maidenhead.
Carry On Laughing. 2nd series.
Under the Round Table - starring Joan Sims, Bernard Bresslaw, Kenneth Connor, Peter Butterworth and Jack Douglas. Broadcast 26 October.
The Case of the Screaming Winkles - starring Jack Douglas, Kenneth Connor, Joan Sims and Peter Butterworth. Broadcast 2 November.

Kenneth Connor, David Lodge and Jack Douglas play the detective comedy with straight faces: *The Case of the Coughing Parrot*.

And in My Lady's Chamber - starring Kenneth Connor, Barbara Windsor, Jack Douglas, Joan Sims, Peter Butterworth and Bernard Bresslaw. Broadcast 9 November.
Short Knight, Long Daze - starring Joan Sims, Bernard Bresslaw, Kenneth Connor, Peter Butterworth and Jack Douglas. Broadcast 16 November.
The Case of the Coughing Parrot - starring Jack Douglas, Kenneth Connor, Joan Sims and Peter Butterworth. Broadcast 23 November.
Who Needs Kitchener? - starring Kenneth Connor, Barbara Windsor, Joan Sims, Bernard Bresslaw and Jack Douglas. Broadcast 30 November.
Lamp-Posts of the Empire - starring Barbara Windsor, Kenneth Connor, Peter Butterworth, Jack Douglas and Bernard Bresslaw. Broadcast 7 December.
Sid James and the gang hung up their innuendos as *Carry On London!* ends its 18-month run at the Victoria Palace, while the 27th film, *Carry On Behind* was released in December. In terms of quantity, 1975 had been the year of *Carry On* comedy.

1976

On The Way I Lost It - An Autobiography by Frankie Howerd, published by W.H. Allen.
Returning from Australia after a tour in *The Mating Game*, Sid James came across a businessman in Phnom-Penh, Cambodia, owner of a cinema screening nothing but *Carry On* movies 24 hours a day! It was packed and Sid was greeted like the 'second coming'.
Sid James (1913-1976) died at 8.45pm on 26 April at the age of 62. Sid was on stage with Olga Lowe and Terry Scott during a production of Sam Cree's *The Mating Game* at Sunderland, directed by *Carry On* stage director Bill Roberton.

Carry On England. Starring Kenneth Connor, Jack Douglas, Peter Butterworth and Joan Sims. Filmed from 3 May to 4 June at Pinewood Studios.
Carry On Laughing. Jack Douglas, Kenneth Connor and Peter Butterworth star in a Sam Cree stage farce at The Royal Opera House, Scarborough, Yorkshire, from July to September.
England released, October.
Carry On farewells
Martin Boddey (1908-1976)... *Sergeant* and *Nurse*.
William Mervyn (1912-1976)... *Camel*, *Again Doctor* and *Henry*.

1977

The Goodies - comic heroes for a generation - publish *The Making of the Goodies' Disaster Movie* book. It features a colourful, one-page deconstruction of the *Carry On* series with *Carry On Christ*, including convincing caricatures of Butterworth, Bresslaw, Windsor, Hawtrey and Williams.
Both Frankie Howerd and Talbot Rothwell are awarded the OBE.
That's Carry On. Starring Kenneth Williams and Barbara Windsor. New material filmed during April at Pinewood Studios.
Another compilation movie, Herbert Wilcox's *To See Such Fun!*, featured clips from *Cruising*, *Cleo*, *Head* and *Henry*.
Carry On farewells
Ted Ray (1906-1977)... *Teacher*.

1978

Kenneth Eastaugh's *The Carry On Book* is published by David and Charles and deals with the first 28 movies. Barbara Windsor's shower scene from *Abroad* enhances the cover.
In January *Carry On Abroad*, starring the late Sid James, receives its television premiere and attracted 18.45 million viewers - putting the film 16th in a 1992 poll for movie ratings on the box. While at Pinewood the *Carry On* survivors were about to make a new film, fans clearly were already looking to the golden age of Sid James.
February - *That's Carry On* released.
Carry On Emmannuelle. Starring Kenneth Williams, Peter Butterworth, Kenneth Connor, Joan Sims and Jack Douglas. Filmed from 10 April to 15 May at Pinewood Studios and on location in Wembley. Released, November - with the Joe Don Baker/Tyne Daly thriller *Speedtrap* as support picture.
Carry On music men Eric Rogers and Bruce Montgomery both die at the age of 57.
Carry On farewells
Susan Shaw (1929-1978)... *Nurse*.

1979

Carry On Again Nurse announced as the 31st film. An 'X'-rated script by George Layton and Jonathan Lynn (star and writing team of the hit Granada situation comedy *My Brother's Keeper* 1975/76) is commissioned and completed but the filming is cancelled due to the financial loss of *England* and *Emmannuelle*.
While the new film was still very much in the air, *Carry On* legend Peter Butterworth (1919-1979) died in Coventry on 17 January at the age of 59. Starring as Widow Twankey in *Aladdin*, Peter went back to his hotel room after a successful evening performance and his failure to return for the following day's matinee show caused alarm. He was found dead from a heart attack.
In the Joan Collins sex romp, *The Bitch*, a wild orgy with Ian Henry is likened to *Cleopatra* but he admits he only ever saw the *Carry On* version!
Carry On farewells
Julian Orchard (1930-1979)... *Head*, *Camel*, *Doctor* and *Henry*.
Eric Pohlmann (1903-1979)... *Regardless* and *Spying*.
Sydney Tafler (1916-1979)... *Regardless*.

1980

Carry On legend Hattie Jacques (1924-1980) died on 7 October at the age of 56. The thought of another medical *Carry On* becomes redundant.
Carry On farewells
Imogen Hassall (1942-1980)... *Loving*.
Renee Houston (1902-1980)... *Cabby*, *Spying* and *Convenience*.
Ambrosine Phillpotts (1912-1980)... *Regardless*, *Cabby* and *Again Doctor*.

1981

Carry On genius Talbot Rothwell OBE (1916-1981) died at his home in Worthing on 28 February at the age of 64. He had been in poor health for many years and was cremated at West Worthing Crematorium.
The infamous ITV compilation series, *Carry On Laughing*, makes its first appearance, moulding the vintage work of Peter Rogers, Gerald Thomas and Eric Rogers into tasty 25-minute chunks (Editors - Jack Gardner/Peter Boita, Assistant Editors - Chris Lancaster/Adam Unger, Sound - Otto Snel, Research - Sylvia Pyke, Titles by G.S.E. Ltd).
Charles Hawtrey gives his last television interview on Roy Hudd's *Movie Memories*. His work is illustrated by clips from *Good Morning Boys!* and *Carry On Constable*.
Stripes is released - an Americanized *Carry On Sergeant* boasting marvellous work from Bill Murray. The film's success (it grossed over $85 million) leads to several mid-Atlantic comedies with *Carry On* smut. *The Police Academy* films (re-*Constable*) were mega-blockbusters

and the *Porky* films also scored at the box office.
A blast of punk rock in Garry Bushell's *Oi* collection presented 'Oi 3 - Carry On Oi!' (SEC 2). Complete with punk orientated McGill postcard cover by Art Dragon it was 'dedicated to the spirit of Sid James and Che Guevara'.
Carry On farewells
John Gatrell (1907-1981)... *Sergeant*.

1982

Film producer, Stephen Wooley wrote in 1989 that 'I would love to re-invent the *Carry Ons* for example, not as *Carry On*, but as a series with 8 or 9 modern comedians in recognizable situations.' It was in 1982 that a series began that practically fits this critique: *The Comic Strip Presents...* It utilized a collection of top comedy talent in a multitude of parodies on the British way of life as well as film spoofs with a more cynical edge. Indeed, the *Carry On* link was highlighted with Leslie Phillips guest-starring in 'Oxford' and 'GLC', while Robbie Coltrane believed that, 'we're halfway between a *Carry On* film and a Joe Orton play. The *Carry On* element is that we're funny and we use the same cast. The Joe Orton element is that we're producing the only consistent satire done on television today.' Coltrane hit the nail bang on the head. The skilled team also included Rik Mayall, Adrian Edmondson, Keith Allen, Peter Richardson, Dawn French, Jennifer Saunders and Alexei Sayle, while welcoming guests of the calibre of Lenny Henry. Indeed, in 1992, with the first *Carry On* for 14 years, most of the *Comic Strip* gang joined forces with Jim Dale and Leslie Phillips to re-invent the official series.
Carry On farewells
Harry H. Corbett (1925-1982)... *Screaming*.
Lucy Griffiths (1919-1982)... *Nurse, Constable, Doctor, Again Doctor, Loving* and *Behind*.

1983

The 25th anniversary of *Carry On* saw celebration with the compilation television shows, *Carry On Laughing* (Thames/ITV) and *What A Carry On* (BBC - Editor - Jack Gardner, Assistant editor - Olive Pearce, Sound - Chris Lancaster, Dubbing editor - Otto R. Snel, Titles & opticals - G.S.E. Ltd). The Thames series scored better in the ratings despite both using almost exactly the same clips (material from the Rank backed films from *Head* to *England*). The 13 BBC compilations and 16 ITV shows have been broadcast and re-broadcast ever since. The success of the ITV compilation shows led to a special seasonal version on 22 December: *Carry On Laughing's Christmas Classics* hosted by Kenneth Williams and Barbara Windsor. Rumours were still rife concerning a new film.
The year also saw the start of another comic classic,

the *Blackadder* cycle. Delighting in the *Carry On* style of employing a regular cast for different interpretations of history, *Blackadder* boasted the sublime Rowan Atkinson and priceless Richard Curtis/Ben Elton scripts. Rik Mayall, Hugh Laurie and Stephen Fry wandered in and out, while the Dickens Christmas special in 1988 saw shades of the *Carry On* special for 1969. The influence on self-confessed *Carry On* fan, Ben Elton, was highlighted with a guest turn for Kenneth Connor in *Blackadder II*.
The television debut of *England* heralds an interview with Jack Douglas who reveals that he is writing the script for a new medical *Carry On* film.
Kenneth Connor, interviewed on *Movie Memories*, is 'waiting for the next *Carry On*'.
Carry On farewells
Norman Chappell (1929-1983)... *Cabby, Henry* and 7 episodes of *Carry On Laughing*.

1984

British Cinema History by James Curran and Vincent Porter (eds.) features the Marion Jordan article 'Carry On - Follow That Stereotype'.
Carry On farewells
Francis de Wolff (1913-1984)... *Cleo*.
Frank Forsyth (1905-1984)... *Sergeant, Nurse, Constable, Cabby, Jack, Spying* and *Screaming*.
Derek Francis (1923-1984)... *Doctor, Camping, Loving, Matron* and *Abroad*.
Arnold Ridley (1895-1984)... *Girls*.

1985

Barbara Windsor starred in the Minehead Butlin's summer season, *What A Carry On!*.
Just Williams - An Autobiography by Kenneth Williams, published by J.M. Dent.
Carry On farewells
Wilfrid Brambell (1912-1985)... *Again Doctor*.
Gordon Rollings (1927-1985)... *Doctor*.
Phil Silvers (1912-1985)... *Camel*.

1986

Gerald Thomas made a welcome return to dramatic film-making with his Australian Second World War adventure, *The Second Victory*, starring Anthony Andrews. The script was written by Morris West from his own novel.
Ben Elton's love of *Carry On* innuendo informed his inspired and underrated series *Flithy, Rich and Catflap*, full of Rik Mayall's deconstruction of double entendres and Ade Edmondson's 'ooers!'. Barbara Windsor guest-starred in the first episode, while Mayall and Planer re-teamed for 1992's *Columbus*. The hugely popular semi-sequel, *Bottom*, continued the innuendo attack and one episode, 'Digger', even resurrected

Loving memories of a marriage agency.
In *Movies From the Mansion - 50 Years of Pinewood*, Chris Kelly introduced some choice clips from *Sergeant*, *Constable* and *Camping*. Peter Rogers was joined by valued 'remnants' Joan Sims, Kenneth Connor and Barbara Windsor at Pinewood Studios for the usual 'funny stories' interview. Marvellous.
Carry On farewells
Dandy Nichols (1907-1986)... *Doctor*.

1987

Tongue-in-cheek suggestion from *Photoplay* magazine implies that Peter Rogers and Gerald Thomas are to film a comedy version of the Hitchcock classic *The Birds* to be entitled *Carry On Carrion*.
A *Carry On* reunion at Barbara Windsor's pub at Amersham brings together Bernard Bresslaw, Terry Scott, Jack Douglas, Anita Harris and Gerald Thomas. Kenneth Williams and Kenneth Connor were both unable to attend due to working commitments, Joan Sims was ill, Jim Dale was at home in America and Charles Hawtrey proved ever elusive. The gathering was to promote the release of 13 Rank *Carry Ons* on 'The Video Collection' sell-through market and also to unveil plans of the new film *Carry On Texas* - a parody of the American super-soap *Dallas*. An apparently hilarious script from Dave Freeman and Dick Vosburgh had been written and Kenneth Williams was already cast in the top billing role of R.U. Ramming. Barbara Windsor was scheduled for Lucy Ramming, the poison dwarf, Joan Sims, Miss Ellie and Jack Douglas, a jittering Jock Ramming. Russ Abbot, Victoria Wood and Lenny Henry were among the new names quoted for a place in the film. Basically a British version of *The Beverly Hill-Billies* with a English family striking oil in Dallas, the film was budgeted at £2 million. However, the very promising plans were quickly curtailed by a threatened law suit from Lorimar Productions. Peter Rogers clearly lacked the courage of his convictions: *Spying* and *Cleo* came through while riding on threatened law suits!
The video release of the *Carry Ons* was also promoted by Bernard Bresslaw and Jack Douglas on the BBC's *Breakfast Time* with Frank Bough. 'The Video Collection' trailer featured some brief bits from *Doctor*, *Again Doctor*, *Loving*, *Convenience* and *Girls*, and some pretty dubious impersonations of Kenneth Williams, Frankie Howerd and Windsor Davies - 'So Carry On, you know it makes sense!'.
The *Carry On* legacy was included in a television celebration - *The Golden Gong - 50 Years of Rank's Films and Stars*. Peter Rogers, Kenneth Williams and Joan Sims shared some familiar memories, while clips from *Camel*, *Khyber* and *Camping* got presenter Michael Caine rolling in the aisle.

In a celebration of British cinema, *Wogan's Film Fun*, Terry Wogan welcomed a brief appearance from Kenneth Williams, Kenneth Connor, Bernard Bresslaw and Barbara Windsor. Complemented by a priceless clip from *Constable*, the team stole the show. A spine-tingling salute to the late greats of British film featured Sid James and Hattie Jacques in a clip from *Loving*.
Carry On farewells
Sydney Bromley (1919-1987)... *Cowboy*.
Irene Handl (1902-1987)... *Nurse* and *Constable*.
McDonald Hobley (1917-1987)... *Orgy and Bess*.
Harry Locke (1915-1987)... *Nurse*, *Doctor* and *Again Doctor*.

1988

Following the abandonment of the *Dallas* parody, Peter Rogers turned to another popular soap opera, *Neighbours*, and his variation on the theme, *Carry On Down Under*. However, no sooner had this idea appeared than it was dropped for a more familiar and safe subject. In a return to profitable terrain, Rogers announced that the new film would be *Carry On Nursing*. Not the Layton/Lynn X-rated *Carry On*, but a new script written by Don Maclean. Kenneth Williams had apparently tentatively agreed to star as the surgeon while Barbara Windsor was set to don the ward sister's uniform. The production date was set for Pinewood Studios in the first week of June. However in this, the 30th year of *Carry On*, two of the leading lights were to pass away. Kenneth Williams (1926-1988), the most prolific *Carry On* film star of them all, died in his London home on 15 April at the age of 62. His funeral took place at St Marylebone Crematorium, North London and a Memorial Service was held at The Actor's Church, St Paul's, Covent Garden. Kenneth Connor, Barbara Windsor and Gerald Thomas were in attendance. Kenneth's death saw national mourning.
In contrast, legendary Carry Oner Charles Hawtrey (1914-1988), died quietly and alone in a Deal nursing home on 27 October at the age of 73. The *Carry On* series could never be the same again.
Carry On fan, Morrissey, paid tribute to the school in *Teacher* with the track 'Late Night Maudlin Street' on his debut solo album, *Viva Hate*. The video included a suitable school-based homage to Hawtrey while Joan Sims featured on the promotional film for 'Ouija-board, ouija-board'.
Peter Rogers announced a new series of four, hour-long *Carry On* films for television. Barbara Windsor, Frankie Howerd, Bernard Bresslaw, Kenneth Connor, Terry Scott, Joan Sims and Jack Douglas had allegedly expressed interest in being cast.
Carl St John establishes The Kenneth Williams/Sid

James fan club, 'Stop Messin' About!'

Nat Cohen (1906-1988), junior partner in Anglo Amalgamated and subsequent mogul with EMI, died 11 February at the age of 82.

What A Carry On - The Official Story of the Carry On Film Series by Sally & Nina Hibbin published.

Barry Took introduced a BBC Radio 2 tribute to Kenneth Williams featuring extracts from *Sergeant*, *Jack*, *Spying*, *Cleo*, *Khyber* and *That's Carry On*.

Carry On farewells

Ameila Bayntun (?-1988)...*Camping*, *Loving*, *Convenience*, *Matron* and *Abroad*.

1989

Tongue-in-cheek reference from Peter Cushing that *Carry On Living* would be a good title for a film during an interview programme *One Way Ticket to Hollywood* for Channel Four. Another tongue-in-cheek comment from Eric Idle during the tenth anniversary celebrations for Handmade Films, explained that the team needed to make *Monty Python's Life of Brian* because in 1979 the cinema audiences hadn't seen *Carry On Crucifying*!.

On 24 October, the National Film Theatre presented a comic/homosexual salute - 'Carry On Regardless - A Tribute to the Genius of Charles Hawtrey'.

Channel Four developed into the airspace for a young generation of *Carry On* fans, primarily thanks to Jonathan Ross who continually expressed his affections (covering his *Last Resort* set with Sid James photos and enjoying a great interview with Barbara Windsor). Channel 4's improvisation show *Whose Line Is It Anyway?* highlighted the trend of young adults admitting to a love of *Carry On*, with hardly an episode going by without *Carry On* being shouted out as a style of film/theatre to improvise. Guests delighted in reading the credits in Clive Anderson's chosen style, with Griff Rhys Jones doing Frankie Howerd(!) and Arthur Smith having a bash at Sid James.

When ITV lost the rights to the 1989 Cup Final to the BBC, they screened *Carry On Again Doctor* to attract audiences back to commercial television.

Clips of *Again Doctor*, *Loving* and *Matron* featured in the Maurice Sellars compilation series *Best of British* for BBC television, while on radio Bernard Cribbins hosted *Make Em Laugh* and featured moments from his own *Jack* and *Behind*.

Harry Enfield's comic documentary *Norbert Smith - A Life* features a brief snippet, *Carry On Banging*. Harry enhanced his parody with a prime cast of Kenneth Connor, Barbara Windsor and Jack Douglas.

Don Maclean is rumoured to be working on a script for *Carry On Again Nurse*, a project which had laid dormant for a decade.

A tearful Charles Hawtrey is featured in a clip from *Carry On Nurse* in an advert for water shades along with the likes of Marilyn, Stan and Ollie and Buster Keaton. The whole thing was backed by Roy Orbison's 'Crying'.

BBC Radio 2's *The Life of Kenneth Connor* includes a vintage *Carry On* reunion with Connor, Leslie Phillips and Gerald Thomas laughing at bits from *Constable*, *Cruising* and *Cleo*. Joan Sims and Bernard Bresslaw ushered in clips from *Cowboy* and *Girls* in another episode.

Carry On farewells

Robert Dorning (1913-1989)... *Emmannuelle*.

Alan Gifford (1905-1989)... *Cowboy*.

1990

In January, Andy Medhurst's salute to low-brow British film comedy at the National Film Theatre included screenings of *Carry On Nurse* and *Cabby*. The season formed part of the NFT's two-year retrospective of British cinema.

In April distinguished director of photography on 10 *Carry Ons* Ernest Steward died.

Modern sitcoms were still using old *Carry On* gags with the Sid James/Angela Douglas towel scene from *Cowboy* cropping up with Gorden Kaye and Guy Siner in *Allo, Allo* while Anton Rodgers and Sylvia Syms incorporated the 'Up yours' banter from *Khyber* into an episode of *May to December*.

Barbara Windsor's autobiography, *Barbara - The Laughter and Tears of a Cockney Sparrow*, is published by Century.

The *Arena* special 'Oooh er, Missus! - The Frankie Howerd Story' featured a clip from *Doctor* and interviewee Eric Sykes stating that Frankie was too good for the series.

The first five *Carry Ons* and *Cabby* were included with such masterpieces of British comedy as *Passport to Pimlico* and *The Lavender Hill Mob* in a BBC2 season.

During his hit one-man show, Frankie Howerd revealed plans for a television special *Carry On Pompeii* which would co-star Barbara Windsor and Joan Sims. Rumours of another *Carry On* also came from Jack Douglas who was trying to find the money from Europe to fund a new feature film which Gerald Thomas would direct. The script would be by Douglas himself and Sir John Gielgud had asked to have a guest-starring role!

Sean Macreavy's wonderfully inspired *Carry On* fanzine, *Infamy*, begins and ends with just one witty and articulate issue.

In December, the *Carry Ons* won the first 'Jester' lifetime achievement award for film comedy. Gerald Thomas, Peter Rogers, Barbara Windsor, Kenneth Connor, Bernard Bresslaw and Liz Fraser accepted the award and Gerald dedicated it to the memory of Sid James, Kenneth Williams, Hattie Jacques, Charles Hawtrey and Peter Butterworth. Sir John Mills introduced a brief tribute to the series with clips from *Sergeant*, *Khyber* and *Camping*. It was only the second award the series had received - in the 1960s, Charles Hawtrey and Barbara Windsor had collected one on behalf of the *Carry Ons* from *Tit-Bits*.

Loose Ends, the Radio 4 comedy programme, presented a Christmas pantomime special, *Carry On Up Yer Cinders*, broadcast 10am, 22 December. It was a far cry from the official series and lacked that spark of affectionate style Harry Enfield had injected. However, Frankie Howerd as one of the ugly sisters made the whole thing worthwhile and Barbara Windsor popped in as Jim Dale as Buttons! Ned Sherrin narrated, future Carry Oner Julian Clary hit the mark as a very camp Kenneth Williams as Cinderella while Claire Rayner was particularly terrible as Hattie Jacques as the Fairy Godmother. Jonathan Ross was brilliantly over the top and wonderfully awful as Frankie Howerd as the other ugly sister and 'the new Sid James', Arthur Smith, starred, unsurprisingly, as Sid James. Rory Bremner also cropped up as Barry Norman, Terry-Thomas and Leslie Phillips. The script, by Arthur Smith, was deliberately awful, but all the best innuendos went to Smith himself and he gloriously sent up the production with his cry of, 'Who wrote this rubbish!'. Relying too heavily on topical gags and the most basic innuendo, *Carry On Up Yer Cinders* hardly set the world alight, but it was good Christmas fun and a funny parody of a parody. Thank heaven for Frankie Howerd! In 1992 Smith would record a location report on the set of *Columbus* for *Wogan*.

The Rank *Carry Ons* are re-released on video in slightly altered sleeve designs on the budget 'Cinema Club' label.

'The Cinema Club' also release three compilation videos made up of thematic collections from the 1980s series *Carry On Laughing*. *Jungle*, *Henry* and *Dick* feature on *Hysterical History*, *Abroad* and *Behind* appear on *Hilarious Holidays* and *Again Doctor* and *Matron* create *Medical Madness*.

Carry On farewells
Eric Barker (1912-1990)... *Sergeant*, *Constable*, *Spying* and *Emmannuelle*.
Jill Ireland (1936-1990)... *Nurse*.

1991

Kenneth Connor is awarded the MBE.

Carry On Regardless is included in Channel 4's excellent season of British comedy, *Beyond Ealing*. Others in the series were Monty Python's *The Meaning of Life*, *Two-way Stretch*, *The Rebel*, *A Funny Thing Happened on the Way to the Forum*, *Billy Liar*, *Entertaining Mr Sloane* and *How I Won the War*.

In May Peter Rogers once again announced plans for a television *Carry On* series. Intended for ITV, these would take the form of a series of half-hour, self-contained stories, akin to the 1975 ATV series *Carry On Laughing*. As usual, *Carry On* greats Barbara Windsor, Joan Sims, Bernard Bresslaw, Frankie Howerd and Jack Douglas were mooted to be the stars and people like Lenny Henry and Victoria Wood were mentioned as possible newcomers.

Stop Messin' About! magazine presents a festival of British comedy at the Scala on 2 June - the show includes *Matron*.

The Video collection re-release *Again Doctor* as a birthday card greetings 'video wishes' (G 0010). Jim Dale and Barbara Windsor enhanced the cover with the legend, 'At your age you should be taking care of your health... this will have you in stitches!' To mark the success of the partnership of Bernardo Bertolucci and Jeremy Thomas (*The Last Emperor*/*The Sheltering Sky*), *Moving Pictures* took a look at the Thomas clan, including Gerald's poetic innuendo at Pinewood. In Novemver the 'lost' television Christmas specials from 1972 and 1973 were finally released on 'The Cinema Club' video label at the meagre price of £5.99

Carry On farewells
Ronnie Brody (1918-1991) ... *Head*, *Henry* and *The prisoner of Spenda*
Donald Houston (1923-1991) ... *Jack*.
Wilfrid Hyde-White (1903-1991) ... *Nurse*.
Carol White (1943-1991) ... *Teacher*.

1992

Frankie Howerd OBE (1917-1992) died on 19 April at the age of 75. Having contracted a virus during a Christmas trip up the Amazon, Frankie was rushed to a Harley Street clinic and released at Easter to enjoy his last few days at home.

The release of the 'last' film *Carry On Emmannuelle* on to sell-through video for the first time. Put straight onto the budget label 'Cinema Club' for just £5.99 it was another historical release made available without fanfares. Aptly enough, as the general public had the chance to see the 'last' *Carry On* in their own homes, shooting began on a new film!

Jack Douglas promotes the new film on Radio 2 with Gloria Hunniford on 22 April. Much surprise is shown that Barbara Windsor is not going to appear! *Carry On Columbus*. Starring Jim Dale and Jack Douglas. Filming began 21 April at Pinewood Studios and on location at Frensham Ponds. The speedy (even by Carry On standards) five-week shoot comes to an end on 27 May. On 6 May, ITC Video release two volumes of *Carry On Laughing* shows - Volume 1, *Orgy and Bess*, *And in My Lady's Chamber* and *Under the Round Table*. Volume 2, *The Prisoner of Spenda*, *The Nine Old Cobblers* and *The Case of the Coughing Parrot*. Two further volumes (both featuring one episode with Sid James) appeared in October 1992 in a tie-in with the release of *Columbus*.

Columbus received its premiere on 2 October at the Leicester Square Odeon with Jim Dale and Gerald Thomas in attendance.

Charles Fleischer astutely saw himself in the Phil Silvers bracket during a discussion about *Columbus* on *Clive Anderson Talks Back*. The *Modern Review* asked 'Can double entendres save the British film industry?'

The Video Club re-package and re-release the 1972 *Carry On Christmas* as *Carry On... Christmas Capers*.

From 22 May to 25 October, jolly holiday-makers were cheered by Bernard Bresslaw and Barbara Windsor in *Wot A Carry On in Blackpool*.

On 18 October Sir Harry Secombe unveiled a plaque in memory of Sid James. Organized by 'The Dead Comics Society', the plaque is situated on Sid's home at 35 Gunnersbury Avenue, Ealing and the event was attended by his widow Valerie, his son Steve and friends and admirers like Jonathan Ross, Peggy Mount, Jack Douglas, Cardew Robinson, Nicholas Parsons and David Lodge.

New Year's Eve saw the first screening of *Seriously Seeking Sid*, a Channel X celebration of Sid James with mega-fan Jonathan Ross. Narrated by Arthur Smith, the documentary included some marvellous clips, old favourites, rare interview footage and some great laughs.

Titter Ye Not! - The Life of Frankie Howerd by William Hall, published by Grafton.

Barry Norman's 'Films of the Year' voted *Carry On Columbus* the worst of 1992! In 1994 Maureen Lipman would select *Columbus* as one of her pet hates in Nick Hancock's *Room 101*.

Carry On farewells

Percy Herbert (1925-1992)... *Jack* and *Cowboy*.

Brian Oulton (1908-1992)... *Nurse, Constable, Cleo, Camping* and *Carry On Christmas* (1972).

Cardew Robinson (1917-1992)... *Khyber*.

Bob Todd (1921-1992)...*Carry On Again Christmas, Again Doctor*.

1993

'Action - British Film Production' held a weekend in celebration of British cinema at Theatr Clwyd, Mold. Saturday, 27 February included a screening of *Cleo* and an interview with guest Jack Douglas by Robert Ross. Gerald Thomas and Peter Rogers presented the British Film Institute with production notes, original scripts, contracts, correspondence and publicity material for the entire series of 30 *Carry On* films from 1958-1978 as well as items relating to 15 other stage/television *Carry On* shows and Rogers/Thomas film productions. This was a year that saw the sad passing of three crucial figures in the *Carry Ons*' history. Bernard Bresslaw (1934-1993) died just before a performance as Grumio in Shakespeare's *The Taming of the Shrew* in Regent's Park. He was 59 years old. His death led to the establishment of the British Comedy subscription magazine, *Cor!*, edited by Robert Ross

Gerald Thomas (1920-1993), director of every *Carry On* movie, died from a massive heart attack at his home in Buckinghamshire on 9 November. He was 72 years old. His screen legacy was saluted on BBC2's *The Late Show*, which featured precious moments from *Cleo, Cowboy, Khyber, Camping, Henry, Convenience* and *Girls*. The show's closing music was the title theme from *Camping*.

Kenneth Connor MBE (1916-1993) died of cancer at his home in Harrow-on-the-Hill on 28 November at the age of 77. Having made his first stage appearance at the age of two, he was still working just two days before his death with an appearance on *Noel Edmond's Telly Addicts*.

In March, the National Film Theatre celebrated five 'Funny Men' with rare television screenings. Both Sid James and Frankie Howerd were saluted, alongside Peter Sellers, Marty Feldman and Benny Hill.

In May, Cilla Black and June Whitfield unveiled 'The Dead Comics Society' plaque to Frankie Howerd at 27 Edwardes Square, Kensington.

For August Bank Holiday, UK Gold presented a weekend of *Carry On* films, screening *Doctor, Loving, Convenience, Girls* and *England*.

In October, EMI released an audio collection of comic songs and sketches by *Carry On* players entitled *Carrying On - Entertainment From the Carry On Team* (EMI - 0777 78959649/ECC28). A double cassette, it includes gems from Kenneth Connor, Jim Dale, Bernard Bresslaw, Hattie Jacques, Barbara Windsor, Joan Sims, Kenneth Williams, Terry Scott and many more. Highlights include Harry H. Corbett's stunning music hall number 'Junk Song', Wilfrid Brambell's plaintive 'Second Hand', Frankie Howerd's robust 'Up Pompeii' and, best of all, Sid James' outstanding 'Ooooter Song'. Pure class.

The Anglo *Carry Ons* were re-released on video in a set of six tapes each containing two films: 'Twice the madness, twice the laughter, twice the *Carry On!*' (*Sergeant* and *Cleo, Teacher* and *Screaming, Regardless* and *Cowboy, Constable* and *Jack, Nurse* and *Cabby, Cruising* and *Spying*). Later such Rogers/Thomas productions as *The Big Job, Watch Your Stern, Twice Round The Daffodils* and *Nurse On Wheels* would be similarly released. In fact, these would be heralded as almost official *Carry Ons* for the first time.

Danny Baker ran a 'best *Carry On* ...' poll on his Radio 5 show. The winner was *Screaming*, although Baker dismissed any film without Sid as 'not a *Carry On*' - his vote was for *Abroad*.

The Kenneth Williams Diaries are published. Edited by Russell Davies, they show the lonely figure which everybody already knew lurked behind the nostril-flaring innuendo. Super sensitive and pouring his heart out on to the page, Williams moaned about his friends and colleagues and cast a shadow over the cheerful, matey Carry On atmosphere that had become legendary. The Kenneth Williams Letters, also edited by Davies, were more morally acceptable, fun and entertaining.

In the last episode of the BBC television series, Hollywood UK, celebrating British film of the 1960s, Peter Rogers and Gerald Thomas wandered round some of the locations of Pinewood Studios and talked about the Carry On series with examples from Khyber, Camping and Jungle. It was screened just before Thomas' death.

At Christmas, the deaths of Kenneth Connor, Bernard Bresslaw and Gerald Thomas were marked with a late-night BBC1 season of Carry Ons featuring Head, Doctor, Matron, Girls and England.

Carry On farewells

Victor Maddern (1928-1993)... Constable, Regardless, Spying, Cleo, Emmannuelle and 3 episodes of Carry On Laughing.

1994

On 9 April, 'Action - British Film Production' held an open day at the home of Carry On, Pinewood Studios. Liz Fraser, Jack Douglas and Valerie Leon represented the series.

The rather clumsily titled, Laugh with the Carry Ons series begins an irregular run. A series of compilations Gerald Thomas had completed just before his death, these covered the remaining films of the original series - namely the Anglo 12 and Emmannuelle. (Chief dubbing mixer - Otto Snel, Dubbing mixer - Michael Carter, Production accountant - Mary Beatty, Production assistant - Audrey Skinner, Co-ordinator - Deborah Hunter, Sound editor - Chris Lancaster, Assistant editor - Adam Unger, Titles & opticals by G.S.E., Editor - Jack Gardner, Associate producer - Philip Jones, Producer - Peter Rogers, Directed & Compiled by Gerald Thomas. Produced by Gerald Thomas Productions Ltd in association with Peter Rogers Productions Ltd and Movie Acquisition Corporation Ltd for Central).

On 15 May, Barbara Windsor and Norman Wisdom unveiled 'The Dead Comics Society' plaque to Kenneth Williams at 8 Marlborough House, Osnaburgh Street, London.

Terry Scott (1927-1994) died from cancer on 26 July at the age of 67. After the cancellation of Terry and June in 1988, ill health forced this fine comic to live his last years in semi-retirement.

On Bank Holiday Monday, BBC Radio 2, Fenella Fielding presented the hour-long Ross Smith

celebration of the series, Carry On Carrying On!. Contributions came from Jon Pertwee, Barbara Windsor, Jack Douglas, Bernard Cribbins and Peter Rogers, while archive gems included comments from Sid James, Charles Hawtrey and Peter Butterworth. The Beautiful South release their greatest hits album under the title, Carry On Up the Charts, featuring the phrase 'Carry On Regardless'. The subsequent tour was entitled 'Carry On Around the Country'.

The two-part South Bank Show on 'Comedy' featured Julian Clary looking at Carry On via his own work in Columbus and vintage material from Jungle.

The South Bank Show later devoted a whole programme to Kenneth Williams, featuring Peter Rogers and Barbara Windsor. Windsor later had another say in her Obituary Show for Channel 4. Camping naturally, was predominant.

Jonathan Ross hosted the comedy quiz show Gag Tags for BBC1 with resident captains Frank Skinner and Bob Monkhouse: Carry On was included with a brief bit of Kenneth Williams camp from Cleo.

The Museum of London used an image of Charles Hawtrey's head superimposed on a caveman's body to advertise their new exhibition - 'See what it was really like half a million years BC (Before Celluloid!)'.

Barbara Windsor becomes a regular in Eastenders and joins Wendy Richard and Dilys Laye in a Carry On ladies reunion. Meanwhile, Johnny Briggs, Amanda Barrie and Sherrie Hewson enhanced Coronation Street. Radio 2 paid belated tribute to Bernard Bresslaw and Kenneth Connor with Dick Vosburgh presenting Bresslaw and Leslie Phillips celebrating Connor.

Carry On farewells

Roy Castle (1932-1994)... Khyber.

Fred Griffiths (1912-1994)... Nurse, Regardless and Loving.

Llewellyn Rees (1900-1994)... Emmannuelle.

1995

Gerald Thomas was honoured with a plaque by The British Comedy Society at Pinewood Studios on 30 April. Carry On fan, Jim Davidson, hosted the event, while Mrs Barbara Thomas and family, Peter Rogers, Jack Douglas, Peter Gilmore, Carol Hawkins, Valerie Leon, Norman Rossington, Fenella Fielding, Suzanne Danielle, Lance Percival, Jimmy Logan, Bernard Cribbins, Angela Douglas, Burt Kwouk, Jacki Piper, Norman Hudis, Brenda Cowling and Patrick Mower were in attendance.

The Paul Daniels game show Wipe-Out asked anybody who cared to spare two minutes to pick out the Carry On actors from a list of names including Charles Hawtrey, Jim Dale, Liam Neeson, Roy Castle, Peter Gilmore, Michael Douglas and Bernard Cribbins - work it out for yourself! A decade earlier, Daniels' game show *Every Second Counts* presented its finalists with the topic 'Movies', asking them to say whether the named actors appeared in *Carry On*, James Bond or Woody Allen movies. Sid James, Kenneth Williams and Joan Sims were the taxing names which rang the *Carry On* bell!

K.P. Nuts used images of Sid James, Kenneth Williams and Charles Hawtrey to sell their wares with captions screaming, 'Keep Your Hands Off My Nuts!!', 'Nuts? Ooo!...Matron!' and 'Oh I say, my nuts are chilli!'. Who said subtlety was dead! Carry On nibbling!.

Cliff Goodwin's biography *Sid James* published by Century.

The Barbican Centre screened the series of films (with the exception of *That's Carry On*) during their season 'Carry On Up the Barbican!' from 11-31 August. For £30, manic fans could forget the summer sun and buy 'The Khyber Pass', allowing access to screenings of the entire 30 film season. Jack Douglas took part in a score of television and radio interviews to promote the season, and I was delighted to join him on a couple of appearances. Every newspaper and journal worth its salt had a piece on the series, while Jack Douglas, Fenella Fielding, Nicholas Parsons and Peter Rogers appeared on *The Big City*. The event even made the BBC's *Nine O'Clock News*. In an interview with *The Evening Standard*, Peter Rogers admitted the time for *Carry On* at the cinema was over, although he was still planning a series of half-hour shows for television. Jack Douglas revealed he was writing a *Carry On* movie script and Angela Grant was working on a novel based on her experiences making *Carry Ons*. The Barbican season's peak came on 13 August when a gala screening of *Khyber* was attended by Peter Rogers, Jack Douglas, Patsy Rowlands, Dilys Laye, Tyler Butterworth, Angela Grant, Patricia Franklin, Valerie James and Steven James. A highlight was a brief production report from the set of *Henry* with priceless interviews with Sid James, Kenneth Williams and Terry Scott - as with all the *Carry Ons*, the out-takes were hilarious gems. *Khyber* had never been funnier and the *Carry Ons* were back on the big screen where they belonged after years of television restriction - one swelled with pride.

The Sid James plaque unveiled in 1992 is stolen but quickly replaced by The British Comedy Society on 20 August.

Music Collection International acquire the rights to 17 *Carry On* movies for audio release under 'The Comedy Club' label. Distinguished thespian and veteran *Carry On* narrator (*Head*, *Doctor*, *Khyber*) Patrick Allen delivered Rick Glanvill's linking narrative, while the covers resurrected those priceless original poster designs. August saw the release of *Khyber*

(GAGMC032) and *Jungle* (GAGMC031). A wonderful idea, a treat for the car and the chance to enjoy *Carry On* anywhere your Walkman goes. Brilliant. And just to jump on the bandwagon, 'The Video Club' re-issued *Head* and *Henry* yet again, incorporating the original poster design for the cover. *Doctor*, *Abroad*, *Camel* and *Emmannuelle* followed later in the year. And just to make the completist's video shelves overflow, Warner Home video re-packaged *Sergeant* (SO38040) and *Cabby* (SO38031)at the budget price of £4.99.

'Comic Heritage' chairman David Graham organized a plaque unveiling event to Hattie Jacques on 5 November at 67 Eardley Cresent, Earl's Court. Eric Sykes was joined by such *Carry On* players as Richard O'Callaghan, Jacki Piper, Lance Percival, David Lodge, Liz Fraser, Melvyn Hayes and Norman Rossington.

In their 'How much is a pint of milk?' interviews, *Empire* magazine asks the likes of Billy Crystal and Keanu Reeves if they have ever seen a *Carry On* film! Damien Hirst's video for Blur's 'Country House' was, according to the *Guardian*, 'all knowingly done in the great English tradition of saucy Max Miller music-hall, *Carry On Camping* and naughty seaside postcards - post-Benny Hill.' *Columbus* players Keith Allen and Sara Stockbridge featured.

Ben Elton's *The Thin Blue Line* allowed Rowan Atkinson to pay homage to the series with the knowing command, 'Carry on, Constable!'.

Columbus recieved its terrestrial TV premiere on 21 December. Heralded as one of BBC's spearhead Christmas movies, it featured in pre-festive trailers and was complemented with a late night season of classics: *Convenience*, *Matron*, *Abroad*, *Dick* and *Behind*. *Columbus* was voted 8th worst film of all time in *Empire* readers' centenary of cinema poll, while a BBC1 season saw *Camping* and *Doctor* take the *Carry Ons* into *Carry On* farewells

Harold Berens (1903-1995)... *Columbus*.
Peter Grant (1935-1995)... *Columbus*.
Dany Robin (1927-1995)... *Don't Lose Your Head*.
Noel Dyson (1916-1995)... *Constable* and *Cabby*.

1996

Radio 2 Arts Programme dedicated two hours to *The Carry On Clan*. Hosted by Barbara Windsor, this boasted brief contributions from such notable Carry On names as Shirley Eaton, June Whitfield, Fenella Fielding and Valerie Leon, celebrated the immortal legacy of the team greats culminating with Williams, Hawtrey and Sid, and reached a peak with several round table discussion snippets with a forum comprised of Barbara Windsor, Jack Douglas, Patsy Rowlands and Kenneth Cope. The Audio Collection continued dishing out priceless soundtrack versions of the Rank era, with Patrick Allen's commentary on *Head* and *Camel*, Peter Gilmore recreating his ambulance man role in assistance of Allen on the *Doctor* tape and the coup of the bunch, Joan Sims running through the narrative for *Camping*. Later in the year *Jungle* was paired with *Khyber* (GAGDMC051), *Camel* with *Doctor* (GAGDMC052) and *Head* with *Camping* (GAGDMC053) to form double bill tape packages at £6-99 each. The British Comedy Society presented *An Evening with Jim Dale*, culminating with a *Carry On* question and answer session featuring Jim, Jack Douglas, Fenella Fielding and Peter Gilmore. Jack Douglas helped launch *The Carry On Companion* at a signing held at The Cinema Store on 16 May, while the author, Douglas and Fenella Fielding celebrated the series on the JoJo Smith hosted show *Funny Business*. In June, *The Stage* run an article detailing the rumour that Peter Rogers was planning the 32nd *Carry On* movie, headlining knock-about children's entertainers The Chuckle Brothers!! God forbid. This quickly became clarified by news from the Pinewood office that these would take the form of hour long television specials. No new *Carry On* films were being considered. Dick Hills, Morecambe & Wise scriptwriter who, with his partner, Sid Green wrote the original story *Call Me a Cab* which, in the hands of Talbot Rothwell became *Carry On Cabby*, died at the age of 70. The *Carry On* cult franchise grew steadily bigger with...wait for it - *Carry On* novels. Doctor Who had enjoyed a lengthy after life in print so why not Sid's innuendo? Six novels by Norman Giller were published in November, wickedly funny tales taking off from where the original movie ended...allegedly. Titles available were *Carry On Doctor* (boasting a shot of Jim Dale and Barbara Windsor from *Carry On Again Doctor* - will people never get it right!), *Carry On... Up the Khyber*, *Carry On Loving*, *Carry On Henry*, *Carry On Abroad* and *Carry On England*. In order to boost the packages, the stories included guest star turns from Frankie Howerd's Francis Bigger (cropping up in *England* & *Abroad*), Charles Hawtrey's James Bedsop (returning for *Loving* as well as finding himself in *Abroad*), a newly created character for Terry Scott in *Abroad* and, at last, finally doing the impossible and casting the late Sid James in *Carry On England*, alongside originally absent favourites Jim Dale, Kenneth Williams (both recreating their Doctor roles - some twenty years early and, supposedly, not looking a day younger), Bernard Bresslaw and Barbara Windsor!! The results were universally considered lamentable. As well as hefty plugs in the novels, the Cinema Club, wallowing in their popular relaunch of the Rank movies, celebrated with a £6-99 *Carry On* calender for 1997 featuring images from *Head*, *Camel*, *Doctor*, *Khyber*, *Camping*, *Jungle*,

Loving, *Henry*, *Convenience*, *Abroad*, *Dick* and *England* while utilizing the basic, slightly adjusted poster for *That's Carry On* with Connor (from the *Girls* poster) and Howerd from *Jungle*, getting in on the act. On television, *Cowboy*, *Loving*, *Matron*, *Abroad* and *England* kept the nation laughing over Christmas while the very first film screened by BBC1 in 1997 was none other than *Carry On Girls*...

Carry On Farewells
Patrick Cargill (1918-1996)...*Regardless* and *Jack*.
Jon Pertwee (1919-1996)...*Cleo*, *Cowboy*, *Screaming* and *Columbus*.
Beryl Reid OBE (1918-1996)...*Emmannuelle*

1997

Carry On's chief editor, Alfred Roome, died at the age of 90. David Benson kept the spirit of Kenneth Williams alive with his excellent, self-penned one-man celebration *Think No Evil Of Us - My Life With Kenneth Williams*. The sublime Steve Coogan uses Des O'Connor ITV chat show to unveil his latest comic creation - the smooth crooning babe magnet Tony Ferrino. He expresses affection for foreign cinema - particularly Korean movies...*Korean Camping*, *Korean Up the Khyber* etc... Classic. New Internet sites, Carry On...On Location (http://members.aol.com/raymortim/carryon.htm) and Rhino's Carry On Laughing Homepage http:vilage.vossnet.co.uk/r/rhino/carry.htm) continue to forge innuendo's way into the new millennium. Cinema Club repackage the Rank era *Carry On* on video, releasing eight tapes each featuring two films. Channel Four's disappointing Sitcom Weekend prompts David Parkinson to remember three 'Kings of Comedy in *Radio Times* - Sid James and Frankie Howerd are joined by Peter Sellers. Jim Dale returns to *Oliver!* and launched the National Lottery with some apt medical innuendo and comments about regular T.V. *Carry On* screenings.

Carry On Farewells
Michael Balfour (1917-1997)...*Constable*
Don Henderson (1931-1997)...*Columbus*
Michael Ward (1909-1997)...*Regardless*, *Cabby*, *Cleo*, *Screaming* and *Don't Lose Your Head*

1998

The 40th anniversary year for *Carry On* began with a post midnight BBC1 New Year's Eve screening of *Carry On At Your Convenience* and there was a hive of activity for planned celebrations. Having bought the rights to the Rank movies Carlton were eager to jump onto the bandwagon with European/Eastern block marketing, *Carry On* greetings cards and even a pin-ball machine, UK Gold continued to repeat the films at alarmingly regular intervals, Pinewood Studios was inundated with proposals for definitive television documentaries and the entire canon was feted as essential cultural information for an understanding of the British way of life. The Pinewood Studios Gala Dinner in celebration of Carry On's 40th year is organized by the British Comedy Society for 26th April – the 71st birthday of Jack Douglas and 22 years to the day since Sid died. A blue plaque to the 31 films in the series is unveiled by Peter Rogers while specially dedicated tributes to Sid, Williams, Jacques and Hawtrey are unveiled by Jack Douglas, Barbara Windsor, June Whitfield and Leslie Phillips respectively. Other key figures in attendence were Shirley Eaton, Fenella Fielding, Alan Hume, Richard O'Callaghan, Jakcki Piper, Norman and Rita Hudis, Liz Fraser, Bernard Cribbins, Anita Harris, Jack Gardner, Dave Freeman, Norman Rossington, Lance Percival, Peter Gilmore, Bill and James Pertwee, Valerie Leon, Alan Curtis, Norman Mitchell, Burt Kwouk, Frank Thornton, Alan Hume, John Clive, Brian Rawlinson, Jeremy Connor, Suzanne Danielle and Angela Grant. Comic heritage honour Terry Scott with a plaque at BBC Television Centre on 10 May, with other plaques going to Dick Emery, Jimmy Edwards and Michael Bentine. BBC2 dedicate a special two part Reputations to the life and work of Kenneth Williams, ten years after his death. Channel 4 present a Carry On Night with documentaries and screenings in celebration of the film's 40th anniversary. In December Carlton screen their official 40th anniversary documentary What's A Carry On? and the Museum of the Moving Image launches their special exhibition. Douglas Gamley, pianist and composer on Cruising, died in April at 74. June Whitfield is made a CBE and Leslie Phillips an OBE. Anthony Sher is set to play Sid James in Terry Johnson's Cleo, Camping, Emmanuelle (sic) and Dick at the National but a conflict over interpretation sees Geoffrey Hutchings take over. Adam Godley played Kenneth Williams, Gina Belman was Imogen Hassall and Samantha Spiro Barbara Windsor. The Carry On Winning fruit machine is produced.

Carry On Farewells

Patricia Hayes (1909–1998) ... Again Doctor

Joan Hickson (1906–1998) ... Nurse, Constable, Regardless, Loving and Girls

Davy Kaye (1928–1998) ... Cowboy and At Your Convenience

Betty Marsden (1919–1998) ... Regardless and Camping

Robin Ray (1934–1998) ... Constable

James Villiers (1933–1998) ... Sergeant

1999

April sees the first official Carry On day at Pinewood pay tribute to Nurse with guests Peter Rogers, Noman Hudis, Shirley Eaton and Christine Ozanne. A Christmas event follows with Jack Douglas, Patsy Rowlands, Alexandra Dane, Brian Rawlinson, Hugh Futcher and Norman Mitchell as Santa Claus. Camping is the first of the series released on dvd and includes the What's a Carry On? documentary. The best-selling CD The Carry On Album is released, with newly recorded Montgomery and Rogers scores conducted by Gavin Sutherland. Lledo release a series of model vehicles: a Sergeant army truck, a Teacher school coach, a Constable police van, a Cabby taxi, a Camping camper van and a Matron ambulance.

Carry On Farewells

Deryck Guyler (1914–1999) ... Doctor

Michael Nightingale (1922–1999) ... Regardless, Cabby, Jack, Cleo, Cowboy, Head, Camel, Camping, Matron, Girls, Dick, England, Emmannuelle and 2 episodes of Laughing.

Bill Owen (1914–1999)... Sergeant, Nurse, Regardless and Cabby

Norman Rossington (1928–1999) ... Sergeant, Nurse, Regardless and Christmas (1972)

2000

Carry On stage director Bill Roberton dies. 25th April, ITV screen the film version of Johnson's play. Now re-titled Cor, Blimey! The central cast of Hutchings, Godley and Spiro, are joined by Hugh Walters as Hawtrey and, Chrissie Cotterill as Sims. Barbara Windsor plays herself in the last scene.

Carry On Farewells

Peter Jones (1920–2000) ... Doctor and England

Brian Rawlinson (1931–2000) ... Cruising, Cleo and Cowboy

Kenneth Waller (1927–2000)... Behind

2001

Channel 4 documentaries, Ball-Breakers On the Box, and Can We Girls Carry On? take a positively feminist glance at the series. Pinwood plaques are unveiled to Bresslaw, Butterworth, Connor, Scott and Peter Rogers. Legends documentaries on Hattie Jacques and Frankie Howerd are screened. Kenneth MacDonald, the 'heavy' in Cleo, Camping, Emmanuelle and Dick, and Cor, Blimey! dies at 50. On 28th June Carry On legend Joan Sims dies at 71. Short animations, The Carryoons, are launched, with the vocal talent of Jack Douglas, Samantha Spiro (as Windsor), David Benson (as Williams) and Jeremy Conner as his father, Kenneth. Royal Doulton issue Sid, Hawtrey, Jacques and Williams toby jugs.

Carry On Farewells

Jimmy Logan (1928–2001) ... Abroad and Girls

Norman Mitchell (1918–2001) ... Cabby, Spying, Cleo, Screaming! and Emmannuelle

2002

Heroes of Comedy shows salute Sid James and Hattie Jacques.

Carry On Farewells

Pat Coombs (1930–2002) ... Doctor and Again Doctor

Claire Davenport (1936–2002) ... Emmannuelle

Stanley Unwin (1911–2002) ... Regardless

ALLEN, Keith
(Actor) - *Columbus*

BARKER, Eric
(Actor) - *Constable, Emmannuelle, Sergeant, Spying* (Original idea) - *Cruising*

BARRIE, Amanda
(Actress) - *Cabby, Cleo*

BAXTER, Ronnie
(Director) - *Christmas* (1969), *Christmas* (1972)

BOITA, Peter
(Editor) - *Emmannuelle, Laughing* (compilation series), *Sergeant*

BRESSLAW, Bernard
(Actor) - *And in My Lady's Chamber, Abroad, Again Christmas, At Your Convenience, Behind, Camping, Christmas* (1969), *Christmas* (1973), *Cowboy, Dick, Doctor, Follow That Camel, Girls, London, Loving, Matron, Screaming, Up the Jungle, Up the Khyber, Lamp-Posts of the Empire, Short Knight, Long Daze, Under the Round Table, What A Carry On!* (TV), *Who Needs Kitchener?, Wot A Carry On in Blackpool*

BRYAN, Dora
(Actress) - *Sergeant*

BUTTERWORTH, Peter
(Actor) - *And in My Lady's Chamber, The Baron Outlook, Abroad, Again Doctor, Behind, Camping, Christmas* (1969), *Christmas* (1972), *Christmas* (1973), *Cowboy, Dick, Doctor, Don't Lose Your Head, Emmannuelle, England, Follow That Camel, Girls, Henry, Laughing* (stage),

London, Loving, Screaming, Up the Khyber, The Case of the Coughing Parrot, The Case of the Screaming Winkles, Lamp-Posts of the Empire, The Prisoner of Spenda, Short Knight, Long Daze, The Sobbing Cavalier, Under the Round Table, What A Carry On! (TV)

CANNON, Esma
(Actress) - *Cabby, Constable, Cruising, Regardless*

CARLIN, John
(Actor) - *The Baron Outlook, Emmannuelle, England, The Case of the Screaming Winkles, Lamp-Posts of the Empire, The Nine Old Cobblers, One in the Eye For Harold*

CASTLE, Roy
(Actor) - *Up the Khyber*

CHAMBERLAIN, Cyril
(Actor) - *Cabby, Constable, Cruising, Nurse, Regardless, Sergeant, Teacher*

CHAPPELL, Norman
(Actor) - *Cabby, Henry, The Case of the Coughing Parrot, The Case of the Screaming Winkles, Lamp-Posts of the Empire, Orgy and Bess, One in the Eye For Harold, Short Knight, Long Daze, Under the Round Table*

CHURCH, Tony
(Scriptwriter) - *That's Carry On*

CLARY, Julian
(Actor) - *Columbus, Up Yer Cinders*

CLEGG, Tom
(Actor) - *Cleo, Cowboy, Loving,*

Regardless, Screaming, Spying

COLIN, Sid
(Scriptwriter) - *Again Christmas, Spying*

CONNOR, Kenneth
(Actor) - *And in My Lady's Chamber, The Baron Outlook, Abroad, Again Christmas, Behind, Cabby, Christmas* (1972), *Christmas* (1973), *Cleo, Constable, Cruising, Dick, Emmannuelle, England, Girls, Henry, Laughing* (stage), *London, Matron, Nurse, Regardless, Sergeant, Teacher, Up the Jungle, The Case of the Coughing Parrot, The Case of the Screaming Winkles, Lamp-Posts of the Empire, The Nine Old Cobblers, Norbert Smith - A Life, One in the Eye For Harold, Orgy and Bess, The Prisoner of Spenda, Short Knight, Long Daze, Under the Round Table, What A Carry On!* (TV), *Who Needs Kitchener?*

COPE, Kenneth
(Actor) - *At Your Convenience, Matron*

CORBETT, Harry H.
(Actor) - *Screaming*

CORNELIUS, Billy
(Actor) - *Again Doctor, Behind, Christmas* (1972), *Dick, Don't Lose Your Head, Girls, Screaming, One in the Eye for Harold, Short Knight, Long Daze, Under the Round Table*

CREE, Sam
(Scriptwriter) - *Laughing* (stage)

CRIBBINS, Bernard
(Actor) - *Columbus, Jack, Spying*

CRYER, Barry

(Scriptwriter) - *Orgy and Bess, Wot A Carry On in Blackpool*

CURTIS, Alan

(Actor) - *Abroad, Henry*

DALE, Jim

(Actor) - *Again Doctor, Cabby, Cleo, Columbus, Cowboy, Doctor, Don't Lose Your Head, Follow That Camel, Jack, Screaming, Spying*

DANE, Alexandra

(Actress) - *Again Doctor, Behind, Doctor, Loving, Up the Khyber*

DANIELLE, Suzanne

(Actress) - *Emmannuelle*

DANN, Larry

(Actor) - *Behind, Emmannuelle, England, Teacher*

DAVIES, Windsor

(Actor) - *Behind, England*

DE GAYE, Phoebe

(Costume designer) - *Columbus*

DOUGLAS, Angela

(Actress) - *Cowboy, Follow That Camel, Screaming, Up the Khyber*

DOUGLAS, Jack

(Actor) - *And In My Lady's Chamber, Abroad, Behind, Christmas* (1972), *Christmas* (1973), *Columbus, Dick, Emmannuelle, England, Girls, Laughing* (stage), *London, Matron, The Case of the Coughing Parrot, The Case of the Screaming Winkles, Lamp-Posts of the Empire, The Nine Old Cobblers, Norbert Smith - A Life, One in the Eye For Harold, Orgy and Bess, The Prisoner of Spenda, Short Knight, Long Daze, The Sobbing Cavalier, Under the Round Table, What A Carry On!* (TV), *Who Needs Kitchener?*

DOUGLAS, Sally

(Actress) - *Cleo, Cowboy, Follow That Camel, Jack, Screaming, Spying*

DU PREZ, John

(Composer) - *Columbus*

ELLIOTT, Courtenay

(Costume designer) - *Abroad, At Your Convenience, Behind, Dick, Girls, Henry, Loving, Matron, Up the Jungle*

EATON, Shirley

(Actress) - *Constable, Nurse, Sergeant*

FIELDING, Fenella

(Actress) - *Regardless, Screaming*

FORSYTH, Frank

(Actor) - *Cabby, Constable, Jack, Nurse, Sergeant, Screaming, Spying*

FRASER, Liz

(Actress) - *Behind, Cabby, Cruising, Laughing* (stage), *Regardless*

FREEMAN, Dave

(Scriptwriter) - *The Baron Outlook, Again Christmas, Behind, Christmas* (1972), *Columbus* (and as actor), *London, The Case of the Coughing Parrot, The Case of the Screaming Winkles, The Nine Old Cobblers, The Prisoner of Spenda, The Sobbing Cavalier*

FURSE, Judith

(Actress) - *Cabby, Regardless, Spying*

FUTCHER, Hugh

(Actor) - *Abroad, Again Doctor, At Your Convenience, Behind, Don't Lose Your Head, Girls, Spying*

GARDNER, Jack

(Assistant Editor) - *Abroad, Again Doctor, At Your Convenience, Behind, Camping, Cowboy, Dick, Doctor, Emmannuelle, England, Follow That Camel, Girls, Henry, Loving, Matron, Up the Jungle, Up the Khyber*. (Editor) - *Laugh with the Carry Ons, Laughing* (compilation series), *Laughing's Christmas Classics, That's Carry On, What A Carry On* (compilation series)

GILMORE, Peter

(Actor) - *Again Doctor, Cabby, Cleo, Columbus, Cowboy, Doctor, Don't Lose Your Head, Follow That Camel, Henry, Jack, Up the Khyber*

GOLDSTONE, John

(Producer) - *Columbus*

GRANT, Angela

(Actress) - *Girls, Follow That Camel, Up the Khyber*

HARRIS, Anita

(Actress) – *Doctor, Follow That Camel*

HARRIS, Max

(Composer) - *England, Short Knight, Long Daze, Under the Round Table*

HARTNELL, William

(Actor) - *Sergeant*

HASSALL, Imogen

(Actress) - *Loving*

HAWKINS, Carol

(Actress) - *And in My Lady's Chamber, Abroad, Again Christmas, Behind, Who Needs Kitchener?*

HAWTREY, Charles

(Actor) - *Abroad, Again Christmas, Again Doctor, At Your Convenience, Cabby, Camping, Christmas* (1969), *Cleo, Constable, Cowboy, Doctor, Don't Lose*

Your Head, Follow That Camel, Henry, Jack, Loving, Matron, Nurse, Regardless, Screaming, Sergeant, Spying, Teacher, Up the Jungle, Up the Khyber

HEWSON, Sherrie

(Actress) - *And in My Lady's Chamber, Behind, The Case of the Coughing Parrot, The Case of the Screaming Winkles, Who Needs Kitchener?*

HICKSON, Joan

(Actress) - *Constable, Girls, Loving, Nurse, Regardless*

HOLLOWAY, Julian

(Actor) - *At Your Convenience, Camping, Christmas* (1973), *Doctor, England, Follow That Camel, Henry, Loving, Up the Khyber*

HOOKS, Linda

(Actress) - *The Baron Outlook, Behind, Dick, England, Laughing* (stage), *One in the Eye for Harold*

HOUSTON, Renee

(Actress) - *At Your Convenience, Cabby, Spying*

HOWERD, Frankie

(Actor) - *Christmas* (1969), *Doctor, Up the Jungle, Up Yer Cinders*

HUDIS, Norman

(Scriptwriter) - *Constable, Cruising, Nurse, Regardless, Sergeant, Teacher*

HUME, Alan

(Camera Operator) - *Constable, Nurse, Sergeant, Teacher* (Director of Photography) - *Abroad, Cabby, Cleo, Columbus, Cowboy, Cruising, Doctor, Don't Lose Your Head, Emmannuelle, Follow That Camel, Girls, Henry, Jack, Regardless, Screaming, Spying*

HYDE-WHITE, Wilfrid

(Actor) - *Nurse*

JACQUES, Hattie

(Actress) - *Abroad, Again Doctor, At Your Convenience, Cabby, Camping, Christmas* (1969), *Christmas* (1972), *Constable, Dick, Doctor, Loving, Matron, Nurse, Regardless, Sergeant, Teacher, Orgy and Bess*

JAMES, Sidney

(Actor) - *The Baron Outlook, Abroad, Again Christmas, Again Doctor, At Your Convenience, Cabby, Camping, Christmas* (1969), *Christmas* (1973), *Cleo, Constable, Cowboy, Cruising, Dick, Doctor, Don't Lose Your Head, Girls, Henry, London, Loving, Matron, Regardless, Sid, Up the Jungle, Up the Khyber, Orgy and Bess, The*

Prisoner of Spenda, The Sobbing Cavalier, What A Carry On! (TV)

KEYS, Rod

(Editor) - *Cowboy, Don't Lose Your Head, Screaming*

KLAUBER, Gertan

(Actor) - *Abroad, Cleo, Doctor, Emmannuelle, Henry, Spying*

KNIGHT, Rosalind

(Actress) - *Nurse, Teacher*

LANGTON, Diane

(Actress) - *The Baron Outlook, England, One in the Eye for Harold, The Prisoner of Spenda, Teacher*

'LARRY'

(cartoonist) - *Camping, Doctor, Girls, Up the Khyber*

LAYE, Dilys

(Actress) - *Camping, Cruising, Doctor, Spying*

LEON, Valerie

(Actress) - *Again Doctor, Camping, Christmas* (1972), *Girls, Matron, Up the Jungle, Up the Khyber*

LOCKE, Harry

(Actor) - *Again Doctor, Doctor, Nurse*

LODGE, David

(Actor) - *The Baron Outlook, Behind, Girls, Dick, England, Regardless, The Case of the Coughing Parrot, The Case of the Screaming Winkles, The Nine Old Cobblers, One in the Eye for Harold, The Prisoner of Spenda, The Sobbing Cavalier*

LOGAN, Jimmy

(Actor) - *Abroad, Girls*

LONGDON, Terence

(Actor) - *Nurse, Constable, Regardless, Sergeant*

LUDSKI, Archie

(Editor) - *Cabby, Cleo, Jack, Spying*

MADDERN, Victor

(Actor) - *Constable, Cleo, Emmannuelle, Regardless, Spying, The Nine Old Cobblers, Orgy and Bess, Under the Round Table*

MARDEN, Richard

(Editor) - *England*

MAYALL, RIK

(Actor) - *Columbus*

MAYNARD, Bill

(Actor) - *At Your Convenience, Dick, Henry, Loving, Matron*

MERRIMAN, Eric

(Scriptwriter) - *London*

MITCHELL, Norman

(Actor) - *Cabby, Cleo, Emmannuelle, Screaming, Spying*

MITCHELL, Warren

(Actor) - *Cleo*

MONKHOUSE, Bob

(Actor) - *Sergeant*

MONTGOMERY, Bruce

(Composer) - *Constable, Cruising, Nurse, Regardless, Sergeant, Teacher*

NIGHTINGALE, Michael

(Actor) - *Cabby, Camping, Cleo, Cowboy, Dick, Don't Lose Your Head, Emmannuelle, England, Follow That Camel, Girls, Jack, Matron, Regardless, The Case of the Screaming Winkles, Lamp-Posts of the Empire*

NOLAN, Margaret

(Actress) - *At Your Convenience, Cowboy, Dick, Girls, Henry, Matron*

OSBORNE, Brian

(Actor) - *The Baron Outlook, Abroad, Behind, Dick, Girls, England, Matron, The Case of the Coughing Parrot, One in the Eye for Harold, Orgy and Bess, The Sobbing Cavalier, Under the Round Table, Who Needs Kitchener?*

OULTON, Brian

(Actor) - *Camping, Christmas* (1972), *Cleo, Constable, Nurse*

OWEN, Bill

(Actor) - *Cabby, Nurse, Regardless, Sergeant*

PERCIVAL, Lance

(Actor) - *Cruising*

PERTWEE, Jon

(Actor) - *Cleo, Columbus, Cowboy, Screaming*

PHILLIPS, Leslie

(Actor) - *Columbus, Constable, Nurse, Teacher*

PIPER, Jacki

(Actress) - *At Your Convenience, Loving, Matron, Up the Jungle*

PURSALL, David

(Scriptwriter) - *England*

RAWLINSON, Brian

(Actor) - *Cleo, Cowboy, Cruising*

RAY, Ted

(Actor) - *Teacher*

RICHARD, Wendy

(Actress) - *Again Christmas, Girls, Matron*

ROBERTON, Bill

(Director) - *Laughing* (stage), *London*

ROBIN, Dany

(Actress) - *Don't Lose Your Head*

ROGERS, Eric

(Composer) - *Abroad, Again Doctor* (and as actor), *At Your Convenience, Behind, Cabby, Camping, Cleo, Cowboy* (and as actor), *Dick, Doctor, Don't Lose Your Head, Emmannuelle, Follow That Camel, Girls, Henry, Jack, Loving, Matron, Screaming, Spying, Up the Jungle, Up the Khyber*

(Musical Arranger) - *That's Carry On*

ROGERS, Peter

(Producer) - *Abroad, Again Doctor, At Your Convenience, Behind, Cabby, Camping, Cleo, Constable, Cowboy, Cruising, Dick, Doctor, Don't Lose Your Head, Emmannuelle, England, Follow That Camel, Girls, Henry, Jack, Loving, Matron, Nurse, Regardless, Sergeant, Screaming, Spying, Teacher, Up the Jungle, Up the Khyber, That's Carry On* (Executive Producer) - *And in My Lady's Chamber, The Baron Outlook, Christmas* (1972), *Christmas* (1973), *Columbus, The Case of the Coughing Parrot, The Case of the Screaming Winkles, Lamp-Posts of the Empire, The Nine Old Cobblers, One in the Eye for Harold, Orgy and Bess, The Prisoner of Spenda, Short Knight, Long Daze, The Sobbing Cavalier, Under the Round Table, Who Needs Kitchener?*

ROOME, Alfred

(Editor) - *Abroad, Again Doctor, At Your Convenience, Behind, Camping, Dick, Doctor, Follow That Camel, Girls, Henry, Loving, Matron, Up the Jungle, Up the Khyber*

ROSSINGTON, Norman

(Actor) - *Christmas* (1972), *Nurse, Regardless, Sergeant*

ROTHWELL, Talbot

(Scriptwriter) - *Abroad, Again Doctor, At Your Convenience, Cabby, Camping, Christmas* (1969), *Christmas* (1972), *Christmas* (1973), *Cleo, Cowboy, Dick, Doctor, Don't Lose Your Head, Follow That Camel, Girls, Henry, Jack, London, Loving, Matron, Screaming, Spying, Up the Jungle, Up the Khyber*

ROWLANDS, Patsy

(Actress) - *Abroad, Again Doctor, At Your Convenience, Behind, Dick, Girls, Henry, Loving, Matron, The Nine Old Cobblers*

SAGAR, Anthony

(Actor) - *Cruising, Loving, Nurse, Regardless, Sergeant, Screaming*

SCAIFE, Ted

(Director of Photography) - *Constable*

SCHWARZ, Lew

(Scriptwriter) - *And In My Lady's Chamber, Lamp-Posts of the Empire, One in the Eye for Harold, Short Knight, Long Daze, Under the Round Table, Who Needs Kitchener?*

SCOTT, Terry

(Actor) - *Again Christmas, Camping, Christmas* (1969), *Henry, Loving, Matron, Sergeant, Up the Jungle, Up the Khyber*

SEDDON, Jack

(Scriptwriter) - *England*

SELBY-WALKER, Emma

(Costume Designer) - *Don't Lose Your Head, Follow That Camel, Screaming, Up the Khyber*

SHIRLEY, John

(Editor) - *Constable, Cruising, Nurse, Regardless, Teacher*

SHUTE, VALERIE

(Actress) - *Again Doctor, Camping, Henry, Loving, Matron*

SILVERS, Phil

(Actor) - *Follow That Camel*

SIMS, Joan

(Actress) - *And In My Lady's Chamber, The Baron Outlook, Abroad, Again Doctor, At Your Convenience, Behind, Camping, Christmas* (1972), *Christmas* (1973), *Cleo, Constable, Cowboy, Dick, Doctor, Don't Lose Your Head, Emmannuelle, England, Follow That Camel, Girls, Henry, Loving, Matron, Nurse, Regardless, Screaming, Teacher, Up the Jungle, Up the Khyber, The Case of the Coughing Parrot, The Case of the Screaming Winkles, The Nine Old Cobblers, One in the Eye for Harold, The Prisoner of Spenda, Short Knight, Long Daze, The Sobbing Cavalier, Under the Round Table, Who Needs Kitchener?*

SOMMER, Elke

(Actress) - *Behind*

STEWARD, Ernest

(Director of Photography) - *Again Doctor, At Your Convenience, Behind, Camping, Dick, England, Loving, Matron, Up the Jungle, Up the Khyber*

STONE, Marianne

(Actress) - *At Your Convenience, Behind, Dick, Doctor, Don't Lose Your Head, Girls, Jack, Nurse, Screaming, The Case of the Screaming Winkles*

TARRANT, Alan

(Director) - *And In My Lady's Chamber, The Baron Outlook, Again Christmas* (and as producer), *The Case of the Coughing Parrot, The Case of the Screaming Winkles, Lamp-Posts of the Empire, The Nine Old Cobblers, One in the Eye for Harold, Orgy and Bess, The Prisoner of Spenda, Short Knight, Long Daze, The Sobbing Cavalier, Under the Round Table, Who Needs Kitchener?, What A Carry On!* (and as producer)

THOMAS, Gerald

(Director) - *Abroad, Again Doctor, At Your Convenience, Behind* (and vocal characterization), *Cabby, Camping, Cleo, Columbus, Constable, Cowboy, Cruising, Dick, Doctor, Don't Lose Your Head, Emmannuelle, England, Follow That Camel, Girls, Henry, Jack, Loving, Matron, Nurse, Regardless, Sergeant, Screaming* (and vocal characterization), *Spying, Teacher, Up the Jungle, Up the Khyber, That's Carry On* (Comedy Consultant) - *Again Christmas, Christmas* (1969) (Producer) - *And in My Lady's Chamber, The Baron Outlook, Christmas* (1972), *Christmas* (1973), *Laughing's Christmas Classics, The Case of the Coughing Parrot, The Case of the Screaming Winkles, Lamp-Posts of the Empire, The Nine Old Cobblers, One in the Eye for Harold, Orgy and Bess, The Prisoner of Spenda, Short Knight, Long*

Daze, The Sobbing Cavalier, Under the Round Table, Who Needs Kitchener?

(Compiler) - *Laugh With the Carry Ons*

THOMPSON, Jimmy

(Actor) - *Cruising, Jack, Regardless*

VOSBURGH, Dick

(Scriptwriter) - *Orgy and Bess, Wot A Carry On in Blackpool*

WARD, Michael

(Actor) - *Cabby, Cleo, Don't Lose Your Head, Regardless, Screaming*

WHITFIELD, June

(Actress) - *Abroad, Columbus, Girls* (and dubbing Valerie Leon's vocals), *Nurse*

WILLIAMS, Kenneth

(Actor) - *Abroad, Again Doctor, At Your Convenience, Behind, Camping, Cleo, Constable, Cowboy, Cruising, Dick, Doctor, Don't Lose Your Head, Emmannuelle, Follow That Camel, Henry, Jack, Laughing's Christmas Classics, Loving, Matron, Nurse, Regardless, Screaming, Sergeant, Spying, Teacher, Up the Khyber, That's Carry On*

WILSON, Ian

(Actor) - *Cabby, Cleo, Jack, Regardless*

WINDSOR, Barbara

(Actress) - *And in My Lady's Chamber, The Baron Outlook, Abroad, Again Christmas, Again Doctor, Barbara, Camping, Christmas* (1969), *Christmas* (1972), *Christmas* (1973), *Dick, Doctor, Girls, Henry, Laughing's Christmas Classics, London, Matron, Spying, Up Yer Cinders, Lamp-Posts of the Empire, The Nine Old Cobblers, Norbert Smith - A Life, Orgy and Bess, The Prisoner of Spenda, The Sobbing Cavalier, That's Carry On, What A Carry On!* (TV/stage), *Who Needs Kitchener?, Wot A Carry On in Blackpool*

WYER, Reginald

(Director of Photography) - *Nurse, Teacher*

BOOKS

'Matron!' 'Oh! Hello!'
'Charming!'
'Stop messin' about!' Cor!
'Get Away!'

Bright, Morris and Ross, Robert
Carry On Uncensored, *Boxtree, 1998*
Bright, Morris & Ross, Robert The
Lost Carry Ons, *Virgin, 2000*
Bright, Morris & Ross, Robert Mr
Carry On, *BBC Worldwide, 2000*
Campbell, Mark Carry On Films,
Pocket Essentials, 2002
**Curran, James and Porter, Vincent
(eds.)** British Cinema History,
Weidenfeld, 1983
Davies, Russell (ed.) The Kenneth
Williams Diaries, Harper *Collins, 1993*
Davies, Russell (ed.) The Kenneth
Williams Letters, *Harper Collins, 1994*
Eastaugh, Kenneth The Carry On
Book, *David and Charles, 1978*
Freedland, Michael Kenneth
Williams, *Weidenfeld, 1990*
Gifford, Denis The Illustrated Who's
Who in British Films, *Anchor, 1978*
Goodwin, Cliff Sid James, *Century, 1994*

Hall, William Titter Ye Not! – The Life
of Frankie Howerd, *Grafton, 1992*
Halliwell, Leslie Double Take and
Fade Away, *Grafton, 1987*
Hibbin, Sally and Nina What A Carry
On – The Official Story of the Carry
On Film Series, *Hamlyn, 1988*
**Housman, David and Frank-Keyes,
John** Funny Business , *Boxtree, 1992*
Howerd, Frankie On The Way I Lost
It, *W.H. Allen, 1976*
Le Mesurier, John A Jobbing Actor,
Elm *Tree Books, 1984*
Murphy, Robin Sixties British Cinema,
BFI, 1992
Quinlan, David Quinlan's Illustrated
Directory of Film Comedy Stars, *B.T.
Batsford Ltd, 1992*
Ross, Robert The Complete Frankie
Howerd, *Reynolds & Hearne, 2001*
Ross, Robert The Complete Sid
James, *Reynolds & Hearne, 2000*

Pertwee, Bill Stars in Battledress,
Hodder & Stoughton, 1992
Sellar, Maurice, Best of British – A
Celebration of Rank Film Classics,
Sphere, 1987
Sims, Joan High Spirits, Transworld,
2000
Staveacre, Tony Slapstick! The
Illustrated Story of Knockabout
Comedy, *Angus & Robertson, 1987*
Warren, Patricia The British Film
Collection, British Cinema in Pictures,
B.T. Batsford Ltd, 1993
Whitfield, June … And June
Whitfield, *Bantam Press, 2000*
Williams, Kenneth Just Williams –
An Autobiography, J.M. *Dent, 1985*
Windsor, Barbara Barbara – The
Laughter and Tears of a Cockney
Sparrow, *Century, 1990*
Windsor, Barbara All Of Me,
Headline, 2000

SOCIETIES

'Matron!' 'Uh! Hello!'
'Stop messin' about!' Cor!
'Get Away!'

**The British Comedy
Appreciation Society**
'Laughter Lines' 1A Woodbury, Castle
Road, Woking, Surrey GU21 4ET
The British Comedy Society
28 Clarendon Road, Borehamwood,
Hertfordshire WD6 1BJ
Comic Heritage
30 Highcroft, North Hill, Highgate,
London N6 4RD
Cor! - The British Comedy Magazine
24 Richmond Road, Basingstoke,
Hampshire RG21 5NX
**The Hattie Jacques
Appreciation Society**
34 Freemantle Avenue, Sutton Trust,
Estate, Hull HU9 4RH

**The Kenneth Williarns and
Sid James Society – 'Stop
Messin'About!'**
27 Brookmead Way, Orpington, Kent
BR5 2BQ
**Steptoe & Son
Appreciation Society**
47 Cornwell Crescent,
Stanford-Le-Hope, Essex SS17 7DC
**The Tony Hancock Appreciation
Society**
426 Romford Road, Forest Gate,
London
The Tony Hancock Society
77 The Avenue, Acocks Green,
Birmingham B27 6NL

**The Tony Hancock Society
incorporating The Tony Hancock
Appreciation Society**
30 Deans Way, Ash Green, Coventry
CV7 9HF
Laugh (UK)
52 Pembury Avenue, Worcester Park,
Surrey KT4 8BT
Laugh (USA)
P.O. Box 5566, Fort Wayne, Indiana
46896-5566 USA
Laugh (Australia)
P.O. Box 394, Caufield East, Victoria
3145 Australia
Wot a Carry On
43 Hunters Drive, Seaton,
Workington, Cumbria CA14 1RN

VIDEOS

'Matron!' 'Oh! Hello!'
'Stop messin' about!' 'Cor!' 'Charming!' 'Get Away!'

British Comedy Legends: Sid! The Very Best of Sid James (PNV 1019)

British Comedy Legends: "Stop Messin' About!" The Very Best of Kenneth Williams (PNV 1021)

Carry On Abroad (CC1079)

Carry On Abroad/Carry On England (CC 7573)

Carry On Again Doctor (CC1067)

Carry On At Your Convenience (CC1066)

Carry On Behind (CC1069)

Carry On Cabby (Warner Brothers – The Big Picture S038031)

Carry On Cabby/Carry On Nurse (PES38322)

Carry On Camping (RCC3059)

Carry On Christmas 1973 (CC1168)

Carry On...Christmas Capers (CC7059)

Carry On Cleo (Warner Brothers – The Big Picture S038032)

Carry On Columbus (SO35579)

Carry On Constable (Warner Brothers – The Big Picture S038033)

Carry On Constable/Carry On Jack (PES38323)

Carry On Cowboy (Warner Brothers – The Big Picture S038034)

Carry On Cruising (Warner Barothers – The Big Picture S038035)

Carry On Dick (CC1075)

Carry On Dick/Carry On Henry (CC 7570)

Carry On Doctor (CC1068)

Carry On Doctor/Carry On Again Doctor (CC 7569)

Carry On...Don't Lose Your Head (CC7000)

Carry On...Don't Lose Your Head/Carry On Henry/Carry On Dick – comedy box set (CC7679)

Carry On Emmannuelle (CC7017)

Carry On Emmannuelle/Carry On Girls (CC 7574)

Carry On England (CC1076)

Carry On...Follow That Camel (CC1170)

Carry On...Follow That Camel/Carry On...Don't Lose Your Head (CC 7572)

Carry On Girls (CC1072)

Carry On Henry (CC1065)

Carry On Jack (Warner Brothers – The Big Picture S038036)

Carry On Kitchener – features Who Needs Kitchener?, The Sobbing Cavalier and One in the Eye for Harold (ITC8142)

Carry On Laughing – Hilarious Holidays (CC7002)

Carry On Laughing – Hysterical History (CC7003)

Carry On Laughing – Medical Madness (CC70,01)

Carry On Loving (CC1074)

Carry On Loving/Carry On Behind (CC 7575)

Carry On Matron (CC1070)

Carry On Matron/Carry On At Your Convenience (CC 7576)

Carry On Nurse (Warner Brothers – The Big Picture S038037)

Carry On Orgy and Bess – also features And in my Lady's Chamber and Under the Round Table (ITC8140)

Carry On The Prisoner of Spenda – also features The Nine Old Cobblers and The **Case of the Coughing Parrot** (ITC8141)

Carry On Regardless (Warner Brothers – The Big Picture S038038)

Carry On Regardless/Carry On Cowboy (PES38325)

Carry On Screaming! (Warner Brothers – The Big Picture S038039)

Carry On The Screaming Winkles – features The Case of the Screaming Winkles, **The Baron Outlook, Lamp-Posts of the Empire and Short Knight, Long Daze** (ITC8143)

Carry On Sergeant (Warner Brothers – The Big Picture S038040)

Carry On Sergeant/Carry On Cruising (PES38326)

Carry On Spying (Warner Brothers – The Big Picture S038041)

Carry On Teacher (Warner Brothers – The Big Picture S038042)

Carry On Teacher/Carry On Screaming! (PES38326)

Carry On Up the Jungle (CC1071)

Carry On Up the Jungle/Carry On...Up the Khyber (CC 7571)

Carry On...Up the Khyber (CC1073)

The Golden Years of British Comedy – From the 60's (4Front/Vision Video 046 540 4)

Laugh with the Carry Ons – Volume 1 (LUM2139)

Norbert Smith – A Life (Polygram 083 388 3)

Internet

Carry On-Line
www.carryonline.com

Carry On Laughing
www.carryonlaughing.com

Carry On Locations
http://carryon.moviefever.com/

Carry On Signing
http://members.tripod.com/autograph_heaven/index.html.

That's Carry On
www.markp.f9.co.uk/thatscarryon/

The Carryoons
www.carryoons.com